AFRICA IN HISTORY

Basil Davidson has been studying and writing about Africa and its peoples since 1951. He is the author of many books on Africa, most of which have been translated into several languages. He also wrote and presented the much-praised eight-part television series *Africa*, which has been broadcast in countries around the world.

ALSO BY BASIL DAVIDSON

History

The Lost Cities of Africa

Black Mother: The Atlantic Slave Trade

The African Past: Chronicles from Antiquity to Modern Times

The African Genius: An Introduction to Social and Cultural History

African Kingdoms (with the Editors of Time-Life)

A History of West Africa AD 1000–1800 (with F.K. Buah and J.F. Ade Ajayi)

A History of East and Central Africa to the Late 19th Century (with J.E. Mhina)

African Civilization Revisited

Contemporary Affairs

Report on Southern Africa

The New West Africa (edited with A. Ademola)

The African Awakening

Let Freedom Come: Africa in Modern History

The Liberation of Guiné: Aspects of an African Revolution

In the Eye of the Storm: Angola's People

Black Star: The Life and Times of Kwame Nkrumah

Modern Africa

The Fortunate Isles

The Black Man's Burden: Africa and the Curse of the Nation-State

Fiction

The Rapids

AFRICA IN HISTORY
Themes and Outlines
Revised and Expanded Edition

Basil Davidson

PHOENIX

A PHOENIX PRESS PAPERBACK

First published in Great Britain
by Weidenfeld & Nicolson in 1966
Revised paperback edition first published in the USA
by Collier Books in 1991
Revised paperback edition first published in Great Britain
by Phoenix in 1992
This paperback edition published in 2001
by Phoenix Press,
a division of The Orion Publishing Group Ltd,
Orion House, 5 Upper St Martin's Lane,
London WC2H 9EA

Second impression September 2003

Copyright © 1966, 1968, 1974, 1984, 1991
by Basil Davidson

A CIP catalogue record for this book
is available from the British Library.

Printed and bound in Italy by
Grafica Veneta S.p.A.

ISBN 1 84212 246 0

CONTENTS

2 Ancient Glories

Origins of Ancient Egypt, its growth and achievement—Links of Pharaonic Egyptians with neighbouring peoples— Emergence and history of the kingdoms of Kush on the Middle Nile, Napata and Meroe; and of Axum in Ethiopia—The old civilization of the Berbers— Punic and Roman North Africa and early links with West Africa

3 The Factors of Growth

Development and diversity of community life in ancient times south of the Sahara—Growth and importance of trading centres—Further evolution of Iron Age political systems—Outline of some of the largest of these systems in western and central-southern Africa up to the sixteenth century—The Christian kingdoms of Nubia and Ethiopia—Rise and early consequences of Islam

7 Conquest and Colonial Rule

*Geographical exploration of inner Africa—
New missionary endeavours—Rise of
European imperialism and its meaning for
Africa— Rivalries for African possessions;
from coastal encroachment to the continental
'scramble' and full-scale invasion—Brief
review of the colonial period in the first two
of its three main phases: 1900–20 and
1920–45*

8 Towards Liberation

*The forerunners of modern African
independence movements, north and south of
the Sahara, before 1945—Outline of the third
main phase of the colonial period after 1945—
Growth of nationalism and the emergence of
independent states—Anti-colonial struggles of
the 1970s—The legacy of the past and new
problems of economic and social transition—
Southern Africa and South Africa—Conclusion*

TEXT FIGURES

Lines from a late fragment of local history
written in Kotoko, a language of Chad,
utilizing an Arabic script, about 1900

MAPS

ACKNOWLEDGEMENTS

The author and publishers wish to thank the following, who have given permission for copyrighted material to be reproduced: Dr Gabriel Camps (page 50, from *Aux Origines de la Berbérie: Monuments et rites funéraires*); Prof. P. Shinnie (page 140, from *Medieval Nubia*); Sudan Antiquities Service (page 42, from *Kush*, vol. 7; and page 140, as above); Oxford University Press (page 29, from A. Gardiner, *Egypt of the Pharaohs*); and the following, who kindly provided material for reproduction: Dr A. D. H. Bivar (page 251); Prof. J-P. Lebeuf (page 254); Prof. J. Leclant (page 45); Library of Congress Collection, Washington (page 217). The maps were specially drawn by Mrs M. Verity.

Preface to this Revised and Expanded Edition

Africa Rediscovered

A blessing arrived with the need for a new revision and enlargement of this book, the fourth since its conception. I undertook this welcome task in 1990; and 1990, in several ways, was for Africa a time of reconsideration and renewal signalled to a worldwide audience by South African statesman Nelson Mandela's liberation from prison.

When Nelson Mandela stepped free from his defeated jailers on 11 February 1990, twenty-seven harsh years after they had first seized him, an immense public in many countries, perhaps in all countries everywhere, gave him their welcome and support. Sanity and courage might again take the lead in South Africa. Relief from persecution in South Africa, if it could now be brought about, might act as a liberating force for the whole continent.

Mandela's release was received as a moment of affirmation in the record of Africa's history, which has long been one of subjection to foreign powers. It was a moment of celebration of Africa's self-development, of Africa's indigenous history prior to that subjection. Specifically it was a moment to recall that the facts of Africa's own history have always been, and remain, an entirely convincing denial of the mythologies of modern racism, in the name of whose lies and legends so many have suffered persecution in South Africa, as in the entire continent.

The history of racist persecution is an old one. In the times of the slave trade, and above all of the Atlantic trade in African captives taken into slavery in the Americas, the 'justifications' were expressed in the language of brutality and ignorance. Africans were 'savages living in primeval darkness'; and so long as they were 'baptized' by the casual waving of a Christian priestly hand above their heads while they lay in chains, the profits of enslaving them were profits to be taken. But the moral sophistications of England and France in the nineteenth century demanded a more persuasive and respectable justification.

In 1830 the colonial partition of the African continent began with the outright French invasion and eventual colonization of Algeria; and in that same year the doctrines of modern racism— of the natural and inherent superiority of 'white' peoples over 'black' peoples—began to take shape as an intellectual and allegedly scientific discourse, initially in the work of the German philosopher Georg Hegel.

The advocates of this discourse—Hegel most typically, but duly followed by a host of other 'justifiers'—declared that Africa had no history prior to direct contact with Europe. Therefore the Africans, having made no history of their own, had clearly made no development of their own. Therefore they were not properly human, and could not be left to themselves, but must be 'led' towards civilization by other peoples: that is, by the peoples of Europe, especially of western Europe, and most particularly of Britain and France.

These assertions were convenient to western Europeans who were about to invade and dispossess the peoples of Africa, whether of land or freedom; and they spawned an abrasive progeny of myths. Typically, these myths projected the picture of an Africa inhabited by 'grown-up children': by beings who, in the words of the famous nineteenth-century explorer Richard Burton, might be normal when children, but regressed ever backwards once they reached adulthood. Now this was a picture, aside from its inherent absurdity, that denied all previous European understanding of Africa and its peoples. Previous European scholarship knew that the foundations of European civilization derived from classical Greek civilization. That scholarship further accepted what the Greeks had laid down as patently obvious: that classical Greek civilization derived, in its religion, its philosophy, its mathematics and much else, from the ancient civilizations of Africa, above all from Egypt of the Pharaohs. To those 'founding fathers' in classical Greece, any notion that Africans were inferior, morally or intellectually, would have seemed merely silly.

So the 'justifiers' of colonial invasion and dispossession of Africa, coming to the fore in the high age of European imperialism, had to sweep aside what the Greeks had believed, because justification for invasion and dispossession otherwise became impossible. Only the saving hand of Europe, it was accordingly said, could lead Africa out of its 'darkness'. So it was clear, to quote the words of another great 'justifier', Professor H. E. Egerton, when Chair of Colonial History at the University of Oxford, that colonial invasion and dispossession 'must be the right way of dealing with the native problem', the word 'native' now being affixed to Africans as a token of proper contempt. With that solution, Professor Egerton assured his students and readers (who generally believed him), 'what had happened' with colonialism was 'the introduction of order into blank, uninteresting, brutal barbarism'. How those passionate adjectives pile up! The intellectual 'justifiers' never quite succeeded in stifling the voice of reason; other kinds of 'justifiers', needless to say, had no such problem.

Such views still had currency in the early 1960s when the gates of a South African prison closed on Nelson Mandela. But when at last he walked free, in 1990, those views were under wide attack even in white South Africa itself. Few in fact believed them any longer; and those few were small minorities embattled behind the barricades of privilege. In a crucial restoration of Africa's history, the scholarship of the second half of the twentieth century had proceeded 'from what is near', as al-Biruni recommended a thousand years ago, to 'what is distant', and had done this with such success that a reliable outline of Africa's history is now available even for remote times, as well as with clarity and precision from the fifteenth century onward. And this has proved to be a history of development, of self-development, from one level of achievement to another.

This liberation from a reductive and perverse mythology has given Africa its true place in the world of human endeavour. It has swept away many strange fantasies. It has made short work of the pseudo-science that sought to justify the colonial invasions just as an earlier version had sought to justify the servitudes and horrors of the slave trade. It has cleared the ground for rigorously factual analyses of Africa's actual achievement, for better or for worse, across the centuries. It has enabled us today to estimate the African achievement without prejudice or denigration, as without exaggeration or sentimentality.

What follows here is a general introduction to this world of knowledge about Africa's record in the past, and about the background of the Africa we see today. It seeks to portray the basic themes that have shaped and informed the self-development of black peoples, and to body forth the essential unities of thought and experience that underlie the rich diversities of this vast continent's cultural and social processes since ancient times. It owes its authority, let me add, to that wide community of scholars and researchers in many languages without whose wisdom no such book as this would be possible. The failings in this book are of course my own; but I thank those many colleagues once again.

In the present considerable enlargement I have taken account of new materials, whether historical or archaeological, and of new interpretations, whether fully accepted or still in contention, from research and discussion in the 1970s and the 1980s: in matters, for example, such as the origins of urbanism and regional trade in the Western Sudan; the introduction and use of locally minted coin currencies along the East Coast; and, for recent years, the origins and nature of the acute political and economic problems of most of Africa in the 1980s. As well as updatings in all the chapters, I have reorganized and expanded sections bearing on southern Africa, and especially South Africa, in the light of recent studies and events.

It is our duty to proceed from what is near to what is distant, from what is known to that which is less known, to gather the traditions from those who have reported them, to correct them as much as possible and to leave the rest as it is, in order to make our work help anyone who seeks truth and loves wisdom.

Abu'l-Rayhan Muhammad al-Biruni, AD 973–1050

ONE

Old Myths: New Truths

Africa's Place in History

This book's purpose is to record the history of the Africans as the subject in its own right that it has become, and to do this within a continental framework from early times. There could be different ways of composing this record, since it rests upon copious quantities of evidence from sources of many kinds: archaeological, written and orally recorded. But the essential themes and outline of this grand and complex story are no longer in doubt. Much new evidence happily arrives year by year, adding to the story and revising it; but the basic outline that has emerged since the 1950s has shown itself strong enough to absorb these updatings and additions. We stand on firm ground, even if much remains to be explored and explained.

Any outline dealing with this complexity of development calls for some kind of periodization, of division into successive historical periods, just as has the history of other continents. All such divisions are of course a subsequent encasing of 'what happened' into mental constructs of a later time and conception, and would have meant nothing to the peoples of the past. In Europe now, for example, the term 'Middle Ages' or 'medieval' has a useful and familiar meaning: we know that it helps to describe the years of European feudalism, for example, in their relation to what came before feudalism and what came after. But the Europeans of the Middle Ages would have been more than

surprised to hear that they were 'medieval', just as the peoples of
Africa, through that same span of years, certainly had no notion
of living in an 'Iron Age', whether 'early' or 'late'. But for us the
term 'Iron Age' has a lot to be said for it, as will be seen, and
does indeed describe a 'period'—an interval of time distinct from
what preceded and followed it. The periodization used in this
book is explained along the way, and may be found in brief
summary in date lists gathered at the end, which I have christened
chronologues, thinking that mere dates and names are seldom
useful.

It may be asked whether one can really think that this long
history, as a process unfolding over two millennia, has moved
from one developmental phase to another in a manner that can
be seen and so described. Many have doubted any such thing,
Africans among them. Looking at the question a few decades
back, an elderly historian of the West African city of Bobo-
Dyulasso enlarged upon the difficulties of making sense of Africa's
past. He recalled the downfall of the Western Ummayads, of the
Caliphate of Cordoba in Spain, and opined that Africa had greatly
changed since then. Considering that this event fell in the eleventh century AD, it was scarcely an understatement; but the mufti
of Bobo, concerned to argue the length and intricacy of Africa's
history, was aware of the fact. He proceeded to rub it in.

As a further warning to anyone who should think it easy to
write African history, he observed that any attempt to bring together the events of the last thousand years would be like trying
to trap wind in a sieve, for 'everybody who attained to distinction
spared no effort at extinguishing the flame of his rival . . . [and]
everybody was in contradiction with the others . . . [while] many
a year would drag on fruitlessly because of the numerous quarrels
and wars among them'. In saying this, of course, the learned
mufti was rather at the other extreme of overstatement. Yet the
warning is a useful one, for it is true that scholarship is only at
the beginning of a deep understanding of the African past. Much
remains to be discovered. Much remains to be agreed.

It is none the less already possible to know a great deal about

African history. Whether in the field of scientific archaeology, the study of languages or the movement of ideas, the assembly of historical tradition or the elucidation of records written by Africans, Europeans, Asians and Americans, fruitful labour and learning in several countries over the past few decades have produced a large body of explanatory work, and have proved that the writing of African history need be neither the repetition of romantic legend nor the mere listing of faceless names and battles long ago.

These historical advances have swept away some old myths and established some new truths. The seductively agreeable belief so dear to nineteenth-century Europe that all in Africa was savage chaos before the coming of the Europeans may linger here and there, but not among historians concerned with Africa. The happy conviction of European conquerors that they were bringing civilization to Africans against whom the Gates of Eden had barely closed may still have its adherents, yet not among those who have looked at the evidence. Far from being a kind of Museum of Barbarism whose populations had stayed outside the laws of human growth and change through some natural failing or inferiority, Africa is now seen to possess a history which demands as serious an approach as that of any other continent. What we now have, more and more clearly, is the bodying forth of a broad and vivid process of human development.

Pessimist though he was, the mufti of Bobo rightly conceived his problem in terms of a very long span of years. And this process of development may now in fact be seen as a continuum evolving with no decisive break from the pastoral populations of the green Sahara more than six thousand years ago, or from the rise of agriculture in the valley of the Nile, or even, though very mistily now, still earlier again from Stone Age peoples of the most remote antiquity. Anyone who might try to explain everything that has happened since then would undoubtedly be trapping wind in a sieve.

But all this, after all, is true of other continents besides Africa; and the writing of history would in any case become a hopeless venture if it involved explaining everything. What now exists for Europe is a fairly solid outline of the past that is filled with interesting and meaningful detail, and divided for the sake of convenience into a number of fairly well accepted periods. It is this kind of outline and periodization, though as yet with far less detail and definition, that is now beginning to exist for the very different history of Africa as well.

The book that follows here is not, of course, an attempt to offer a complete review of what is known and thought about the African past. No such effort could succeed with a single volume unless this were to be a mere catalogue of facts and hypotheses; and even then the treatment would have to be unreadably dense. Besides, there is already beginning to be available a number of good histories of single countries or regions; a list of some of them will be found further on. This means that the specialist and even the non-specialist will be aware of many omissions in these pages. I am well aware of them myself. They will be forgiven, I hope, for the sake of clarity and readability within a short volume designed to offer a continental view of the past. What follows here, accordingly, is an attempt to trace a broad outline of African growth and change over some twenty centuries; to present a general and yet reasonably balanced summary of those years; and to suggest the long-range historical explanation of Africans and their development which modern scholarship can now increasingly reveal, and which, in the measure that its leading themes can be well and clearly shown, may really 'help anyone who seeks truth and loves wisdom'.

The winning of this new view of Africa, historical Africa, has been compared with the nineteenth-century's geographical exploration of the 'unknown continent'; and there is something to be said for the comparison. For a long time now, labouring in solitude and often in great obscurity, many good enthusiasts have given themselves to the task of African historical exploration. Like the pioneering travellers of old, they tend to vanish for months or even years, unnoticed and unsung, forgotten by all but their families and their friends, only to return suddenly one day with an effect of glamour and discovery that must be much the same as the impression made by Mungo Park, nearly two hundred years ago, when he came home from West Africa and told his London audience that he had seen the Niger flowing to the east and not, as European geographers then believed, the west.

Only recently, as I was beginning this book, a modern Mungo Park who is otherwise a French archaeologist of many years' experience arrived on my doorstep in the middle of the morning. He came actually from Waterloo Station in the heart of London and not from the heart of Africa. Yet he brought with him all the same the gleam and glint of distant places, as well as the news that beneath the ruins of a certain West African site, a medieval city of the Western Sudan, there lay a neolithic settlement no smaller than one kilometre square. And a year later, as I was finishing this book, there came a letter from central Africa with another piece of news still more exciting in its context: 'Have you heard', it laconically inquired, 'that Hamo Sassoon in Tanzania has a date for Engaruka of AD 1450?' Thanks to many such pioneers, the truths of old Africa at last take firm and rounded shape.

This enfolds the whole continent. A rigid dividing of Africa into historical regions can be useful for purposes of detailed study; it will no longer satisfy a balanced view of the past. For while it is true that the Sahara has long placed a barrier between northern Africa and the rest of the continent, and that the great rain forests, further south, have sometimes proved to be a still greater barrier in relation to central-southern Africa, it is also true that all these regions really belong together, and that what is particular to each of them is general to them all in their foundation and emergence. So that there can be little more sense in studying southern Africa in separation from central and northern Africa than in trying to understand northern Europe apart from central and southern Europe.

This is not of course to deny the obvious fact that some of Africa's large regions have developed in ways distinctive from

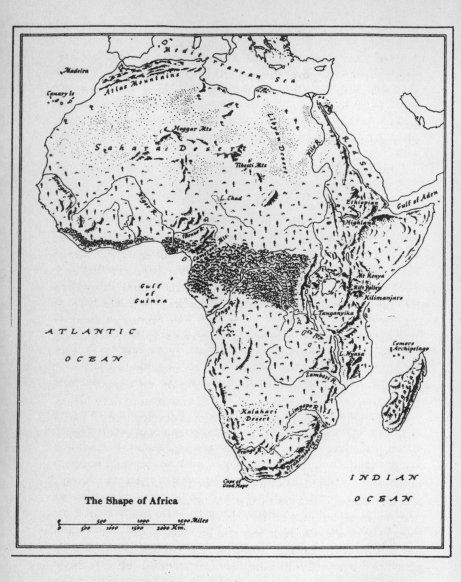

The Shape of Africa

those of other regions. Yet the essential truths and probabilities
yielded by research over the past few decades repeatedly insist on
two great underlying themes, manifest or hidden, concerning all
African development no matter what the region may be. These
themes are unity and continuity of cultural growth among them
all, and from an immense depth of time.

The Peopling of a Continent

If the learned mufti of Bobo had trouble with the last thousand
years, this is nothing to the jungle of tentative terminology in
which the description of the Stone Age is still ensnared. Fossils
and artifacts of a great variety of types have been labelled after
the sites of their first discovery, and the labels then attached to
similar types of fossils and artifacts no matter how much distance
may lie between. But the confusion has long become worse con-
founded by necessary revision and reservation to the point where
any brief survey of the Palaeolithic, however simplified, can only
be of small value. A few points, even so, may be useful.

Ironically enough, given Africa's more or less complete historical eclipse in recent times, Africa is now seen to have played
a part of crucial importance in early human development. Thanks
largely to the African evidence, several large and revolutionary
revisions have had to be made to the simple scheme of nineteenth-
century anthropology. It used to be said that man and the apes
had developed from a common ancestor as late as the Pleistocene,
and that one of the tasks of physical anthropology would be to
find the essential 'missing link' between the two. It used to be
thought that *homo sapiens* was the first tool-maker, and that it
was precisely this capacity to think well enough to make tools
which differentiated him from his less successful relatives. Now
it seems clear, on the contrary, that *homo sapiens* was in fact the
tardy product of natural selection from a large number of different
types of man-like ancestors, or hominids, and that some of these
hominids were themselves capable of the manufacture and use

of simple stone tools and weapons. The general picture at present is one of technical development among man-like creatures that begins nearly 3 million years ago, spreads gradually across the world and leads by definable stages to the disappearance of all these hominids, one after another, and the sole survival of *homo sapiens*.

That is probably, in this context, about as much as can usefully be said upon a subject of dense obscurity and diversity of opinion among the specialists—that is, the physical anthropologists, who study the origins of humanity through the evidence of fossilized bones and stone tools. The specialists have worked with success and courage to recover the truths of human evolution, and their controversies, often richly human in the clash of personalities and ambitions, have added spice to their work. We are wonderfully better informed on all these matters than we were thirty or forty years ago.

Briefly, proto-human, part-human and fully human evolution occurred through a geological era known as the Quaternary, nearly all of whose enormous span of years—up to, say, ten or twelve thousand years ago—has been assigned to an era or 'period' called the Pleistocene, which began, more or less vaguely, some 3 million years ago. In that immense wilderness of years, barely imaginable even with a huge effort, the evidence for the earliest development of the ancestors of *homo sapiens*—of you and me— comes insistently from Africa, just as Charles Darwin much more than a century ago said it would. In 1967, writing in *Tarikh*, the pioneering twentieth-century anthropologist Dr Louis Leakey gave Africa three "firsts" in this respect. His conclusions have not been fully accepted by colleagues then or since, but in their general substance these conclusions appear to stand as a useful basis for further speculation and research.

From fossil and tool evidence that he and others found in eastern and southern Africa, Leakey thought that it was 'the African continent which saw the emergence of the basic stock which eventually gave rise to the apes, as well as to man as we know him today'. This had evolved, he said, in the Nile region during the Oligocene era between 30 million and 40 million years ago. Second, it was in Africa that 'the main branch which was to end up as man broke away from those leading to the apes'; and this separation, he considered, took place in the Late Miocene or early Pliocene (the latter era beginning some 12 million years ago). Third, during the Pliocene in East Africa, 'true man separated from his man-like (and now extinct) cousins, the *australopithecines* or "near men" of some two million years ago'.

The Pleistocene development can be followed to some extent through successive types of stone tools. After about a million years ago the quantity of such tools has vastly increased; and they are being used by increasingly man-like creatures. The most frequent of these tools is called a hand-axe: in appearance it is a large oval of chipped flint which may weigh anything up to several pounds and must have required a powerful but also skilled hand to use it. Hand-axe folks are known to have inhabited the whole of the continent but for the rain-forest zones of the Congo and western Africa, as well as many countries outside Africa.

Technical improvement remains snail-slow, but it continues. The later stages of the hand-axe millennia are times of great increase and spread of proto-human occupation. They reach a crucial point of change, at least so far as Africa is concerned, about fifty thousand years ago with the emergence of populations who have learned how to make fire, who live in caves or rock shelters, know how to carry burdens and are equipped with better tools, notably choppers and scrapers. These heavy-browed creatures spread across most of Africa south of the Sahara. But the interesting point here, no doubt, is that several major regional variations in physical appearance seem already to have been present when *homo sapiens* first appeared. Little is clearly certain, as yet, about these distant and obscure processes of natural selection. But there seems little doubt that the main pigmentary and other physiological variations of mankind were evolved, at least in some distinctiveness, during the earliest times.

By 10,000 BC the last of the hominids not directly ancestral to ourselves—the Neanderthals—have vanished from the scene, and *homo sapiens* alone holds the field. The small-statured 'Bush-man' type of his ancestors has taken over in the extreme south of Africa, larger humans are dominant elsewhere, while the Neanderthals and neighbours in North Africa have given way to incoming migrants from neighbouring lands who are also a form, or rather several forms, of early man. All these new folk, certainly much mingled in their further procreation, are recognizably human in ways that the older types were not: they bury their dead with care and have some use for paint and decoration. They live in large groups, and begin to solve the problems of regulating community life among comparatively large numbers of people.

The regional variation of *homo sapiens* continued, one may note, through all these transformations: as between north and centre-south, no doubt, partly because the Saharan belt remained uninhabitable, much as it is today, throughout a great deal of the Middle Stone Age. But at some time after 10,000 BC, the climate of the Sahara grew cooler and less dry. Pastures appeared. Rivers flowed. Much land became fertile. This marked another turning point, and may be regarded as a highly progressive period in African prehistory. Some of the peoples of North Africa pushed southward into this welcoming Sahara, while others in central-western Africa probably pushed northward; and throughout the Saharan region there began an interchange of peoples, ideas and equipment that was accompanied by a corresponding impulse towards the improvement of tools and techniques.

This spread and mingling of peoples through the wide plains of the Sahara continued in later times. Between about 5500 and 2500 BC there occurred another 'wet phase', the Makalian, which was evidently very favourable to the fruitful mixing and multi-plication of peoples. For about three thousand years the Sahara teems with life. The rivers of its temperate and pleasant climate are wide, reliable and many, and are filled with many varieties of fish. Its hillsides are covered with forests of oak, cypress and other handsome trees. Its grassland plains are alive with wild game. Its people raise great herds of horned cattle.

At least seven thousand years ago these peoples of the then

green Sahara begin to practise elementary forms of farming. They build the African cradle of the Neolithic or New Stone Age. With this development the earliest growth of civilization in Africa passes a major landmark in its social and economic as well as cultural evolution. Among its achievements will be the laying of primary foundations for the high civilizations of the Nile Valley after 3500 BC. Pharaonic Egypt will be the child of this Saharan Neolithic.

So it is that Africa has been a continent of very early and possibly decisive importance for human development, including the much earlier development of those types of hominid or 'not-yet-Man' who possessed the evolutionary potential that was to be fully realized in *homo sapiens*. Thus we know that human stocks in Africa have evolved from or alongside hominid types which had existed in Africa for an immense period of time, and that this evolution continued down the centuries until it eventually promoted civilizations of the highest value.

These human stocks varied in culture and appearance. By the dawn of the Saharan Neolithic, around 5000 BC (and the true date may be found to have been earlier still), there were indigenous types to which a number of unsatisfactory labels are often attached—'Bushman', 'Negro', 'Negroid' or the like—but which, leaving the labels aside, were all the product of this long and varied evolution. We may be content to call all of them Africans, and the more so because recent analysis of blood groups has gone far to suggest that nearly all shared, however distantly, the same remote ancestors.

It has become similarly clear that the once familiar attribution of the term 'white' to North African stocks (as of the term 'black' to other African stocks) is really little more than another mystification of the racist sort. All such categorizations should be dismissed. Consider only the strange case of the 'Hamitic Hypothesis', another myth dear to the epoch of imperialism. In countless books and lectures it was preached that any signs of past progress detectable among Africans must have been the fruit of outside intrusion, of intrusion from the north: more exactly of 'white' intrusion from Europe. This derivative form of the 'Africans-have-no-civilization' myth was best offered in a scientific guise by a British anthropologist, C. G. Seligman, in a book of 1929 (*The Races of Africa*, much admired then and after).

Offered as a proven truth, this particular myth asserted that a people or peoples known as Hamites were responsible for any process of history that might be identifiable in Africa, because the Negroes (the Africans) were too primitive to be able, on their own, to embark on any such process. Apart from positing recent Semitic influence, Phoenician or Arab, Seligman taught that 'the civilisations of Africa are the civilisations of the Hamites'. And who were these indispensable Hamites? For Seligman, the answer was obvious: the Hamites were not in origin Africans at all. On the contrary, they were 'Caucasians, i.e. belong to the same great branch of mankind as almost all Europeans'. Just to make sure, he went on to explain that 'the incoming Hamites were pastoral Caucasoids—arriving wave after wave—better armed as well as quicker witted than the dark agricultural Negroes'. The idea was not new, but more than convenient at a time when travellers and researchers were beginning to light upon archaeological and other signs of obvious past progress in the African interior.

The 'Hamitic Hypothesis' was great nonsense. No serious Africanist believes in it or even in the mere existence, then or since, of any people or culture properly definable as Hamitic. This scientific abolition of the Hamites was confirmed by J. H. Greenberg in his essential *Languages of Africa* of 1963, and has continued ever since. 'Even the linguistic use of the term Hamite', Greenberg affirmed with an authority unchallenged in this context, 'should be abandoned'. As for 'Caucasoid', another mystification, it can only mean 'pertaining to Caucasian'; and as for 'Caucasian', it either signifies a mountain range in eastern Europe or else another myth, invented this time by a man called Blumenbach in 1800, whose strange idea was that the mountain range in question had been the birthplace of the white race of mankind. All such labellings, as I said, should be abandoned. They belong to the debris of the past.

What one needs to hold in mind is the gradual crystallization of a few main stocks out of an extremely complex process of natural selection through tens of thousands of years, this process being itself the sequence to another and immensely longer period of selection among a range of hominids who were not apes, but who were not fully fledged men either. With this crystallization of human types there also came, little by little, a gradual emergence of specialization in the use of tools and weapons, as one or another branch of humanity adjusted itself to the particular environment in which it lived. The almost universal hand-axe of a million years ago gave way, in short, to a far better armoury of tools and weapons wielded by different types of men for different purposes in different places. By the dawn of the Neolithic this diversification was already far advanced.

In the Heart of Africa

What Desmond Clark has called the 'feedback relationship' between biological evolution and cultural change was certainly present in Stone Age times. Favourable conditions enabled this or that group to develop improved techniques for getting food: in doing so, they changed their way of life. In changing it they themselves gradually became different from their ancestors, handier, more skilful, better able to think and to act by thought. Putting it another way, one can say that progress requires a fruitful interaction of environment and invention, of men's relations with nature and of men's relations with each other.

In Old Stone Age times the rate of progress was as quietly slow as countless ages. With the coming of early farming and settlement, the pace quickened enormously. Just how quickly the biological-cultural feedback could now operate is suggested by the astonishing speed of social and technical advance in the Nile Valley. Long sunk beneath the waters of the Nile and its lakes and marshes, the land of Egypt began to emerge some ten thousand years ago. Only by about 8000 BC, in the words of H. W.

Fairman, did there begin 'that deposition of alluvium over the deep-lying water-laid gravels and silts that resulted eventually in the formation of the real, habitable Egypt; it can hardly be much more than seven thousand years ago that this process of deposition had reached the stage that continuous areas of land began slowly to form in and emerge from the swamps and marshes', and human settlement became possible.

Yet by 4000 BC the descendants of these earliest settlers in this 'new' land of Egypt were already cultivating regular crops. By 3500 BC they had formed themselves into early states. By 3200 there came the unification of Lower and Upper Egypt, and the beginnings of a brilliant urban civilization. All the essential foundations of Pharaonic Egypt, whether material or intellectual, were now already in existence; and soon after 2600 the Pharaoh Cheops could order the building of the Great Pyramid of Gizeh, 756 feet square at the base and one of the greatest structures the world has ever seen. The time-span from *homo habilis* with his earliest tools to Neolithic man with his farming cannot in any case be much less than 2 million years. Yet not much more than two thousand years separate the earliest farmers who settled along the river Nile from the mathematically precise builders of the monuments of Egypt.

This same process, though with less startling results than along the uniquely beneficent banks of the Nile, was present elsewhere. The peopling of Africa with most of the ancestors of its modern inhabitants, from the far south to the far north, was more or less complete by two thousand years ago. These ancestors were, of course, very few in number when compared with the size of later populations who knew how to grow food. One estimate has put the total population of the greater part of Africa, two thousand years ago, at only about 3 or 4 million people. In considering how their development took place, and how the feedback between biological evolution and cultural change worked to make it possible, the green Sahara and Sudan of the temperate Makalian Phase (c. 5500–2500 BC) is a helpful place to begin. There are two reasons why it is helpful. The first is that the green Sahara

and Sudan were evidently the first African regions where early
forms of cultivation were practised on any scale. The second is
that it was probably from this partially fertile though desiccating
region that techniques of farming were carried elsewhere for adaptation in the rest of the continent.

Egypt remains something of a special case in this respect as in
others. This was partly because of its proximity to earlier farming
cultures in the Near East but even more because of its unpar-
alleled advantage in the Nile floods. Yet from the standpoint of
African development, Egypt clearly belongs to the Saharan-
Sudanese region of the Makalian Phase. Its earliest recognizable
farmers, those of the Tasian Culture, were close neighbours of
the Middle Nile, while the next farming culture, the Badarian,
seems quite certainly to have consisted of peoples who had come
into the Nile region from the west or south-west. 'The peopling
of pre-dynastic Egypt', to quote Fairman again, 'must have been
largely the result of the desiccation of the Sahara.' The ancient
Egyptians belonged, that is, not to any specific Egyptian region
or Near Eastern heritage but to that wide community of peoples
who lived between the Red Sea and the Atlantic Ocean, shared
a common 'Saharan-Sudanese culture', and drew their reinforcements from the same great source, even though, as time went
by, they also absorbed a number of wanderers from the Near
East.

Herodotus saw the matter very clearly when travelling through
Egypt not long after 450 BC, for he had no difficulty in concluding
that Egypt's cultural origins lay in continental Africa. On the
subject of circumcision, for example, he remarked that 'as between the Egyptians and the Ethiopians [by which he meant
those since called Negroes], I should not like to say which learned
from the other . . .', a remarkably up-to-date statement of the
case. Here in this ancient community of cultures between the
Atlantic and the Red Sea, one may indeed trace the ground-
stratum of many obscure but persistent unities of thought and
attitude among African peoples now living far apart and apparently in total isolation from each other. Thus it was not simple

diffusion from Pharaonic Egypt, but still earlier diffusion from the Saharan-Sudanese community, which can probably explain why the ram and python should be symbols of religion all round the Sahara and far beyond it, or why many related social attitudes and institutions should be present among widely separate African peoples.

Based largely on datings achieved by the Carbon-14 test,* the chronology of early Saharan development of stock-raising and crop-growing has made great advances over the last dozen years or so. It now appears that the late fifth and early fourth millennia BC saw the development of comparatively widespread populations capable of food-production on an impressive scale at the 'Neolithic' level. In some areas, notably the Hoggar region of the central Sahara (now in southern Algeria), these peoples engraved and painted splendidly on stone, and have left many galleries of pictures of themselves, their gods, their cattle, and the wild animals which flourished then. There is even an increasing body of evidence which tends to the conclusion that the crucial stages of this early development were achieved in the Saharan region before they appeared in the valley of the Nile.

In this period, accordingly, there were many peoples in this wide region who were genotypically of stocks native to continental Africa, North Africa and the Nile Valley, and who undoubtedly possessed a close affinity in material and spiritual culture. But they lived in a land with no future for themselves. Earlier even than 2000 BC the Sahara began to lose rainfall, rivers and rich pastures, and therefore its capacity for supporting large stable populations. There occurred a steady movement of Saharan peoples into more favourable lands nearby. The migrants who went northward out of the Sahara merged with those populations of Mediterranean type, themselves the distant product of long min-

---

*This isotope of carbon loses radioactivity at a measurable rate, and so provides a broadly reliable means of dating ancient materials. The dates, of course, are only approximate indications of chronological time. But as approximations they have proved remarkably reliable.

gling between Mediterranean newcomers and Aterian natives, who were already in North African lands; and after 2000 BC there emerged the strong group of peoples whom we know as Berber, a term which properly applies only to the languages they speak, and not to any specific physical characteristic.

Firmly established along the North African littoral, among the mountains of Morocco and far southward into the fringes of the Sahara, these Berbers also made contact with Bronze Age neighbours in Spain; partly through this contact, they entered a Bronze Age of their own. By the thirteenth century, and even earlier,* the Egyptian rulers had to face the invasion of Libyan Berbers who were well equipped with bronze swords, spears and even body-armour. Skilled horsemen, these North Africans were expert in the use of the war chariot and also, possibly, of the merchant cart. How soon they began trading across the Sahara we do not yet know, but some evidence suggests that Berber carts draw.1 by horses or donkeys may have traversed the Sahara by several well-marked trails from Morocco to the Senegal River and beyond, and from Tunisia through the central Sahara to the middle waters of the Niger, at least by 500 BC.

Those Saharans who pushed eastward into the good lands of the Nile came up eventually against stiff Egyptian resistance. At least two of the pharaohs of the nineteenth dynasty (c. 1308–1194)—and there must have been many earlier cases—were obliged to meet the threat of Saharan invasion. The second of these, Merenptah (1224–14), even had to face a regular coalition between several Berber peoples and five groups of 'peoples of the sea' who included, if their name Akawasha is anything to go by, some of those famous Achaeans of distant Greek memory and legend. In a great battle at Pi-yer, a place lying in or near the delta of the Nile, Merenptah's army slew six thousand Libyans as well as many of their allies, and took nine thousand prisoners. Even if the inscriptions exaggerate, the clash was obviously a

*Sethos 1 (1308–1290 BC) had to fight at least two big battles against Libyan intruders.

memorable one. Behind it lay the driving pressures of an arid
land, again recorded in one of Merenptah's inscriptions where
he reviles the invading Berbers for having come to Egypt 'in
search of food for their mouths'. These invasions continued as
Egypt grew weaker. By the reigns of Rameses IX and Rameses X
(1227–1107 BC) there were regular Libyan settlements south of
the Fayum and near Thebes. After 950 BC a line of Libyan princes
grew powerful enough to impose their rule on Upper Egypt for
nearly two hundred years.

There was a third movement of dispersal. Other Saharans
edged their way southward into the heart of the continent and
mingled with the peoples whom they found there. Stock-raising
cultures emerged on the Ethiopian plateau and in East Africa.
The Sudanese fringes of the south-western Sahara began to support a Neolithic way of life which was in many ways the product
of local experiment and invention. Here in western Africa new
crops were cultivated, including sorghum and rice, together with
a number of other crops such as Guinea yams and melons, while
in Ethiopia the early type of cereal called *eleusine* began to be
grown. Little by little, new habits of cultivation moved southward
to the verge of the dense forests of the tropical rain belt; but here
there came a pause. Regular farming appeared in the forestland
only at a much later date, perhaps little earlier than 500 BC; and
it is not difficult to see why. Given the richness and variety of
fruit and edible vegetables in the forestlands, Old Stone Age
hunting and food-collecting folk could still live as well as Neolithic farmers, and with less labour for their pains, without growing any food. For them, there could be little incentive to
supplementing the abundance of nature. Not until populations
greatly expanded did this easy-going situation alter.

An 'Iron Age' Begins

Beginning in about 500 BC or soon after, though for reasons as
yet far from clear, this expansion among long-established peo-

ples was soon associated with another development of critical
importance, the gradual replacement of stone by iron for essential weapons and tools. Once iron had appeared, the whole
perspective was changed. Iron-pointed spears were an arma-
ment that could take small groups of wandering men through
unknown country they had never dared or cared to enter before.
Iron-tipped hoes were a big improvement on stone cultivators in
lands where the tsetse fly—evidently present in much of central-
southern Africa since the earliest times of man's appearance—
forbade the use of draught animals. Iron-shod axes could master
the forestland as stone tools had never done. With the spreading use of iron, peoples also spread, and populations grew.
Making its rise some two and a half thousand years ago, early
iron-working helps to mark the foundation of the Africa we know
today.

The appearance of iron-working, and its closely associated phenomena of early farming and population growth throughout most
of Africa south of the Sahara, began at different times in different
regions. North of the Sahara, as we shall see, the use of iron
became general in the Nile Valley after about 500 BC and was
quite extensively used in the Berber lands, in Kush on the Middle
Nile, and in the rising state of Axum in north-eastern Ethiopia.
By 200 BC, or possibly a little earlier, the metal founders of Meroe
on the Middle Nile had built a major handicraft industry in iron,
and must have sent their products far and wide. Bronze and iron
objects would certainly have crossed the desert lands to the grassland countries south of the Sahara before this time: the horse
and chariot merchants would have carried them there, a means
of communication which no doubt explains the occasional find
of Pharaonic Egyptian metal objects south of the Sahara. But the
actual setting up of iron-extractive and forging industries south
of the Sahara seems not to have occurred until about 500 BC.
Several early iron-making sites are now identified in the grassland
plains immediately south of the Saharan desert fringe, none more
interesting than a Nigerian series in the Niger-Benue confluence
area.

This earliest-found iron-making polity in western Africa has been named the Nok Culture after the village where its artifacts, mainly figures in terracotta, were first recovered by accident during modern tin-mining excavation in the 1930s. These figures are remarkable for their great artistic qualities, combining as they do a rare sensitivity to human character and features with a sophistication of style that seems extraordinary for the times in which they were made. Historically, though, the Nok Culture has proved even more rewarding for its clear evidence of being transitional between a Stone Age food-collecting culture and one that cultivated food. Carbon-14 dating suggests that this polity ranged between 900 BC and AD 200. The first of these dates is certainly too early for the transition to the use of iron and perhaps also for the transition to growing food; and the iron-making transition may be placed, with some assurance, as being around 500 BC, possibly a little earlier than any other sites now identified in northern Ghana, central Mali and western Uganda. Others will surely come to light.

Whether by the same process of diffusion or by local invention, and most probably by a combination of the two, the knowledge of how to get and use iron then moved with astonishing rapidity into southern Africa. This knowledge had certainly appeared among peoples of the central-southern plateau country, north and south of the Zambezi, by AD 200 or 300 and probably before. Large areas of continental Africa now entered their Iron Age, though by gradual stages. It is this development, above all, that is closely associated with a comparatively rapid growth in population, and more especially with the expansion of the great family of Bantu-language peoples who now inhabit most of Africa south of the Sahara.

Some progress has been made lately in explaining this remarkable 'Bantu spread' across central, southern and eastern Africa. Linguistic evidence suggests that the people who spoke 'original Bantu'—the supposed mother-language of what were eventually to become the several hundred languages of the Bantu

'family' spoken today*—emerged in the Nigeria-Cameroons region several thousand years ago. From there it is inferred that
iron-using cultures migrated slowly southward into the western
Congo grasslands, while others went east and then south into the
eastern Congo grasslands; and that their chief area of early population growth and subsequent diffusion, beginning from there
around two and a half thousand years ago, was in the southern
Congo Basin. From this general region they appear in any case
to have spread fairly rapidly through the plateau grasslands of what
are now Angola and Zambia and neighbouring lands to the south,
gradually displacing or absorbing the Late Stone Age cultures
which already existed there. If the detailed truths of this 'spread'
have yet to be established, the fact of the 'spread' is not in doubt.

Two new factors helped the Bantu to grow in numbers and
spread across the land, diversifying as time went by into a host
of separate peoples speaking different though related languages.
The first of these factors was the better command of environment
provided by the knowledge of how to get and use iron. This
knowledge was certainly spreading among them by AD 200. Its
influence may be thought to have worked in two ways. It helped
to improve the food supply. But an improved food supply helped
in turn to provide a surplus for specialists such as miners, me-
talsmiths and other artisans who would, in their turn, continue
to swell the supply of tools and weapons. This 'two-way interaction' enabled the Bantu to grow from few peoples into many.
Another factor was the arrival of Indonesian sailors on the coasts
of East Africa, bringing with them at least one new crop of high
value. This was a better banana than any that Africa itself possessed. The Asian banana took root in East Africa and spread far
inland, once again improving the available food supply.

*It may be useful to note that the word *Bantu* consists of a root,—*ntu*, which means
'human-ness', and a plural prefix *Ba*—; i.e., *people*; while the singular is *Muntu*. On
this and related subjects, an essential book is C. Ehret and M. Posnansky (eds), *The
Archaeological and Linguistic Reconstruction of African History*, U. of California Press,
1982. Read at all costs on the 'Bantu Spread,' C. Ehret, 'Linguistic Inferences About
Early Bantu History,' in that volume.

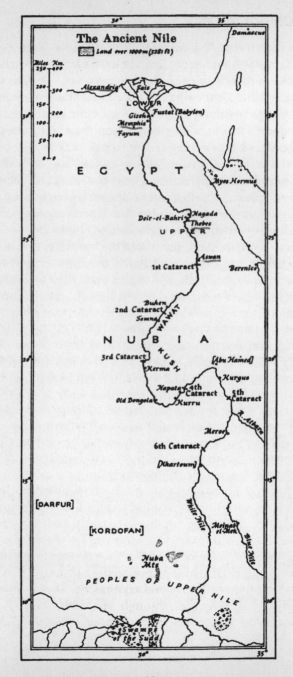

The Ancient Nile

Land over 1000 m (3281 ft)

Damascus

Alexandria
Sais
LOWER
Gizeh
Fustat (Babylon)
Memphis
Fayum

E G Y P T

Myos Hormus

Deir-el-Bahri
Nagada
Thebes
U P P E R

Aswan
1st Cataract
Berenice

Buhen
2nd Cataract
Semna
WAWAT

N U B I A

KUSH

3rd Cataract
[Abu Hamed]
Kerma
Kurgus

Napata 4th Cataract
5th Cataract
Old Dongola
Kurru

Meroe
R. Atbara

6th Cataract

[Khartoum]

[DARFUR]

[KORDOFAN]
White Nile

Meinas
el-Meh
Blue Nile

Nuba
Mts

P E O P L E S   O F   U P P E R   N I L E

Swamps
of the Sudd

22

These sea-faring Indonesians, coming by way of southern India, colonized the large East African island of Madagascar during the early centuries of the Christian era. The use of iron had reached Indonesia after 300 BC, no doubt with much the same expansive effect on population as in Africa; and the departure of many emigrants may perhaps be fixed at the beginning of the period of Hindu rule in the second century AD. Quickly absorbed along the mainland coast, where they have left some traces of their presence in the shape of out-rigger canoes and other equipment, they established themselves firmly in Madagascar and formed the initial stock from which the Malagasy people of today are mainly drawn. One modern view even thinks it possible, judging by the movement of non-African food crops, that they may also have sailed round the Cape of Good Hope and reached the coast of West Africa. Much in all this, however, is still controversial.

By about AD 800, with these events, the population picture had greatly changed. The whole of continental Africa had entered a thriving Iron Age but for a few regions where Bushmen and their like continued a Late Stone Age kind of life, hunting and gathering their food, painting and engraving on rock as the Iron Age Bantu-language peoples seldom did: a way of life that has continued, little altered even to this day, in remote segments of the Kalahari and among some of the Pygmies of the Congo forestland. Everywhere else populations had greatly multiplied, developed their farming and metal-using technology, worked out their characteristic religions, embarked on new forms of social and political organization ranging from powerful states like ancient Ghana to intricate systems of village democracy among a wide range of different peoples, and laid foundations for the growth of their civilization into recent times. From this Early Iron Age until the colonial period of the nineteenth century, the course of continental Africa's development remains, with a few important exceptions, steady and continuous. Unbroken by any major outside intervention through ten centuries and more, highly various in form, repeatedly successful in its settlement and mastery of a difficult and sometimes harsh environment, this development offers a remarkably special but also remarkably unified chapter in the history of mankind.

In telling the story of these centuries it is to some extent necessary to regard the Sahara Desert as a line of division. For while it is true that the Sahara was never a complete barrier in historical times, but rather a much-used zone of inter-communication, the fact remains that the peoples to the north of it—already differentiated from their fellow-Africans during Middle Stone Age times—nonetheless developed separately from the peoples to the south of it; and, to the extent that they developed separately, they developed differently. There was always much traffic between the two. Many migrants and many influences passed back and forth, especially during medieval times. Yet from the outset of the Neolithic in the Nile Valley and the north there was already a marked separation; and this increased with time. While the peoples of the North developed as part of the whole Nile–Near Eastern–Mediterranean complex of cultures, those to the south were left in isolation to problems and solutions of their own. Before returning to the fortunes of the continental Iron Age, this is accordingly the place to consider what happened to peoples who lived on the northern side of the great desert.

TWO

Ancient Glories

Gift of the Nile

In nothing more clearly than in the way they conserved their history did the ancient Egyptians reveal their masterful grip on the categories of space and time; not even in their mathematics, their monumental architecture, their making of calendars, or their elaborate machinery of government and collection of wealth. In the fifth century BC Herodotus thought them 'the best historians of any nation of which I have had experience', pointing out that at Memphis they had given him a written record of the names of no fewer than 'three hundred and thirty monarchs who succeeded Min . . . the first king of Egypt'. And about a hundred years after that, true to the habit of thinking big and thinking long, an Egyptian called Manetho established the framework of thirty-one dynasties that still serves us, if with some additions and amendments, more than two thousand years later.

Yet Egypt, until lately, has figured little in the thought of scholars who have studied African history, and this in spite of the fact that Egyptian records already provide a host of dates that are useful to early African history. This attitude of leaving ancient Egypt out of the history of Africa has been generally defended, if at all, by reference to the racist hierarchies of nineteenth-century thought. The Egyptians of the Pharaonic Age were not Negroes, it was argued, and therefore they were not Africans; and so their civilization, no matter how firmly and enduringly planted on the soil of Africa, should be left outside the African context. This view has little to be said for it. If it now seems perfectly clear that the vast majority of pre-dynastic Egyptians were of continental African stock, and even of central-western Saharan origins, there is likewise serious dispute among the authorities even as to whether the hypothetical 'dynastic race' associated with the foundation of Pharaonic Egypt had come from outside Africa. These early populations undoubtedly included the descendants of incoming migrants from the Near East. But to argue from this that the vast majority of the inhabitants of old Egypt, not being 'Negro', were therefore not African is as little tenable as to argue the same about the Berbers and the Ethiopians, whom nobody has yet proposed to erase from the list of African peoples. The old racist categories of 'white' and 'black' can indeed make no sense in this or indeed any other connection. Thus the Berbers have been often referred to as a 'white race'. Yet it is 'quite impossible', in Capot-Rey's most expert view, 'to speak of a Berber race. Either one means, in using this term, a language spoken with much the same grammar and vocabulary from the Mediterranean to the Niger, or one means a moral and material civilization.' Whatever their pigmentation or physical appearance, the Egyptians of Pharaonic times were an intimate part of African history.

Yet their part in African history was just as certainly a special one. And this special nature of Egyptian civilization, of the 'gift of the Nile' as Herodotus called it, detached itself from the general African context as early as the fifth millennium BC. Then it was that farming peoples of the Lower Nile and the delta evolved out of their obscurity, and, across a few brief centuries, built an urban civilization which had all the essential characteristics and acquirements of Egypt's later glory. Just how this was done remains to be discovered, and perhaps will never be known; yet the more one learns of this 'pre-dynastic Egypt' the more wonderfully impressive its achievements must appear. Almost overnight, as it were, primitive farmers seem to acquire the arts of writing, calendar calculation, obsessively ambitious building in stone and the capacity to accumulate wealth in such a way as to yield, at least for ruling groups and governing families, a civilization of unprecedented comfort and sophistication.

The change took in fact several hundred years; yet the suddenness of all this growth and lavish diversity has suggested a crucial political intrusion into the Nile Valley, which may have been associated with the arrival of new rulers from elsewhere, presumably from the urban civilizations of Mesopotamia. Some of the traditions, as well as some of the artistic and archaeological evidence, have been argued in support of this. 'It would seem probable', in Emery's view, 'that the principal cause [of the change] was the incursion of a new people into the Nile Valley, who brought with them the foundation of what, for want of a better designation, we may call Pharaonic civilization'. The late Gordon Childe was among those who have thought otherwise. He agreed that 'new ethnic elements from outside the valley' may have helped towards the unification of Egypt after 3400 BC, but 'they certainly did not introduce ready-made a culture superior to the native pre-dynastic'.

Most recent evidence combines to show that the earliest developments in Egypt derived not from Asia but from Africa; and the Chicago Oriental Institute has lately produced strong grounds for thinking that the earliest Pharaonic kingship likewise derived from the Saharan regions. This also coincides with what the Greek historians of classical times thought. They knew Egypt well, and had speculated much on the nature and origin of the Egyptians. Diodorus of Sicily—a member, that is, of the Greek settlement long established on that island—summed up their conclusions in his histories written around 50 BC. 'As historians relate', he recalled, 'the black peoples were the first of all men; and the proofs of this statement, say those same historians, are manifest'. As for the Egyptians themselves, the Greek historians of those times—of the last four or five centuries BC—accepted what the Egyptians had told them: that 'the Egyptians are colonists [i.e., immigrants] sent out by the Ethiopians', meaning by 'Ethiopians' not the peoples of the geographical Ethiopia we know today but, generally, the inhabitants of inner Africa south of Egypt. And why should the 'Ethiopians' have done this? Because 'what is now Egypt, our historians maintain, was not land but sea when the Universe was being formed; afterwards, as the Nile during the times of its inundation carried down the mud from Ethiopia [i.e. from inner Africa], land was gradually built up from the deposit'. The racist ideologues of nineteenth-century history-writing simply ignored all this. Yet what Diodorus wrote in 50 BC remains astonishingly close to what scientific research has now confirmed.

As to Asian influences, no doubt the truth lies somewhere between the two extremes of thought on this point; and, as Childe implied, the change derived really from a crucial climax of development peculiar to the Nile peoples—rapidly expanding their agriculture, their use of metals, and their accumulation of surplus food and other wealth, so that new rulers merely took advantage of a revolution which was already in the making, and was now ripe for consummation. African history suggests many examples of the closely interwoven process of conditions-ripe-for-change and the fortunate arrival of immigrant groups who knew how to profit from the fact. Where such examples lie near to our own times, and can be studied in some detail, they generally indicate that the immigrant influence was of secondary importance; and one may well think this of pre-dynastic Egypt as well. For even if those legendary 'Followers of Horus' had really come hot-foot from the courts and pavements of Mesopotamia, bearing news of new fashions and inventions, they could never have revolutionized Egypt unless most Egyptians had been ready for the change. Even after the change, moreover, dynastic Egypt copied little or nothing from foreign contemporaries, but continued to evolve new ideas and fashions of its own.

The change was certainly dramatic. Two states emerged in Egypt, one along the Nile and the other in the delta, both being the product of wealth accumulation from skilful use of the river's annual floods. These two states were never quite to lose their separate identities. But after about 3200 BC they were brought together under a king who wore the double crown; and from henceforth for millennia the hieroglyphic titles of the ruler of Egypt included not only the Horus falcon-figure of pre-dynastic times, but also the dual sign of the cobra of Lower Egypt and the vulture of Upper Egypt. Like those of the two states or great provinces on which it rested, this newly united country drew its governing power and revenue from the control of water supply, from taxation of landowners and peasants and from other forms of tribute, including military service. It took over and reshaped the administrative services of the two pre-dynastic states, and developed a large corps of clerks and tax-gatherers, commanders and governors, artists and technicians. It brought a wider peace and security to the peasants of the Nile, although the price they paid was not a small one.

'I am told you have abandoned writing and taken to sport, set your face to working in the fields and turned your back to letters', wrote a clerk of high dynastic times, chiding a colleague who had given up the stylus. 'But do you not remember the condition of the farmer who is faced with paying his harvest-tax when the snake has carried off half the corn and the hippopotamus has eaten the rest? Then the mice abound, the locusts come, the cattle devour, the sparrows bring disaster; and what

Ancient Egypt's three main scripts: Hieroglyphic (dating from before 3000 BC); Hieratic, a priestly 'short-hand' evolved soon afterwards; and Demotic, a much faster cursive developed shortly before 600 BC.

remains on the threshing floor is taken by thieves . . . And now the clerk lands on the river bank to collect the tax. With him are guards with staves and Nubians with rods of palm, and they say, "Hand over the corn", though there is none. And the farmer is beaten, bound and ducked in the well . . .' White-collar jobs, then as in other times and places, seemed the safest way to a quiet life.

Yet the benefits of strong central government made Egypt flourish. Aside from the stupendous evidence of temples, pyramids and tomb furniture, all bearing witness to a hitherto unknown success in accumulating wealth and using labour power, there is the scarcely less impressive fact of duration. After the great breakthrough into unification, complete by 3200 BC, there follow many centuries of brilliant development and growth. But there is no radical change. Its direction firmly set along the path chosen at the outset, Egyptian civilization continues unswervingly until the end. The 'gift of the Nile' enjoyed a wonderful strength and continuity, and used these advantages to marvellous effect; yet the framework was so strong and successful that it discouraged experiment. Egyptian history has rested on the counterpoint of these two opposing factors: steady growth, but also a certain stagnation.

The impact of this grand and long-enduring civilization on the rest of Africa was powerful at several points. By the fourth dynasty (c. 2620–2480 BC) its rulers were sending quite large maritime expeditions down the Red Sea as well as pioneering traders into the fertile lands of the south and west. For the sixth dynasty, beginning c. 2340 BC, there are several well-attested expeditions far to the south-west through country that was still green and watered, including one that 'went down with three hundred asses laden with incense, ebony, grain, ivory [and others goods]' and must have travelled far towards the fringes of the Congo forest. On the long western frontier with the Berber communities of the Sahara and Libya there must likewise have been many exchanges, though the records apparently say nothing of

far western travels; just as there were certainly many wars of
defence against Libyan raiders and would-be settlers.

So far, such travels and expeditions were little more than exchanges within the Saharan-Sudanese community of peoples.
After the end of the third millennium, however, Egypt began to
exercise a direct military and political power over her southern
and to a lesser extent her western neighbours. First of all, around
2200 BC, there came a time of confusion and reorganization
which Egyptologists, extrapolating from Manetho's neat dynastic
lines, have called 'the First Intermediate Period'. Asians raided
the flourishing towns of the delta, and there were revolutionary
upheavals among Egyptians themselves. 'The bowman is ready,
the wrongdoer is everywhere', runs a nostalgic text of this period.
'A man goes out to plough carrying his shield . . . Men sit in
the bushes until the benighted traveller passes by, and plunder
his load. Thieves grow rich . . . He who had nothing is now a
man of wealth, while the poor man is full of joy. Every town
says: let us suppress the powerful among us . . . The children of
princes are dashed against the walls.' But when all this Jacobin
upheaval is over, with the beginning of the eleventh dynasty in
2130 BC, the great system takes control again; and Egypt is once
more ruled by a single strong power dispensing law and order
throughout the Upper and Lower Kingdoms.

Only now there is a significant difference. Power has shifted
three hundred miles upstream from Memphis to Thebes. The
Pharaohs turn their attention to the southern country beyond the
cataracts, the land of Nubia and the source of gold, and send
victorious expeditions both to raid the Nubians and subject them,
as well as to fix their southern frontier and control all passage
through it. They build huge forts and fill them with frontier
guards. And during this Middle Kingdom—onwards from about
2130 for three and a half centuries—Egyptian civilization makes
its first deep impress on the farming peoples of the various lands
of Nubia, of Wawat and Irthet and Kush and the like, that lie
beyond the second cataract. Then comes a Second Intermediate

Period which terminates with the uprising by Asian settlers who make great use of horse-drawn chariots, a technique that now spreads rapidly westward through the still habitable Sahara; but these Hyksos people fail to hold their conquests, or were absorbed.

Once more the great system absorbs disaster and comes out intact. The Hyksos interlude, now thought to be Phoenician, is followed by a powerful dynasty, the eighteenth, whose rulers include some of the most majestic names in Egyptian history. It is rather as though the whole intricate system had required a thorough bureaucratic shake-up, every now and then, in order to recover its ambition and efficiency. The recovery now was even more imposing than under the Pharaohs of the eleventh and twelfth dynasties who had followed the First Intermediate Period of confusion. Egyptian armies pressed far southward, and the greater part of Nubia became an Egyptian colony. Tutmosis I of this New Kingdom, which lasted from about 1580 until 1050 BC, completed the work of his predecessor Amenophis and brought all the country of Nubia between the second and fourth cataracts within Egyptian control. He and others sent new naval expeditions down the Red Sea, fought off Libyans in the west and Asians in the east, and established an empire that was larger and had more influence on its neighbours than ever before.

This New Kingdom radiates power and influence for nearly five centuries, but is far gone in political decline by 1000 BC. The system continues as before, just as do the irrigation technologies which have given it birth, but Egypt passes from one stiff crisis to another; and it is from now that the factor of stagnation becomes fatal to recovery. As before, a long period of centralized rule through a highly stratified bureaucracy, military and civil, is followed by revolt and invasion. Libyan princes seize power in parts of Egypt, and we have Manetho's twenty-second dynasty, beginning with Shoshenk I in 945. These Libyan princes rule for about two centuries, often with success, until their power in turn fritters itself away. While Lower Egypt has been ruled by a rather shadowy 'four kings of Tanis', making the twenty-third dynasty, and one or two still more shadowy kings of the twenty-fourth dynasty, a new power has gathered south of the cataracts. Upper Egypt and then Lower Egypt are invaded by the rulers of the South, the Kushites, who have often lived under more or less direct Egyptian rule, but have never lost their separate identity, ever since the conquests of Amenophis and Tutmosis in the sixteenth century BC. Kashta begins this Kushite conquest at some time in the first half of the eighth century. Piankhy (751–30) and his brother Shabako (716–695) complete it. Kush becomes a world power.

Deeply imbued with the ideas and beliefs of Egyptian civilization, these early Kushites of the lands we now call Nubia might have held Egypt for much longer than a hundred years if they had been left alone. But they were not left alone. In the 660s the Assyrians came south into the delta with iron-equipped armies that drove their bronze-armed enemies before them. They fought the Kushites and set up against them a ruler of the delta city of Sais. The Kushite Pharaoh Taharqa (689–64) felt the full weight of these Assyrian blows, and his successor Tanuatamun (664–56) was the last of the Kushite rulers of Egypt. The Saite kings took over after Assyrian and Kushite withdrawal, and stayed in power until 525. Then the Persians under Cambyses followed where the Assyrians had led but, unlike the Assyrians, pressed home their victories into the greater part of Egypt. In 332 they in turn were followed along the invading trail by the Greeks under Alexander of Macedon, and the long period of Greek rule under a line of Ptolemaic rulers began. Then came the Romans, and after the Romans more confusion, and after this confusion the Muslim Arab conquest and reorganization of the seventh century AD.

Pharaonic Egypt disappeared utterly from sight, its rich tombs rifled of their precious furniture, many of its monuments engulfed in sand, even its language surviving to some degree only among a small minority of Egyptian people; and would not be drawn into the light again for another thousand years and more. Yet the achievements and inheritance of this grand civilization had fed and given vigour in countless ways to the onward movement of other civilizations in many lands.

The Blameless Ethiopians

The ancient Egyptians thought it obvious that they themselves were the only true men, but were ready to admit the existence of three lesser branches of the species, Asians, Nubians and Libyans. The ancient Greeks, taking a barbarian view of the matter, gave precedence of dignity and worth not to the Egyptians, in spite of the manifest superiority of Egyptian civilization over anything else they knew in that particular line, but to all those peoples who lived, lost in mystery, in 'Africa beyond Egypt'. These Africans they called Ethiopians rather as later Europeans would indiscriminately call them Negroes; and it was to the land of the 'blameless Ethiopians' that Homer's gods repaired once a year to feast for twelve days.

Of these peoples beyond Egypt the Greeks in fact knew little or nothing, then or later, and even the valiant Herodotus failed to visit them. 'The furthest inhabited country towards the southwest', he observed in about 450 BC after visiting southern Egypt, 'is Ethiopia.' By this he meant Kush in Nubia and lands immediately to the south of Kush. 'Here gold is found in great abundance, and huge elephants, and ebony, and all sorts of trees growing wild. The men, too, are the tallest in the world, the best-looking, and the longest-lived.' Considering that Herodotus had to rely on travellers' tales during a period when relations between Kush and Egypt were anything but good, this is not a bad description of the land and peoples of the Middle and Upper Nile. For there was much gold in these lands and many elephants, as we know from other evidence; while even to this day there are peoples dwelling along the Middle and Upper Nile, who, if not particularly long-lived, are unusually handsome and tall of stature. Yet apart from a few reports of this kind, the Greek writers have nothing to say about the lands beyond Egypt, a fact which helps to explain why European scholarship of later times, so often closely tied to the writings of later Hellenism, also had nothing to say on this interesting subject. Only these last sixty years have brought any real advance in the study of Kush.

Two great centres of metal-using civilization emerged among the blameless Ethiopians, and both are now recognized as having been of high importance for subsequent history. The first, whether in order of time or weight of influence, was that of Kush in Nubia; while the second, parent of modern Ethiopia, was that of Axum in the mountains along the south-western side of the Red Sea.

The origins of Kush lie in the remote settlement of early farming peoples along the Middle Nile above the first and second cataract, riverain peoples whose cultures were closely akin to those of the early pre-dynastic Egyptians, but were modified from time to time with the arrival of neighbours who moved in during and after the third millennium BC. Still probing for closer definition, archaeologists have as yet to be content with merely alphabetical or site labels for them. They more northerly of these peoples came under Egyptian influence during the Middle Kingdom after 2000 BC. Amenophis I (1991–62) began this conquest by securing Wawat, the northernmost province of old Nubia (as the Egyptians called it, though the Nubians of later times had yet to appear); and it is from about this time that southern Nubia begins to be called Kush in the Egyptian records. Sesostris continued the conquest. His armies 'passed beyond Kush and reached the end of the earth', or perhaps as far as the third cataract or some way beyond, but secured no permanent hold there. At some time before the Hyksos invasion of the Second Intermediate Period (c. 1750–1550), when the whole of Nubia regained its independence, a new state emerged in the Kerma region, immediately south of the third cataract; and it is mainly in this Kerma state— undoubtedly an important early culture of inner Africa, highly distinguished for its painted pottery, but of which little is securely known—that the ancestral origins of the later Kushite system may probably be traced. Meanwhile, recent excavation at Qustul by the Chicago Oriental Institute points to the origins of Egyptian kingship as having occurred not in the Delta in the north, but here in the south. Again, the conclusion is that Egypt of the Pharoahs was first and foremost the product of inner-African initiative, just as the historians of classical Greece reported.

With the end of the Hyksos interregnum and the rise of the New Kingdom in Egypt, expeditions were renewed towards the south as well as in other directions; and the vanguards of the great conquering Pharaoh Tutmosis I, who pushed far southward through Kush and established his frontiers at Kurgus between the fourth and fifth cataracts, may even have gone as far as the region of modern Khartoum. From 1500 until about 800 BC the greater part of Nubia, composed of the two great tribute-paying provinces of Wawat and Kush, lay under close Egyptian supervision.

Yet its people remained distinct from the Egyptians. They went on living by their own ideas and customs. Even the highly Egyptianized Pharaohs of the twenty-fifth (Kushite) dynasty lie in their tombs, at Kurru near the fourth cataract, in a posture used traditionally by their Nubian forebears but not by the Egyptians whose gods these Kushite rulers had nonetheless largely accepted. Although strongly marked and shaped by Egyptian culture, early Kushite civilization cannot properly be considered a mere emanation of Egypt or even a second-class copy.

The two main phases of Kushite development were associated with successive capitals at Napata, near the fourth cataract, and at Meroe, some two hundred miles farther south. The first of these phases began with the obscure rise of Kushite political power based largely on the control of the sources of Nubian gold, after the New Kingdom of the Pharaohs had begun to disintegrate in the eleventh century BC. While Libyan princes ruled from Thebes, the capital of Upper Egypt, chiefs in Kush could safely raise their heads in Nubia. They were perhaps further encouraged

in this, during the late tenth and ninth centuries, by their local
priests of the god Amun and of other gods associated both with
Thebes and Nubia. Their power grew. Early in the eighth century, as we have seen, the chiefs of Kush were strong enough to
begin the invasion of Egypt itself.*

These Kushite Pharaohs ruled Upper Egypt for a century, and
the whole of Egypt for more than fifty years; yet the impact of
all this on their homeland seems to have been remote and even
insignificant. Their own peoples continued to live as they had
lived before. The kings and soldiers had gone down into Egypt,
conquered and held it until the coming of the Assyrians and then
returned again. Though the Kushite court at Napata, at least after
the death of Piankhy (730 BC), became heavily Egyptianized in
its rites and manners, in its architecture and use of Egyptian
hieroglyphics, the Napatan empire must be regarded, Adams tells
us, as 'from first to last a Nubian culture and a Nubian population
which for a brief time'—from about 730 until the death of Aspelta
(568 BC)—'took upon itself an artificial veneer of pharaonic tradition'. So far as most Nubians were concerned, the whole Egyptian enterprise might have been little more than a raid upon the
big scale, exciting and adventurous but yielding no important
change. Yet something new had in fact occurred; and this was
of the first importance. In their furious delta battles of the 660s,
the Assyrians had fought with weapons of a new kind, weapons
of tempered iron instead of bronze and stone. However little
noticed at the time, a new age in Africa had begun.

Content with their bronze, the Egyptians had ignored the
spreading use of iron in nearby Asia. They had known iron for
many centuries, but had made little effort to reduce its rarity or
to master the skills of getting and working it. Prized as curiosities,
iron weapons had formed no significant part of Egyptian military
equipment. A fine dagger with an iron blade was buried with

*Egypt had in fact lost control of Kush under Rameses XI in the eleventh century BC.
Pinhasi, the 'King's son', or viceregal governor of Kush, threw off his allegiance and
invaded Thebes with a Nubian army, thus prefiguring the more famous and enduring
Kushite invasion of three centuries later.

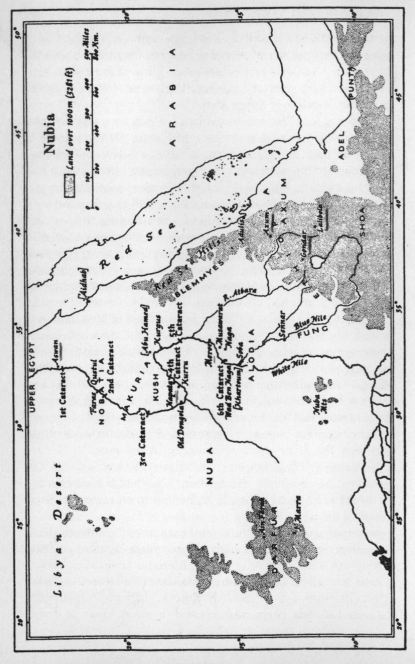

Nubia

☐ Land over 1000m (3281 ft)

0 100 200 300 400 500 Miles
0 200 400 600 700 Km.

Libyan Desert

Red Sea

ARABIA

UPPER EGYPT

1st Cataract · Aswan

Tarsa Qustul
N O B A T I A
2nd Cataract

Faras [Abu Hamed]
M A K U R I A
Xurgus
KUSH
Kageba 4th Cataract
Old Dongola · Kurru

3rd Cataract

NUBA

DARFUR
Jiu Tagu
J. Marra

[Aidhab]

Red Sea Hills

BLEMMYES

5th Cataract

R. Atbara

Meroe · Musawwarat
Naga
6th Cataract Soba
Wad Ben Naga
[Khartoum]
ALODIA

White Nile

Nuba
Mts

Blue Nile
Sennar
FUNG

AXUM

Adulis

Axum · O
H · Gondar
Lalibela

SHOA

ADEL
(PUNT?)

Tutankamun, who died in 1339 BC, yet not for another thousand years did iron tools and weapons become common among the Egyptians. Here again one may observe how the pace of technological change, once set in motion, grows by rapid progression. For while it had required at least a thousand years for the highly evolved and in many ways matchless civilization of Egypt to pass from regarding iron as a curious rarity to accepting iron technology as a necessary part of daily life, it needed less than half that time for the knowledge and practise of iron winning and working to emerge across Africa as far west as the Atlantic, and as far south as the grassland plains beyond the Congo Basin.

The effects of iron-working upon Kushite civilization, basically a riverain farming culture, can as yet be gauged only by inference. About a hundred years after their retirement from Egypt, a new centre of Kushite civilization emerged at one of their southern cities, Meroe, lying about one hundred miles north of Khartoum, although not for another two centuries would Napata lose its old importance. Gradually, however, the weight of political and economic interest shifted southward. Detectable reasons for this include the continuing desiccation of the Napatan region and its consequent shortage of timber and pasture. Perhaps Persian and other military pressure from the north, during the sixth century BC, may have had something to do with the move. There is also the suggestive fact that the region of Meroe, unlike that of Napata, has large deposits of good iron-bearing ore; and this was a period in which the demand for iron was spreading steadily. Within some three hundred years of the southward move, the metalworkers of Meroe had in fact turned their city into what appears, by the archaeological evidence, to have been an important iron-founding centre.

Whatever the precise reason for the southward move may have been, they were accompanied by a growing anti-Egyptian reaction among the Kushites of the towns. Meroitic civilization—what Adams has called 'the Meroitic Renaissance'—became far more self-consciously and deliberately Kushite than its Napatan predecessor had ever been, and revealed 'a whole series of devel-

opments and accomplishments which are by no means prefigured
in the late Napatan era, and which are symptomatic of a marked
return of cultural vigour'. Its gods and rituals were primarily those
of Meroe, not Egypt. While good Egyptian hieroglyphics continued to be used in temple inscriptions, the Kushites now began
writing their own language in an alphabetic script which has yet
to be understood. The fine painting of pottery reached a new
excellence and the styles used were largely Kushite. Meroe became very much a civilization in its own right; and this civilization was one of considerable depth and range of culture.

The history of Meroitic Kush covers at least six centuries of
energetic and often quite distinctive development in many fields,
especially those of town and temple building, metal manufacture,
and the elaboration of international trade with countries as remote
as India and even beyond. Shinnie's important excavations of
1968–72, digging into residential quarters outside the walls of
the royal buildings at Meroe, indicate a first major settlement
there around 600 BC, which was considerably earlier than expected. This early date suggests rather clearly that Kushite culture
had taken an early urban form, far towards the south, even during
the imperial period of Napata or very soon afterwards; and this,
in turn, was then confirmed by Hintze's excavations at Musawarat
as-Safra, not far from Meroe, where the earliest buildings, there
mainly religious in kind, also appear to date from the sixth century
BC. What we are confronted with, in short, is a culture of great
historical depth even before its major development at Meroe in
the fourth century.

At any rate from the fourth century BC, there unfolded here a
far-reaching process of inventive development whose influence
on neighbouring African lands is yet to be traced, but upon
existing evidence was probably important. From Meroitic Kush
the caravan trails went eastward to the ports of the Red Sea—to
'Aidhab, for example, still to be fully explored archaeologically—
and links with the Indian Ocean trade; northward to Greek-
ruled and then Roman-ruled Egypt and links with southern Europe; and south-eastward into the mountains of Ethiopia, and,

at least after AD 100 or thereabouts, to the empire of Axum. There is much to suggest that other trails may have led westward towards the Niger.

Like some other geographically remote civilizations of antiquity, Kush was forgotten by a later world. There is a stray reference in the Book of Kings to the Pharaoh Taharqa (fifth of the Kushite dynasty), and another in the Acts of the Apostles to an envoy of the queen of the Ethiopians (that is, of the Kushites of Meroe) who was converted by one of Christ's apostles on the road that 'goeth down from Jerusalem to Gaza'. But misleading use of the Greek term 'Ethiopian', together with a general indifference to the historical claims of Africa, tended to sink the Kushites deep within a sea of scholarly indifference. Even when the nineteenth century brought a new interest in ancient civilizations, the early travellers and excavators were understandably dazzled by their brilliant discoveries in Egypt; and Kush was generally regarded, insofar as it was thought about at all, as no more interesting than a provincial poor relation.

The last seventy years, but above all the last twenty years, have wrought a change in this. Much remains to be understood about the Kushites of Meroe and their highly specific civilization, but enough is already clear to frame a picture of extraordinary diversity, creative skill and technological success. They combined a stubborn attachment to their own traditions with the speculative and syncretic approach to new ideas and fashions that may be characteristic of all strong trading cultures. Their temples and palaces owed a great deal to Egyptian examples, but nonetheless had styles and ornaments which were purely Meroitic. Much of their religion, like their language, their alphabetical script and the best of their pottery, was all their own. Yet they had always welcomed innovation, and they continued to do so. As time went by, and the Ptolemaic Greek rulers of Egypt were displaced by the Romans, and trade across the Indian Ocean grew with greater skills in using the monsoon winds, the Kushites of Meroe and its sister-cities borrowed repeatedly from their neighbours and trading partners. One or two of their later buildings remind one

Alphabetical script consisting of 23 symbols and a sign for word-division, invented by the Meroites in the third century BC.

of Syrian Palmyra. Not a few of their copper vessels seem to have been Chinese imports or at least to reflect Chinese styles. There is a Greek air about some of their art, while their four-armed lion-god Apedemak would almost look at home in an Indian temple. Yet the total effect remains powerfully distinctive and specific.

The high period of this civilization lay in the five centuries after the reign of Nastasen, whose period appears to have initiated or at any rate crystallized that profound cultural reaction against Egyptian ways and customs which led to many of the best achievements of Meroitic art and thought. Nastasen's exact dates are still contested, but he certainly ruled for about twenty years in the first half of the fourth century BC. It was not long afterwards, and perhaps under Arnekhamani (c. 235–18 BC) who built the Lion Temple at Musawarat as-Safra, that the priests and traders of Meroitic Kush appear to have begun to use their own cursive script, * and pottery was painted with great beauty. By this time, too, Meroitic iron-using manufacture was getting into its stride, while Meroitic political and military power reached far to the south and west, eastward to the Red Sea, and northward beyond Napata to the region of the first and second cataracts. By 200 BC Meroitic Kush had become a large and powerful empire, endowed with the means of far-ranging trade and the benefits of a self-confident and capacious native culture; and these benefits it continued to enjoy until the fourth century, when nomad incursions and an invasion from the Tigrean kingdom of Axum combined to bring the achievements of Meroitic Kush to an end.

The second outstanding civilization of the lands 'beyond Egypt', that of Axum, took its rise at about the same time as Meroitic Kush, though little or nothing was known of its origins until systematic archaeological investigation began in 1952. Here again there was the same remote interweaving of a local culture, that of the people of north-eastern Ethiopia, with commercial, religious and political ideas from elsewhere, in this case from old Arabian civilizations across the Red Sea. In later times this distant process was nicely symbolized by Ethiopian adaptation of the biblical story of the Queen of Sheba's visit to King Solomon. That lady of Sabaea in southern Arabia went up to Jerusalem at some time in the tenth century BC 'with a very great company, and camels that bear spices, and gold in abundance, and precious stones', and afterwards came home again in good heart. She also

---

*Though the earliest attested example of Meroitic script is from a later century, its development and use seem to have appeared in the third century BC.

came home with a son by King Solomon, according to the Ethiopian legend; and this son was Menelik, founder of the dynastic line of the legendary Lions of Judah that eventually ruled over Ethiopia. The little difficulty caused by a gap in time of many centuries between the dates of Solomon's reign and the rise of the kings of Axum, forerunners to those of Ethiopia, naturally failed to worry the story-tellers of long ago.

Yet the legend secretes a core of truth. It is now known that a strong trading polity was established along the coast and in the hinterland of north-eastern Ethiopia by the fifth century BC, and that this polity owed much to southern Arabia. Its altars were engraved in the boldly beautiful script of southern Arabia, and the language used was from the same source. Its gods were likewise from across the water. Yet even in the fifth century BC this culture had an originality of its own, as many objects recovered in the 1950s clearly show; and this local originality increased as time went by.

After the fourth century BC, Ethiopian-Sabaean culture entered a transitional period during which the main outside influence ceased to be southern Arabian and became Greek: now it was, for example, that the ocean trade between Ptolemaic Egypt and the lands of India and the Far East made extensive use of the north Ethiopian port of Adulis. Ethiopia's early trading links with Kush and Egypt were multiplied by many contacts with the ports of the Indian Ocean and beyond. Adulis became a centre of world trade, and the Ethiopian capital of Axum, in the hills behind Adulis, felt the influence of all this. Writing of the later years of the first century BC, Strabo could note that no fewer than 120 ships were known to have sailed from the Egyptian Red Sea port of Myos Hormos on business connected with the Indian Ocean trade, while an Egyptian-Greek sailor's guide of the great period of Axumite expansion described Adulis as a vital link in the long chain of ports which lay between the central coast of East Africa and the Red Sea.

This great period began soon after AD 50 when Axum became the seat of a new line of kings. By now the cultural break with

This fragment of an inscription from an altar near Axum shows the Sabaean form of script used by the Ethiopians early in their history, and from which Ge'ez was developed.

Arabia was complete, and Axumite civilization was as distinct from its early Sabaean relatives as was Meroitic Kush from Napata or Egypt. Its gods, like Almaqah the moon-god, might still be the old gods of Arabia, but altar and other inscriptions were now in Greek or in Ge'ez, language of the Axumites and parent of later Ethiopian. Zoscales, reputedly the first of these new kings, was followed by other powerful monarchs who raised in Axum those towering stelae—usually though misleadingly called obelisks—which overtopped all other standing stones in this land of megalithic profusion, and whose sole tall survivor is still the admiration of the world.* Some of the names of these kings are

*More will be known about them when excavations begun by the late H. N. Chittick can be continued and fully published.

known from their fine gold and silver coins and from other
sources, but no sure dates are available until the fourth century
AD with King Ezana; and even Ezana's dates have been lately
questioned by scholars who believe that he may have reigned in
the fifth century and not in the fourth.

It was Ezana, at all events, who completed the downfall of
Meroe. After centuries of trading intercourse between Meroe and
Axum, the two had grown far apart. During the early part of the
fourth century, if not before, new peoples came filtering into the
settled lands of Kush. A famous inscription of Ezana's calls them
the Kasu and the Red Noba; they were in any case the last of all
those many peoples who had moved out of the dry lands of the
Saharan west and found the comfort of the Nile Valley to their
taste. These Noba or Nubians seem to have settled down alongside the urban Kushites without much trouble, although here
the records are entirely lacking. But with Axum they were repeatedly at war. Ezana's inscription tells self-righteously how he
was provoked by the Noba, time and again, until he decided to
make an end of their presumption. Gathering his armies, Ezana
marched down the Atbara, the ancient road to Meroe, and defeated the Noba 'at the ford of Kemalke', pursuing them thereafter
for three and twenty days.

The precise direction of this running fight is not clear from
Ezana's inscription, but Hintze has lately argued, to me convincingly, that it went westward and south-westward over the
Butana scrublands to the Blue Nile around Sennar. Here the
Axumites ravaged the 'towns of masonry' of a Noba people who
understood iron-working, wheat-growing and cotton production,
who raised temples to their gods, and who possessed camels and
Nile shipping: all of which suggests that these Noba, by this time,
were a long-settled people. Later phases in Ezana's campaign
took him down the Atbara to the Nile, whence he sent expeditions
to ravage the Noba and the Kushites to the southward and also
to the northward.

It was during this southward expedition that Meroe itself was
evidently destroyed, along with other towns less securely iden-

tified. And this is the last glimpse we have of ancient Kush. Its cities do not recover. Its rulers vanish from the scene. For this complete disintegration a single military invasion, very clearly, could not have been the major cause. Other possible causes were the decline of Meroitic trade with the north, because of bad relations with Roman-ruled Egypt; with the Red Sea, for the same reason; and with the south-east, because of Axumite rivalry after the first century AD. Yet we know next to nothing about the quantities and variations of Meroitic trade. Was the decline caused by dynastic discord, by an 'over-militarization' of the state? Again the evidence fails. All that we know with some assurance is that the decline set in at some time around AD 200, was fairly rapid, and affected the urban centres while scarcely touching the villages of the countryside.

Far more probably than to any other cause or assembly of causes, the decline of this ancient and majestic polity owed its chief origin to the structure of the Meroitic state. This, so far as the evidence can show, had two basic components. The first consisted in a state system and politico-administrative hierarchy, capped by a divinely sanctioned ruler with his immediate family and flanked by holders of titles both hereditary and appointive: this was the 'body of the state' and was largely parasitical upon the internal economy. Its principal foreign concern lay in the export of raw materials and primary products, including captives for foreign enslavement, in exchange for foreign consumer goods imported for its own use and comfort. The second component consisted of a population which in its great majority, if with exceptions in Lower Nubia where the towns had become larger, lived by cultivation, cattle-raising and short-distance trade.

This kind of structure certainly became known in later African history, and what we know about such structures points to a conclusion that may well be valid for Meroe as well. It is the kind of structure which has generally led to what is nowadays called 'under-development': to a *process*, that is, of widening economic stagnation and then of actual regression in relation to its external markets and suppliers, and therefore to their political and military power. In the case of Meroe, as it happened, these foreign neighbours were strong and could be hostile, whether they were Roman in the north or Axumite in the south-east. In these circumstances it would seem that only a structural revolution could have saved the Meroitic state from extinction.

Now it was the turn of Axum in Ethiopia. A new Axumite phase—again, it appears, within a basic structure very like that of Meroe—opened in the third century. Soon after that the rulers of Axum were ready to grapple with the outside world and make their mark. The cultural evidence is very clear. It is also very special. Ezana, or perhaps his predecessor, accepted Christianity as one of the state religions. Ezana's coins show both pagan and Christian symbols, and from this time onward the separation from its neighbours of Axumite civilization, merging later into the Amharic civilization of medieval Ethiopia, became ever more marked. While the Ethiopians developed their own strong Christianity, their neighbours remained pagan or accepted Islam. Wars of commercial or political rivalry became religious wars as well. Out of this cultural isolation in north-eastern Africa the Ethiopians were to fashion their own unique traditions of religious custom and of art.

It would be valuable to know how far these advanced Iron Age civilizations of Kush and Axum were linked with other African peoples to their west and south. Little can as yet be said about this. The Meroites certainly traded far westward, and possibly it was in this way that the Chad-Niger peoples first learned the art of making sculpture in metal by the lost-wax process.* It would be no surprise to find that West Africans sojourned in Kush, or Kushites in West Africa; and further excavation in the cities of Kush, as well as decipherment of Meroitic inscriptions, may one day make it possible to begin to write this closed chaper in trans-African relations.

Southward movement from Kush was impeded by the nature

*This involves the coating of a clay model with wax, and then the displacement of the wax by molten metal. The wax, being thus melted, is 'lost'.

of the Upper Nile country, and especially by the nature of the enormous swamps of the Sudd. If Kushites travelled to the land of modern Uganda and saw the Mountains of the Moon, or Ugandans to Kush, the records are silent on the fact. Yet this was probaby one route by which the ancient world of the Mediterranean heard a little of the truth of inner Africa; and here again the Meroitic records, when at last they are properly examined and understood, may throw some useful light. Further eastward, the Axumites undoubtedly travelled far into the continent, whether for trade or plunder, and perhaps it was from Ethiopia that the developing Iron Age cultures of East Africa, at least after about AD 700, adopted such techniques as that of hillside farming by the use of stone terraces and water channels. A better understanding of these matters may even show that the important copper-producing centre of the Katanga in the eighth and ninth centuries AD may have enjoyed some distant link, through intermediaries, not only with copper buyers along the East Coast but also among the urban peoples of the north. The present state of the question suggests in any case that all these regions—whether in north-eastern, western or central Africa— were at least indirectly linked together over a long period in the past. In this, as in so much else, a certain underlying unity of ancient African cultures seems once more affirmed. And what in this respect was true of Kush and Axum, of the 'blameless Ethiopians,' was likewise true of their neighbours in the west and north-west, the Berbers of the Sahara and the lands of the Maghreb, modern Tunisia, Algeria and Morocco. They, too, developed a notable civilization which had many links with the cultures of their African neighbours.

Early North Africa

Not far west of Algiers there stands a monumental and majestic tomb of circular design: a great mound piled firmly on the ridge of the coastal hills, and visible from far away. The guidebooks

call it the Tomb of the Christian Woman; but there is really
nothing Christian about this strongly columned dome of masonry
with its single internal corridor winding inward to a solitary cham-
ber. It dates in fact from the pre-Christian period, and is the
greatest of many thousand Berber tombs scattered along the length
and breadth of north-western Africa. Its architectural origins lie
neither in Europe nor in the Middle East. They belong to the
distant centuries of Berber emergence.

Between those origins and the Berber king who was buried in
the Tomb of the Christian Woman—probably the Bocchus who
ruled in the central Maghreb during the second century BC—
there reaches the long and often mysterious development of a

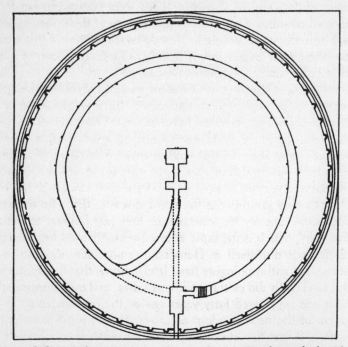

*Plan of the winding tomb-corridor inside the 'Tombeau de la Chré-
tienne'. An earlier straight passage is reconstructed by the dotted lines.*

civilization which owed much to the ancient people of the fertile Sahara, something to the Bronze Age cultures of south-western Europe, especially Spain, and a great deal to its own unfolding growth.

Here in north-western Africa there occurred a synthesis of cultures of Saharan origin together with native cultures deriving from Mediterranean forebears. By the middle of the second millennium BC these emergent Berber peoples—peoples, that is, who may be grouped together by their common use of the Berber language in its variants—had become an active part of the whole North African scene. They dominated the smiling Mediterranean coastland and its inland hills, while their poor relations sojourned throughout the Sahara from the shores of the Atlantic to the borders of the valley of the Nile. They were famous far beyond their own countries for the speed and beauty of their horses; and it was from them, according to Herodotus (in matters of this kind more often right than wrong), that the Greeks first learned the skill of harnessing four horses to a chariot.

Something of the inner and abiding strength of this old Berber culture may be glimpsed by measuring the tales of Herodotus against the findings of modern research. Writing in the fifth century BC, the 'father of history' described how a people called the Auses, who lived in the southern part of modern Tunisia, 'hold an annual festival in honour of Athene, at which the girls divide themselves into two groups and fight each other with stones and sticks; they say this rite has come down to them from time immemorial, and by its performance they pay honour to their native deity, which is the same as our Greek Athene.' For a long time this was dismissed as Herodotian embroidery or pure invention. Yet anthropologists have lately shown that a ceremony of this kind really did exist in southern Libya, and even continued until it was suppressed forty years ago by the modernizing government of the new kingdom of Libya. In this most venerable ceremony it was the custom up to about 1960, very much as Herodotus explained, for the young girls of Ghat and El Barkat in the Fezzan, and perhaps elsewhere as well, to gather for a

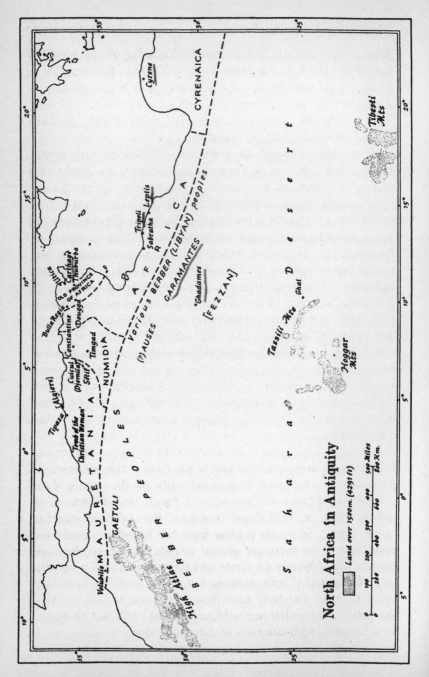

North Africa in Antiquity

Land over 1500m. (4291 ft)

| 0 | 100 | 200 | 300 | 400 | 500 Miles |
| 0 | 200 | 400 | 600 | 800 Km. |

'feast of salt' in their best clothes and wearing all the jewellery they could lay their hands on. Got up like this, they paraded in military style with flags and musicians, each being armed with a stick or whip, and celebrated the salt harvest with a mock battle. Even if they did not know it, they were acting in a play that was at least two and a half thousand years old.

While it was only with Herodotus that the Berbers enter written history, they had long had a script of their own, ancestral to the *tifinagh* still used by the Tuareg Berbers of the Sahara, though it is also true that inscriptions of Old Berber have as yet yielded very little of historical value. Herodotus in the fifth century had many different names for their branches or tribes: Garamantes, Nasamonians, Machyles, Auses, Mauretanians and others, corresponding to cultural or political divisions which had come into existence in much earlier times. These ancient divisions are faithfully reflected today by the still existing divisions of North Africa, with distinctive peoples of Berber origin (if later mixed with incoming Arabs) occupying Morocco, Algeria, Tunisia, the Fezzan and Libya; for it appears that the Berbers were never united, except perhaps in very early years, into a single group or even into a single confederation of peoples. Onwards from the first millennium BC they occasionally combined against foreign enemies or rivals, but never sank their differences for more than brief periods.

Although they appear in written history only in the fifth century BC, they were already a vital part of the African side of the whole Mediterranean trading circuit of antiquity. By the middle of the second millennium BC they were in touch, and sometimes in military alliance, with those 'peoples of the sea' who helped to ravage Egypt. So much is clear from the Egyptian records; but aside from these there are several strands of evidence for their contact with Mycenaean Crete and Greece, not least a magnificent 'flying gallop' rock-painting from the Tassili n'Ajjer mountains. Even in that early time they were quite possibly crossing the Sahara, somewhat less wild and hostile in its nature than it soon became, with caravans of carts and riders.

With the coming of the Phoenicians to the western Mediterranean, the Berbers were drawn fully into the commerce of the ancient world. The process was of course a gradual one. Phoenicia's earliest settlements along the Berber shore were intended as little more than staging-posts which could securely link the Phoenician trading colonies in Spain, great exporters of tin and copper, with their homeland ports at the eastern end of the Mediterranean. But these energetic businessmen took root in their little colonies. Their North African entrepôts grew into trading states in their own right. Carthage, the greatest of them all, has a traditional founding date at the end of the ninth century BC; but as a city rather than as a staging-post for Spain, it probably dates only from the seventh. Within another hundred years, however, Carthage had become a city of the first importance, its trading strength being drawn no longer from Spain but from the African interior.

By the fourth century many Phoenician ports had sprung into being along the North African littoral, ports such as Leptis and Sabratha, whose principal *raison d'être* was not to act as intermediaries in the east-west Mediterranean trade, but as intermediaries in the trade between the African interior and the rest of the ancient world. It was thus the wealth of the inner-African trade that properly explains the splendour of Leptis, Dougga, Thuburba Majus, and other trading cities whose majestic ruins evoke admiration today. They bought gold, ivory and other African goods from Berber neighbours, who in turn had carried these things across the Sahara from West Africa, linking North and West Africa in the same way as their descendants were to do, though with still greater success, after the Muslim Arab conquests of more than a thousand years later.

These trading Berbers were seldom much influenced by Phoenician city life. United in their several kingdoms of the Maghreb, Fezzan and Libya, they allied themselves with Carthage and its sister-cities, or quarrelled with them according to the shifting fortunes of the day. The most famous of the kings of Numidia—roughly, western Tunisia and eastern Algeria—even led a Berber

army as an ally of Carthage against the Romans in Spain. This
outstanding man, Massinissa, afterwards warred with Carthage
as well as sending several contingents of his cavalry, and one of
elephants and riders, to fight in Roman wars against Philip of
Macedon. Carthage responded by siding with Massinissa's most
powerful Berber rival, Syphax, king of the Mauretanians of Morocco.

In 146 BC the long struggle between Rome and Carthage ended
with the ruin of the latter. The Carthaginian 'home territory' in
eastern Tunisia became a Roman province. For the Berbers, this
was merely exchanging one probable enemy for another. As with
the Phoenicians, they were ready to trade with the Romans provided that it paid, or even to fight for them, but they were unwilling to give up their independence. In the end the Roman
republic was able to master Numidia and turn it into a client
state, yet only with great difficulty; while further west, in Morocco, Roman order never became secure. Only with the rise of
the Roman empire and its highly organized military power did
Tunisia and Algeria, and to a lesser extent Morocco, come under
strong Roman influence. Then through four remarkable centuries there was peace and great prosperity. Many cities were
founded. Many of them flourished. Many Berbers of the coastland became city dwellers and citizens of Rome.

This was much more than mere Romanization. Those who
visit Carthage today may well receive from its almost entirely
Roman ruins the impression that Rome completely supplanted
Phoenician or Phoenician-Berber civilization. The impression is
misleading. Little was destroyed by the legions of the Roman
Republic except Carthage itself, the capital of African Phoenicia.
Elsewhere the cities remained much as they had been before.
Then with the growing power and prestige of Rome there came
a long and highly successful synthesis. Roman government and
Roman settlement gradually reshaped North African civilization
without fundamentally changing it. Along these fertile coast-
lands, rich in grain and cattle, Phoenician-Berber cities acquired
Roman habits, gods and customs—and, what was perhaps most

important of all, Roman markets—while continuing to stand on
the cultural soil of their old pre-Roman traditions. New Roman
colonies, staffed and defended by Rome's veterans of foreign wars,
grew into cities that were among the finest in the world; but they
were Roman with a big difference, and the difference was African.

Leptis, for example, had come into existence as a junction for
the Saharan-Mediterranean trade during the fifth century BC.
From the first it was heavily influenced by its large dependence
on Berber contacts with the interior. On these it thrived, and the
treasury at Carthage looked to Leptis for a substantial annual
contribution to the costs of the capital and empire. But the Libyan
Berbers also looked to Leptis for a living. During the upheavals
of the Roman conquest, they even tried to capture it. And when
Rome acquired a Leptian emperor in the person of Septimius
Severus, Berber links were further strengthened by the positioning
of a permanent Roman garrison at Ghadames in the heart of
Garamantian Berber country. This garrison was designed to guard
the trade-route south into the Fezzan, but it strikingly confirmed
the interest of the coastal cities in their hinterland.

There followed years of growth and great expansion. The North
African coastlands became a land of milk and honey, 'a country
that was nothing but one shaded grove', as an Arab writer would
later picture it, 'one unending series of villages'. Many of the
powerful fragments of this Romanized civilization of North Africa
are still there to tell the tale. One can follow their fortunes almost
year by year.

Cuicul, or Djemila by its Arabic name, is a good example. In
AD 96 or 97 the emperor Nerva ordered veterans to set up a colony
in a fine steep-sided valley bottom that could guard the mountain
road between Sétif and Constantine. These veterans called their
settlement by its Berber name, married local girls and steadily
prospered. Within fifty years their modest huts had given way to
large houses, and soon these were so crowded within the walls
that their new theatre, another evidence of civic pride, had to be
built 150 yards beyond their outer rampart. In AD 161 they added

a superb arch between the rampart and the theatre. In 183 they built a comfortable bathing establishment two hundred yards beyond their south gate. The line of the old rampart now became lost within a vast aggregate of suburban dwellings. Many more large public buildings were added during the thriving Severan period of the third century AD: a forum, fountains, public lavatories, new temples and meeting halls. By now the population was around ten thousand strong. It was a population, we may be sure, that was well pleased to be Roman in its citizenship, but was no more Roman in its origins or its everyday language than most of the peoples of Roman Britain or Roman Gaul.

With the rise of these grand and comfortable cities, Timgad and Leptis, Tipaza and Dougga, Cuicul, Thuburba and many others, the trans-Saharan trade passed into a new phase of growth and orderly organization. No doubt it was in this period, after the second century AD, that the earliest trading polities beyond the Sahara began to respond to steadily strengthening commercial demand from the north. The trade grew for several reasons. The cities of the north had become ports of entry to the almost inexhaustible markets of the Roman Empire. Widening use of the camel went hand-in-hand with security along the trade routes, at any rate within Roman borders, and with the opening of new wells and the conservation of old ones. Beyond the *limes*, moreover, Roman power interested itself in keeping the peace along these routes. There were even two or three Roman expeditions far into the desert country towards the Sudan beyond it, though none of these seems to have gone further than the Tibesti and Hoggar mountains of the eastern and central Sahara. Generally one has the impression, if from scanty factual evidence, of a well-ordered system of trade through many Berber intermediaries who were in regular and frequent contact with those Africans of the Western Sudan who dealt in gold and ivory, and who, having begun to develop their Iron Age (possibly by Berber transmission) around 500 BC, were moving into the development of early forms of state.

Not all went smoothly. The massive ruins of Cuicul, lying within their bastion of tall Algerian hills, may once again be called in evidence. After the death of Emperor Severus Alexander in AD 235 there came a temporary weakening of Roman power, and poor harvests, and revolts; but the city recovered in about 280 and enjoyed another period of civic comfort in the fourth century. Now its public buildings included many Christian churches, and Cuicul became a place of pilgrimage. With a local end to the Donatist schism in 411, the bishop of Cuicul, Cresconius, built an imposing basilica with five naves; and the pilgrim traffic, now under Byzantine inspiration, grew apace.

This newly Christian civilization was sorely threatened by Vandal invasions from western Europe in the fifth century, but the end came slowly. Cuicul, for instance, continued to be a Byzantine Christian city of importance, sending a bishop to Constantinople in 553, until it was finally destroyed, violently and mysteriously, at the end of the sixth or early in the seventh century, probably by the revolt and ravaging of nearby subject peoples. In breaking up the Roman system, however, the Vandals opened the way for more than the destruction of cities like Cuicul. Lacking any firm base, but unable to engraft themselves into the urban culture of Roman North Africa, and thereby carry on the empire, or at least a part of it, these ambitious raiders signalled the close of an epoch, the end of Antiquity. With their breaking of the gates, there came a final interruption in all that long process of growth which had coupled the Berber Bronze Age of the second millennium BC to Phoenician enterprise and Roman organization.

What came now would be singularly different. In 641 the followers of the Prophet Muhammad seized Babylon in Egypt, capital of that Byzantine province. A year later they had Alexandria; in 647 Tripoli; in 670 most of Tunisia. Everywhere they marched they were triumphant. Their conquering hand was heavy, and loot was often their incentive. After taking Byzantine Babylon, later to become the great Fatimid city of al-Khaira or

Cairo, its conqueror wrote to Caliph Omar that he had within
his hand a city of 4,000 palaces, 4,000 public baths, 400 theatres,
12,000 spice-dealers' shops and 40,000 Jews paying tax, the latter
being already an important community here. Exaggeration as to
numbers, no doubt; but not perhaps a large one. Babylon-in-
Egypt was no mean successor to its then legendary forerunner.

Much loot was seized; yet there were advantages in this conquest for the Egyptians, and especially for those who belonged
to the Egyptian national branch of Byzantine Christianity, the
Coptic Church of venerable foundation. These Egyptian Christians, whose language (and then whose liturgy) was to prove the
last survivor of the language of the Pharoahs, were glad enough
to lose their 'Greek oppressors' of Byzantium, fellow-Christians
though these were; when the Arabs attacked, the Copts stood
neutrally by. For this they were rewarded with a certain tolerance.
They secured their religious enfranchisement from Byzantium
without being oppressed by the Muslims, or not at least in any
systematic way, even when Egyptian conversion to Islam was
otherwise far advanced. They exploited their literary and administrative skills, rare among the Arabs of that time, or at any rate
among the conquerors, to secure most of the jobs in government.
Collaboration paid off, and they were also able to seize the property of many Melkite (Byzantine) monasteries and churches
whose Greek Christians had fled. This Muslim tolerance was
likewise extended to the Jews of Egypt, and the latter were now
able to lay the foundations for their great influence and prosperity
during the high days of Fatimid rule (tenth to twelfth centuries
AD).*

After a hundred and fifty years of uncertainty or upset, this
new peace came widely in North Africa to offer a new security
for men long wearied of the dangers of the time; and Islam
triumphed here, as it sometimes would elsewhere, as much by

*Cf. especially S. D. Goitein, A Mediterranean Society, vol. I. Economic Foundations,
University of California Press, 1967.

its message of unity and brotherhood—however often honoured only in the breach—as by the vigour of its military arm. The consequences were many. Within another hundred years or so, the trans-Saharan trade was once more on the path of large expansion, and the history of northern and much of western Africa entered a new stage.

THREE

The Factors of Growth

African Solutions

If all he could hope to explain was how one barbarian succeeded another, Voltaire tartly observed to an intending historian of the Turks, where could be the advantage to mankind? The point should be well taken by an intending historian of the Africans. There is little difficulty, as it happens, in setting forth a list of kings or regnal dates for quite a number of African states and empires; and of kings, moreover, who were no more barbarian in the sense of being violent, irrational or vowed to blind destruction than most of their contemporaries in Asia or Europe. The notion that African life before the colonial period was 'blank, uninteresting, brutal barbarism'—to offer the definition of a professor of colonial history, Egerton, at the University of Oxford seventy years ago—is now thoroughly exploded. But any 'scissors and paste' approach to African history, relying centrally on lists of kings, battles and 'big events', would go badly wrong from the start. For it would miss more than half the story. It would suggest, for example, that those African peoples who developed forms of centralized self-rule and empire were the only ones worthy of attention, leaving aside as insignificant those many other peoples who did not.

   This kind of approach would miss not only the great diversity of African social and political experience, but also, and even more, the underlying unities and similarities which give to all of

them, practically without exception, their profound inner coherence and inter-relationship. This political and social unity-
in-diversity may be reasonably compared with the African linguistic scene: more than a thousand distinctive languages, according to the present view, have flowed from four or five root
tongues, *Ursprachen*, of unknown but certainly enormous age.
And on the political and social scene a correspondingly great
diversification has likewise fissured from unities which first took
shape in distant Stone Age times.

Especially within the last two thousand years, the historical
period since the beginning of the African Iron Age, this diversification has supported, and to some extent continues to support,
an extremely wide and complex range of political and moral
authority, so that there is scarcely a single case where one people
governs its behaviour by the same rules and precepts as those of
any of its neighbours. Now the reasons for this seeming confusion
of system and belief deserve some brief examination as a prelude
to our narrative. They make it possible to place many of these
types and sizes of system and authority within a meaningful if
summary perspective which helps to explain their origins and
nature.

If people recognizably like ourselves began to multiply in Africa
about 40,000 years ago, as the anthropologists now assure us was
probably the case, they were far from numerous. They multiplied,
then or thereabouts; but slowly. By the final period of the Makalian Wet phase after 2500 BC, when the Sahara began to draw
a wilderness of desert between continental Africa and the rest of
mankind, scattered groups of hunters and food-gatherers had long
since appeared in all the main regions of the continent; yet even
by this comparatively late period they were still few in numbers.
At the outset of the Iron Age, two thousand years ago, the peopling
of Africa in anything like its later density and universal presence
had only just begun.

The central problems which had to be solved by these early
Africans were thus of two kinds. In the first place they had to
master an often very hostile environment to at least the point

where they could support their own settlement and multiplication: in other words, they had to improve their economic understanding and organization, they had to invent new tools and discover new techniques. Secondly, they had to elaborate sociocultural superstructures of thought and belief such as would enable them to establish and support the self-confident identity not only of numerically large groups of people, but also of many separately distinct societies. Their simple economies could seldom allow them to multiply and stay *in situ*: some of them had to be repeatedly moving and spreading their numbers. What happened, time and again, was that a given group would divide and hive off a lesser group, and this lesser group would march off into new territory, for a long time into territory possessing few or no people of its own; and there they would settle and begin a new life, work out new rules of law and order, redefine their morals and beliefs and then again, as multiplication continued, themselves divide and hive off still other groups who would repeat the process.

Now the principal ways in which this interplay of environment and social relationships worked to establish Africa's patterns of belief and behaviour were much the same, fundamentally, as the experience of other peoples in other continents who were faced with much the same problems. A main starting-point was the 'extended family', a more or less close-knit group of relatives comprising several pairs of grandparents, or possibly great-grandparents, with all their living descendants except those who had married out of the group into another but comparable group. Such groups would be larger or smaller according to the nature of the country in which they lived: larger in fruitful country, smaller in country that was dry or poor in game.

As soon as a group grew markedly above its optimum size, some of its members would have to withdraw and move elsewhere. In withdrawing, however, they were posed not only with the problem of finding another place where they could live in peace, or at any rate support themselves; they also had to solve the problem of authority within their breakaway group. Putting this another way, they had to cement their new and isolated identity. They had to explain to themselves who they were, what they had become; and they had to do it in such a way as to enable their coherence to survive in the face of many dangers and exertions. Their systems of behaviour—their systems of religion, if you will—had to be both mandatory and explanatory. *

Something like this process, greatly simplified in these few words, went on over wide regions of Africa through a very long period of Stone Age and early Iron Age multiplication, spread, and development of community life. Out of it there came a large number of political and social systems based on the structures of lineage and family kinship. Each of these systems supported, and was in turn supported by, its own adherent forms of religion and ritual. These forms were applied to the consecration of accepted custom and authority, and to all those situations where decisive change in custom and authority was found desirable or necessary. That it why African religions have ideally displayed or have been intended to display a completely rounded explanation of life. Their essential *raison d'être* has been to provide the individual with his firm place in society, furnish him with evidence of his own identity, and generally equip him with beliefs appropriate to the acceptance of his social condition and survival within his environment.

In doing this, no doubt, the religions of Africa have performed the same kind of social and political work as other religions in other lands; but they have nonetheless been characteristic of Africa and nowhere else. To grasp even a little of their moral and emotive force, valid for so many peoples over so many years in so many different and testing situations, one must at least to some extent envision the varied manner of their teaching and acceptance: whether by the rehearsal and catharsis of rhythm in the movement of dancing or the power in the patterned playing of drums; whether by sanction in the shape of masks and figures

---

*I have discussed these processes, within their cultural framework and significance, in *The African Genius*, Boston, Little, Brown, 1969, and reprints (*The Africans*, Longman, 1969, Penguin, 1973).

carved in wood and ivory or forged in metal, or by the persuasion of belief conserved in shrines and gods and ancestors, magic and enchantment. All this has been a work of long sophistication and creative practise. Nothing shows it better than the splendid arts with which these religions are organically and inseparably linked. Like the religions of Africa, the arts of Africa are not the crude imaginings of primitive men. On the contrary, they are the embodiment and statement of old and intricate speculations and traditions about the nature of the world and man's possible place in the world. They are the literature, the holy books, the poetry of African belief.

All this, too, has belonged to the underlying structure of every kind of political development in Africa. Immensely varied though they became as time went by, it was the vertical divisions of African society, divisions framed by lineage and kinship loyalties and fixed by ritual and religion, that governed and impelled the machinery of diverse growth within a given environment. These divisions operated at different levels and in different ways; but they were universally present. Some of them promoted social organizations which have remained relatively simple even into modern times, such as those of the Khoi (Bushman) of the Kalahari or the Twa Pygmies of the Congo forest. Others ramified and reconstructed themselves into large political organizations which we call states and empires. But all derived from the same root patterns.

It is possible for the sake of convenience to classify African societies into a number of general types, distinguishing those with much government from those with little, those with centralized forms of rule from those whose cohering authority has been dispersed among heads of clans or extended families. Yet the distinction remains at best an artificial one. There is no true division to be made between African 'states with kings or central governments' and African 'societies without kings or chiefs'. Each of them derives from one form or another of what latter-day sociologists call the 'jural community', recently defined by Middleton as 'the widest grouping within which there are a moral obligation and a means ultimately to settle disputes peaceably'.

It is the elaboration, of course, which makes the stuff of history.
It is there that the drama lies. The 'blank, uninteresting, brutal
barbarism', which was all that Professsor Egerton of Oxford could
see in pre-colonial Africa seventy years ago, gives way on better
understanding to a major chapter in the survival of mankind and
the growth of civilization. For the elaboration has been various
and vigorous in every geographical region of the continent.

In West Africa, for example, the last fifteen hundred years
have seen the growth of large and long-lived systems of central
rule involving great hierarchies of privilege and government, intricate systems of justice, regular recruitment into a wide range
of professional services, civil or military, including a sometimes
numerous and literate bureaucracy. Other West Africans, at the
same time, have continued to live under rules so simple as to
raise the question of whether the rules may be said to constitute
government at all. A people like the Tallensi of northern Ghana
have never desired institutions which could be called central
government, nor persons appointed to political authority, nor use
of writing or written records. Yet it would be absurd to suppose
that the Tallensi or others like them, peoples who have generally
remained on the margins of political change and movement in
Iron Age Africa, have been in some way less gifted or intelligent
than their state-forming neighbours. Their mode of individual
and collective social life, with its niceties of check and balance,
its strength and flexibility, its bare simplicities of form combined
with tolerance for stress and error, allows no place for any such
idea.

It would be agreeable to follow this line of thought; but the
result could be nothing like a compact summary of history. What
we have rather to do here is to select those political forms, changes
and departures which best reveal and illustrate the growing complexity and onward shift of socio-political organization and its
corresponding action on the general scene. In the case of Africa,
where the writing of history has so far made no beaten paths,

any such selection is bound to be something of a personal choice: in what follows, however, I have tried to keep a balanced view of the significant and less significant. Yet it will be useful, before going any further, to say a little more about the variety of Africa's historical development.

Much of this variety can be traced to fairly obvious environmental differences. The peoples of the Sudanese grasslands have developed differently from their near-neighbours of the tropical forest for reasons that are not difficult to isolate; just as it is easy enough to envisage why the peoples of the East African uplands, excellent country for grazing cattle, should have followed a different path of growth from those of the Congo River Basin and its densely tangled woodlands. But not all the reasons for variety are obvious, at any rate when considered from a distance. If the plough developed in the north as early as the fourth millennium BC, it was nonetheless banished from large areas of the rest of the continent by the tsetse fly, a pest which appears to have been present in Africa since the earliest times of human habitation, and has certainly been present since the earliest times of animal domestication. If some peoples developed an imposing socio-political organization on the basis of mining for minerals and trading in the minerals, other peoples had no such opportunity. If the concept of kingship proved helpful to a number of societies, it was evidently useless to others.

Ideas and things received and adapted by Africans from other continents have also played their part, and sometimes not a small one. Here again some peoples were well placed to profit from external influences, or to suffer from them, while others were not. In the Western Sudan, time and again, the steady demands of the trans-Saharan trade drew enterprising and ambitious rulers into an effort to enclose large areas of trade and production within single systems of power and revenue. Famous markets appeared at the cross-roads of commercial exchange. Peoples who lived along or near such trading routes were often impelled, whether as rulers or ruled, into new forms of political organization. Islam, arriving in the ninth century and greatly expanding in the eleventh and twelfth, brought new solutions to new problems of power, and often helped the processes of centralization.

Sea-merchants mooring on the coast offered another kind of stimulus. City-states grew and flourished in the swampland of the Niger Delta, after the sixteenth century, where only fishing villages had been before. Other city-states, still older and more successful, came into being along the coral seaboard of eastern Africa, and were raised to brilliant life and commerce by connection with the traders of the Indian Ocean on the one hand, and with the producers of inland Africa on the other. Southern Bantu-speaking peoples opened tens of thousands of mineral workings, whether for gold or copper or other metals, in response to manufacturing demand from across the eastern seas: and they too, while doing this, likewise changed their forms of political organization.

Some peoples accumulated wealth, at least in the hands of their kings, chiefs and governors, while for others the concept of accumulation remained impossible and undesired. The great lords of the western Sahara grew famous far outside Africa for their stores of gold, their lavish gifts, their dazzling regalia and ceremonial display. When the most powerful of the emperors of Mali passed through Cairo on pilgrimage to Mecca in the fourteenth century, he ruined the price of the Egyptian gold-based dinar for several years by his presents and payments of unminted gold to courtiers and merchants. A sixteenth-century emperor of Kanem-Bornu was even said to have equipped his cavalry with golden bits and his hunting dogs with golden chains.

Of those for whom accumulation was impossible, or simply wrong, the Dinka farmers of the Upper Nile provide a good example. They live in a country which might well have baffled any attempt at settled habitation. North of them lies the grim and thirsty land of Kordofan; southward is the trackless wasteland of the swamps of the early Nile. Their own country is a plain of grass and woodland that is drowned for part of every year by floods from rain and river, and where permanent homesteads and gardens are possible only on slips and stretches of higher ground that seem to float upon the sky-reflecting waters all around. Most of Dinkaland has no minerals, or none that could be reached, little timber and practically no stone. 'Apart from imported metal and beads', writes Lienhardt about this extraordinary people, 'there is nothing of importance in Dinka material culture which outlasts a single lifetime. The labours of one generation hence do not lighten, or make a foundation for, those of the next, which must again fashion by the same simple technological processes, and from the same limited variety of raw materials, a cultural environment which seems unchanging and, until the extensive foreign contacts of modern times, was unchangeable.'

Such apparently 'primitive' peoples were regarded by Europeans who went to Africa a hundred years ago, and later, as the more or less tormented victims of savage ignorance and hopeless superstition. They were often thought of as children who had somehow failed to grow up, whether from lack of cranial capacity or some other supposed physiological defect; and they were accordingly approached as being proper subjects for control by others who knew better. What we now understand about the Dinka should dispel any lingering notions of this sort. For it may easily be seen that a people living in nudity on the brink of starvation once a year, manufacturing nothing that endures and accumulating for inheritance only a few cattle and a few tools or ornaments, are not necessarily a people who have failed significantly to evolve. On the contrary, it becomes obvious upon reflection that the very stability of Dinka life can only be the outcome of successful adaptation to a stubbornly hostile environment, and that any less careful or ingenious a compromise must have rapidly destroyed them. To dismiss this kind of achievement as belonging merely to the 'unrewarding gyrations of barbarous tribes in picturesque but irrelevant corners of the globe', as a Regius Professor of History at Oxford urged us in 1963 seems a curiously provincial impoverishment of the proper study of mankind.

These few remarks by way of prelude to modern African history—to the history, let us say, of the last twelve centuries—

indicate that the record is far richer than any short survey can possibly encompass. With that word of warning, we may now begin to detach the purposive movement of African history by concentrating on a few main themes and sections in the story. One helpful way to apprehend this movement, at any rate in the present phase of historical analysis, is to look at certain ways in which Iron Age societies grew and changed; at the transformation of early political organizations into states and systems of increasing size and complexity of government; and at the forms in which trade and production for trade took shape in the foundation of cities, in the forging of communications and in many efforts at meeting the expansion of demand for African goods both inside and outside the continent. We shall also look at the manner in which vertical divisions in society—lineage and kinship systems—became progressively influenced and overlaid by horizontal divisions, by caste and class systems; and, last but not least, at the way in which major influences from outside Africa made their own specific contributions to the changing scene.

It needs to be remembered, at the same time, that in all these manifold and complex transformations the mere size of any given polity, or its degree of political centralization, offers no reliable guide to effectiveness of development and control of environment. On the contrary, many of the 'small' polities, such as the village governments of the Igbo of eastern Nigeria in historical times, have shown a quite outstanding capacity for political and economic adaptation, social coherence, and ideological self-assurance. The notion that some special virtue lies in the politically 'small' becoming the politically 'large', whether by absorption or conquest of neighbours, may fit the conventional traditions of Europe and America: it has seldom fitted those of Africa. Rather was it in the 'small' societies that the characteristic tone and temper of African community life retained and constantly reshaped the modes and morals of public behaviour, no matter what changes might occur in surrounding circumstance. It was repeatedly the 'small' and not the 'large' societies—the village governments and not the royal or imperial systems—

which framed Africa's insistent interweaving of the duties of the individual with the rights of the community, and produced Africa's specific forms of egalitarian democracy.

I hope to give due value not only to a number of leading themes in the movement of African history, but also to the great diversity of culture which occurs from one end of the record to the other. A little repetition may be unavoidable here and there, as well as an occasional leaping back and forth across the years; but these should do no more than clarify the movement of events. We begin with the years up to about AD 1500, taking the eighth or ninth century as a general starting-point.

Trading Cities

With the emergence of new and stable systems of Muslim law and order in the Near East and North Africa, the arteries of economic growth regained their health. In the Mediterranean, as in all the seas surrounding Arabia, the carrying-trade of Antiquity recovered and was steadily enlarged. Responding to their new opportunities, as well as to the challenge of their new unity and faith in themselves, Muslim merchants pushed their ships and enterprise far across the seas. They established themselves in little trading settlements along the coasts of India, Ceylon, Malaysia and down the eastern coast of Africa, and in the ports of southern China. They multiplied the old Phoenician links between southern Spain, soon to be the seat of material prosperity and soaring intellectual achievement under a succession of Muslim dynasties, and the harbours of the southern and eastern Mediterranean as far as Alexandria and beyond. They reopened large channels of inter-continental communication.

What was true of the seas of water was also true of the ocean of sand. With camel transport a widely used routine, Berber traders became ever more numerous along the trans-Saharan trails. Old wells were dug out again; new wells were driven. There came to be used in the Saharan oases the same technique of underground water-channels, *foggara*, as in the oases of the central Asian desert of Chinese Turkestan, one piece of evidence among many of the constant interchange of ideas throughout the world of Islam. If the Berber middlemen of Phoenician times had used mainly two trails across the Sahara—westward from Morocco through Mauretania and southward from the Fezzan of the Garamantes to the Middle Niger and Lake Chad—their successors of early Muslim times were soon using many more. This wide world of Islam, reaching by many intermediaries from Spain and Morocco in the west to China in the east, now steadily expanded the demand for the goods of West Africa and especially for gold and ivory.

Meanwhile the same demand for ivory and gold, as well as for some lesser commodities like tortoiseshell, made itself felt through eastern and south-eastern Africa from the ports and cities of the Indian Ocean seaboard. Hindu brides bedecked themselves with the carved ivory of Kenya and Tanganyika. Chinese officials went to court in palanquins veneered and decorated with the same material. 'That is where the ivory goes', complained al-Mas'udi in the middle of the tenth century, 'and were it not for this demand, there would be plenty of ivory in our Muslim countries.' Even the smelted iron of East Africa acquired an international reputation. Collecting reports of Africa in twelfth-century Sicily, al-Idrisi was informed that the best steel came from India, but that India had its best iron from south-east Africa. This East African iron, he wrote, was supplied 'to all the lands of India . . . [and] at a good price—[because it is] most superior in quality and most malleable . . .' Slaves from Africa also went that way; judging by the documents, however, these were very few when compared with the Atlantic slave trade of much later times.

Two large regions of old Africa were thus involved in the recovery and expansion of the carrying-trade in medieval times. There arose two correspondingly large and long-enduring networks of commerce that penetrated far into the continent: between North and West Africa, and, in somewhat lesser degree, between the East Coast and the mineral-rich plateau lands of the central-southern interior. Both of these trading networks were major features of the African scene by the tenth century. Even before this, moreover, they had given rise to the expansion of old markets and the founding of new ones. These early market-centres and their later rise to wealth and influence form a continuous aspect of development after about AD 800. They greatly help to shape the course of political change in West and East Africa. Their history illustrates both the capacity of Iron Age response to new trading opportunities, and the way in which this response was itself linked to the elaboration of new political systems.

Later in medieval times the reputation of some of these cities became world-wide and clothed in distant glamour. Long after he had travelled through East African Kilwa in 1331, the Moroccan scholar Ibn Batuta could still remember it as 'one of the most beautiful and best constructed towns in the world'; and he, by that time, had seen the cities of India, China and his own Moorish countries. Writing for an Italian audience early in the sixteenth century, Leo Africanus described Timbuktu as a city of learning and letters where the king, besides disposing of an army of three thousand cavalry and 'countless infantry', supported from his treasury 'many magistrates, learned doctors and men of religion'. 'Here in Timbuktu', he noted, 'there is a big market for manuscript books from the Berber countries, and more profit is made from the sale of books than from any other merchandise.'

These travellers were not exaggerating the comparative comfort of fourteenth-century Kilwa or the bookish leanings of medieval Timbuktu. Yet the beginnings were certainly more humble. So far as the western regions are concerned, they appeared after the Muslim conquest and cultural unification of North Africa; but new growth was necessarily slow. The desert was little more hospitable then than now, perhaps the only real difference for travellers being in the greater number of usable wells; and the distances were as vast as ever. Camels were better than horses, yet no faster on their feet; given the continuing desiccation of the Sahara, they were probably even slower.

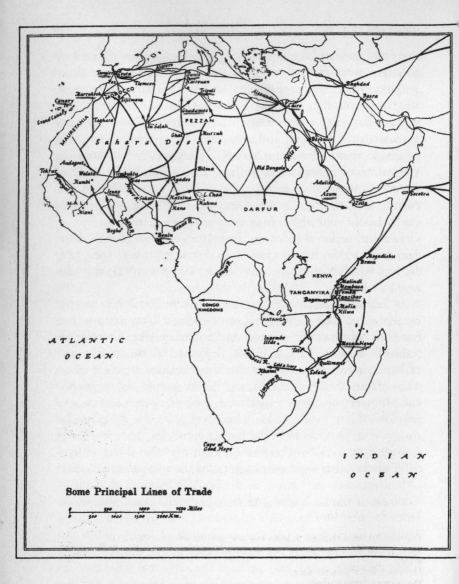

Some Principal Lines of Trade

0   500   1000   1500 Miles
0   500   1000   1500   2000 Km.

74

A good notion of the difficulties which had to be faced by Saharan travellers may be had from Ibn Batuta's celebrated description of his own crossing of the desert. Though made in 1352, when the trans-Saharan trade was nearing the peak of its activity, it was certainly valid for much earlier times. Ibn Batuta took the main western route from Sijilmasa, then the flourishing 'northern terminal' of the Moroccan-Mauretanian trails to and from the Western Sudan. Nowadays Sijilmasa is no more than a site of interest to archaeologists. But in Ibn Batuta's day it stood at the crossroads of the far western trade, and was the major *entrepôt* for Sudanese gold in the Maghreb. Long used in antiquity, Sijilmasa had grown into a large and agreeable town whose abundant dates, in Ibn Batuta's view, were even better than the fabled dates of Basra,* while 'the kind called *irar* has no equal in the world'.

At Sijilmasa, preparing to cross the desert, Ibn Batuta bought camels and a four months' supply of forage. Travelling with a company of Maghrebin merchants, Berber like himself, he reached the salt-making centre of Taghaza after twenty-five days of journeying through the northern fringes of the desert. He found it 'an unattractive village with the curious feature that its houses and mosques are built of blocks of salt, roofed with camel skins', an observation of no small interest in helping one to grasp the antiquity of the trans-Saharan trade. Nearly eighteen centuries earlier, Herodotus had described a place near the Pillars of Hercules where 'the houses are all built of salt blocks'; and Herodotus

---

*The dates of Basra have a literature all their own. Cf. a Somali song (Siraud Haad's 'Lament for a Dead Lover'):

You were the fence standing between our land and the descendants of Ali,
(Now in your departure) you are the sky which gives no rain while mist shrouds the world,
The moon that shines no more,
The risen sun extinguished,
The dates on the way from Basra cut off by the seas.

(From *Somali Poetry*, by B. W. Andrzewski and I. M. Lewis, Oxford, 1964, p. 138.)

was certainly relying on the information of travellers who had passed that way.

Here at Taghaza, the real hazards had only just begun. After observing that the business done at Taghaza, a main point of salt supply both for northern and western Africa, amounted to 'an enormous figure in terms of hundred-weights of gold dust', Ibn Batuta and his companions embarked on the nightmare journey across the true desert that lies beyond. They laid in water supplies for a first stage of waterless travel covering a journey of ten nights, movement by day being generally avoided because of the heat, but were lucky enough to light upon rain pools where 'we quenched our thirst and washed our clothes'. Encouraged by this, 'we used to go ahead of the caravan and whenever we found a place suitable for pasturage we would graze our beasts'. They continued doing this until one of their party went astray and was lost. 'After that', says Ibn Batuta, 'I neither went ahead nor lagged behind.' Two months after leaving Sijilmasa they safely reached the first main 'southern terminal' of the western route in those years, the oasis town of Walata; and with that their troubles were over. Once arrived in Walata, then a thriving market-centre for the trade of the Western Sahara but nowadays exceedingly obscure, Ibn Batuta found a comfortable welcome before embarking on his passage across the Sudanese grasslands to the settled lands of Mali which lay beyond.

We can date the medieval expansion of this West African trade from early in the ninth century. Growing first by Muslim demand in North Africa and the Near East, it increased steadily as the cities of southern Europe embarked on their own expansion after the twelfth century. West African gold now became a staple export to Europe; and without it there would have been no general use of gold as a medium of exchange in high medieval times. Monarchs as far away as England struck their coins in the precious metal of West Africa. Even as late as 1832, plundering the treasury of a conquered dey of Algiers, French invaders came upon a store of no less than 15,500 pounds of gold, nearly all of which must have come across the Sahara. There is a large sense in which the prosperity of the states and cities of the Western Sudan was founded on the export of gold, and supported by it through many centuries. *

Some of the early market-centres are known only by report or by a few bare mounds on the surface of the arid grassland. Audagost, famous at least from the tenth century, remains a puzzle for the archaeologists, but lies probably beneath the much later town of Tegdaoust. Kumbi, largest of all the early cities of the Western Sudan, with a population of perhaps as many as 15,000 to 20,000 in the eleventh century, is nothing more than a mark on the map of the Kaarta region, two hundred miles into the southern fringe of the desert from the modern city of Bamako, capital of the Republic of Mali. Walata remains, remote and humble; so does Timbuktu, though in little better case. Gao and Jenne are still respectable towns, even if their old importance is long since gone. Yet in medieval times these and other cities were a vivid and dynamic part of West African life. They lay at the heart and centre of great events and changes. Through long years their merchants and soldiers faced and conquered the daunting misery of the trans-Saharan trails, linking many West African peoples to the onward drive of Mediterranean prosperity and power, and helping to evolve a civilization which has continued into our own day.

If one large link in this wide system connected North Africa with the plains of the Sudan—taking this Arabic term to mean all the grasslands between the Atlantic and the Nile—another link connected the peoples of the Sudan with the producers of gold and other goods in the near-forest and forestlands to the south. Here, indeed, the system was often independent of North African demand. From the fourteenth century, if not earlier, towns like Niani on the Upper Niger, then the capital of the

*The same is of course true of the states and cities of the Maghreb, in their turn no less dependent on the gold trade of the Western Sudan. For an interesting discussion of this aspect of North African history, see Yves Lacoste, *Ibn Khaldun*, Paris, 1966.

Mali empire, looked south for trade even more than they looked
north. They it was, and others like them, who organized the
import of southern gold and other goods; while markets still further south, markets inside the forestland, came into being so as
to organize the export of their produce, and buy what was needed
in return. Thus it came about that Begho grew into a central
market near the gold-producing country of modern Ghana, and
one that was of quickly growing importance from about 1400
onwards. Similar pressures of trade and production may have
helped the Nigerian city of Benin to emerge as a centre of exchange between the forestland and the plains of the north. Benin
grew into a powerful city in the fifteenth century, its prosperity
being partly based on the exchange of locally manufactured cotton
goods for south Saharan copper and Sudanese horses. By about
1400 or even earlier, accordingly, one should think of the whole
of West Africa as being intricately traced with trading trails and
market centres, an economic fact of basic importance for understanding the political history of this region, and one to which
we shall return.

Much of the same type of long-range trading system forms an
essential part of the groundwork of development in eastern Africa
and its central-southern hinterland. Its links, too, are somewhat
similar, though this East African trade never reached the intricate
complexity and value of its contemporary in the west. What the
Phoenician-Berber connection had achieved in north-western Africa, however, the traders and mariners of Greek-ruled Egypt,
southern Arabia, East Africa and India largely repeated in the
last centuries before the Christian era. By then the steady winds
of the western half of the Indian Ocean, blowing back and forth
between West India and East Africa in regular seasonal variation,
were being used by sailors who had learned how to trim their
sails from peoples further to the east, and mainly from the
Chinese. Writing in about AD 100, or soon after, a Greek-
Egyptian captain of one of the Red Sea ports, probably Berenice,
explained in a mariner's guide how the trade of Egypt was linked
with that of Arabia and India, by way of such ports as Adulis in

the Horn of Africa, as well as with that of the East African coast
as far south as Rhapta. Exactly where Rhapta was remains to be
discovered; its general location, in any case, was the coast of
Tanzania or one of the Tanzanian off-shore islands.

This trade was conducted mainly by the merchants of southern
Arabian cities, although Axum also had a hand in it. These
merchants sent agents down the coasts of Somalia, Kenya and
Tanzania, men who settled there, learned the local languages
and married local women. They bought cinnamon, tortoiseshell,
ivory, rhinoceros horn, a little palm-oil and a few slaves, selling
in exchange Arabian-made iron spearheads and axes, glass and
some wine and wheat; and transacted all this for transport in
Arabian vessels whose visits down the coast seem to have been
fairly regular and frequent. As yet, however, this eastern trade
was still on a small scale. Among the coin finds of the East
African seaboard only twenty-five of the Ptolemaic period (third
to first centuries BC) are so far known, as well as three Parthian
coins (first to second century AD), nine Roman and two Sassanian
(third century AD). Although more early coins may yet be found,
this paucity suggests that East Africa was still outside any major
trading circuit.

In the ninth and tenth centuries there came a change that is
comparable with the commercial expansion in the west, and for
much the same reasons. Islam had now given a sense of unity,
at least against their non-Muslim rivals if seldom among themselves, to all those Arab trading interests and enterprises which
had spread along the coastal countries of the Indian Ocean. Many
of these countries meanwhile began to flourish in a new way,
forming among themselves a wide community of commerce and
production. At the same time the Arab sailors whose exploits
were vividly embroidered in *The Thousand and One Nights*,
Sinbad and his like, took their new faith far down the African
coast. They converted some of the coastal peoples, or at any rate
some of the coastal rulers. They established themselves in settlements that were wealthier, stronger, more ambitious than before,
intermarrying with local women as their predecessors had done.

They drew these ports and settlements into the community of
the Indian Ocean trade, and thereby laid the foundations for a
distinctively East African variant of Islamic civilization. By the
tenth century there were markets of importance as far south as
Sofala in modern Mozambique, building their wealth and power
on trade with ivory and gold producers of the interior.

By the thirteenth century Kilwa and Zanzibar, and probably
Mogadishu on the Somali coast, had acquired mints of their own;
their kings struck copper coins in fair quantity, usefully inscribing
their names but not, unhappily, their dates. The dating here has
become open to question, and the Kilwa mint may have begun
operation late in the eleventh century. A wider and even more
startling story was revealed in 1984–85 with the unearthing of
fresh numismatic evidence. Archaeologists working in the locality
of Pemba Island (next to Zanzibar Island) recovered a horde of
some three thousand silver coins of local minting, whereas previously only a scattering of such coins had been known. As so
often in African archaeology, dates initially suggested have proved
to be too late. These finds indicate that the burgeoning economy
of the East African seaboard moved into a local coin-minting
stage soon after AD 1050.* Material and cultural progress became
very marked by the thirteenth century.

The whole long seaboard was now linked together by a string
of thriving ports and city-states, Mogadishu, Brava, Malindi,
Mombasa, Pemba, Zanzibar, Kisimani Mafia and Kilwa being
among the most prominent. Islamic in their faith, strongly conscious of their membership in the Muslim world, the peoples of
these ports and city-states were nonetheless African, being of
various origins in the north and mainly Swahili in the centre and
south. They traded with all the peripheral countries of the Indian
Ocean, exporting metals, ivory, tortoiseshell, a few slaves, and
buying cottons and luxury goods from as far afield as China.
Some 240 Chinese coins, for example, are so far known from

*M. Horton and C. Clark, *Zanzibar Archaeological Survey 1984–5*, cyclostyled, Min-
istry of Information. Zanzibar, May 1985; M. Horton, 'Recent Archaeological Discoveries
in East Africa', Society of Antiquaries, London, April 1986.

East African hoards and scattered finds, ranging from those of the
T'ang emperors (618–906) to much later times, though mostly
of the Sung period (960–1279). Yet more revealing for the Eastern trade is the amount of pottery and porcelain that was landed
on these shores. This was imported from China and the Persian
Gulf states, though mainly from the latter, in such quantities
over so many years that any casual visitor may pick up many
fragments in a few hours' wandering along the gleaming sands
of the East African coast or its neighbouring islands. These wares
range from cheap kitchen types to fine examples that were often
used for the embellishment of private houses, mosques or the
characteristic pillar tombs of the East African coast; and they have
greatly helped to establish a broad chronology of sites which cover
a time-span of several centuries.

The Portuguese who ravaged and largely ruined these flourishing Swahili cities have made some slight historical amends by
recording what they looked like at the end of the fifteenth century,
the zenith of medieval civilization along this coast. Sailing up
from the Cape of Good Hope in 1498, Vasco da Gama and his
crews were astonished and relieved at Quilimane in southern
Mozambique to find that they had swum once more into a zone
of trade and frequent ocean voyaging. They had news of ships
still bigger than theirs, and pressed on up the coast. At Malindi,
in modern Kenya, they borrowed a pilot who was familiar with
the route to India. Other Portuguese followed where da Gama
had led. Kilwa, they found, was a town 'with many fair houses
of stone and mortar, very well arranged in streets . . . with doors
of wood, well carved with excellent joinery'; and the archaeological excavation of Kilwa, undertaken in the 1960s, has fully
confirmed this description. Mombasa was likewise a 'very fair
place with lofty stone and mortar houses, well aligned in streets
after the fashion of Kilwa'.

The fate of these cities will be told later. Here it is important
to note that their importance lay not only in themselves, but also
in their stimulus upon the peoples of the interior. Just like the
trans-Saharan trade, the Indian Ocean trade was reproduced

between the coast and the inland country by another and internal trading system which came to have a life and meaning of its own.

Many traces of this internal system may be found in the archaeological records of central Africa for as far back as the eighth or ninth centuries AD: *conus* seashells from the East African coast, beads from India and perhaps beyond, fragments of Sung and Ming porcelain at some of the big stone-built sites of the plateauland between the Zambezi and the Limpopo, even an early Dutch gin bottle at Khami near Bulawayo. But mainly the import trade was in cotton goods, and these of course have perished. Every year, recorded a foreign trade commissioner of one of the cities of southern China in 1226, the north-west Indian kingdom of Gujerat and the ports along the Arabian shore dispatched their ships to East Africa with cargoes of cloth for sale. Much of this cloth must have found its way far inland, being paid for in ivory and tortoiseshell but above all, at least in the heyday of this trade during the two or three centuries before 1500, in gold and copper from countless mine workings. All this trade was accompanied in the interior, just as it was along the coast, by far-reaching political changes.

Iron Age Departures

The earliest political systems south of the Sahara that are recognizable as modern states began to appear in the ninth or tenth century, although in some cases their origins were considerably older. They were modern states, that is, in the sense of having at least in embryonic form an institution of effective government, some kind of primitive civil service, an executive arm composed of an available military force (though of vassal levies, not professional soldiers), and more or less regular sources of revenue (though paid in kind, not cash). Their emergence and growth were intimately related to their skills in making and using iron tools and weapons, whether for farming, hunting, mining or subduing their neighbours; to their general development of a horizontal stratification dividing rulers from ruled; and to their grasp of the new trading opportunities which had opened with the Muslim commercial unification of all the lands to the north and north-east.

Their beginnings rise from those little-known transitional cultures which carried Africa into an early Iron Age two thousand years ago: from the Nok Culture, for example, in the Niger-Benue region of West Africa; from a comparable development, as yet vaguely identified by the archaeologists, along the line of plateau southward from the East African Rift Valley; and from other early cultures that were transitional to farming and the use of metals, mainly iron. These transitional cultures embodied and developed many characteristics and customs reshaped from their Stone Age inheritance, whether in the forms of kinship loyalty, religion, or social organization; and they lie at the root of nearly all subsequent political and social growth.

Most of the evidence is archaeological. Yet much is clear in general outline, if not in any reliable detail, from the early writers of Muslim North Africa and Arabia. Having sailed down the East African seaboard in about 917 on the 'stormy seas of the Zanj'— of the Africans—al-Mas'udi could write of the existence of a large state or empire, ruled by a king 'who commands all the other kings of that country' and situated far down the coast, adding details which make it clear that this was the work of a Bantu-speaking people. They had cattle but no horses, mules or camels; they were well provided with cereals and fruit, especially bananas and coconut palms; and they enjoyed the right to depose their rulers if these should seriously abuse their power. This 'empire of the Zanj' was clearly a successor-culture to early Iron Age political departures in the south-eastern region, and is perhaps to be identified with an early phase of the mining civilization of the Monomotapan empire of five centuries later.

There are no documentary references to the Nok Culture (transitional from Stone to Iron Age between about 300 BC and AD 200), nor to any other transitional culture in West Africa; but the oral traditions of Ancient Ghana, written down in Timbuktu long afterwards, speak of as many as twenty-two kings before the beginning of the Muslim era (AD 622), while al-Fazari, writing in AD 772, could already call Ghana 'the land of gold'. By this time, clearly, Ghana was a state of some importance in the Western Sudan. So was the future empire of Kanem-Bornu, lying east of Ghana round the shores of Lake Chad. Some of the famous market cities of the Western Sudan, Audagost, Gao, perhaps Timbuktu, likewise have their rise in about 800 or soon after. If we are to believe Ibn Khaldun, who wrote much later, the Middle Niger city of Gao was certainly in existence by the later part of the ninth century: he refers to it as the birthplace of a Kharidjite dignitary, Abu bin Kaidad; while the first Muslim ruler of Gao, converted early in the eleventh century, is remembered by tradition as the fifteenth of his line. *

All these, like the south-eastern 'empire of the Zanj' reported by al-Mas'udi, were manifestly the product of early Iron Age growth. Having opened their way to cultivation, stock-raising and mining, Africans had spread across the vast and thinly peopled lands of the interior, multiplied in numbers, evolved new ways of mastering nature, and embarked upon barter-trade with their neighbours and even with foreign countries. Already their situation was in one respect crucially different from that of their

---

*One among a group of expensive Muslim gravestones of Spanish marble, recovered from near Gao in recent years, has a date equivalent to AD 1100. Local traditions suggest a slightly earlier date for the acceptance of Islam, at least as a 'religion of convenience', and say that the *dia* dynasty in question had fourteen rulers of Gao before the one who accepted conversion. Further archaeological investigation under the auspices of the Centre of West Africa Studies, University of Birmingham, began in 1973, and throws a more detailed light on Gao Muslim origins.

Other evidence indicates that Gao's foundations as a trading centre, no doubt obscure for a long time, may have occurred as early as the seventh century. By the eighth it was a trading 'port' for Ibadi merchants from Tahert (Algeria): see T. Lewicki, 'L'Etat nord-africain de Tahert et ses relations avec le Soudan oriental etc', in *Cahiers d'Études Africaines*, vol 2, 8, 1962, and ibid., 'Traits d'Histoire du Commerce trans-Saharien . . .' in *Etnografia Polska*, vol. 8, 1964.

Stone Age forebears. These, who had survived by hunting game and gathering food, had lived by an economy of the merest subsistence, neither producing nor being able to produce any surplus above their very modest needs. But Iron Age farmers increasingly faced a new situation. They could produce a surplus, even though this was minimal at first, such as gradually enabled them to settle longer in a chosen place, increase their production of food and handicraft goods, and engage in barter with their neighbours. With the appearance of surplus and its derivative changes there came new political demands; and these the very small-scale 'family rule' of Stone Age times was no longer adequate to meet. Modern politics, the politics of class differentiation, took their embryonic rise. Stone Age simplicity gave way to Iron Age development. Vertical divisions of lineage and kinship authority began to be matched by horizontal divisions, by the emergence of castes of craftsmen, traders, warriors, labourers and kings, but also by the splitting of society into peoples who were rulers and peoples who were ruled. The questions of who should govern whom, and how, became the stuff of conquest, change and revolution. Although the old vertical divisions of lineage and family remained important, they were no longer the only arbiters of everyday authority, nor even the most important of them.

Such crucial points as these come repeatedly from the archaeological record. In 1960, for example, the Water Department of the Northern Rhodesian (now the Zambian) Government set about excavating the site of a proposed pumping station on the hill on Ingombe Ilede not far north of the Middle Zambezi. In so doing, they came upon a number of gold-decorated skeletons and uncovered one of the most important early Iron Age sites so far to be found in central-southern Africa. Comparing these 'golden burials' with those of simple but contemporary burials found nearby, the archaeologists Fagan and Chaplin, who examined this site between 1960 and 1963, have pointed to 'considerable stratification'; and Ingombe Ilede, we may note from the Carbon-14 dates that have been secured for it, flourished during the fifteenth century.* Other Iron Age sites to the south of the Zambezi, and even to the south of the Limpopo, help to support these conclusions.

This Iron Age revolution was slow but irreversible. It brought profound changes. North of the Sahara, at least, many must have despaired. How was anyone to control the explosive potentialities of this new metal whose use was so much greater and wider than copper or bronze, and whose spread seemed impossible to halt? Where was the end to be if every man could own his own spear or sword? Bronze-clad kings and chiefs had monopolized their rare equipment. But the monopoly of iron weapons, once the techniques of manufacture became widely known, was utterly beyond their reach. Like the nuclear powers of our own day, the iron 'monopolists' of ancient times might desperately wish to keep the new knowledge to themselves; the task was beyond them. It is little wonder that Herodotus should have written, as of a perfectly obvious fact, that 'the discovery of iron was a bad thing for mankind'. Under the impact of this rapid multiplication of iron equipment one great empire after another crashed and foundered. Not until AD 700 or 800 did a new but still fragile stability become possible.

South of the Sahara conditions were different. Here the use of iron appears to have been crucial for enabling Stone Age peoples to move into a mainly agricultural economy, to penetrate their dense forests, to live in settled and larger communities, and to complete the peopling of their continent. Here the use of iron cannot have seemed 'a bad thing for mankind', or not at least to

---

*It should be emphasized, perhaps, that C-14 dates are extremely useful guides to chronology, but are also no more than statistical probabilities. A date of AD 900 ± 100 years means only that we have two chances out of three that the actual date of the object in question lay somewhere between AD 800 and 1000. This is not bad, however, when you consider that the odds are 20 to 1 on the 'third chance' lying between AD 700 and 1100. Double-checking, however, remains advisable. The dates originally determined for Ingombe Ilede referred to AD 700–900, and were wrong.

*Though it must certainly have seemed so to any thoughtful Bushman, seeing his people steadily ousted from their traditional hunting grounds by iron-using farmers and warriors.

a majority of people. * Yet as time went by, and the process of
expansion continued on its way, there arose an increasing need
to solve new political and social problems associated with this
gradual transformation of community life, and to establish more
effective systems of law and order such as could absorb and exploit
the impact of new materials, new techniques, and new types of
social relationship. Many solutions were found. Though nearly
all of them were variants on the same essential pattern of Iron
Age diversification and growth, they differed much in their detail
and their development. It is their changing record, above all,
which forms the history of continental Africa between 800 and
1600.

Ghana and Kanem-Bornu

The origins of Ancient Ghana lay among West African peoples,
mainly Soninke of the Mande-speaking group, who lived at a
crossroads of trade between the oasis peoples of the Sahara and
the gold and ivory producers of the grassland and forest country
to the south. This crossroads, a wide area of pastoral plains situated to the north of the Upper Niger and Senegal rivers, is the
now remote region of the Sahel. Its markets were valuable because
they were vital relay-points for trade along the Mauretanian-
Moroccan routes to and from North Africa. Most famous among
them, at least up to the twelfth or thirteenth centures, were
Audagost and Kumbi, cities which have long since vanished from
the map.

There has been general agreement that the strong polity known
as Ancient Ghana took its rise in the western Sahel, along the
southern flank of the Sahara (the word 'Sahel' having derived
from the Arabic for 'shore'), in about the seventh century AD,
and that its large expansion after the eighth century was a response
to new trading opportunities with Muslim traders from the Maghreb. The second point is certainly right. But important archaeological discoveries late in the 1970s have revealed a far

more complex and much earlier development, well before Ancient Ghana, of early state-like communities and even of early
cities.

These discoveries, among the most instructive in all African
archaeology of recent years, have once more pushed historical
process further into the past. They reveal another zone of West
African Iron Age development, this time not in the area of the
Niger-Benue confluence but within the 'delta' region of the Middle Niger: that is, the region upstream from Timbuktu within
the great northern bend of the Niger, and notably in the neighbourhood of the surviving market-city of Jenne. Surveys and
excavation in this 'Middle Niger' region, completed in 1984 at
no fewer than forty-three sites of ancient settlement, proved that
these belonged to an Iron Age culture developing here since about
250 BC, that the settlements grew into urban centres of notable
size and duration, and that they were much concerned with
networks of regional trade established south of the desert. Here,
in short, was another arena of early development that owed no
decisive stimulus to any 'outside' agency.

This meant that long-distance trade and its supporting requirements, above all a degree of urbanism at specific points of initiative and exchange, could no longer be seen to have begun
south of the Sahara with the trans-desert trade of the eighth
century, but, instead, long before. It could now be safely affirmed
that 'the key to political and economic development in the Western Sudan'—in West Africa south of the desert—'lies in the
growth of increasingly complex *indigenous* trade networks
thoughout the first millennium AD': networks, that is to say,
introduced and long sustained south of the desert by purely West
African needs and agencies (my emphasis).*

*S. K. McIntosh and R. J. McIntosh, *Prehistoric Investigations in the Region of Jenne*,
Cambridge Monographs in African Archaeology 1, 1980; and see R. J. McIntosh and
S. K. McIntosh, 'The Inland Niger Delta Before the Empire of Mali: Evidence from
Jenne-Jeno', *Journal of African History*, 22, 1981, and 'Archaeological Reconnaissance
in the Region of Timbuktu', *National Geographic Research*, Washington, D.C., 2,
1986.

The implications were far-ranging. One of them was that semi-legendary traditions in the Western Sudan which placed the rise of Ancient Ghana in the fourth century AD, hitherto thought a good deal too early, were unlikely to be astray of the truth. Earlier still, indeed, there must have existed some form of West African long-distance trading network capable of meeting trans-desert as well as regional West African needs. For it was from the Sahel regions that Berber groups in Antiquity had been able to carry West African goods to the Phoenician cities of the Mediterranean seaboard many centuries before the onset of Muslim times. The expansion of Muslim trans-desert trade after about AD 750 provided a new and major spur to West African state-formation and urbanism; but this was an expansion grafted onto earlier indigenous initiative.

We know little about those early endeavors. Trade along the trans-desert routes was probably much depressed during the Vandal upheavals in the Maghreb during the sixth and seventh centuries, but it picked up again with the establishment of Muslim power in Algerian centres such as Tahert and its neighbours. After 800 there seems to have been rapid expansion, and this clearly had developmental effects on the old trading polities south of the desert. By 1067 the Andalusian chronicler al-Bakri, writing in the then brilliant Andalusian city of Cordoba in southern Spain, but drawing on firsthand information from trans-Saharan travellers and traders, could describe Ghana as a large and powerful empire.

North African demand for gold and ivory was one side of the picture. West African demand for salt was the other. Then as now salt was indispensable to the comforts of life. But salt was a rare commodity beyond the Sahara. Much of it came from deposits like Taghaza far into or across the desert. Even during the middle of the twentieth century, when factory-made salt had become a commonplace, annual caravans to the Bilma oasis, north of Lake Chad, have continued to carry several hundred tons of salt southward into Nigeria and the Cameroons, employing great caravans of several thousand camels at a time. The salt trade was no less important than the gold trade, and was probably much older. So far as the westerly regions of West Africa were concerned, the salt trade likewise found good relay-stations in the old markets of the Sahel.

This meant that Ancient Ghana, approaching maturity in the Western Sudan at about the same time as the Franks were organizing their structurally comparable empire in western Europe, could draw strength and revenue from the movement of two precious minerals: gold from the south and salt from the north. Other commodities were of course added as the years went by: copper and cotton goods, fine tools and swords from Arabian workshops and afterwards from Italy and Germany, horses from Barbary and Egypt, ivory and kola nuts and household slaves from the south; but the staples of the trade, in earlier times and later, were always salt and gold. These were the prizes of political success. These were the means by which the new states and empires could support their soldiers, their governors, craftsmen, courtiers, singers of songs. And the power of these empires became legendary as the years flowed by: writing in the twelfth century at the court of the Norman king Roger II of Sicily, al-Idrisi described how the lords of Ghana would often feed thousands at a time, spreading banquets more lavish than any man had ever seen before.

Thanks to al-Bakri, who wrote in the eleventh century, we can even penetrate a little way into the system of revenue collection that made it possible for these lords of Ghana to promote and buttress their power and patronage. Dominating all the relay-stations of the western trade routes south of the Sahara, they applied two kinds of taxes: one on production, the other on the import-export trade. 'All pieces of gold that are found in this empire', notes al-Bakri, who had excellent sources of information from traders and travellers, and who used these sources with an evident care and caution, 'belong to the king of Ghana, but he leaves to his people the gold-dust that everyone knows. Without this precaution gold would become so plentiful that it would practically lose its value.'*

One may doubt the truth of this last statement: the trans-Saharan demand for gold was so capacious, then and later, that no obtainable amount could have much depressed its value in exchange. But the fact remains that the king of Ghana, at any rate in al-Bakri's time, took care to follow the same course of action as the diamond corporations of a later age: he monopolized the worthwhile pieces so as to control the market. On the import-export trade, moreover, he applied a regular scale of duties, being apparently strong enough to ensure that these could be collected at every market of importance. He took through his agents a certain weight of gold or its equivalent value as import duty on 'every donkey-load of salt that enters the country', and twice as much again on 'every donkey-load of salt that goes out'. A load of copper, coming from the north, had to pay a duty of five *mitqals* (though a distressingly uncertain entity, the *mitqal* in somewhat later times was often the equivalent of about one-eighth of an ounce of gold), while every load of merchandise had to pay as much as ten *mitqals*. These details are of course far from precise. If donkeys were used in the Western Sudan, camels were the only usual means of desert transport; and we have no idea how a camel-load was broken down into donkey-loads for purposes of taxation. But the main system firmly emerges. Ghana was a state and empire based on a grouping of peoples whose Soninke overlord had the titles of *ghana*, 'war chief', and also of *kaya maghan*, 'master of the gold', and whose primary interest lay in controlling a large but crucial area of trade in several staples. At least to some extent its revenues were expressed in gold; and with these the king supported his court and lavish ceremonial,

---

*In this royal monopoly one must of course see the traditional role of an African king as an essential regulator in the distribution of realized wealth. The king accumulated but he also distributed: without the power to exercise this distributive function, he could not have commanded the authority that was invested in his kingship. At the same time, he took steps to safeguard his trade monopoly by obstructing any private enterprise.

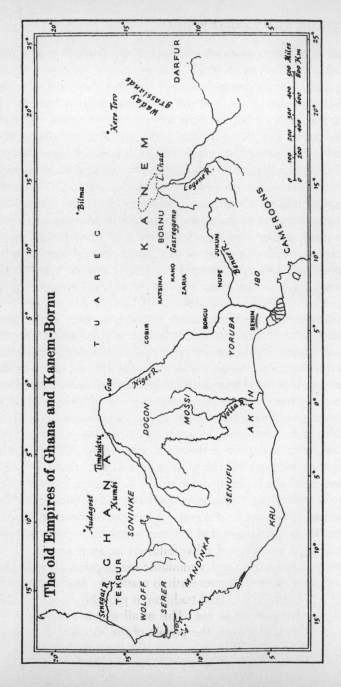

The old Empires of Ghana and Kanem-Bornu

rewarded his vassal chiefs and lesser kings, handed round the gifts and gave the 'free dinners' on a massive scale such as custom looked for from a mighty ruler.

Endowed with strong ritual powers necessary to this new post–Stone Age situation, the Soninke king (like other Iron Age rulers) was also in some sense 'divine'. He personified the spiritual being and welfare of his people conceived as a community of the ancestors, the living, and the yet unborn. But while this sanctity made him powerful, it also hedged him round with many limitations on the exercise of his power, which could seldom become despotic. In other words, with the growth of Iron Age patterns of social reorganization and central rule, a new hierarchy of ancestral powers came to be modelled on a new hierarchy of rulers, although, of course, appearances made it seem that the kings were an emanation of ancestral powers conceived as mandatory powers, and not the other way round.

Grown famous by its wealth, Ghana attracted rivals and invaders. For three centuries after the Muslim conquest of the north, the Berbers of the western Sahara had been content with peaceful trade. Early in the eleventh century they embarked on their own path of conquest. These obscure peasants of the far west, inheritors of the Berber Bronze Age of remote Antiquity, became fired with the hope of a new and better life. Gathering amid their pastures on the Mauretanian plains, infused with conquering ambitions by Islamic leaders of devotion and austerity, they rode out to pillage the rich and comfortable. Some of them went northward and eventually took possession of Moorish Spain, ruling from Seville through a dynasty which lasted from 1061 to 1147; others, still earlier, turned southward and invaded Ghana. An unreliable tradition had it that their principal leader established himself and a few followers on an island in the river Senegal, and lived there a monastic life of preparation for great deeds, after which they set forth to master the lands of the south and southeast. The 'island tradition' is probably apocryphal, but the monastic retreat is not. This at all events gave them their name among Muslims, the people of the monastery, al-Murabethin, whom our own histories call the Almoravids. They warred on Ghana in about 1052, seized Audagost a few years later, but were unable to capture its capital—almost certainly then at Kumbi, some two hundred miles north of modern Bamako—until 1076. These were remembered as years of devastation. Ibn Khaldun wrote three centuries later that the Almoravids had 'spread their dominion over the Negroes, ravaged their lands and plundered their goods, submitting them to a poll tax and compelling many of them to become Muslims'.

Restless raiders, the Almoravid Berbers could not maintain their power. They withdrew or they scattered. But they had weakened the old Ghanaian system beyond recall. Others now reached for a share in the spoils of a time of confusion. In about 1230 a people from Takrur (the northernmost part of modern Senegal) seized the last Ghanaian capital, and the empire came at last to a close, having endured as a principal factor in the onward movement of West African development for nearly half a millennium.

Chronologically, Ghana was accompanied by another imperial system in the easterly lands of the Western Sudan, that of Kanem-Bornu. The rise of this second system was less dramatic and, perhaps a little later, less influential too, because Kanem had no neighbouring or native source of gold, the commodity above all else that North Africa expected from trade with West Africa. Yet the general importance of Kanem for the easterly regions of the Western Sudan was not much less than that of Ghana for the westerly regions. Moreover, Kanem endured until recently: its ruling dynasty, the kings of the Sefuwa family, came to power at some time in the ninth century or not much later, but their last representative quit the throne of Bornu (lineal successor of the Kanem-Bornu empire) only in 1846.

The strength of Kanem, reaching east and north and west of Lake Chad, and some way to the south as well, rested on the same kind of trading foundations as that of Ghana. Northward lay valuable deposits of salt, notably at Bilma, and also of copper; southward were the sources of forest goods and the fine cotton stuffs of southern Nigeria. Between these two, centred in the lands of Kanem, were the relay markets necessary not only for trade along the eastern trails across the Sahara, mainly to the Fezzan, Tunisia, Tripoli and onward to Egypt, but also for trade through the grasslands of Waday and the hills of Darfur to the cities of the Nile.

Having endured into very recent times, the ancient organization of Kanem (or more properly of Kanem-Bornu, since the centre of its power shifted in the course of time from Kanem east of Lake Chad to Bornu west of the lake) has conserved useful traditions about its kings and their reigns. For the earliest times, they seem to point to the local peoples of the Chad region as being among the makers of a remarkable culture which flourished in settlements along the Logone River. This culture has generally been called 'Sao'. But the term is misleading if it suggests a distinctive people, for Sao evidently meant no more than 'heathen' to the Muslim converts who took over power in the eleventh century, and may be compared with the word 'kaffir' applied by Muslims to peoples of south-eastern Africa. Exactly who the makers of the Sao culture were is still in dispute: at all events they were excellent artists in metal and terracotta, and enjoyed an urban but non-literate civilization of some distinction. They form part of the background to the growth of Kanem.

Originating in a council of powerful family heads, the Sefuwa chiefs institutionalized their system of rule into an early form of central government during the ninth century. Late in the eleventh century their ruling monarch, Humé (c. 1085–97), accepted conversion to Islam for reasons we shall discuss at a later point; and from about this date one may reckon the emergence of the first Kanemi empire. It now disposed of a more or less systematic hierarchy of administrative power through governors and sub-governors, some of whose titles, such as *chiroma* and *galadima*, were taken over by Hausa chiefs in the fifteenth and sixteenth centuries and still survive in northern Nigeria.

Three main periods may be distinguished in Kanem history. There is the early period of formation when the Kanembu under their early chiefs were striving for leadership in the grassland country around Lake Chad. With the eleventh-century conversion of the Sefuwa to Islam, there comes an increasing involvement in the trade of the region, together with a successful effort at establishing a single overall system of law and order throughout a wide region of trade and pasture. This is the period of the 'old empire' based on Kanem to the east of Lake Chad. It collapses in the fifteenth century with the rebellion of some of its subject peoples, notably the Bulala, and there follows a time of confusion while sovereignties are violently contested. This terminates with the rise of a new empire whose main seat of power has shifted west of the lake, and lies in the land of Bornu. In 1571, after many adventures, the greatest of all the kings or *mais* of Kanem-Bornu, Idris Alooma, at last comes into his rights and launches out upon a grand career of political achievement that was contemporary with the reign of England's Queen Elizabeth. Idris Alooma unites the whole grassland country from the borders of the Darfur in the east, and perhaps Darfur itself, to the kingdoms of eastern Hausaland; maintains diplomatic missions in Tripoli and Cairo; exchanges gifts with the Ottoman sultan in Istanbul; and rules as the most successful West African monarch of his day.

West of Bornu the early states of Hausaland composed another segment of the general process of state-formation that had certainly begun to crystallize, throughout the grassland country, by the end of the first millennium AD. Here the traditions may not be far astray in assigning the origins of the early Hausa states to the eleventh or twelfth century, a period of much change and movement in this region of the Sudan which saw the political expansion of the Kanembu and their allies and possibly, as other traditions suggest, a southward migration out of this region of some of the ancestors of the Yoruba of western Nigeria. There is likewise some evidence for this period of small colonizing groups pushing westward from Hausaland into the lands south of the great bend of the Niger, groups that took the lead over local Gur-speaking folk and eventually built in the course of time the highly stable and enduring states of the Mossi of modern Upper Volta. By the thirteenth century, at all events, a number of Hausa settlements had appeared, each centred on its own walled or palisaded village, its *birni,* and governed by its own council of notables and chiefs.

In later times Katsina took the lead over Gobir, Zaria and the rest. After Katsina, Kano became the greatest of all the Hausa cities; and by the sixteenth century this seat of government, trade and Muslim scholarship was among the most important in West Africa. These Hausa states never formed more than a loose confederation of partners or rivals, sometimes on good terms with one another, at other times competing for a bigger share of the north-south trade which had so greatly helped their foundation and growth. Not until the early nineteenth century, with conquest by Fulani under the lead of Uthman dan Fodio, did the greater part of Hausaland come within the boundaries of a single overriding authority, that of the first Amir al Mu'minim (Commander of the Faithful) of Sokoto, Uthman's notable son Muhammad Bello.

Mali and Songhay

With the collapse of Ghana there followed for the Western Sudan one of those times of confusion which the historians of Pharaonic Egypt have called 'intermediate periods', marking in this way both the end of one system of law and order and the prelude to another. In Egypt, as it happened, the end of the First and Second Intermediate Periods brought the rise, respectively, of the Middle and New Kingdoms, each of them being an advance upon its predecessor in terms of power and efficiency of organization.*
One may detect much the same kind of progression in the Western Sudan: Mali, which followed Ghana, grew more powerful

---

*Though not, one may note, of art or sensitivity of culture. Pharaonic art became, with one or two interludes of creative beauty, more and more vulgar and ostentatious as the centuries rolled by. This tendency towards steady artistic decline appears indeed to stand upon a general rule for all imperial systems. The exercise of power over other peoples is evidently fatal to metropolitan standards of taste, as to other standards as well.

and highly organized, while Songhay, which in a looser sense may be said to have followed Mali, likewise outdid Mali in administrative sophistication and political power.

Ghana split apart into a number of successor states, under new or established rulers, as previously subject peoples took advantage of upsets of the times and made their bids for independence. Among these were the Mandinka of the little state of Kangaba on the banks of the Upper Niger. They it was who formed the core of a new empire which took its rise in the thirteenth century and remained effective over a wide region for nearly two centuries. Their initial success is explained by tradition as being due to the strength and skill of some of their early rulers, notably the renowned Sundiata Keita. But the conventional date of Mali's appearance on the scene is generally assigned to a great battle at Kirina, fought in about 1240, when Sundiata triumphed over his main enemy. This was Sumanguru, king of a people from Takrur who had seized the capital of old Ghana and were themselves trying to build a new empire.

Though historically respectable, these explanations need to be viewed against the special and in some ways specially favourable circumstances of the Mandinka at that time. Their position was an unusual one in that many of them were intermediaries in the trade between the grasslands and coast to the south, producing a wide variety of goods from gold to dried seafish, and the big Sudanese markets to the north. At any rate from the fourteenth century, Mandinka traders organized in little companies or combines, and, travelling far and wide, became active elements in the whole West African trade. They called themselves Dyula, a title and meaning which have survived to this day; cemented their internal unity by allegiance to Islam and the efficiency of their organization by recognition of a 'company chief' or Dyulamansa; and became in time the founders of market-towns, cities and even states. But their origins almost certainly go back to the early gold and other trade of Ghanaian times. They occupied a favourable middleman position, and they exploited it.

Together with this, the Mandinka may have had other circumstances in their favour. They and their immediate neighbours were among West Africa's most successful—and perhaps earliest—cultivators of the soil, producing rice and other foods in the rich hinterland of the Casamance and Gambia rivers. This strong agricultural base seems likely to have played an important part in their growth in numbers and their rise to power. Together with their trading skills and opportunities, the Mandinka occupied a country which had become rich. With the collapse of Ghana, their chance of large political power was opened. They grasped it with a sure hand.

Having defeated Sumanguru at the battle of Kirina—a clash so memorable that magical legends of what happened there circulate even to this day in the villages of the Western Sudan—the vigorous Sundiata Keita ruled for about twenty-five years and died, according to Ibn Khaldun, who is our best source of information on the chronology of the Mali kings, in about 1260. It was he who transformed the little state of Kangaba into the core of an imperial system. Like other leaders of Sudanese states greatly involved in trade, Sundiata had accepted conversion to Islam, no doubt as a gesture of friendship to the Muslim loyalties of Kangaba's northern trading partners. Yet Sundiata, again like many leaders of this time and later, nonetheless owed the greater part of his political success and authority to a powerful exploitation of traditional religion. Characteristically for rulers of his kind—the founders of large or wealthy states in the Sudan, but not the men who ruled these states in the time of their maturity—Sundiata is remembered not as a good Muslim but as a powerful man of magic and enchantment. One may usefully note a close parallel in this respect between Sundiata of Mali and the founding emperor of the Songhay, the no less famous Sunni Ali of two centuries later.

Sundiata's successor, Mansa Uli, made the pilgrimage to Mecca (as some of his predecessors may also have done), and, like Mansa Qu and several other rulers next in line, worked at the consolidation of Sundiata's conquests. After Mansa Abu Bakr, who appears to have been a grandson of Sundiata, the throne was seized by a man of servile origin, Sakuru, in about 1298. This usurper founded no dynasty but proved a capable ruler. 'Under his powerful government', according to Ibn Khaldun, who collected his information on the subject about seventy years later, 'the possessions of the people of Mali were expanded, and they overpowered the neighbouring nations . . . Their authority became mighty. All the nations of the Sudan stood in awe of them, and the merchants of North Africa travelled to their country.' Mandinka achievements had become the biggest single political factor in the Western Sudan.

These achievements were now carried to their furthest point by the most renowned of all the Mali emperors, Mansa Musa, who came to the throne in 1312 and died in 1337. Under Musa this empire reached from the shores of the Atlantic, west of Takrur, to the borders of modern Nigeria, and from the margin of the tropical forests northward into the Sahara. Gathering information in Cairo a few years after Musa had made his lavish way through that city on pilgrimage to Mecca, al-Omari was told by a fellow-Egyptian* who had lived for thirty-five years at Niani, the Mali capital, that 'the kingdom is square in shape, being four months [of travel] in length and at least as much in breadth': an exaggeration unless the travel was on foot, and yet not a large one even if it were by horse. Mali was not counted as one of the great empires of the Muslim world, and the maritime nations of southern Europe also began to recognize it as such. Completing his remarkable atlas of Africa in 1375, the Majorcan cartographer Cresques shows the lord of Mali seated in majesty upon his throne, holding an orb and sceptre, while the traders of all North Africa march sturdily towards his markets.

This central age of Mali was afterwards remembered as a golden age of prosperity and peace. Much of the grassland country west

*With Cairo the grand commercial centre of East-West exchanges during the great age of Islam between the tenth and early fourteenth centuries, Egyptians had many and varied direct contacts with the cities of the Western Sudan. This long commercial intercourse forms an aspect of African history, during European medieval times, which remains to be properly explored. For a glimpse of its possible historical rewards, see S. D. Goitein. A *Mediterranean Society*, op. cit.

of Kanem-Bornu lay within the rule of a single overriding system of law and order, and the system was both strong and tolerant of local variation. Less than twenty years after Musa's death the globe-trotting Ibn Batuta, still restlessly wandering after nearly thirty years of eager observation up and down the Muslim world, found complete and general safety in the land. Its inhabitants, he considered, had 'a greater abhorrence of injustice than any other people', while their sultan showed no mercy to anyone who should be guilty of it. 'Neither the man who travels nor he who stays at home has anything to fear from robbers or men of violence.'

This was also a period of commercial expansion, much of it the work of Dyula enterprise. These Dyula traders penetrated southward into the forest country, travelling the roads with their own armed escorts, establishing themselves at regular relay-stations, patiently linking one zone of production with another. In the course of time they accomplished for the western regions of West Africa what Hausa, Yoruba, Ibo and Kanuri traders achieved for the eastern regions; and the story of Dyula enterprise runs like a vivid thread through the records of West Africa from the early times of Mali to the republics of today.

Mansa Musa is remembered for much else besides military success and the growth of trade. He brought back an architect from Arabia and caused new mosques to be raised in Timbuktu and other cities. He presided over the introduction of building in brick where *pisé*, or pounded clay, had formerly prevailed. He patronized Muslim scholarship, making himself far more the exponent of proselytizing Islam than any of his predecessors. This was the time when Timbuktu and Jenne began their long career of scholarship and learning; and from now onwards the reputation of their schools of theology and law spread far into Muslim Asia. Government became more methodical; administration began to become literate. Mansa Musa, al-Omari could note from first-hand witnesses, had 'secretaries and offices'. Yet government was still very much a personal affair: 'legal cases go up to the sovereign who examines them himself.'

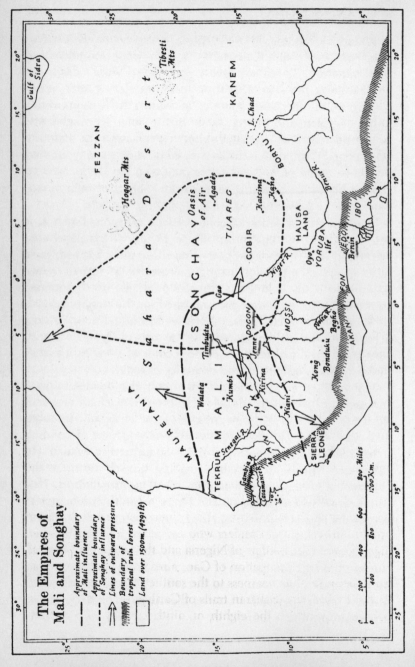

The Empires of
Mali and Songhay

— — — Approximate boundary
of Mali influence

- - - - Approximate boundary
of Songhay influence

⟹ Lines of outward pressure

Boundary of
tropical rain forest

▢ Land over 1500m. (4291 ft)

Gulf of Sidra

FEZZAN

Hoggar Mts

Tibesti Mts

KANEM

L. Chad

S a h a r a   D e s e r t

BORNU

Benue R.

IBO

SONGHAY

Oasis
of Air

Agadès

TUAREG

Katsina
Kano

HAUSA
LAND

GOBIR

Niger R.

Oyo
Ife
YORUBA
EDO
Benin

MALI

MAURETANIA

Timbuktu

Gao

DOGON

MOSSI

Volta R.

Begho
AKAN
Bonduku

Kong

FON

Walata

Kumbi

Jenne

KIRINA
Kirina

Niani

Gambia R.

Senegal R.

TEKRUR

MANDING

Casamance R.

SIERRA
LEONE

800 Miles
1200 Km.

800
600
400
200
0

102

Only with the later rise of Songhay does imperial administration begin to operate by a regular delegation of authority to a civil service. It operates by a shift in the exercise of power that forms another principal theme in the political history of Africa: a shift from the exercise of power by ascription, by inheritance, to the exercise of power by appointment, mainly by royal appointment. Associated with the growing personal authority of kings, and thus with a reduction of traditional democracy, this shift occurred in a wide variety of kingdoms in many parts of Africa, whether Muslim or not. Yet its clearest manifestations south of the Sahara may be seen in Muslim-propelled reforms during the late fifteenth century in Songhay, Kanem-Bornu and some of the Hausa city-states, notably Kano. With these reforms, the kings raised armies and bureaucracies which were at least partly composed and commanded by their own servants or bondaged men: of men, that is, who stood outside the traditional descent-lines of political loyalty, and who, because they stood outside them, could be relied upon for a stronger personal loyalty to the king. This was the same kind of process, however different in form, that took place in western Europe at the close of early feudal times. Kings became, among their peers, far more than *primus inter pares*: relying on their personal servants, they ruled by a 'right' which they soon found it convenient and possible to call divine. And in the same way, many of the so-called 'divine kings' of Africa did in fact create a good part of their 'divinity'.

The next main landmark in the records of the Western Sudan was the growth of the trading city of Gao, downstream from Timbuktu on the Middle Niger, and its transformation into the seat of an empire which gradually eclipsed Mali. The Songhay today are a people numbering about three-quarters of a million farmers, fishermen and traders who live along the banks of the Niger between the borders of Nigeria and the lake region west of Timbuktu. Their occupation of Gao, already an ancient trading centre because of its nearness to the southern terminal of one of the old Berber trans-Saharan trails of Carthaginian times, seems to have occurred in the eighth or ninth century. There they formed a strong little city-state under a line of rulers who accepted Islam at the beginning of the eleventh century while conserving, in the manner of their kind and situation, their old faiths as well. Mansa Musa brought Gao within the Mali system, no doubt because of its profitable relationship with the trans-Saharan trade, and exacted tribute from its rulers. But Gao soon grew strong enough to make a bid for independence, and afterwards for empire, being favoured in this by the weakness of the Mali emperors who followed Mansa Musa. In 1375 the second of a new line of Songhay rulers in Gao, known as the Sunni or Shi dynasty, successfully refused to pay tribute to Mali; and in 1400 the Songhay cavalry, increasingly on the warpath, even made a raid on the city of Niani, capital of Mali.

In 1464, with the appearance of Sunni Ali, the Songhay embarked on the systematic conquest of their neighbours. Here again one may see how the power of local loyalties and religions became interwoven with the political and commercial ideas and enterprises of Muslim groups who dominated the market-towns. Generally, the towns became Muslim, at any rate so far as their leading families were concerned, while the peasants of the countryside, caring little or nothing for trade but much for their own traditions, remained faithful to their old beliefs. Out of this dichotomy there often came a shuttling of power between town and countryside. The Songhay empire, like Mali and Kanem before it, emerged under a strong ruler who rested his power mainly on the peasants of the countryside. But he was followed, just as in Mali and Kanem, by other rulers whose mainstay increasingly became the men and merchants of the largely Muslim towns. This was a factor that goes far to explain the instability of these medieval empires. Their kings could prosper and pay their way so long as they could use the Islamic system of belief and government, for promotion both of central rule and long-range trade and credit. But this very reliance on the towns tended to alienate the peoples of the countryside. In times of crisis, the town-centred empires could quickly fall apart.

Sunni Ali was repeatedly successful. He drove off a varied host

of eager raiders, among them the Mossi from the south and the
Tuareg of the north, riveted his government on many peoples of
the Middle Niger grasslands, brought Timbuktu under his firm
control and, together with Timbuktu, controlled a vital segment
of the whole commercial network of the central region of the
Western Sudan. At the same time, he devised new methods of
administration; defined provinces to which he appointed governors; regulated his hierarchy of command through many long-
term administrative appointments; created the beginnings of a
professional army and even of a professional navy on the Niger;
and presided over a large extension of the area of watered cultivation. Organizationally the Songhay of Sunni Ali was already
an advance on Mali, just as Mali had been in this respect an
advance on Ghana.

Of this undoubtedly great man the records in Arabic have little
good to say, while the seventeenth-century writers of Timbuktu
excoriate him as a cruel tyrant. It is not difficult to see why.
Although the evidence shows that he well understood the need
to mollify his Muslim townsmen and tolerate their special loyalties, Sunni Ali remained much more a man of the countryside
than a man of the towns, much more a potent force in Songhay
traditional religion than a good Muslim. He repeatedly played a
skillful game of balancing the often opposed ideas and interests
of townsman and peasant; but the townsmen were not yet strong
enough to have the upper hand in the empire. Some of them
undoubtedly tried. When the Tuareg of the north successfully
took and held Timbuktu during Sunni Ali's time, the leading
families of that city seem to have shown little energy in defending
themselves. Probably they saw in the Tuareg a useful Muslim
ally in promoting the independence of Timbuktu against Songhay
overlordship. Sunni Ali, at any rate, believed that they had deliberately betrayed their formal loyalty to him in order to advance
their own freedom of action. Retaking the city in one of his
furious campaigns, he fell upon the *qadis* of Timbuktu with a
ruthless hand, and was for long afterwards remembered there
with horror and dismay.

For the same order of reasons, but in reverse, the records of Timbuktu have fulsome praise for Sunni Ali's outstanding successor, the Askia Muhammad Turay, who founded a new line of rulers—taking their title from a Songhay military rank—and largely switched from reliance on the peasants to reliance on the towns. This, as we have seen earlier, was the same kind of break with tradition which had occurred with Mansa Musa of Mali, and it was to have something of the same general consequences. So long as the towns of Songhay remained strong and prosperous, the empire survived and grew. Once they failed, Songhay collapsed even more rapidly than Mali had done.

Not content with commanding the wide region of the Middle Niger, Askia Muhammad thrust both east and west. He had returned from his pilgrimage in 1496 with authority to act as caliph of Islam in the Western Sudan, and he now proceeded to play the part. He pushed an army as far west as Takrur, submitting its non-Muslim rulers to his tribute and command (at least in theory, for they were far from Songhay); fought off the Middle Niger raiders once again, the Mossi and the Dogon and their like; and then ordered his generals eastward. These overran the western Hausa states, Gobir and Katsina, and were halted for a while only at the gates of Kano. Having taken Kano, and exacted regular tribute from this city through a tax-collecting governor established for the purpose, they turned north and marched across the plains to the great oasis of Aïr. There they attacked the Tuareg in their native stronghold, temporarily drove them out and settled in Aïr a colony of Songhay settlers whose descendants may still be found there. Having done all this, Askia Muhammad had achieved a success comparable with that of Mansa Musa of Mali. Once again the greater part of the central regions of the grassland country were brought within a single over-riding system of law and order.

In 1528, now more than eighty years old and growing blind, Askia Muhammad was deposed. He died a few years later, and was buried in a tomb at Gao which is still in a fair state of preservation. He was followed by a son who reverted to Sunni

Ali's policy of basing himself mainly on the peasants of the countryside. But the towns were now stronger than before. This ruler was sharply and quickly removed from power. Henceforth until the end of the century it was to be the men of the towns who exercised predominant influence in the empire, although most of the Askias remained careful to placate their country folk by permitting the observance of traditional customs and ceremonials. Under Askia Dawud (1549–82) there was more expansion, and through nearly half a century the Songhay empire was little disturbed by internal upheavals or revolts. Then in 1591 came invasion from Morocco, disaster in battle, widespread rebellion of subject peoples, and irreversible collapse. With this the long and memorable era of medieval empire in the central and western regions of the West African grasslands drew at last to a close.

South of the Sudan

These few examples may serve to show how the subtle yet persistent pressures of Iron Age transformation carried many peoples of the Sudanese grasslands from simple systems of political organization to more complex systems, and how this ripening process continued over a long period more or less contemporary with the European Middle Ages and Renaissance. This is the period, taking shape roughly between AD 1000 and 1300, and displaying its full potential between AD 1300 and 1600, of what I shall call the Mature Iron Age in Africa.

Throughout this period, one may note in passing, there are several interesting parallels with Europe. Although Sudanese peoples never evolved systems based on the effective private ownership of land, such as in feudal Europe, they undoubtedly built systems based on taxation and tribute, on lord-and-vassal relations, on forms of slavery akin to European serfdom, that were not unlike some of the contemporary social structures of Europe. Here and there these African systems have been directly compared with European feudalism. But while this comparison can be

useful as a stimulus to thought and argument, it will be misleading if made without serious reservation. These African societies never developed the autocracy of feudal rule that reposed
on the alienation of land from those who used it. There occurred
here no such decisive stratification of society.

Built on the collective ownership of land with market-cities
playing no *dominant* general part in their economy, these kingdoms remained much more broadly democratic, even when allowing for the steady growth of royal power after the middle of
the fifteenth century, than their contemporaries in Europe.* Yet
the parallel between the position of the towns in western Africa
and western Europe remains interesting. For if it is true, to glance
at another comparison, that the Western Sudan produced no
parliamentary forms of a kind that were structurally close to those
of western Europe, it is also true that the question of political
representation was always present, often arduously and urgently
present, and was certainly among the knottiest of problems ever
laid before the rulers of states such as Mali or Songhay. As
between the men and merchants of the towns and the chiefs and
spokesmen of the countryside, there developed an increasingly
acute rivalry for power in councils of state, at least from the time
of Sundiata Keita in the thirteenth century. The triumph of the
townsmen of feudal England in winning at that very time their
first right of representation with the calling of Simon de Mont-
fort's Parliament, in 1265, would have been well appreciated in
the cities of the Western Sudan. With a deeper understanding
of this long period there will be more parallels and comparisons
of this kind.

The same processes of maturing Iron Age transformation were
at work in the forestlands to the south of the Sudan as well as in
the upland countries of central-southern Africa. Here too it is
possible to speak of the gradual development of a Mature Iron
Age between about AD 1000 and 1600. The transformation took

---

*The non-kingly states were of course far more democratic still, at least so far as men
and not women were concerned.

effect in very different conditions, and its consequences were accordingly diverse, yet here too there were parallels with northern experience. This remains a subject of much complexity; but one possible method of tracing the crystallization of states in many African countries is to isolate those institutions which seem to have a common origin. Among these institutions there is that of spiritually sanctioned kingship, or rule by a supreme though by no means divine chief whose powers were conceived as given by God, and whose person was thought of as embodying divine sanctions for the welfare of his people. Such kingships became common to the emergence of many of the states of Africa south of the Sahara, often with attributes and customs that were remarkably close to each other.

This being so, it is tempting to suppose that such institutions of government were diffused southward from a northern source, at first into the tropical rain forests and afterwards into the plateaulands of central-southern Africa, by peoples who carried Iron Age ideas and habits into these distant countries. And it does indeed appear likely that some such process of diffusion took place. The general southward shift of Iron Age technology, traced by types of pottery and other artifactual evidence, together with the spread and multiplication of Bantu-speaking peoples through central into southern Africa during the first millennium AD, lends force to this view. Local traditions of southward movement add their meed of confirmation. In the case of West Africa, for example, it is reasonable to suppose that the political origins of many later and fully historical states were in being by the eleventh or twelfth century, if not earlier; and a number of local traditions can be interpreted as bringing these origins from the north, from the Western Sudan. Thus Akan traditions generally bring the ancestors of state-forming chiefs and groups from 'somewhere in the north'. These are the traditions which have enabled the nationalists of modern Ghana to link their state to the ancient Sudanese empire of Ghana far away in the north-west. Old Yoruba traditions likewise bring the state-forming ancestors of Oduduwa, their legendary founding hero, from far in the east (even, in some versions, from Arabia); and these may also be taken as possibly indicating a Sudanese origin. And when it is recalled that the rulers of the Akan and the rulers of the Yoruba shared some of the characteristics of Sudanese types of kingship, this diffusionist case looks remarkably complete, repeatedly buttressed as it is by other examples of the same kind.

Yet it will be unwise to push the case too far. Institutions of 'divine kingship' are certainly first identifiable in Pharaonic Egypt. They may have passed from there to the Sudan and thence again onwards, with the development of Iron Age politics, into continental Africa further south and west. But little or nothing is known of the process. Meanwhile, to suppose a simple diffusion from Egypt of such notable characteristics of Iron Age society would be to risk adopting an extreme position comparable with the opposite view, popular until recent years, according to which the links between ancient Egypt and continental Africa were of no consequence at all.

There is a second reason for caution. Traditions of southward migration, no matter how common they may be (and they are very common), can seldom or never be taken as indicating the displacement of large numbers of people, or the mere substitution of one population or culture for another. Wherever they contain a core of truth, these traditions should rather be taken as pointing to the movement of small but strong groups who set forth in search of a new homeland. Finding it, they conquered or otherwise settled down with its indigenous people, acquired governing power through their superior techniques and organization, and thereby conserved their own traditions at the expense of the traditions of the peoples among whom they had settled.

But this does not mean that one culture was automatically displaced by another. For the migrating groups would be without women, or with few women. Arriving in their new home, they would take wives from their new but indigenous fellow countryfolk. So that within a generation or two there would occur a profound intermingling of the two cultures, the immigrant and the indigenous. People A, in other words, moved southward and settled down with People B, whether by conquest or agreement. But out of this combination, as People A and People B inter-married and inter-grew, there would soon emerge a new people, People C. There thus occurred a frequent process of diversifi-cation; and this goes far to explain the great variety of cultural forms and systems which came into existence alongside each other.

We know little of this process, largely because it began to occur so very long ago. Just how long ago this really was is tentatively indicated by the modern study of African languages. Their time-scale appears to be immensely long. English and High German separated from their parent tongue some seventeen or eighteen centuries ago; yet it would seem that the languages spoken by the Yoruba of Oyo and their near-neighbours, the Edo of Benin, may have divided from *their* parent tongue almost twice as many years before the present. Even so, a few points seem clear enough. While People C in the above example will have inherited some of the new techniques of government and handicraft skill brought in by People A, they will have inherited a great deal more from People B, the indigenous stock. In the measure that People A took wives from People B, for example, People A's language will have disappeared, since it was the mothers who decided what the children spoke, not the fathers; and with the loss of its language, much of People A's culture will have gone as well. *

Thus we may take it as certain that the vast majority of the inhabitants of fourteenth-century Ife, Benin or other strong states of the forest country were descended from ancestors who had lived in those countries since remote Stone Age times. If they modified their culture with the arrival of migrants from the north, the migrants will have changed their own much more. So the resultant cultural patterns were neither exotic nor entirely local. On the contrary, they were the creative product of a marriage

---

*A conclusion to be accepted, however, with due caution. In 1804–11 the Fulani conquered Hausaland and afterwards adopted the Hausa language. Thirty years later the Kololo (Tswana) conquered Bulozi (Basutoland); but after the Lozi regained control, thirty years later again, they spoke siKololo and have since continued to do so.

between local conditions and new social and political solutions whose origins may have lain elsewhere, but whose forms had become peculiar to the city-states of Bono, Ife, Benin and their like. Hence the southward diffusion of such institutions as spiritually sanctioned kingship, if this diffusion really did happen, must be regarded as anything but a simple transfer of ideas and structures.

If one probes a little further into this intriguing problem as to why states emerged in this or that part of Africa, one is constantly faced with the need to isolate and explain those crucial changes which called for a shift from older and much looser forms of community life to new and more structured forms. It was not the appearance of 'divine kings', after all, that led to the formation of states, but the formation of states that led to the appearance of such kings. Expressing this another way, the need for more centrally organized forms of rule arose not merely or mainly from the habits of dominant cultures that moved southward across Africa. Far more important, in fixing the change to new forms of organization, were local changes in social and economic need. Behind the 'divine kings', in short, lay the pressures of Iron Age transformation.

But what were these pressures? When trying to answer this question, one comes repeatedly across an apparently quite central factor: the growth of trade and production for trade. Here, of course, there is also need for caution. To reduce these intricate processes of transformation to the growth of trade and production for trade might be not much less of an over-simplification, perhaps, than to suppose that the transformation was the mere work of southward diffusion from Egypt and the Sudan. But there is no doubt that the factor of trade and production for trade, wherever it can be traced, is often illuminating and instructive.

If one applies this explanation to Bono, for example, the results are immediately helpful. One of the traditions of Bono has it that gold began to be exploited in that country during the founding reigns of Asaman and Ameyaa, traditionally in the thirteenth century but probably in about 1400, and that this discovery brought wealth and progress in its train. As so often, the traditions manifestly turn things upside down. They make the exploitation of gold, or of the gold trade, a product of the reigns of Asaman and Ameyaa, the founding rulers, whereas the truth is likely to have been just the reverse. Gold must have long been known in the Akan forestlands, and sporadically mined as well. These lands were already several hundred years into their Iron Age. But the rise of Bono followed the rise of Mali, and the rise of Mali had promoted a rapid expansion of southward trade through the Mandinka agents whose professional name was Dyula. With increasing demands for gold the peoples of the gold-producing country must have been faced with many new and difficult problems. Who was to mine the gold, for instance, and who was to trade in it, and how were they to be protected from competing neighbours? There came the need for tighter political organization, and the state of Bono was founded.

Something of the same explanation seems applicable to many other early states. If the Yoruba states emerged from cultural cross-fertilization between Early Iron Age populations in Yorubaland and immigrant groups from the Western Sudan, possibly from the Chad region, it appears likewise true that this coincided with an extension of north-south trade through the rising power of Kanem-Bornu and of Saharan commerce in the north. Neighbouring Benin, to offer another example, is traditionally said to have drawn its political institutions from Ife and other Yoruba states. Yet these institutions took forms of their own that were native to the Edo-speaking people of Benin. And the resultant political structure of Benin was appropriate not only to this intermarriage of ideas but also to the needs of growing trade with the north, based quite largely on the exchange of Benin cotton goods and tropical products for Saharan copper. Trade and production for trade, and all the new social and economic problems and needs they brought in their train, appear once again as a root stimulus of major changes in political organization, and for the development of a Benin state.

This movement, two-way assimilation, and transformation of

Early Iron Age structures into Mature Iron Age structures may be traced right through the continent as far as the Cape Province of South Africa. By at least 1400 the evidence of far-reaching local adjustment to new techniques of farming, mining, trading and state-formation may be found throughout the Bantu-speaking areas of central and southern Africa, which means, by this time, throughout the greater part of this vast region. Entering their Iron Age some two thousand years ago, peoples of the central plateau (Zambia and Zimbabwe today) had undoubtedly reached this point of socio-political reorganization by the tenth century, where they were producing quite large quantities of minerals and exchanging them with their neighbours. There is no lack of archaeological evidence both north and south of the Zambezi, while the rise of the prestigious plateau kingship of the Shona, associated with Great Zimbabwe some time after AD 1250, shows how greatly this economic development impinged on social structures. All this was in process by about AD 900. Not long afterwards, far away on the East Coast, ports like Sofala and Kilwa were growing strong by the purchase of central African ivory and gold in exchange for Indian, Arabian and even Chinese goods. Reacting in turn from the consequences of this trade, the gold-producers also changed their socio-political institutions.

The archaeology of the large stone structures at Zimbabwe, not far north of the Limpopo in modern Zimbabwe, offers another demonstration of this process. This shows that the earliest settlement there was of an iron-using people, not yet building in stone, whose appearance dates from the second or third century AD. In about 1100, with trade and production for trade beginning to exercise their influence on the stratification of society, there came a clear cultural change, and the first stone structures were erected. Already, as the archaeological records indicate, there were groups who ruled and other groups or peoples who were ruled. Thus the miners seem to have been socially and culturally distinct from the people for whom the many stone structures were built. A state based on spiritually sanctioned kingship had come into existence. Later again, after 1400, with the East Coast now at its zenith, this early state was transformed into a much larger group of states, the empire of the Monomotapa. And with this the same dynamic was clearly at work as with Mali and Songhay in the Western Sudan. Like their western contemporaries, what the lords of Monomotapa desired was to impose a single system of rule and revenue across a wide region of production, trade and tribute revenue. It was in this respect that these big political structures in medieval Africa were like the imperial *regna* of medieval Europe, such as Charlemagne's empire of the Franks.

One should add at this point another word of caution. Although changes in social relations linked to the development of trade and production for trade do often help to explain the growth of new political structures in the period between AD 1000 and 1600, they are by no means everywhere satisfactory. Several states of some importance emerged in fifteenth-century Uganda, as we shall see. But excavation of their sites has yet to reveal much evidence of long-distance trade, while here and there, as notably at the Mature Iron Age site of Bigo, there is so far no sign at all. Nor, to offer a West African example, does it seem that trading factors played any leading part in the foundation of the Mossi states. In explaining such political phenomena as these, one is forced back on the evidence of cultural diffusion by immigrant groups who brought state-forming ideas and techniques with them, and on general suppositions about the likely effects of introducing these ideas and techniques.

In any case it will have been true that the pressures of Iron Age change acquired a dynamic of their own, and that this dynamic could and did operate even where there were no precious metals to mine and trade in, or where the peoples concerned lay far outside the circuit of any large system of exchange. For it was these pressures of Iron Age growth, after all, which had carried central-southern Africa into its Early Iron Age at a time when large-scale trade or production for trade still lay in the future, and when the problems were the clearing of forest, the tilling of land, and settlement defence by the superior strength of iron tools and weapons over those of wood and stone.

Summing up, then, Iron Age transformation of most African communities south of the Sahara and south of the Sudan had matured by about 1400 to a point consistent with steady internal development of the potentialities inherent within themselves: inherent, that is, within metal-using cultures based on subsistence farming, on the collective ownership of land, and on a certain amount of production for exchange. These Mature Iron Age cultures possessed an underlying unity of content. For they were the outcome of the same social factors operating within comparable conditions and in solution of comparable problems. But they were highly various in form. Before looking at their history, even in outline, we must first catch up with some contrasting developments elsewhere.

The Christian Epic

By 1400 there were peoples in north-eastern Africa who had long experienced a very different cultural history from their southern or even their northern neighbours. They owed little in their ideological framework to the traditional religions of Africa and even less to Islam, but much to a devout and penetrating Christianity. Many of the outward forms of their political systems, as well as their religious concepts, customs and sense of separate identity, had by this time been Christian for nearly a thousand years.

At some time in the fourth century a philosopher of Christian Tyre, one Meropius, was voyaging at the southern end of the Red Sea with the aim of improving his mind as well as those of two young relatives, Aedesius and Frumentius. Unhappily for Meropius, the Roman ship in which they were voyaging put into an Ethiopian port at a time when the Axumites, who were now the major power at the southern end of the Red Sea, considered themselves in dispute with the Romans. Their local people boarded the Roman ship and forthwith massacred the crew, and Meropius as well. But Aedesius and Frumentius, being examples to all good children, were not found idling on board ship: on the contrary, they were preparing their lessons under the shade of a nearby tree, and were accordingly spared for service to the Axumite king, Ella Amida, the father of the Ezana who would afterwards invade Kush. Pleased with these worthy young men, Ella Amida showed them his favour. Aedesius became his cupbearer and Frumentius his secretary. And it was to be through Frumentius, afterwards raised in Alexandria to be first bishop of Axum, that Christianity eventually became a state religion of the Axumite kingdom, and afterwards the chief religion of the peoples of Abyssinia (later Ethiopia).

We see this clearly with Ezana, Ella Amida's successor, for Ezana's coins bear the symbols of Christianity as well as those of the traditional Axumite religion. Unfortunately there are as yet no certain dates for Ezana's reign. His invasion of Kush and destruction of Meroe and its sister cities, well attested by a fine but not dated inscription, has been generally attributed to about 325, which would place the arrival of Meropius at the beginning of that century. Recently, however, it has been suggested that Ezana's conversion really fell a good deal later, perhaps in about 420, and his invasion of Kush a little after that. The point is important because the difference of a century in the destruction of Meroe must weigh heavily on any full evaluation of the impact of Meroitic Kush upon its western and south-western neighbours. In this immediate connection, however, we need note only that Ezana's invasion of Kush, whether in the fourth or fifth century, did not bring Christianity to the Middle Nile. The epic of Christian Nubia sprang not from Axum but from Egypt.

After Ezana's invasion, the cities of Kush appear to have passed into the hands of the Noba and 'Red Noba' upon whom Ezana had chiefly warred. Like other nomads, they took to city life and liked it: they mingled with the urban Kushites and a new culture arose from this union. Politically, the old Kushite empire fell back into its ancient provincial divisions. These were the Kush of northern Nubia, of the villages and towns south of Aswan; the Kush of Middle Nubia, of the old Napatan kingdom near the fourth cataract; and the Kush of southern Nubia, of Meroe itself. Into all these, though the details still escape us, neighbouring peoples infiltrated and gradually settled, including the Nuba of the western desert and the Blemmye of the eastern desert. Prudently avoiding premature identification, archaeologists have gathered the peoples of this immediately post-Kushite culture under the safely anonymous name of X-Group.

From about the fifth century the X-Group Nubians increasingly acquired a taste for settled life as well as the opportunity of indulging it, took over many Kushite customs and beliefs and inter-married with Kushite townsfolk. By the sixth century they had somewhat reconstructed their three small states—northern, middle and southern—whose culture was in quite a large degree the continuation of Kush at a lower level of civilization. While the X-Group people conserved a characteristically Kushite interest in foreign goods, especially of the luxury sort, together with a nice mingling of Kushite and nomad art styles, funeral procedures and the like, they failed to re-create the literacy of the Meroitic age.

This development occurred only with the conversion of the Nubian states, whose monks at first wrote in Greek and then (but using a Greek script) in Old Nubian, an achievement lessened for a later world by the lamentable loss of most of their writings. Yet a good deal is known of the conversion, while excavations in 1961–64 have had splendidly fruitful results at Faras in the discovery, among other things, of an eleventh-century list of no fewer than twenty-seven bishops of the diocese of Pachoras, many splendid frescoes, and a fine cathedral. Like much subsequent Christian endeavour in Africa, the conversion owed more than a little to acute rivalry between two branches of the Church: not between Roman Catholics and Protestants, as in later days, but between Monophysites and Melkites, the one being under the patronage of the Emperor Justinian and the other under the patronage of the Empress Theodora. Two missions set out from Alexandria in about 542 but the Monophysites, thanks to influence at court, managed to get the Melkites held back by the

Roman (that is, Byzantine) governor of Upper Egypt. Their man Julian was the first to pass beyond the cataracts and arrive in Nobatia, the northernmost of the three kingdoms established on Kushite foundations by the urbanized X-Group.

Julian spent two years in Nobatia, suffering greatly from the heat like other visitors then and since, and being obliged, according to a contemporary account, to take refuge during the day 'in caverns full of water, where he sat undressed and girt only in a linen garment such as the people of the country wear'. By about 580, thanks to the labour of Julian and later missionaries, all three Nubian kingdoms had accepted Coptic or Byzantine Christianity: Nobatia in the north with its capital at Qustul and then at Faras; Makuria in the middle, reaching along the Dongola region of the Nile with its capital at Old Dongola; and Alodia (or Alwa) in the south with its capital at Soba, another old Meroitic city which lay a few miles up the Blue Nile above the latter's junction with the White Nile at Khartoum. These Nubian kingdoms were generally at peace with one another, and a union was made between Nobatia and Makuria at some time before 710.

Having become Christian in the sixth century, the Nubians remained so for many centuries of often remarkable and brilliant development in their civilization. Just how great this was could not be clearly seen, and only then in outline, until the archaeological discoveries of the 1960s that followed on an international effort to excavate and understand a large number of sites above Aswan, before the waters of the High Dam closed above them. As a result of this and previous archaeological work by many hands, Adams has been able to suggest a broad chronology of Christian Nubia from the sixth to the thirteenth centuries, though emphasizing that only about a dozen of more than 250 known Christian sites in Lower Nubia, not to mention many others in Upper Nubia, can as yet be dated on the basis of direct or documentary evidence. After a brief period transitional from X-Group culture, Christian Nubia became well established soon after 600, grew strong enough to dominate Upper Egypt by 745, and entered a long period of peace and prosperity. Church-building flourished and fine arts were practised during the ninth, tenth and eleventh centuries.

During all this time these remote kingdoms of the Middle Nile were cut off from the rest of the Christian world by the Muslim occupation of Egypt (640–42). Yet they were strong enough to resist Muslim encroachment and even to threaten Muslim positions in Egypt, making a treaty with the caliph of Bagdad in 836 and occupying southern Egypt in 962. Not until 1173 did there come the first big Muslim raid by Saracen cavalry from the north. A startling panorama of the wealth and distinction of the religious life was revealed in 1961–64 by Polish excavations at Faras (old Pachoras) under the leadership of Michalowski. *

Like many other international expeditions working in the 1960s in the tremendously rich area above Aswan, now flooded for ever by the waters of Lake Nasser rising against the new High Dam, Michalowski and his colleagues were only in the nick of time. Yet by 1964, with the waters already closing in on them, they had uncovered an outstanding Christian complex of architecture and art. This included a great church or cathedral founded probably at the end of the seventh or the beginning of the eighth century, and much extended and embellished in the late ninth and early tenth. Long engulfed in dry protecting sand, its walls still gleamed with more than a hundred painted murals, many of which were rescued for the museums of Khartoum and Warsaw. Its numerous inscriptions in Old Nubian, Coptic and Greek, including a list of twenty-seven bishops of Pachoras, have thrown a vivid light on the Christian history of Nobatia.

How far into inner Africa did this Christian culture make itself felt? The answer is still uncertain, even if probability suggests that the old westward trails of Kush were also followed by the caravans of these Christians. Perhaps they were also followed by their monks as well. In 1958 it was suggested that the brick ruins at 'Ain Farah, seven hundred miles west of Faras in the hills of Darfur, might possibly have been the site of a Christian monastery

*See K. Michalowski, *Faras*, Warsaw, especially the volumes of 1962 and 1965.

at some time before the fifteenth century. Other archaeologists have disagreed, and believe that the brick buildings there were always what they undoubtedly became after the fifteenth century: a chiefly residence along the 'spine' of the hill above the pool (the '*ain*') together with a mosque, and a larger mosque below, the latter being the structure suggested as perhaps orginally a church.

The 'western connections' of Christian Nubia, as of Kush before it, remain to be established. But many monasteries are certainly attested. They were the pillars of a wealthy city culture. What travellers thought of these cities may be glimpsed in words reported by Maqrisi, telling the impressions of Ibn Selim al-Assuani after seeing Soba, capital of distant Alodia. 'Fine buildings, roomy houses, churches with much gold and with gardens lie in this city . . . The land is more fruitful and bigger than Makuria . . . They have much meat . . . good horses and camels . . . '

By 1250, however, Nobatia in the north was far in decline, and in 1275 the Mamluk soldier-kings of Egypt established Muslim superiority there. Further south, in Makuria, Christianity persisted for a while longer, and for longer still in the southernmost kingdom of Alodia, overthrown by the Fung sultans of Muslim Sennar only in 1504. But from this time onward the inheritance of the Christian kings and monks of Nubia disappears rapidly from the inner lands of Africa where they had conserved it for so long. The engulfment was strangely complete, but not perhaps surprising. These monks and kings had stood for a valid and vigorous culture, that of the Nubians of the Middle Nile. Yet they were identified like the Kushites before them with the life and manners of their towns. Drawing a reasonable parallel with what happened in countries of West Africa where Muslims occupied that position, one may think that these Nubian Christians can seldom have been very sure about the loyalty of the peoples of the countryside, immersed as these must often have remained in the older beliefs of pre-Christian times. Underlying that dichotomy, too, there will have been something of the same conflict of interests as occurred in the Western Sudan. The support of monasteries, for example, implies the existence of secular labour: all round the base of the hill that supports the possible monastery site of 'Ain Farah, in distant Darfur, there are simple hut foundations of a numerous village population. When Muslim missionaries and invaders appeared on the scene they would surely have found willing listeners among the humble folk who laboured for the monks. And when the monks were gone, together with their literary habits and comparatively privileged way of life, their books destroyed or lost, their records ruined or consigned to the flames, there was indeed nothing left but a few brick buildings and a handful of broken pottery to suggest the Christian beginnings of this place.

The Nubian kingdoms vanished from the scene: unhonoured and unsung, or almost so, until the twentieth century. Yet Ethiopia survived both as an independent kingdom and a Christian culture, though not easily. Like Nobatia, Makuria and Alodia, it was cut off from the Mediterranean by the Muslim conquests of the seventh century. A hundred years later the Ethiopians had even lost their Red Sea ports to the soldiers of the caliph. But they still possessed good mountain country in which to rally and recuperate. They re-took their ports in the tenth century and became once more a maritime power; fought off their pagan neighbours of the inland country; and eventually, though at a date that is far from certain, attained a new strength and stability. During these 'dark ages' their capital was moved from Axum to Lasta by the first of a new line of rulers called the Zagwe. There began the gradual transformation of the old Axumite empire into its Tigrean and eventually Amharic successor. Famous churches were built in Lasta by King Lalibela, great hollowed monuments of solid rock of which the largest, the Church of the Redeemer of the World, is a hundred feet long and seventy-five feet wide, its interior divided into five cavernous aisles.

Overthrown in about 1270, the Zagwe dynasty was followed by another line of kings claiming descent from Solomon. In fact, however, the first of these Solomonic kings was Yekuno Amlac, prince of the inland Ethiopian province of Shoa; and it is from now onwards that a distinctively Amharic culture becomes dominant. The capital is shifted from Lasta in the centre to the less precipitous land of Shoa to the southward. There is a rebirth of learning and literature. Not only are Greek and Coptic religious works translated into Ge'ez, often embellished with fine illumination, but there is also a beginning of the writing of history. Biographies of local noblemen are made. Most striking of all, the *Kebra Nagast* (Glory of the Kings), an often legendary history of the Solomonic rulers of Ethiopia, is composed in Ge'ez. More and more contemporary chronicles are put into writing by court scribes and monks.* Prominent among the kings who preside over this energetic growth of a truly national culture and self-consciousness are Amda Sion (1314–44) and Zara Yaqob (1434–68), warriors and reformers who carry on the wars against Muslim raiders or neighbours with more than usual success, while ruling at home with an iron hand.

'In the reign of our king Zara Yaqob', recalls a chronicle written soon after 1500, 'there was great terror and great fear in all the people of Ethiopia, on account of the severity of his justice and of his authoritarian rule.' The people of the ancient city of Axum are described as welcoming the king 'with rejoicing'; and they do not go unrewarded. 'After arriving within the walls of Axum, the king had much gold brought to him, and this he scattered in carpets spread along his route as far as the city gate. The amount of gold was more than a hundred ounces . . .' More information now becomes available because European travellers began visiting this distant Christian ally. The first such traveller was probably a papal delegate entrusted with the task, an impossible one as it proved, of submitting the Ethiopian church to the authority of Rome rather than Alexandria; while an Italian painter, Niccolò Brancaleone, arrived a few years later and decorated many churches, getting into trouble at one point for painting the infant

---

*A good short anthology in English is R. K. P. Pankhurst's *Ethiopian Royal Chronicals*, Oxford, 1967.

Jesus on Mary's left arm, considered less honourable in Africa than the right arm, but generally exercising an influence on the development of Ethiopian art.

These stray visitors were followed by others from Portugal, Pedro de Covilham in 1488, seeking Prester John, and several more soon afterwards. Of these the most useful to history was Fernão Alvares, who sojourned in Ethiopia between 1520 and 1526 and, as the chaplain of a Portuguese diplomatic expedition, wrote an invaluable description of what he saw and heard. In 1541 the fourth son of Vasco da Gama led a military expedition to the succour of an Ethiopian king then facing disaster at the hands of a strong Muslim invader from Adel, a powerful state which neighboured Ethiopia on the east.

Having weathered so many years of danger and assault, Ethiopia came to rest on strong foundations. They were foundations of a special kind, once more emphasizing this mountain country's cultural separation from the life of its neighbours. They supported a structure of lord-and-vassal stratification which was far more rigid than elsewhere, and gave Ethiopia a remarkably 'feudal'

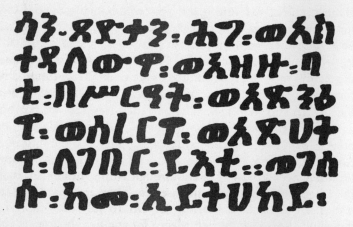

Ge'ez script from an Ethiopian manuscript: Compare with Sabaean on p. 45.

social atmosphere and appearance. At the head of the state was an anointed king surrounded by a court of priests and officials and army commanders who were drawn from ruling families. Like feudal sovereigns, this monarch could seldom afford to remain for long in any one place. He had repeatedly to move his armed camp from one region to another, exacting fealty from nobles and governors, ensuring their payment of tribute and participation in military campaigns, while exiling rivals within his own family to the chilly eminence of hills with flat tops but very steep sides.

The result was a close-knit system of rights and duties into which every significant person in the state was bound. 'In this feudal country', wrote a French traveller of the nineteenth century whose words apply as well to earlier times, 'men are united by an infinity of ties which would count for nothing in Europe. They live together in a reciprocal dependence and solidarity which they value highly and consider a matter of pride, and which influences all they do.' This highly personal system of rule, matched to the needs of a sturdy people often fighting for their lives, proved strong enough to endure through all of Ethiopia's many times of trouble and invasion. It was essentially against this sytem that the Italian invaders of the 1930s were to strike their heads, and not until long after the Second World War would there be any serious inroads into its all-pervading influence. What is perhaps most impressive about the long tale of Ethiopian history is precisely this resilient continuity of attitude and action since the remote times of Axum.

In the Name of Allah

Of the headlong rush of Islam through North Africa and Spain, the dates speak almost for themselves. They are dramatic dates; even, at first sight, impossibly so. On 16 July 622, four men travelling on two camels left Mecca for another obscure Arabian town, Medina. Within as few as twenty-two years the movement of religious and political revolution thus set going by Muhammad had won the whole of Arabia and Syria, engulfed Egypt, seized the Byzantine fortress of Babylon at the southern apex of the delta of the Nile, captured Alexandria, and was everywhere preparing new departures.

Expeditions swept eastward and westward. In 670 'Uqba ibn Nafi established Muslim rule over most of Ifriqiya—Tunisia—and founded Kairouan, weaving with confident prophetic hands the fabric of an entirely new civilization, rejecting what displeased him, suppressing what offended him, and turning what still seemed valuable, such as the Roman pillars and capitals embodied in the Friday mosque of Kairouan, to Muslim use and purpose. By 683 Muslim pioneers had seen the ocean waves of the Atlantic. In 711 Tariq thrust his way into Spain across the straits and northward through the Spanish kingdom of the Visigoths. A year later Musa ibn Nusayr went further still. In 713 'Abd al-Azziz ibn Musa rode beyond the Tagus and harried into central Portugal at the head of battle-hardened troops. A year later again, 714, raiding Muslims were far into France and watering their horses in the Upper Rhône; and it was not until 732, in the decisive battle of Poitiers near the Loire, that Charles Martel at last set limits to the flood of conquest and incursion, defeating 'Abd al-Rahman al-Ghafiq and opening, but under Muslim pressure and example, a new period of history in western Europe.

Yet the really impressive aspect of these and other advances over many hundreds of miles to west and east was not, after all, their speed. Raiding bands of highly trained cavalry could always burst through frontiers and city gates if their leaders were sufficiently determined, and this the early Muslim leaders almost always were. Far more remarkable were the political stability and economic recovery which followed in their wake. In Africa, Spain and Asia these victories laid the groundwork for a civilization that could and did unite men of religion, learning and philosophy from the Mediterranean to Arabia, from the plains of the Western Sudan to the hills of China, and bore a light of tolerance and social progress through centuries when Europe, impoverished, provincialized and almost illiterate, lay in distant battle and confusion.

But when one pauses to inquire how it could possibly come about that slender regiments of hard-riding Arabs or Berbers were capable of founding a civilization such as this, a number of interesting if as yet insufficiently explained phenomena need to be remembered. To begin with, the Muslim conquests came in the wake of long insecurity and turmoil. Two centuries earlier the barbarian raiders of the north had shattered the great imperial systems which had governed Roman Africa, the Near East and western Europe since times long before. Yet these newcomers, Vandals and Goths, Franks and Visigoths, had failed either to engraft themselves into the Roman system and relaunch it under new management, or to build any other wide system of their own. In their attitudes and group behaviour they remained much what they had always been: men of clannish loyalty for whom the notions of a universal culture, a culture capable of embracing many peoples and glowing with the vision of a new society, long remained beyond their grasp. It was by intellectual and spiritual limitations such as these that they fell greatly short of their Muslim rivals; and it was largely because of this kind of difference, one may think, that the Muslim cause triumphed where its enemies faltered and failed.

The difference goes back to the beginnings of Islam. Thus the 'Constitution of Medina', either an original document composed soon after the *Hijrah* or 'migration' from Mecca to Medina or a conflation of several early documents, lays it down that the Muslims 'are a single community distinct from other people'. But distinct, be it noted, by religious conviction and not by clan or national origin. This is a central point. For what Muslim generals could offer the peoples over whom they came to rule was not only subjection to a foreign victor but also the promise of membership in a new and broad community, the *umma* of Islam, within whose boundaries all men could be at least theoretically of equal dignity and worth. The promise, perhaps needless to

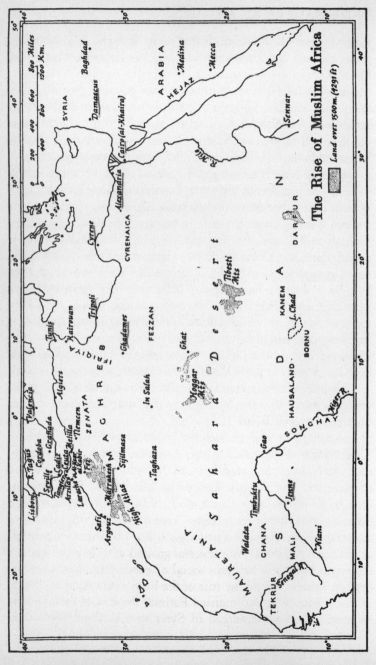

The Rise of Muslim Africa
Land over 1500 m. (4921 ft)

say, was not always kept. For a long time there remained a
powerfully exclusive sentiment among the victorious Arabs, and
this the Caliphate encouraged by trying to keep the Arabs as a
military class apart from their conquered peoples. Yet as soon as
conquered peoples became converted or acceptable within the
umma, as many of them gradually did, Muslim rulers could
appear not simply as conquerors but also as renovators, as leaders
who could point the way to a better order of society.

Only along these lines can one probably hope to explain how
the faith of their Arab conquerors could take root and flourish
among peoples who owed nothing to the Arabs, knew little of
the Arabs and seldom or never spoke Arabic, and who had often
thought of the Arabs as their rivals or foes. Only from this approach, perhaps, can one begin to grasp the attraction of Islam
for heterogeneous or harried populations which had long lacked
a common focus or had never achieved one. Any parallel between
Muslim imperialism and the European imperialism of modern
times would seriously miss the point. The latter remained—as,
to some extent, the conquests of Rome had also remained—a foreign imposition, but the Muslim systems gradually acquired local
garb and became the full possession of those they had enclosed.

Even the egalitarian message of Islam could have availed for
little without the measure of reality that followed. But within a
hundred years this civilization had established a community of
ideas among a host of diverse populations. Out of this, of course,
there flowed the political divisions of Islam. Having rooted in
many soils, Islam flowered in many variants. Local loyalties soon
thrust up through the surface of a system which, for all its ideological promises, could in fact do little or nothing to change
the inner structure of the societies it affected. These local loyalties
found local spokesmen. They argued their differences in terms
of religious orthodoxy, but the real ground of difference was less
theological or doctrinal than social or geographic. Such fissures
became critical during the rule of the fourth caliph, 'Ali, in spite
of the fact that 'Ali had married Fatima, the Prophet's daughter.
A dissenting group emerged in Syria in 657 when Mu'awiya,

governor of that country, became 'Ali's successful rival. From this there came an enduring schism between the Sunnis, who accepted Mu'awiya and his Ummayad successors, and the Shi'as, who did not. Yet all remained Muslim and continued, at least against the rest of the world, to assert their common identity. Another split with a basically social origin occurred when a group of nomads rejected 'Ali's claims and established the Kharidjite brotherhood, a puritanical movement of the oases and distant plains. This denounced the easy-going tendencies of the towns and cities, and was to become of some importance in northern and western Africa.

A hundred years later the fissuring process repeated itself, in the field of politics, when the centre of greatest Muslim power shifted from Damascus to Bagdad with the emergence of the Abbasid Caliphate. Within another hundred years a political map of Islam shows the *umma*, the Islamic community considered in its widest sense, as divided among many local dynasties, the most ambitious of which were the Abbasids and the Western Ummayads in North Africa and Spain. This east-west opposition deepened in the tenth century with the rise of the Fatimids, who drew their initial strength from the Berbers of central Algeria but soon, reaching out for power, pushed their rule far to the east. In 969 the Fatimid armies replaced Abbasid rule in Egypt, and then in Syria and Hejaz. In 973 the Fatimid caliph Al-Mu'izz shifted his capital from the Maghreb to Egypt, and established himself in a new city, al-Khaira, next door to old Fustat (itself the site of the Egyptian Babylon of Byzantine times); and Cairo began its long and often spectacular career.

The Fatimid caliphs ruled in Egypt for two centuries, but soon lost their North African and then their Syrian-Arabian lands. So far as the first of these were concerned, the Fatimids had forfeited Berber support in moving eastward. New Berber kingdoms appeared in Tunisia and Algeria, ruled by chieftains of the Sanhaja confederation. Looking for a means of removing these chieftains, the Fatimid caliph in Cairo worked a revenge on the countries from which his ancestors had come. He urged a group of Beduin nomads under the leadership of the Bani Hilal to invade those fertile western lands. These trotted on their way in dust-trailing bands of hungry raiders, settled like locusts (as Ibn Khaldun was later to describe them) in the watered meadows and orchards of Ifriqiya, and spurred on that profound and prolonged process of Arabization which was to submerge Berber culture in much of Tunisia and Algeria. Westward in Morocco, the Bani Hilal and their companions had little or no effect. Here the deepening of the *umma* into local variants had already taken another important turn with the rise of a southern Berber movement of a different sort. Unlike the Fatimid Berbers, who had gone eastward to the blessings of city life, the Almoravid Berbers of the Mauretanian grasslands were inspired by quite other ideas.

They were inspired by those profoundly moving though Utopian ideas of equality and justice set in being up and down the Muslim world by the Prophet and his immediate followers, but never afterwards entirely forgotten. Like other Muslim reformers before and since, the Almoravids sought to overcome the stratified and fissured nature of the society whose benefits they desired to possess; or this, at any rate, formed the idealist side of the preaching they followed. Like the others, they failed; and it is worth pausing for a moment to consider the reasons for their failure. This failure would repeat itself among other Africans in later times. Centuries afterwards, in the Western Sudan, the great reforming movement associated with the Fulani leader Uthman dan Fodio would draw its inspiration from a Utopian picture of the Abbasid era of the tenth and eleventh centuries, seeing in it the prototype of that 'Rightly Guided Caliphate' in which all Muslims had once enjoyed equality and justice. But the Almoravids, living in the very wake of the Abbasid era, knew better than this. For them the 'golden age' of Islam could not possibly lie in Abbasid times. Rather it lay during the earliest years when, in von Grunebaum's words, 'the ten years of the Prophet's rule in Medina and perhaps the thirty years following his death' were conceived as having formed 'an age in which human society had come as near perfection as could be hoped for . . .'

The golden age was an illusion. Islam possessed no ideological tool that was adequate to the levelling of a society embarked upon a course of deepening internal division between rich and poor, weak and strong. Even the first caliph after the Prophet, 'Umar, who reigned between 634 and 644, had found himself obliged to recognize hierarchical differences among the faithful. These differences became sharper as Islam faced the wear and challenge of power. By the outset of the ninth century, as we are told by a somewhat later writer, Ibn al-Faqih, the Muslim societies of the Near East were divided into four classes: 'the ruler, whom merit has placed in the foremost rank; the vizier, distinguished by wisdom and domination; the high-placed ones, whom wealth has placed aloft; and the middle classes, who are attached to the other three classes by their culture; while the rest of mankind is mere scum who know nothing but food and sleep.'

The scum no doubt objected; their opinions were no longer asked. What the Rightly Guided Caliphate was really like, in those Abbasid times which formed an age of happiness for Muslim reformers nine centuries later, may be seen in an eleventh-century description by the great historian al-Biruni. Hierarchical distinctions had in fact reached an extreme of social prejudice and privilege. 'When the Abbasid rulers had decorated their assistants, friends and enemies indiscriminately with vain titles . . . the empire perished, for in this they went beyond all reasonable limits—[for after] the caliphs had bestowed titles, there were other men who wanted the same titles and who knew how to carry their point by bribery. Thus it became necessary a second time to create a distinction between this [aspiring] class and those who were [already] attached to the court, so the caliphs bestowed triple titles, adding besides the title *Shah-in-Shah*. In this way the matter became utterly opposed to common sense, and clumsy in the highest degree. So that he who mentions them gets tired [of reciting their titles] almost before he has begun, he who writes to them loses his time in writing, while he who addresses them runs the risk of missing the hour for prayer.'

Behind this towering structure of titled ranks there lay impov-

erishment for the mass of the people, for 'the scum who know
nothing but food and sleep'. And it was this 'progressive impoverishment of the country', once more in von Grunebaum's words,
that provided 'the mainspring of "revolutionary Shi'ism" ', so
that political and social conflicts were again fought out in religious
terms. Here and elsewhere and at other times, established religion
had become a bulwark of the rich and wealthy; and lesser people
were not fooled. 'No, certainly I shall not pray to God as long
as I am poor', wrote one of their spokesmen around AD 1000.
'For why should I pray? Am I mighty? Have I a place, horses,
rich clothes and golden belts? While I possess not a single inch
of earth, it would be pure hypocrisy to pray.' Nine hundred years
later, celebrating the virtues of the Abbasid era, Uthman dan
Fodio and his companions would ignore the views of 'the scum'
of those early times, their memory and their protests drowned in
the torrent of the centuries. But the Almoravids were closer to
the scene of Abbasid crisis, and it was essentially against this kind
of crisis, though occurring in the westerly regions of Islam, that
they carried their revolt.

Not the first or last of their kind, these lean and hardy coun-
trymen looked out from barren pastures and saw the promise of
a better life. Under their leader Ibn Yasin, a man of Sijilmasa,
they identified their vision of relief from want and hunger with
a reduction of their neighbours' comfort; and here again, like the
earlier Muslim conquerors, they found a response from peasant
peoples who laboured under the yoke of local lords and landowners. For they overran the fertile plains of Morocco within a
few years and then, invited across the water by Andalusian Muslims facing Christian armies, within another twenty years brought
all of Muslim Spain within their power.

The culture of al-Andalus, of Muslim Spain, had matured
long before this. Originating in the conquest after AD 710, its
chief and in many ways beneficent achievement lay in the formation and unfolding growth of the Emirate of Cordoba and its
Western Ummayad rulers from the remarkable 'Abd al-Rahman
I (AD 756–88) down to Hisham III al-Mu'tadd, whose brief and

inglorious reign saw the end of the great Caliphate in AD 1031.
There followed a time of troubles and acute dynastic conflict,
then the Almoravid conquerors from Morocco; after them the
Almohads, also from Morocco; and finally Christian supremacy
in the fourteenth and fifteenth centuries. But seven centuries of
Muslim power had stamped an African imprint deeply into the
life of much of Spain, above all of southern Spain. And for much
of this time the culture of these Muslim cities, fed and fuelled
by a wealthy agriculture, glowed brilliantly in Europe, opening
a bridge across the Mediterranean that was wider and more influential than any other till very recent times.

Islam south of the Sahara was to owe nothing to Arab conquest
but much to Berber influence. Except for the Almoravid raids
and ravagings of the eleventh century, there was no movement
of North African conquest until the Moroccan invasion of Songhay in 1591. Neither of these major incursions may be thought
to have done much to help the cause of Islam. On the contrary,
both tended to undermine it. Yet Islam spread gradually and
persistently in the Sudan west of Lake Chad from the tenth
century onwards, being partially barred from the Eastern Sudan
only by distance or the Christian kingdoms of the Middle Nile.

This south-westward spread took shape in a slow extension of
the Islamic community to include the settled populations of some
of the leading cities and market-centres. The pattern for this had
almost certainly existed in times long before the Muslim era,
since the trans-Saharan trading system of Phoenician and even
pre-Phoenician times had no doubt planted little Berber communities in the markets of the south. But now the difference was
that Islam could more effectively bind all these communities
together, whether in the Western Sudan, among the oasis relay-
stations of the desert country, or in North Africa. Increasingly,
the trans-Saharan trade came to be conducted by Muslims of
many ethnic origins, forming a vast and intricate network of
exchange that brought wealth and power to the rulers of many
African states, and fed the western world for centuries with goods
of prime value.

To what extent did Islam find converts among the mass of West Africans? Here the picture is somewhat different from elsewhere. Briefly, one can distinguish four main periods in the history of Muslim influence. There is first of all a long period of slowly expanding trade through Muslim enterprise, accompanied by the gradual conversion of Sudanese traders by their Berber partners from the Maghreb, mainly from the small Ibādi state of Tāhert and its neighbours. Islam reaches the markets of the Western Sudan by at least the ninth century. But it makes little initial impact. The rulers of Ghana do not accept Islam as one of their state religions. Only at the beginning of the eleventh century are there a few such conversions, the earliest of any importance of which we know being that of the king of Gao, traditionally in 1010, followed by that of the king of Kanem-Bornu in 1086. These are tactical conversions, motivated as much by commercial convenience as by appreciation of the political and religious achievements and teachings of Islam. They do not touch the people of the countryside, while even the people of the towns whose rulers have accepted Islam regard this innovation with a doubtful eye, at the same time holding fast to their own traditional faiths in a duality of beliefs that will continue. In its time and place, the same duality will apply to much of the African history of Christianity as well.

A second period begins with the thirteenth century. It follows a long confusion which includes the Almoravid invasions, the fall of Ghana, the rise and rivalry of the successor states of Ghana, and the emergence of Mali. But with Sundiata (c. 1235-60) the expansion of Islam begins to be enmeshed with the expansion of Mali. Under Mansa Musa (c. 1312-37) the correspondence is clear. Musa becomes caliph of 'the western parts'; and Islam now appears as the great religion of progressive government. It opens the way to a literate bureaucracy, to effective diplomatic links with distant powers, and to the inner reorganization of power and authority along lines which cut across the separatist loyalties of traditional religion. Out of all this modernizing trend there comes the foundation of solid schools of Islamic learning in

Timbuktu, Niani, Jenne and elsewhere. These schools will flourish for three hundred years and will attract Muslim scholars from
many countries and many trends of thought.

At the same time Islam remains the great religion of commerce.
From Mali the Dyula traders push out along the trading trails.
They are staunch promoters of Islam, the religion which has not
only assured them of their livelihood through the traders of the
Sahara, but has also given them an up-to-date and efficient set
of commercial customs and credit procedures such as have not
been available before. By 1400 and probably much earlier, strong
little Muslim trading communities exist in most of the important
market-centres of West Africa right down to the coast itself. They
will make few converts outside their own kind, but they form
pressure-groups which grow into an influential component of
West African life.

This long period of steady expansion continues, if with many
ups and down, until the Moroccan invasion of Songhay at the
end of the sixteenth century. For reasons we shall look into at a
further point, the whole trading network of North and West Africa
is by now badly disrupted and partly ruined. There follows, in a
third period, an anti-Muslim reaction which is also an anti-town
reaction. The peoples of the countryside, true to the old faiths,
raise their heads again and take the lead, among them many
whom the town-based Islamic empires have thrust down into a
servile condition. This continues until the eighteenth century
when a fourth period opens with the revival of Islam by bold
leaders and ambitious peoples, hand-in-hand with a political
reorganization which continues in one form or another until
sharply checked by European invasion.

Historically, then, the influence of Islam in West Africa must
be considered, aside from its spiritual aspect, as having primary
significance in two main fields: in the techniques of commerce,
and in those of the government of cities, states and empires of
growing power and importance. In both respects, moreover, Islam
may be seen as having acted as an effective solvent of traditional
society, repeatedly blurring the lines of ethnic separatism, dis-

placing the old 'tribal' equalities with new hierarchical structures and servitudes, and generally, with an impact increasingly noticeable after the sixteenth century, deepening the horizontal stratification of West African society.

In all this, one may repeat, the Almoravid invasions were an eccentric interruption, not to be repeated for another five centuries. Perhaps that is the chief reason why the great Ummayad period in al-Andalus, the period of early Muslim development of this memorable trading system across the desert, is remembered with such honour and respect by the Muslim schoolmen of West Africa, and why, for example, the mufti of Bobo-Dyulasso, who was born as late as 1897, should have noted the downfall of the Ummayads as marking the end of something like a golden age. Yet the trading system that was so greatly extended during the early centuries of Islam in West Africa—with its main routes reopened to half the world, with the capacities of camel transport ever more widely understood, with the wells of the Sahara constantly repaired and multiplied—brushed aside the Almoravid interruption and continued to gain in strength until the end of the sixteenth century. Then it finally levelled off in face of maritime competition, and gradually was lost to sight in modern times.

Islam may therefore claim to have brought much to West Africa. A commercial map applying to the period of 1300–1600 shows many regions of the western continent, north or south of the desert, as being directly or indirectly linked with a worldwide commercial system, built by men who recognized the essential unity of Islam, no matter how much they might at times contest each other's political authority. Throughout these centuries it seemed natural to religious potentates in Mecca to nominate a supreme representative or caliph in the Western Sudan, choosing for the purpose whatever powerful man might present himself from that quarter. And to the scholars of Cairo, Damascus and beyond it seemed likewise natural that Mali, largest of the Sudanese empires, should be reckoned among the leading states of the Muslim world.

As elsewhere within the *umma*, a widening of conversion led to local variation and diversity of form. Although West African Muslims have often shown themselves to be in strict orthodoxy to the Quran, there was never a time when the actual practice of Islam did not differ, and sometimes differ greatly, from the customs of Egypt and North Africa. Ibn Batuta, visiting Mali in the fourteenth century, was shocked by such things as the nudity of unmarried women and the sociable self-confidence of wives, while the great brotherhoods of Islam such as the Qadiriyya or Tijaniyya have often taken special forms in the Western Sudan. On top of this, or rather underlying it, there was the constant rivalry and conflict between Islam and the religions of West Africa. Some converts became devout Muslims. Many more settled with their conscience by a more or less uneasy compromise. After 1010 King Kossoi of Gao felt it wise, and no doubt he also felt it necessary, to maintain non-Muslim ceremonies at his court. But this persisted. Even great rulers who became caliphs were obliged to do as much. The prestigious Askia Muhammad of Songhay (1493–1528) also supported non-Muslim ceremonies and festivals at his court. Such customs were similarly continued under another powerful Songhay ruler, Askia Dawud (1549–83). Those who came before him were expected to prostrate themselves and sprinkle their heads with dust, a custom already noted with distaste by the visiting Ibn Batuta two centuries earlier. Upbraided for this by a devout *imam* of Timbuktu, who observed to the Askia that he must be mad to allow such heathen customs at his court, Dawud is said to have replied: 'I am not mad, but I rule over mad, impious and arrogant folk. It is for this reason that I play the madman . . .' Paris, in short, was worth a Mass.

We have already touched on this dichotomy between the Muslim towns and the non-Muslim or anti-Muslim countryside. Like other rulers in the Western Sudan, Dawud was faced in 'the Muslim question' with the most serious of all his many problems of political power. However devoutly orthodox he himself might have wished to be, however much he may have appreciated the literary, administrative and political advantages of Islam over traditional religion, he could not ignore the delicate balance of statesmanship that was alone capable of upholding him between the two sides. He had to consider on one hand his North African alliances and the interests of his towns and cities, while not forgetting too completely the contrary alliances and interests of all those rural peoples over whom he also ruled, and often with a heavy hand. In this Dawud succeeded, like other outstanding rulers before him; but more than one Sudanese monarch came to grief in leaning too far one way or the other.

By contrast with this continually ramifying influence in the west, Islam in East Africa achieved no more than local influence. Yet what it did achieve was done with a memorable distinction. Conversion of island and coastal populations from Somalia in the north to Mozambique in the south, a process which had got into its stride by the twelfth century, helped to carry these trading settlements into closer partnership with the whole Indian Ocean community. It instructed East Africans in the manners and methods of long-range commerce and of ruling by the profits of trade. It endowed their developing civilization of the seaboard with a notably Islamic accent of its own. At one or two points, moreover, Arab settlement was sufficiently dense to mark a brief but interesting non-African presence. This may be seen, perhaps better than anywhere else, in the ruins of the once majestic Husuni Palace on Kilwa Island. Believed by Chittick, its excavator, to have been built between about 1260 and 1330, this large place of commerce, residence and leisure on the brink of the Indian Ocean was equipped with lavish sanitary arrangements and an octagonal open-air bath, evidently supplied with fresh water, which has reminded archaeologists of Abbasid examples. For the most part, however, Arab settlers were quickly lost by intermarriage among Swahili or other communities. These accepted Islam and came to value greatly their membership in the Muslim world. But they retained their own languages, evolved their own literature, and built an urban civilization which remained emphatically their own.

Part of a Christian text, in Old Nubian, written in a fine hand using the Coptic form of the Greek alphabet.

FOUR

Tropical Achievement

A Mature Iron Age

'It seemed a perfect Arcadia', wrote the nineteenth-century explorer Joseph Thomson when first traversing the green and temperate lands that lie to the north of Lake Malawi. 'Imagine a magnificent grove of bananas, laden with bunches of fruit, each of which would form a man's load, growing on a perfectly level plain from which all weeds, garbage, and things unsightly are carefully cleared away.

'Dotted here and there are a number of immense shady sycamores, with branches each almost as large as a separate tree. At every few paces are charmingly neat circular huts, with conical roofs, and walls hanging out all round with the clay worked prettily into rounded bricks, and daubed symmetrically with spots . . .'

Perhaps the reality was less idyllic, as reality tends to be when looked at closely. Yet Thomson's travels took him through the land of the Nyakyusa, and not even close inspection in modern times has altogether removed the Nyakyusa from Arcadia, or at any rate from something very like it. These are the people, after all, of whom Monica Wilson has reported a firm and primary attachment to *ukwangela*, the 'enjoyment of good company', the 'mutual aid and sympathy which spring from personal friendship' and imply 'urbane manners and a friendliness which expresses itself in eating and drinking together; not only merry conversation,

141

but also discussion between equals, which the Nyakyusa regard as the principal form of education'.

Not all Iron Age peoples can have possessed such geniality and tolerance as the Nyakyusa, whose good fortune counted a fine and fertile countryside as well as immunity from the ruinous horrors of the East Coast slave trade in the nineteenth century. Others lived in harsh country and hungered every year, harried their neighbours or were harried in return, exacting tribute or being obliged to pay it, engulfed and barbarized in wars of migration and restless movement as northern peoples swept southward, or southern peoples thrust to the north. Yet the picture of old Africa as predominantly brutal and chaotic in its manners remains so widely accepted by the world at large—even to the point where many who question this picture are inclined to do so with a self-excusing air—that it may be good to remember the Nyakyusa and their love of peaceful argument, genial manners and tolerance of error. They have not been unique in having these attitudes.

How far is the term 'Mature Iron Age' permissible? There is as yet no generally agreed periodization of African history such as exists for Europe with its convenient parcelling into Antiquity, Middle Ages, Renaissance and the rest. But the interpretation of African history, and its ordering into a meaningful sequence of events, requires a phasing process as much as any other history. So far as continental Africa is concerned—largely, Africa south of the Sahara—the thousand years before about AD 1000 were the period of the installation and gradual spread of initial Iron Age societies. This period may reasonably be called an Early Iron Age. In or around AD 1000 there occurs a series of events or developments, not confined to one or other of the regions of sub-Saharan Africa, which mark a change to a new period, although the terminal date is no more satisfactory than other dates of the same kind, and calls for as many reservations. By AD 1000 the North African states had long ceased to be primitive Iron Age societies. So had some of the societies of the Western Sudan, while Early Iron Age describes the Christian kingdoms of Nubia and Ethiopia no better. In general, though, a notably large number of societies in most regions had developed by about AD 1000 to the point where they could embark on forms of organization which were not only new, but were also an unfolding realization of the potential which had been inherent within earlier forms. These were, in short, mature forms; and the gradual attainment of this maturity was carried into many fields of enterprise and effort.

This growing maturity of form is manifest in many directions. By 1400, for example, there were sculptors in wood, ivory, metal and terracotta in many African lands whose conceptual grasp of contemporary thought and belief had carried them to remarkable and daring experiments and styles. To be sure, the Mature Iron Age societies which produced such artists were still enclosed within an economy of subsistence, modified only by a varying though never dominant production for exchange. There was no revolutionary break. Yet these societies had mastered all the technical and ideological problems essential to their survival. They could now, with a general development which gathered strength after about AD 1000, move towards fresh growth and even relative abundance. This they did in a number of ways.

They developed their methods of tropical or sub-tropical cultivation. They extended their systems of irrigation and of soil-conservation where these were needed. They brought into the realm of widespread knowledge a host of herbal cures. They became skilled in mining. By about 1500, Mauny guesses, the miners of West Africa had produced perhaps as much as 3,500 tons of gold (and would produce as much again in 1500–1900); and they had done it, so far all the evidence shows, by methods of prospecting, shaft-sinking, extraction and refinement that were technical achievements of their own. In Southern Rhodesia, according to Summers, 'there is scarcely a modern gold mine . . . which is not on the site of an "ancient working" ', adding that 'it has been deduced that originally the zone from the surface down to about 20 feet was exceptionally rich in gold, and it seems very probable that immense quantities were exported'.

Copper was another important metal for noble decoration and exchange, and was greatly mined at many places; so was tin, enabling good brass alloys to be made; while iron-working, with the exception of a few groups such as the Khoi in South Africa who had remained in a Stone Age culture, seems to have been practised by every people who could find the ore. Nor was it even necessary that iron ore be locally present for its potential uses to be understood. The Canary Islands off the West African mainland had no iron ore, but their pre-colonial—that is, pre-Spanish—inhabitants, the Guanche, who had derived from the mainland shortly before the time of Christ, used iron objects acquired by trade with the mainland. Moreover, they were mining sulphur shortly before the Spanish conquest, according to Abreu Galindo (*História de la conquista de las siete islas de Canárias, 1602*; reprint, A. Cioranescu [ed.], Santa Cruz de Tenerife, 1977.)*

Being by modern standards pre-scientific, these societies were still the home of magic and enchantment. They adopted magical or supernatural explanations for real phenomena they could not otherwise elucidate. Such explanations became interwoven with their religions, just as their religions were inseparably part of their process of social crystallization and self-identification. Magical and supernatural beliefs, in short, were necessary parts of the 'social cement' which held these societies together. This being so, they projected *systems* of belief, thought, and behaviour. That is why it is almost always wrong to conceive of Iron Age Africa as submitted to a chaotic or haphazard wizardry. On the contrary, Iron Age Africa was almost always submitted to a systematic wizardry having hard-and-fast limits, coordinates and rules. While they might temper this 'pre-scientific science' of com-

*I am grateful to Michael R. Eddy for these points, a correction to the accepted view, and to previous editions of this book.

munity relations with a nicely shrewd scepticism—well displayed
in the Niger Delta proverb which recalls that once a spirit grows
too violent, 'people can tell him the wood he is made of'—these
societies depended for their survival on such rules being thoroughly understood and strictly applied. Nothing was punished
so severely as their abuse: it was precisely for abuse of the rules
of magical and supernatural belief and behaviour that persons
presumed to be witches were tormented.

Looking back on the way these communities were ordered,
one may sometimes be as struck by the blind or squalid cruelty
with which such rules could be applied as by the torments and
ordeals of what Bishop Stubbs, but without irony, used to call
'the dear delightful Middle Ages' of Europe. Iron Age Africa was
clearly not a paradise. Yet to isolate its darker side as evidence
of unusual cruelty or natural human inferiority would be even
more misleading than to suppose that the European Middle Ages
knew only racks and thumb screws. If anything, the comparison
between Africa and Europe is likely to be in Africa's favour.
Throughout the medieval period most African forms of government were undoubtedly more representative than their European
contemporaries. Most African wars were less costly in life and
property. And most African ruling groups were less predatory. So
far as the comparison has any value, daily life in medieval Europe
was likely to be far more hazardous or disagreeable for the common man and even, with exceptions, for his wife.

All these things, in any case, were part of their social context
and have to be viewed as such. One might even say about Africa,
if one wished to moralize, that they were a possibly unavoidable
part of the price that had to be paid for man's being able to master
the arts of survival and expansion in this most huge and difficult
continent. However that may be, the work of populating and
mastering Africa was largely over by the later centuries of Iron
Age maturity: a large and many-sided achievement in adaptation,
new discovery and bold initiative that may well be seen as the
central and imposing contribution of Africans to man's general
mastery of nature and the world.

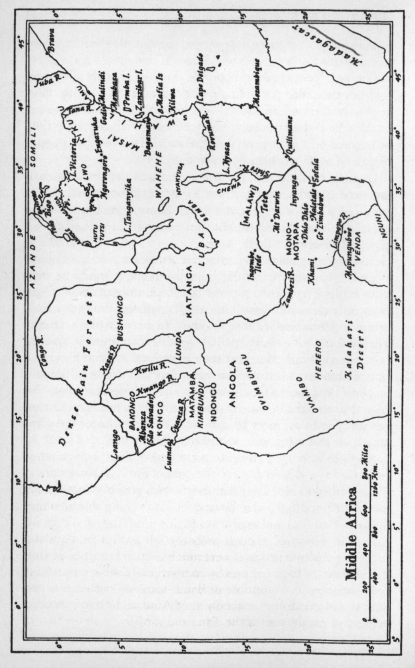

Middle Africa

Rift Valley Kingdoms

Early Iron Age cultures appeared in central-southern Africa within a few centuries of their expansion along the Middle Nile, in western Africa and in northern Ethiopia, indicating a very rapid spread of metal-using technology once the necessary skills were known. Mere southward diffusion from Meroe or other Sudanese centres appears too simple an explanation for this revolutionary advance. Certain correspondences between all these early metal-using cultures do indeed suggest a common source for all of them, but the general trend among most researchers today is to allow for a large and perhaps crucial element of local invention or inventive adaptation.

Much of the available evidence points to this spread of iron-using culture as being identified with the spread of Bantu-speaking peoples whose 'nursery' was the southern Congo Basin. These peoples undoubtedly had iron-using technology two thousand years ago, and steadily expanded in numbers with better farming and command of terrain. By about AD 300 their migrating groups had reached the Limpopo and crossed southward into modern South Africa. In the other direction they had expanded to parts of East Africa. Southern Uganda, central and western Kenya and central and western Tanzania all had sedentary farming and iron-using populations, interspersed with Stone Age hunters, by the eighth or ninth century. Here, again, of course, one must be careful not to think of migrating groups as being large columns continuously on the march. The spread was a gradual one. It was mainly obtained by the repeated hiving off of junior groups from parent groups, as Iron Age populations grew steadily more numerous and required more land.

In later centuries, though probably not until after about AD 1300, these farming peoples were much disturbed, moved around and changed in their cultures by complex population movements on a major scale. A number of Bantu-speaking peoples are said to have dispersed in a generally southward and south-westward direction from the area of the Tana and Juba rivers on the fringes

of modern Kenya and Somalia, although these traditions are far
from reliable, and probably refer to the movement only of small
groups who mingled with indigenous Late Stone Age populations
established long before in central and western Kenya and Tanzania. One estimate places the arrival in central Kenya of the
Embu, for instance, in about 1425, and of the Kikuyu in the
Fort Hall area of Kenya in about 1545, but such dates are really
without value. To these Bantu migrations there were added many
others by a number of non-Bantu peoples from the north and
north-east, among these being the immigrant ancestors of the
Kalenjin and the Luo, and later the Masai. All this helps to
explain why the modern population map of eastern Africa shows
a maze of peoples whose languages, appearance, customs and
traditions go back to different roots in the distant past. Such was
the complexity of this great to-and-fro of diverse peoples over
many years—'movements on a scale', as Oliver has described
them, 'which has not occurred in Europe since the Dark Ages'—
that much about their history is still mysterious, and may probably remain so. As an example of the difficulties, there is the
case of Engaruka.

Engaruka is a ruined settlement or series of village settlements
of many hundred stone-built huts or small houses terraced along
the eastern slopes of Mount Ngorongoro near Tanzania's frontier
with Kenya, and about three hundred miles from the sea. In this
remote place nothing is apparent to explain why Engaruka came
into existence, and nothing to show why it lapsed into ruin. For
anyone who cares to slash his way through the bush and thorn
that overwhelm this extensive settlement, clambering terrace by
terrace from its valley river to the ridge of the hillside where it
terminates, there is only the insistent stumbling certainty of its
presence, mutely unique in its acres of tumbled stone, its cairns
and lines of house foundations, its scatter of level platforms, its
hint of walls and paths half-buried in the grass and thorn.

Manifestly a product of Mature Iron Age development in these
eastern highlands, and having some obvious cultural links with
lesser settlements of the same general type, Engaruka is interesting

both for its relatively large size and for the absolute silence which enshrouds its past: nothing but a little vague and dubious tradition has anything to say or to remember on the subject.* No doubt it became the victim of some of those southward-moving peoples, probably the Masai, who came into these lands during the Mature Iron Age and damaged much of their cultural fabric; but whether this was five hundred years ago or less remains a matter on which, at the moment, anyone may make his guess. The Engaruka settlements mark in any case a point of Iron Age maturity, and remain even today beneath their veil of bush and thorn, a powerful indicator of the depth of culture that can lie behind the apparent simplicity of East African village life.

Elsewhere we can reach stronger ground, thanks to the survival of much traditional history and other useful evidence. The Early Iron Age farmers of Uganda, for example, had evidently acquired a simple form of government by chiefs before the thirteenth century. Some time around 1300 there came the rise of a kingdom or kingdoms under shadowy dynasties of local rulers of which the most famous are the Chwezi. Towards 1500 these were infiltrated by migrating groups of Luo-speaking folk from the region of the Upper Nile. These Luo were looking for good land. They found it in the pleasant country of Uganda. Here their ruling clans, supported by a large number of 'commoner clans' into which local people were progressively absorbed, were able to impose themselves and to found states and dynasties of their own.

Being cattle-raising wanderers, these newcomers did not necessarily bring with them a higher level of culture than already existed in the East African lands where they settled. Often enough, as Engaruka suggests, they destroyed a great deal which they were quite unable to replace. Even from the little evidence that Engaruka has so far yielded, it seems clear that its builders and inhabitants had achieved a far greater mastery of environ-

---

*Excavations by Hamo Sassoon have thrown some fresh archaeological light on this subject. See a report on his work during 1964 in *Azania*, Journal of the British Institute of History and Archaeology in East Africa, vol. 1, 1966, p. 79. See also P. Robertshaw, 'Engaruka Revisited: Excavations of 1982', *Azania*, vol. 21, 1986.

ment, a far better use of labour and a much higher standard of living, than the wandering nomads who came from the north with their hunting spears and cattle moving on the hoof. In Uganda, however, the newcomers settled down and took over and developed existing political forms; their long-surviving traditions indicate that they were successful in promoting long periods of peace and stability. One branch of the Luo, for instance, founded or at least helped to found the Bito line of kings, who are remembered as having ruled over Bunyoro for eighteen generations. Another line of kings is remembered to have ruled over Buganda for twenty-two generations. The old kingdoms of Ankole, Koki and Kiziba have comparable traditions. Sometimes the process of political change, and the acceptance of rule by chiefs, has continued into very recent times. Even under colonial rule the chiefs of the Alur, another people of Luo origins, were still extending their authority over neighbouring folk who had previously lived without any 'central government' of their own, but who now saw a new value in the arbitration of chiefs, accepted Alur chiefly rule without resistance, or even asked for it to be extended among them.

South from Uganda, along the pleasant upland pastures which form the inland flank of modern Tanzania, the same process of development into Mature Iron Age forms was repeated with the rise of kingdoms in Ruanda and Burundi. Incoming wanderers, under strong chiefs, evolved new patterns of authority in combination with iron-using farming peoples who had previously lived in states that were far more loosely organized, or were organized so little as barely to deserve the name of states at all. There gradually crystallized a sharply hierarchical structure of society in which ruling clans were supported and supplied by subject clans or subject peoples. In the southern Ugandan kingdom of Ankole, for example, the Hima ruled and reckoned their wealth and happiness in cattle, while the Iru farmers fed the cattle of their Hima lords, worked for them, and were generally without political rights of any value. Much the same situation obtained in Ruanda between the Tutsi minority of cattle-rich noblemen and the Hutu majority of peasants.

The structure of these kingdoms as it developed after about 1500 may be reminiscent of systems of feudal vassalage in western Europe a little earlier. Tutsi and Hima rulers were linked to their followers by links of vassalage or 'clientage' that were specifically defined, named and understood. As time went by, somewhat similar links were developed between Hima and Iru, Tutsi and Hutu, though the 'lower classes' never managed, any more than in Europe, to achieve anything approaching equality of rights. And again, with the passage of time, the kings became more powerful and despotic by a shift in authority from ascription to appointment. They raised soldiers and governors from men who were their own personal servants or appointees, rather than from men who owed their rise to nobility of birth. But this development acquired no momentum here until the nineteenth century and its time of troubles.

Before the nineteenth century, however, these lord-and-vassal systems composed a structure that was based, at any rate ideally, on a two-way exchange of benefits. While Tutsi nobles gossiped among their equals, sipping honeydew and arguing the wisdom of the ages, or leaned upon their spears while composing verse in praise of their courage, virtue and authority, the humble Hutu laboured at their gates in producing food and bearing burdens. Yet the Hutu and their kind also had their expectations. For the Tutsi nobles and their like were under obligation to assume not only the responsibilities of government, but also those of defence. Just as the yeomen of medieval France preferred to bind themselves to strong masters, seeing in this their best assurance of safety and protection, so also did the farming peoples of these inland kingdoms think it wise to make themselves the tribute-paying vassals of men for whom warfare and government were a professional duty, and not only a guarantee of privilege. Rising in the fifteenth or sixteenth centuries, these Rift Valley kingdoms were able to remain stable and independent until European co-

lonial invasion overturned the world they knew and left their
peoples with the need to build another.

Around Great Zimbabwe

While it has long been known that the many large stone structures
of the gold-bearing country between the Zambezi and Limpopo
rivers (once Southern Rhodesia, now independent Zimbabwe)
were the work of indigenous African peoples, only in the 1960s
was their chronology securely established. Renewed excavations
and a large number of Carbon-14 datings show that building in
stone began around AD 1100, and developed to a mature stage,
with the creation of the vast complex at Great Zimbabwe, around
1300. The builders were one or other group of the Shona-
speaking people who inhabit most of Zimbabwe today. The recovery of oral tradition indicates that another stage began around
1425, when Mutota, king of the Karanga, organized a vast and
victorious campaign of conquest designed to extend his rule over
the whole inland plateau between the Zambezi and the Limpopo—the main gold-bearing area—and afterwards through
Mozambique to the harbours of the East Coast trade.*

All this was substantially achieved by Mutota and his son Matope, so that the latter became the most powerful sovereign in
the central-southern continent during the 1470s, and was honoured as such by the rulers and chiefs of the East Coast ports.
These called his empire *Wilayatu 'l Mu'anamutapah* after his
indigenous title of Mwanamutapa, or 'Lord of the Plundered
Lands'; and use of this title was duly taken over by the Portuguese
who corrupted it to Monomotapa and believed, for a while, that
they had found the legendary empire of Prester John.

After the death of Matope in about 1480 this large structure

*The indispensable and perhaps definitive book on the archaeological origins and
development of Great Zimbabwe and related structures is P. S. Garlake, *Great Zimbabwe*,
London, 1973.

was riven by internal rivalries. Two of the Monomotapa's strongest 'barons', Changa and Togwa, rebelled against his overlordship, and Changa, after some years of fighting, was able to establish himself as the ruler of a separate kingdom in the southern part of what is now Zimbabwe, leaving the northern part to the continued rule of the Monomotapan line of kings. Changa himself became known by the title of Changamire, perhaps after Changa *Amir*, or the Governor, as the traders from the coast had known him; and Changamire then became the dynastic title of Changa's successors as kings or *mambos* of their land. Far from the sea and the Zambezi, this kingdom of Urozwi—the land where the Rozwi ruled—remained beyond reach of Portuguese ravages. But it was different in Monomotapa to the north. Here the bold and predatory Portuguese, coming up the Zambezi in the sixteenth century in search of gold and silver, were able to set up permanent markets as far as the neighbourhood of Mount Darwin and, gradually, to impose their military and political authority. In this they were partially successful, as elsewhere, by means of intervening on one side or the other of dynastic or 'baronial' wars. A decisive battle in 1628 enabled them to displace the ruling Monomotapa with a convenient nominee of their own, and a year later this virtual puppet, Mavura, duly signed a treaty which gave the Portuguese a free run in looking for minerals and, if they could find any, in mining and exporting them. This was an early example of an Afro-European treaty of the 'concession type', disastrous to the concession-givers, which was to become common in later times.

Continuing over many years, Portuguese intervention—whether officially or by the hand of local settlers—went far to ruin the Monomotapan system of government, production and trade. In a valuable report of 1667 Barreto listed three reasons why so little gold could now be taken from these lands. They make sad reading. The first, he said, was the reluctance of chiefs to allow any digging for gold, lest the Portuguese should seize the land. The second was the lack of population. And the third, a constant theme in Portuguese rule, formed in Barreto's opinion

the principal reason for decay: this was 'the bad Portuguese con-
duct' that drove people from their homes into exile in other lands.

Southward in later Mashonaland, the second Karanga state
continued to be ruled by kings of the Rozwi clan. These were
the lords of Khami, Dhlo Dhlo and of other stone-built settlements. They fared much better. A few Portuguese came this way
but never gained the decisive power they enjoyed in the north.
Around 1690 they were finally driven out by Changamire
Dombo, who considerably strengthened the Rozwi state; and they
were never able to return. The seventeenth century seems to have
been one of peace and progress, although it is interesting that
the massive buildings at Great Zimbabwe, long deserted by then,
were evidently not reoccupied by the Rozwian rulers. Except
among the eastern hills—at Inyanga and its neighbouring sites—
there is little sign of defensive works in any of these structures.
The hill-top 'acropolis' of Great Zimbabwe may look like a fort;
but in reality it was a place of sanctity guarded merely from the
profane. Khami near Bulawayo was certainly the dwelling of a
powerful chief, but it has nothing that resembles fortification.
Naletale is much the same. Immune through many peaceful
decades, and no doubt defenceless and largely disarmed, the
Karanga were to be quickly and cruelly smashed and ruined in
the 1830s by northward-moving Ngoni invaders from Natal,
themselves seeking to avoid white-settlers' aggression.

Further south again, beyond the Limpopo, the same kind of
progress from early to mature Iron Age systems occurred with the
so-called Mapungubwe Culture. Here, along the southern bank
of the Limpopo, in what is now the northern Transvaal, Shona
peoples established themselves after about AD 1000 and built a
series of Iron Age polities which were further developed by new
groups from north of the Limpopo in later centuries. They reproduced the skills and customs of their neighbours to the north,
working finely in cast and beaten gold, producing good hand-
turned pottery, trading their products for Indian cottons and other
Indian Ocean imports, and burying their kings with a wealth of
golden ornament. Towards 1600 they were displaced by another

set of rulers from across the Limpopo, relatives of the Karanga called the Venda, who remained here until they too were ruined by the devastations of the early nineteenth century.

And the same state-forming process, in one degree or another, went on right across South Africa as far as its southernmost seaboard. Many new political systems appeared in the fourteenth or fifteenth century. Even as far as the mouth of the Umzimvubu River, only three degrees north of the latitude of the Cape of Good Hope, there was a place of trade between the peoples of Pondoland and sea-merchants from the Swahili coast. Almost the whole of south-eastern Africa was enclosed within Iron Age states formed by Bantu-speaking people whose presence in South Africa had pre-dated white arrival by at least twelve centuries.

These states were very old at the time the Dutch arrived in 1652. Their institutions included the familiar vertical divisions of lineage and family-descent groups, as well as horizontal divisions into 'age-sets' and 'age-regiments' composed of men and women born at about the same time and bound to the same loyalties and duties. This two-way stratification of society was further complicated, as it was elsewhere, by horizontal divisions such as those between craftsmen and farmers, or between ruling groups and subject groups. There was the same type of kingship, with its firm belief that the health and welfare of the king were inseparably and spiritually linked with the health and welfare of the whole society. There were the same notions of religious identification with ancestors, of beneficial magic and harmful witchcraft, of methods of making war or keeping the peace. Well before 1400 the community of Iron Age ideas and structures reached from the fringes of the Sahara to the Antarctic-facing shore of southern Africa. At least five hundred years before the Dutch landed at the Cape of Good Hope, this community had almost touched its greatest possible geographical extension.

In the Congo Basin

A few other examples may be useful in illustrating the socio-political evolution that was nearly everywhere present in these central-southern regions.

The origins of the kingdom of Kongo, 'great and powerful, full of people, having many vassals', as the Portuguese described it four and a half centuries ago, are told in many traditions. Some of them say that the founders of this well-knit political system near the mouth of the Congo River had moved from the inland country beyond the river Kwango. Another and more likely version is that they came from the northern bank of the Congo estuary late in the fourteenth or early in the fifteenth century. This was again the pattern of a small but powerful intrusive group which imposed its superior organization on indigenous people.

Early in the sixteenth century King Affonso of Kongo dictated many letters to kings of Portugal; here are the last lines and official signature from one of them.

They conquered, inter-married and gradually gained the upper hand of recalcitrant neighbours until by 1483, when the Portuguese captain Diogo Cão first anchored in the waters of the Congo, these Kongo people (or BaKongo, *Ba* being a prefix indicating the plural) had built a large and closely articulated state in the northern region of modern Angola. Their king in Cão's time entered willingly into trade with the Portuguese, exchanged ambassadors with Lisbon, and received Christian missionaries with curiosity if not conviction. In this way they opened with Portugal a brief but friendly period of partnership.

From his capital at Mbanza, which the Portuguese later baptized São Salvador, the strong king of the Kongo (also Christian in more than name after about 1506) ruled the metropolitan lands of his empire, the country between the Kwilu and Congo rivers. North of the Congo River were several small tributary states; southwards lay several others. The Portuguese misinterpreted this lord-and-vassal hierarchy in terms of their own feudalism, and in 1512 presented the Mani-Kongo, the lord of these lands, with a list of noble titles which they thought he would do well to copy and which, nominally at least, he did adopt. A Portuguese report of 1595 can thus describe the organization of metropolitan government as including the authority of 'six Christian dukes, who may even be called little kings . . . and as well as these there are Catholic counts and marquises who obey the king's orders with very strict obedience. He dismisses any of them who do not carry out their responsibilities, and replaces them by other men.'

At the beginning the Portuguese found it necessary and even desirable to respect the sovereignty of this Kongo kingdom and its neighbours. They presented themselves as friends and allies, just as they had done along the coast of Senegal, at the mouth of the Gambia, at Elmina and at Benin. They remained for some time content with this state of affairs, while extracting from Kongo the greatest possible number of captives for enslavement elsewhere. Yet almost from the beginning the overseas slave trade had its grim effect in violence and deepening despair. As early as 1526 the baptized King Affonso of Kongo is writing to his 'royal brother' in Lisbon that 'we cannot reckon how great the damage is . . . and so great, Sire, is the corruption and licentiousness that our country is being completely depopulated . . .' It made no difference. Slaving continued.

Events took a somewhat different course further south. Here, in the coastal country of the powerful Mbundu kingdom of Ndongo (whose king's title was *ngola*: hence the Angola of later times), the Portuguese ran into opposition and rejection. The reasons were not far to seek. It was by raids on Mbundu country that the Kongo rulers had obtained many of the captives whom they sold into Portuguese slavery. From the first, then, the Portuguese appeared along the coast of Ndongo as obvious enemies, and were treated as such. Yet the Portuguese, whether as royal agents or private adventurers, were not to be put off. Inspired partly by a fixed illusion that the mountains of Ndongo possessed rich silver mines, they at first attempted the same tactics of peaceful penetration by which they had acquired their influence in Kongo. Failing with these, they turned to outright invasion. From 1575 the wars went on for a weary century and more. Their little armies were repeatedly thrown back and scattered. Portuguese gangs roved the countryside, seizing captives wherever they could. Ndongo was steadily and disastrously depopulated. Shifting inland, its leaders set up a new state in Matamba, associated with the heroic name of Queen Nzinga, who fought the Portuguese for many years before coming to terms with them. By the 1680s the Kongo kingdom, like Ndongo, was far gone in ruin.

East of these Congo-Angola states were others of the same type, though varying in local structure and having no direct contact with Europeans. Many of their peoples, like those of the riverain populations of western Africa, were highly gifted in the plastic arts, while they shared with other tropical Africans their love of dancing and versatility in the use of rhythm. The Bushongo of the Kasai were among several who developed a fine art in raffia-weaving, a skill that still partially survives. Their state appears to have entered its mature form, with spiritually sanc-

tioned kingship, a hierarchy of chiefs, some division of labour
and a complex ideology of moral and political behaviour, some
four centuries ago.

These developments in social and political organization involved the slow transformation of scattered communities of Early
Iron Age farmers, for a long time very small in numbers, into
much larger communities which became states with kings and
central governments. No exact date or place can be assigned to
the origins of this 'Congolese revolution', although its effects were
far-reaching. Traditions suggest that the homeland of these
changes lay in the ancient Luba country of the northern Katanga
grasslands, and that the critical period of onward-moving development occurred between 1400 and 1500.

One may hazard a few guesses which can be nourished, so
far, by no exact proof. This wide grassland belt of the Katanga,
it may yet be seen, was one of the seminal points of remote
African growth. There is first of all the evidence, by no means
conclusive and yet insistently persuasive, that the Katanga was a
very early 'nursery' of the Bantu-speaking peoples some two thousand years ago. There is next the evidence, this time not open
to doubt, that the Katanga was the scene of early metal-using
states in the first millennium AD: of states near Lake Kisale that
were perhaps the most advanced of their kind for the whole Early
Iron Age in Middle Africa, mining and smelting copper for their
own use but also trading in it with near neighbours and, quite
possibly, with distant neighbours too. There is thirdly the large
probability that populations grew less slowly in these fertile and
well-watered grasslands than elsewhere in Middle Africa, and
that this was the growth which gave a decisive impulse to the
settlement of the whole region with Iron Age peoples.

For by about 1400, at all events, we have echoes in the old
traditions which suggest that earlier processes of state formation
were already going through a new phase of growth. Soon afterwards there was certainly a strong Luba state in the area near
Lake Boya. The traditions say that its 'founding hero', or 'first
ruler', was Kongolo. This ruler and his successors belonged to a

Luba clan known as the *balopwe*, clearly a much extended family having special powers and prestige, with its members being recognized as intermediaries with the world of the ancestors and the gods, just as with the Rozwi rulers of the Shona kingdoms to the south of the Zambezi. From now onwards it is the *balopwe*, with their methods of centralized rule, who play the crucial role in political development throughout this wide belt of grassland which lies between the Congo rain forests and the plateaux of the south.

With the *balopwe* of the Luba, in short, we have another branch of that characteristic pattern of centralizing rule, through spiritually sanctioned kings and a hierarchy of governors and under-governors down to headmen at the village level, which may be seen in many regions. But it may well be that it was here, though long before 1400, that the seeds of this typically African form of kingship were first sown in Middle Africa. There is in any case a series of remarkably close resemblances between the kingly laws and obligations, customs, regalia and beliefs, of these Luba kingdoms in the southern Congo and those of southern Uganda, Ruanda, Burundi, Malawi, Zambia, Zimbabwe and the western Congo-Angola complex; and the evidence suggests that it was the Luba kingdoms, at least in early form, which appeared first. All these kings were powerful for spiritual as well as military reasons: above all, indeed, for spiritual reasons. They were appointed, respected and eventually interred with special ceremonies of much the same kind. And they tended to exercise their hegemony over subjects and subjected neighbours with much the same attitudes and methods.

Within the region of the Congo-Angola-Zambia grasslands, moreover, the Luba impetus comes very clearly from the record of remembered history. Successive migrations by groups under junior chiefs or disappointed contenders to the throne of one or another Luba state carried waves of Luba *balopwe* far and wide across these countries. Towards 1600, for instance, a Luba *mulopwe* called Kibinda Ilunga went away to the west with a band of followers, and founded a new state among the Lunda of the

southern lands of the river Kasai. The traditions say that Kibinda
did this by marrying a local queen, whose name was Rweej, and
explains how the issue of this marriage, Luseeng, and Luseeng's
son Naweej, built a mighty empire. These traditions, no doubt,
legitimize a Luba conquest in this way; whether by conquest or
peaceful infiltration, however, there is no doubt that a Luba-
Lunda empire did emerge. Naweej is remembered today as the
first emperor of Lundaland: as the first Mwata Yamvo, 'Lord of
the Viper'. By 1700 the empire of Mwata Yamvo was undoubtedly
a major factor in Middle African politics.

Its formation set other movements in being. Lesser segments
of the Kasai Lunda, unwilling or unable to live under the rule
of Kibinda and his successors, shifted westward into what is now
Angola. They included the followers of a brother of Queen Rweej
whose name is remembered as Kinguri, the founding hero of the
Imbangala of inland Angola; while another brother of Rweej is
likewise said to have moved southward with his followers and
formed the Lwena people who live today along the headwaters
of the Zambezi.

At least three other important migrations affected Zambia.
Towards 1650 the ancestors of the Lozi appeared in the country
that is now called Barotseland. They seem to have come from
Luba-Lunda districts in the north. At about the same time the
ancestors of the Bemba, under their founding hero Chiti Maluba,
crossed the Luapula River eastward out of Lubaland, and came
eventually to rest in what is now north-eastern Zambia. And
again at about the same time another state of Luba-Lunda origin,
under a line of rulers entitled Kazembe, took shape astride the
modern Katanga-Zambia border.

In all this too we have the theme of material advance. Economic factors are among those that explain these successive and
successful movements, new settlements and the founding of states
based on a mingling of migrant and already settled peoples. The
westward move of Lunda and Luba into Angola seems clearly
linked with the growth of long-distance trade with the Portuguese
along the Atlantic coast after about 1600. The southward move-

ments may well have been impelled by the search for wider farming lands now that several American crops of great value, notably maize and cassava, had been carried inland from the ports of Angola, and were beginning to be widely cultivated. By 1700 one may reasonably suppose that all these populations, with the exception of scattered remnants of Bushman hunters, were growing less slowly than before, and perhaps much less slowly, although their total numbers will have remained only a small fraction of what they are today. And this will have been true not only for the peoples mentioned in these pages but also for others along their periphery as far as the Ovambo and Herero of the far south-west.

Their political development illustrates the flexibility and pragmatism that were possible, here as elsewhere, even within the ideological limits of an age of faith when politics and religion stayed bound inseparably together. Always conservative in essence, if only because they drew their strength from the solutions and beliefs of tradition, these systems were often highly experimental in form. After Kibinda Ilunga had imposed Luba rule on the Lunda of the Kasai, around 1600, the result was not a mere copy of *balopwe* practices further east. The Mwata Yamvo, to be sure, had all the religious prestige and spiritual authority of the Luba rulers; and yet the pattern of his state revealed a new syncretism. Through means that remain to be fully understood, the Lunda rulers took a different attitude to lesser chiefs whom they subjected and obliged to pay tribute. In Lubaland the subject chiefs had remained outside the Luba kingdoms, being treated as little more than defeated vassals. But the Lunda chiefs, adopting Luba methods and modifying them, absorbed their defeated rivals into the Lunda system and made them organically parts of it. They obliged the chiefs whom they defeated to adopt Lunda titles of office, and to pay tribute to the Mwata Yamvo through the agency of royal representatives who were permanently in residence at these provincial courts. But they did not otherwise deprive these chiefs of their local power or humiliate them. On the contrary, they enhanced their prestige by giving them membership in the hierarchy of Lunda imperialism. Stability and peace were achieved throughout a broad region of the Congo grasslands, and for a long time.

One may note, in passing, that although these developments were specific to Middle Africa and its southern periphery they were in many ways comparable to events elsewhere on the continent, and especially in the forest and near-forest areas of West Africa. What the most distant connections between these two great regions really were we do not know. Linguistic parallels suggest that such connections certainly existed. Some specialists would have it that 'original Bantu' had its earliest homeland in the Niger-Benue confluence area. Others have seen reason for believing that iron-working technologies in Middle Africa derived in the first place from the Nigerian region. But whether by contact or separate invention, political and social evolution in West and Middle Africa often followed much the same path. The modes of spiritually sanctioned kingship show as much. So do many forms of religious belief. Artistic conceptions, notably in woodcarving, point to common attitudes: the attitudes, in short, of an underlying common culture fructified by great diversities of style and form. Even political methods emphasize this basic unity. The royal commissioners of the Mwata Yamvo, for example, placed as they were in residence at the courts of subject chiefs or kings, had functions in no way essentially different from those of the *ajele* commissioners of the *alafin* or ruler of Oyo, a contemporary kingdom in western Nigeria.

The theme of underlying cultural unity can be extended. Eastward in Malawi there was the same crystallization of states originating in an Early Iron Age when trade had been of minimal importance or no importance at all, but whose later patterns of organization reflected a growing commercial factor. Here the principal people were the various branches of the Malawi (or Marave as the old European travellers generally knew them), a cluster of Iron Age populations speaking much the same language, and whose traditions also bring their founding ancestors from Lubaland. Their coming, however, was earlier than the

migrations of the Bemba and Lozi of Zambia, and they seem to
have had some distant relationship with the Shona peoples to the
south of the Zambezi, or at any rate with the ruling clans of the
Shona. Together with the Shona, whose traditions likewise claim
an origin in the north, the Malawi were able to link the inland
countries of Middle Africa with the East Coast, just as the Luba-
Lunda peoples linked it with the West Coast, in a long-distance
trade of great duration and political influence.

Among the notable ancestors of the Malawi, remembered by
tradition, was a ruler called Kalonga, and he it was who gave the
Malawi the title of their most powerful line of kings. Soon after
1600, according to reports by the Portuguese, who were now
beginning to collect a good deal of political information about
these inland countries, Kalonga Mzura was in command of all
the country between Lake Malawi and the mouths of the Zambezi. Here the story of Portuguese intervention in Angola repeated
itself in different form. In 1608 the Portuguese were able to strike
up an alliance with Kalonga Mzura, and to obtain from him a
force of four thousand warriors for use against the Shona south
of the Zambezi; in return for this, Kalonga Mzura was able to
secure Portuguese aid in defeating his principal local rival, a
Malawi chief called Lundi who ruled the Zimba. Later, in 1623,
Mzura switched alliances, and began helping the Shona against
the Portuguese. But in this policy he failed to make much progress, and turned his attention back to the extension of his domains north of the river. In the 1640s he welcomed Portuguese
traders to his capital near Lake Malawi, and asked them for
'technical aid' in the form of carpenters who could build sailing
ships for use upon the lake. Perhaps needless to say, no shipwrights ever arrived, just as, for somewhat different reasons, they
had failed to arrive in Kongo when King Affonso had asked for
them.

Mzura's empire of the Malawi did not long survive him, although in this case the reason for collapse lay in domestic circumstances and not in Portuguese intervention. By 1700, if not
before, the Malawi had reverted to the separate independence of

their several sections, foremost among whom were the Chewa. Travelling through this country in 1831–32, the Portuguese explorer Gamitto remarked that 'all these people are totally independent of each other'. It remains to be noted, however—and this is another theme which could be generalized—that the tradition of Malawi unity in ancient times has been lately called in aid, by modern Malawi nationalists, as a powerfully emotive influence for the building of a modern state.

How far did the trading enterprises of this period connect these peoples and their neighbours with the city-states of the East Coast? There is no doubt that an important trade route linked Kilwa with the northern end of Lake Malawi. It was certainly used for a long time. Yet there is little to show what effect it had on the people through whose territory or near whose territory it passed. A little is known of the history of the interior of central and southern Tanzania before the nineteenth century, and a little more may be guessed; in general, though, the impression is one of scattered or isolated peoples who lived on the margins of the pressures that were now developing around them. Largely because of the steady southward-drifting infiltration of nomad peoples originating in the Horn of Africa or along the Upper Nile, the Mature Iron Age in Tanzania and Kenya was the scene of much conflict and confusion, as well as the overthrow of a number of settled farming communities or polities. In all this there were gains and losses. Many influences, but above all the dangers of warfare and the opportunities of long-distance trade, tended to reinforce the power of chiefs or to bring chiefs into existence where none had ruled before. Military unity could be greater where chiefs ruled. Long-distance trading enterprises similarly called for the unity of decision and organization that chiefs could provide. In this process chiefs tended to become kings, and kings tended to become military rulers who were increasingly able to defend their peoples from raid or invasion, or to take fuller advantage of the trade that was evolving with the coast.

The peoples who lived in these kingdoms might forfeit, as many of them undoubtedly did, much of the tolerant equality of everyday life that continued to characterize such groups as the Kalenjin, Luo and Kikuyu. Yet at the same time they were better placed than many of the smaller 'chiefless peoples' to fend off the attacks of rivals and invaders. Perhaps it was precisely the Kalenjin, Luo and Kikuyu who were able to have it both ways: they were numerous enough, well enough organized in village governments and possessed of country that was sufficiently good for defence, to enable them to withstand outside pressure except along their boundaries, where they were harassed by the Masai. At the same time they were able to continue to enjoy the blessings of popular self-government in ways that were increasingly denied to the peoples of powerful kingdoms such as those of the Ganda and their neighbours in Ruanda and Burundi.

Yet migrations and incursions undoubtedly had a powerful impact throughout this region. Some of its peoples were successful in standing outside the region of pastoral invasion, or at least of warding off attack. Old states remained stable here and there, while new ones were formed. But the repeated population movements seem to have had a widely disruptive effect, and new troubles were now added to them. These began with Portuguese piracy along the coasts. They were extended by the war-like pressures of internal migration. They were worsened for a number of peoples and states by the northward-moving Ngoni invasions of the early nineteenth century, still more by the somewhat later East Coast slave trade, and by other such ruinous interruptions. But troubles such as these were not everywhere present. And wherever slaving or other outside interference remained absent or of small importance, the stability achieved in the fifteenth and sixteenth centuries continued until recent times. Such was the ordered condition of much of the inland country, even in the early nineteenth century, that goods could be carried from one side of Africa to the other. Two Afro-Portuguese dealers made the crossing from Angola to Mozambique in 1806–11 and proved that it was safe and easy so long as one had the necessary permits. Hazards arose not from political chaos but from political organization: without the 'visas' of the Kazembe and the Mwata Yamvo, nothing could be done.

Living at the Katangan court of the Kazembe a hundred and sixty years ago, these traders found the land agreeably supplied with cereals, vegetables, fish and fruit, and the government strong and tolerant. The Portuguese traveller Gamitto, who arrived there in 1831, thought the Kazembe of his day a sensible man though very splendid in his style of life. Gamitto discovered all that 'ceremonial, pomp, and ostentation', as he put it, which were thought necessary to the prestige of kingship. But the pomp was not an empty one. It stood for a power that was real. The chaos came later.

West Africa in the Sixteenth Century

Even a brief summary can do something to suggest the complexity and many-sided growth of western Africa during this period when the 'old society', the society of Iron Age maturity, touched or approached the peak of its achievement. Still more than elsewhere, one is confronted with the interplay of a multitude of peoples and political patterns, with the decline of ancient politics and the rise of others in their place, and with a wealth of oral and written record that is more and more illuminated—though somewhat distorted—by the reports of visiting Europeans.

All this combines into a scene of arresting scope, its details painted with a riveting impression of reality, its dramas played out by kings and priests whose characters can be sometimes traced, its onward shift and movement turning on events whose meaning can often be defined. This was a period when the old civilization of western Africa, lettered or unlettered, had deepened to a profound self-confidence and social resonance whose returning echoes one may catch in many fields of effort, whether religious or artistic, political or economic. The mere bird's-eye

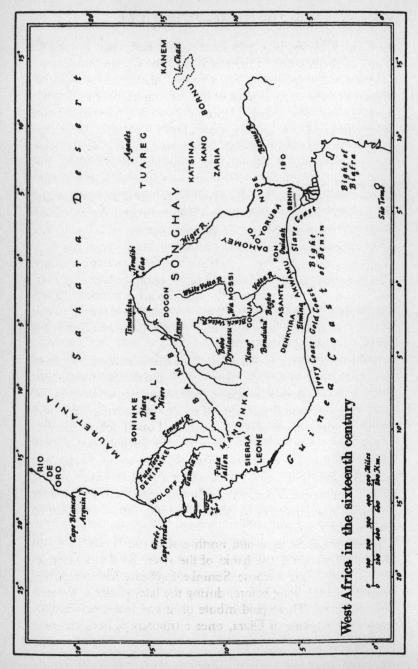

West Africa in the sixteenth century

0   100   200   300   400   500 Miles
0   200   400   600   800 Km.

view which follows here goes from west to east, moving from the shores of the Atlantic to the margins of the Congo forest.

Much of the western region, whether inland or near the coast, still showed the deep imprint of the old empire of Mali, itself in far decay but yet remaining strong enough in its ancient centres of Mandinka population to support a noble reputation. In Senegal the principal successor-state of Mali remained the Wolof empire, consisting mainly of the three provinces of Walo, Cayor and Baol; these held the coast and much of the near-coastal country between the Senegal and Gambia rivers. 'Here at the Senegal', reported D. Pacheco Pereira in 1506, 'you find the first black people. This is the beginning of the kingdom of the Wolof, a hundred leagues long and eight broad', a lineal exaggeration, as modern cartography shows, but substantially accurate enough. 'The king of the Wolof', adds Pereira, again perhaps not exaggerating much, 'can put into the field an army of about 10,000 cavalry and 100,000 infantry. They go naked save for the nobles and men of honour who wear blue cotton shirts and trousers of the same material.'

North of the Senegal River were nomadic peoples who lived by a slave economy which was to persist into the present century. Though chiefly Berber by origin, these Mauretanian peoples had come under the political control of southward-moving Arabs from Morocco during the fourteenth century. Loss of political control meant loss of local culture. These western Berbers, unlike their relatives of the eastern Sahara, gave up their own language and took to using Arabic instead, while at the same time adopting some other aspects of western Arab culture. All this was to have important consequences for the spread and nature of Islam in these western regions.

South of the Senegal and north-east of the Wolof states, in the Futa Toro along the banks of the river, lay the old state of Takrur under rulers whose Soninke forebears had established themselves here, long before, during the later phases of the empire of Ghana. These paid tribute or at any rate a nominal allegiance to the king of Diara, once a tributary of Mali and now a tributary of Songhay. But there now occurred in Takrur a change of a kind that was to become characteristic of much that happened in the grassland country of the Western Sudan after the collapse of Songhay in the 1590s. A people of the countryside, peasants hitherto strange to town life, came invading into Takrur and built a new state.

Three hundred miles towards the east in the dry savannah lands of Termes and Nioro a group of Fulani cattle-breeders revolted against their allegiance to the emperor of Songhay, the famous Askia Muhammad, and set out to find a new home. Led by their chieftan Tengella, these wanderers began with a raid on Diara. Here they clashed in 1512 with a Songhay army under the Askia's brother, and Tengella was killed. There is some reason to think that these Fulani had been encouraged on their raiding path by the Mali emperor, seeking to undermine his Songhay rival. One of Tengella's wives, at all events, belonged to the Mali royal family. His son by this marriage, Tengella Koli, now assumed control and led his people southward into country that was still under Mali sovereignty. They arrived in Badiar, near the modern frontiers of Senegal and Guinea, and made common cause with a Mandinka group. Together these marched north-eastward into Futa Toro. By about 1550 they had established there a new line of kings, the Denianke, who ruled in Futa Toro until 1776, when they themselves were displaced during the revival of Islam in the eighteenth century. Though not Muslim, the Denianke state may be regarded as the forerunner of many later states in which once-nomadic Fulani were to play a leading part.

South of the Gambia the Mandinka and related peoples remained in control of a country which had been theirs, or at least under their general influence, since time immemorial. These peoples now began trading profitably with the Portuguese. Even 150 leagues up from its mouth, Pereira noted in 1506, ships' crews could carry on a good trade in cheap cotton goods and other items in exchange for gold. When these countries were at peace, he estimated, gold exports to Portugal were worth five or six thousand *dobras* of fine gold. Like so many other monetary calculations, this is vague enough; yet the total was evidently thought to be surprisingly satisfactory. Already the long-standing monopoly of the Western Sudan in trading West Africa's gold in North Africa and Europe had begun to be broken.

The same Pereira, like others after him, speaks of many small states along the eastward-bending coast towards modern Ghana. By this time the whole seaboard and forest country as far as Yorubaland and the empire of Benin was divided among a multiplicity of communities, sometimes closely linked to one other, which had built themselves into states ruled by chiefs or chiefly families. Their principal trade was in selling fish and other coastal products to their neighbours of the inland country, but the sixteenth century now called them to a maritime commerce which was entirely new. The coast of Guinea, as Dike has said, became for the first time a 'frontier of opportunity'.

Europeans found them keen men of business. Although interested in buying cottons and metalware, Africans could and did produce these goods for themselves. The Portuguese found their cottons well worth buying for sale in Europe, while an English captain observed in 1556 how 'they can work very finely in iron', manufacturing spear-heads, fish hooks and short swords, 'some of them as long as a woodknife and exceeding sharp on both sides'. Most of these little coastal states, accustomed to securing their interests in competition with their neighbours, were well able to defend themselves against European bullying, even though this was often tried; and their relations with visiting ships' crews were generally pitched in terms of alliance and partnership. The Plymouth adventurer John Hawkins turned this to his advantage in a slaving voyage of 1562. He struck up alliance with two kings of Sierra Leone so as to attack their neighbours, and was rewarded for the efforts of his soldiers with several hundred war-captives whom he carried to the Spanish Main and sold as chattel slaves for a handy profit. In later times there would develop a belief in Europe that only the climate and coastal fevers deterred European settlement along the coast. It was wide of the truth.

The fevers, though not the climate, certainly cost many lives among Europeans who had developed none of the partial immunity achieved by local populations. But the real and enduring deterrent to any forced European foothold was the superior strength of African states until the nineteenth century.

Footholds secured by African agreement in pursuit of trading partnership were another matter. The Portuguese built Elmina Castle by initial consent in 1482, and against the payment of rent. Many other castles were afterwards built on much the same terms. From the African standpoint they were of merely local importance. What mattered to coastal Africans was not these minor European ventures but the major pressures of powerful states of the inland country. These inland or near-coastal states continued to dispute the control of central Guinea until the rise of the Asante empire in the eighteenth century. It was they, not the Europeans, who dominated the fortunes of the little seaboard states.

In the sixteenth century the main powers in central Guinea were still the old states of the Akan, exploiting their near-coastal or forest cultivation and trading in gold with the Dyula, Hausa or Kanuri merchants of Bonduku, Kong and other commercial centres to the north-west and north-east. Most of these states now fell within the orbit of two or three of their number. By 1650 Denkyira and Akwamu were the powers that counted most in the territory of modern Ghana. Yet the coastal trade with Europeans had its effect on the Akan and their neighbours, gradually and from small beginnings, in the same way as with the Mandinka further west. Little by little, the inland trade shifted round upon itself, as the sea-merchants grew more numerous; it was turned about-face, as Fage has put it, and began to look southward as well as north.

The foundation of Gonja, in the north-central part of modern Ghana, is a good illustration of the consequences. Towards 1550 the ruling *mansa* of Mali dispatched a company of cavalry from the country of the Upper Niger into the grasslands north of the Akan country where the gold was mined. He was interested in the reasons why the northward flow of gold was beginning to run short. His pennoned riders, semi-professional, well equipped, the 'armoured fighting vehicles' of that day and age, bore southward from the region of Bobo and Jenne into the countryside of the Black Volta, west of the Mossi states, where they established themselves not far north of the forest. Though unable to do anything about improving the flow of gold, they remained in these grasslands and founded several chiefdoms. Others of their fellow-countrymen are said to have joined them early in the seventeenth century, including a warrior-chief called Jakpa who was either a historical personage or the legendary personification of several such 'founding heroes'. To this day the imams of Wa in the old country of Gonja recall their origin in Jakpa and his trading companions, while the principal imam of Wa still bears the title of Dyula-Mansa, 'Lord of the Mandinka Traders', or, as the Hausa have it, Shehu-Wangara, the 'Sheik of the Wangara [that is, Mandinka] People'. The name of the modern city of Bobo-Dyulasso indicates the same background, for it means the 'House of the Dyula Traders of Bobo'. Kong's history is another variant on the same theme.

Other large changes, still within the purely West African framework and owing nothing of importance to the European presence along the coast, occupied the scene in what are now the Western and Eastern regions of Nigeria, and in Dahomey. The late sixteenth century saw the rise of a new power among the Yoruba, that of Oyo lying just to the north of the deep forest. Its origin is remembered as the outcome of disaster. This occurred when the trading state of Nupe, north of the Benue River, conquered the Yoruba of Oyo around 1550, and drove their chief, headed by the Alafin, or king, of Oyo, into exile. When these came home again they set about organizing an army based on the cavalry which had made their northern neighbours strong. Alafin Orompoto is said to have begun with a thousand mounted men. His successors went further. They extended the principle of maintaining long-service troops who were composed of heavily equipped cavalry maintained by the state and quickly to hand in case of need; and in this way they made themselves unbeatable in the grasslands to the north of the forest. By the end of the sixteenth century their rule was powerful throughout the thinly wooded country to the west of the Niger as far as the hills of Togo, for they had also established themselves among the Yoruba of Dahomey—the Yoruba of Ketu—as well as bringing the Fon people of that country under their dominion.

Once more, at this point, there is to be noted the influence of trade, and of production for trade, upon the formation of powerful states. The northern Yoruba had long been fortunate in the fertility of their land and the skill of their craftsmen: two qualities between which there lay, of course, an obvious connection, since fertility meant surplus, and surplus meant both the demand for handicraft goods and the capacity, through non-farming specialists, to supply them. With the steady growth of north-south trade, these northern Yoruba were able to play the role of intermediaries between the producers of the eastern forest country of Guinea and the traders of the Western and Central Sudan, the Sahara and North Africa, as well as dealing profitably in their own products. Out of this dual activity, as producers and traders on their own account and as intermediaries in the long-distance trade between south and north, they built a prosperity which enabled them to nourish and to realize some large political ambitions. Though formed later than their southern neighbours, the Yoruba towns of the north, and especially Oyo, were thus able to take a lead throughout the greater part of Yorubaland by about 1600, and to retain this lead for a long period. They could afford, for example, to buy regular supplies of Sudanese horses for a mounted army, a factor of critical importance in country where the tsetse fly prevented the breeding of horses, and this gave them a clear military superiority.

The *alafins* of Oyo remained strong for nearly two hundred years. Wherever their cavalry could operate, their power became legendary. To give an idea of the strength of the Oyo army, wrote an Englishman resident in Dahomey at the end of the eighteenth century, the Dahomey people (then tributary to Oyo) used to say that when the Oyo people want to go to war, their general 'spreads the hide of a buffalo before the door of his tent, and pitches a spear in the ground on each side of it. Between these spears the soldiers march until the multitude which pass over the hide have worn a hole in it. As soon as this happens, their general presumes that his forces are numerous enough to take the field.' The Dahomey people, he added, 'may possibly exaggerate, but the Oyo are certainly a very populous, warlike and powerful nation'.

They were also capable of building a large and long-enduring political system without the use of a literate bureaucracy. They extended the power of their *alafin* over many of the little states to the north of the dense forest country, operating through a system of permanent officials whose powers may be likened to those of colonial commissioners or 'residents' in later times, but whose authority was deepened by their being able to act within the community of Yoruba language and tradition. The Oyo ruling families retained a king-making capacity, but their social and political organization absorbed many of the administrative advances of the sixteenth century. These included a sharper division of executive powers within the *alafin*'s governing council.

South-east of the Yoruba, Benin was unaffected by the rise of Oyo but had troubles of its own. Oba Ewuare, who became ruler in about 1440, appears to have strengthened the power of his dynasty. Oba Esigie strengthened it again after 1504, moving from the exercise of power through hereditary chiefs to the exercise of power through chiefs of his own appointment. Yet the rule of Benin and its tributary states, like that of Oyo, was still a matter of delicate adjustment among an intricate hierarchy of chiefs rather than the expression of a single individual will. This process of adjustment had formed a barrier against autocracy that was common to nearly all Iron Age systems in Africa. By the sixteenth century, moreover, Benin's trading community seems to have become strong enough to make its weight felt in government for the first time.

This was reflected in the reforms introduced by Oba Esigie, who reigned between 1504 and 1550. These revealed the growing importance of trade as well as efforts by the Oba to reduce the influence of hereditary noblemen. 'Town chiefs' were created. Bradbury tells us that they were chosen from among those who had made their own way in life, achieving 'wealth, prestige and following through warfare, farming and trade'. But at the same time the 'peerage' was further watered down by the creation of 'palace chiefs' who owed their position to royal preferment, while the traditional Uzama nobles—the old 'earls and barons' of Benin—were deprived of their rights of nominating the next oba, this being now decided by primogeniture.

With all this, the kings of Benin appear repeatedly to have strengthened their control and royal exploitation of trade, and certainly of foreign trade. 'Town chiefs' might prosper on trading concessions by the king's monopoly, but the kings saw to it that there would be little or no development of private enterprise at the expense of the state's overall command of the profits of trade. The point may seem a small one, but it is crucial to any consideration of the reasons why this mercantile system failed to develop into early forms of merchant capitalism. Other powerful kingships in this period followed the same restrictive policy and continued to follow it in a later period. As Ivor Wilks has shown in his pathfinding research into the history of the Asante kingdom (region of modern Ghana), the same restrictive process would again occur late in the nineteenth century.*

But the kings of Benin followed their own *raison d'état*, and grew more powerful and majestic. Endowed with divine attributes, passing his days in the majesty and mystery of a labyrinth of decorated halls where he was surrounded by the tokens of his power, the oba now stood for a concept and practice of kingship that were to make political adjustment still harder to achieve. When the Dutch took over the main European trade with Benin from the Portuguese in the seventeenth century, they found the king a very great man. His palace and apartments had galleries

*I. Wilks, *Asante in the Nineteenth Century*, Cambridge, 1975, esp., in this context, chaps. 14 and 15.

'as big as those on the Exchange at Amsterdam', being supported by 'wooden pillars encased with copper where their victories are depicted', while the city had many wide streets and large houses. 'I saw and spoke to the king of Benin', a Dutch visitor remembered of the year 1702, 'in the presence of his great counsellors. He was seated on an ivory throne under a canopy of Indian silk. He was about forty years old and of lively expression. According to custom I stood about thirty feet away from him. So as to see him better, I asked permission to draw closer. He laughingly agreed.'

Unlike the *alafins* of Oyo, who could usually be deposed by their traditional nobles if they were judged incapable of rule, the obas of Benin gradually came to exploit a petrification of authority and custom. Benin's royal sculpture in brass reveals this as well as anything else. After the great period of the sixteenth century, as William Fagg has pointed out, royal styles show an increasing heaviness and crudity of concept, loss of energy and experiment, and a notable decline in the quality of craftsmanship. There was indeed a growing rigidity in the means and attitudes of government, and this, later on, was to make it doubly hard for the rulers of Benin to understand the nature of the European imperial challenge of the nineteenth century, and attempt an intelligent adjustment to it. The end of this ancient and famous state was to be a wretched one.

Northward of these forest and near-forest kingdoms, the political reorganization of the grassland country was now increasingly moulded by methods and techniques evolved or borrowed from those of the great Songhay and Kanem-Bornu systems. These changes once more illustrate a shift of power from men who exercised it by right of birth to men who exercised it by right to royal appointment. What M. G. Smith has called this 'double exposure of Hausa to influences from Bornu and Songhay' induced among the leading Hausa city-states, notably Katsina, Kano and Zaria, 'a period of intensive political and military development, as well as religious and economic change'. At Kano, for example, Sarkin (that is, King) Muhammad Rumfa (1465–99) took several leaves out of his Bornu neighbour's book.

He formed new regiments under his close command. He glorified
his kingship with new ceremonial. He built himself an imposing
palace. And in line with the deepening stratification of the leading
grassland states, reflected by these changes, he imposed new taxes
and obligatory labour-service on the *talakawa*, the freemen of
Hausaland. Now were sown those seeds of Hausa discontent
which were to ripen many years later into Fulani-led rebellion.

With developments like these one may again trace the expanding influence of Islam, another constant theme in the history
of the Sudan. Though egalitarian in its spiritual teaching, Islam
like Christianity went hand in hand with the practical dividing
of rulers from ruled, rich from poor and strong from weak. Many
of its political and social teachings both fitted the deepening
stratification of society and helped to carry it further. A place
might still have to be made at court for the rites of the old religions;
in practice, the kings ruled more and more by Islamic order and
coercion, and less and less by the sanctity and ritual of local
tradition. Hence the emergence of long-service regiments drawn
from enslaved war-captives or others of servile caste: their loyalty
would hold firm, or so it could be hoped, where royal adherence
to Islam had undermined the older lineage loyalties of 'divine
kingship'. To Sarkin Rumfa and his like, again in M. G. Smith's
words, 'the ritual support which the chief lost when he became
Muslim was made good by new sources of power, especially by
eunuch administrators and squads of slaves who could serve as
guards, police, soldiers or messengers'. Local kingship fealty and
the *levée en masse* were passing away in the grassland country.
But the reasons for this were also the reasons why the states grew
stronger, and why their productive power increased and their
trade expanded.

Based on their flourishing towns, as centres of trade and craftsmanship, the Hausa states could now play an important role as
distributing agents for much of the commerce of the eastern
region. Travelling among them early in the sixteenth century, a
youthful North African who was later to be captured by Christian
pirates and baptized as Giovanni Leone, or Leo Africanus as he

is generally called, found 'civilized handicraft-workers and rich merchants' in Kano, a city encircled then as now by a great wall of earth and timber, while the king of another Hausa state, Guangara, drew 'a great revenue from dealing in goods and from commercial taxes'. Perhaps most successful of all the Hausa city-capitals, Kano was now a well-ordered market-centre surrounded by a dense neighbourhood of villages producing textiles as well as food.

Kanem-Bornu remained a large and influential state. Early in the sixteenth century its rulers regained much of their previously lost authority to the east of Lake Chad, and began encroaching on Hausa lands to the west. In 1580 there came to the throne a ruler who built a new empire. This was the renowned Idris Alooma (1580–1617), who raised Kanem-Bornu to a new eminence, carried further the process of administrative reform, opened embassies north of the desert and entered into friendly relations with the Ottoman sultan of Turkey. In these and other ways the sixteenth century witnessed a summit of political achievement. There would now follow a long period of profound upheaval and transition to new challenges from the outside world.

But the kingdoms and empires were not, of course, the whole of the picture of political development in these centuries; they were not even, in some respects, the most familiar or interesting part of it. It may be reasonable to dwell on their development from one stage to another for the benefit of readers whose own history has been overwhelmingly one of centralizing government, class stratification, and the attempt to apply checks and balances to royal or other forms of despotism. These were situations also shared, as we have seen, by many African peoples. Yet there were many others whose development from the numerically frail communities of Early Iron Age times took a different road. In following this road, they often displayed an originality and dynamism which make the outcome of their history far more intriguing than the government of kings, emperors or royal legates.

These 'non-kingly' societies have been variously described, partly because of the vagaries of anthropological jargon and partly

because the very diversity of such 'small societies' makes any
simple explanation difficult. Perhaps their commonest label is
'segmentary'. A segmentary society in Africa (and to some extent
in other continents) is said to be one in which power within a
given community is distributed more or less equally between the
heads of its constituent family descent-lines or internal segments.
This kind of organization reflected the structure of daily life in
villages which ran their own affairs but were prepared to accept
a relationship of loyalty, and mutual obligation, with neighbouring villages. Simplifying, one may say that each village was
inhabited by a single major descent-line whose elders formed its
government, although, with the growth of its population and the
ramifications of its marriages, each village would also have its
own internal segmentary pattern. The conceptual form within
which inter-lineage loyalties took shape usually rested in the cult
of appointed ancestors: of those ancestors, that is, who were regarded as standing in line of communication with the founder-
guardians of the people and the spirit world of their gods.

Now it might at first view appear that this would be an inef-
fectual and even primitive way of managing the affairs of a people
scattered among different villages. Such an extreme dispersal of
political authority surely led to conflict and confusion? Generally,
the truth was otherwise. Within their limits of time and place,
segmentary societies could show a quite emphatic capacity for
dealing with the changes and chances of life. One may quote
the case of the Igbo peoples of eastern Nigeria.

The Igbo possess an unusually fertile land and a corresponding
skill in making it bear fruit. This has been so for as long as the
records indicate: certainly for many centuries. Over this period
the Igbo and their immediate neighbours have continuously expanded in numbers, to the extent, indeed, that they were able
to suffer enormous losses, through the forced emigration of the
Atlantic slave trade, and yet still produce more people than their
land could easily support. This demographic buoyancy called for
a flexible political system. Segmentary politics met the need.
These provided for the easy solution of conflicts both of 'fission'

and of 'fusion': it was relatively simple, in other words, for Igbo segments to break away and form new villages of independent authority, and not much less easy for villages to join together when they wished.

The keynote, in any case, was a vigorous egalitarianism. Though the Igbo respected age, and leadership devolved on the elders, 'respect was not servility and was balanced by the belief that birth did not confer advantage on any man. The Igbo were individualistic and egalitarian, every man considering himself as good as everyone else and demanding a voice in his local affairs. Since everyone had a right to rise in the society, Igbo culture emphasized competition: competition between families, between lineages and between clans. Competition was promoted by Igbo national sports, wrestling and mock battles. Although men were born equal, they could rise to positions of prestige through a combination of wealth and a record of service to the clan.'*

How far this egalitarianism applied to women greatly varied. Generally, all women in Africa suffered, as most of them have continued to suffer, from more or less gross forms of discrimination imposed by men. The origins of this systemic discrimination can be argued about; but by historical times it had in any case reached an often suffocating severity, and was increasingly worsened by the influence, wherever it took hold, of medieval Islam. To that too there were exceptions, especially among the Berbers of the desert oases. The segmentary peoples, as a rule, were also less discriminatory; some of the hierarchical societies, on the other hand, carried gender discrimination to an extreme of oppression. Most of the Igbo societies, so far as the evidence can show, were somewhere in the middle in this matter; and no doubt it was their relative lack of gender discrimination that accounted for the notably enterprising nature of their culture in questions of trade and innovation.

Not all segmentary societies were acutely competitive, though

*J. B. Webster, A. A. Boahen and H. O. Idowu, *The Growth of African Civilization: West Africa Since 1800*, London, 1967, pp. 174–75.

all tended to be egalitarian. Among many of the peoples of Middle
Africa, by contrast, individual competition in the striving to better
oneself above one's fellows could be regarded with a sadly and
even apprehensively discouraging eye. This spirit gave the Igbo
an advantage in adapting to new situations and problems, but it
served them poorly when it came to questions of intra-Igbo unity,
always hard to achieve and seldom durable. Yet it was an attitude,
one may repeat, that was eminently adaptable. Where local unity
became desirable if trading opportunities were to be fully
grasped—as, for example, among the Cross River peoples of the
Niger Delta during the expansion of the Atlantic trade after about
1650—there were local groups who found ways of combining a
certain egalitarianism with the rule of a successful minority. They
did this through an association called Ekpe, a 'secret society' like
the Poro of Sierra Leone or the Ogboni of the Yoruba or many
others of the same type. Ekpe was really a corporation of elders
and wealthy merchants or farmers, and 'secret' only to the extent
that, like Freemasonry in Europe, knowledge of its assemblies
and ritual was open only to members.

Associations such as Ekpe form a subject of their own. They
may be regarded as an adjustment of traditional gerontocracy so
as to enable younger men of substance and ambition to acquire
influence 'before their time': before, that is, they became elders
by sheer weight of years. They may also be regarded as a technique
for uniting the people of any given locality in despite of ethnic
differences. Thanks to their common membership in Ekpe, for
example, the traders of the Cross River ports were able to act
together against European partners or rivals. They could and did
'close the river' to European trade if one or another of them
considered himself the victim of fraud or other misadventure at
European hands. They could and did monopolize the right to
decide prices. They could and did administer law and order,
hand down judgements, carry out sentences, and generally behave as a 'democratic oligarchy': as an oligarchy, that is, to which
every man might gain access in the measure of his ability to pay
the graded fees of membership.

Other segmentary societies that were far from the influence of trade were generally without such aids to commercial or political unity. Yet they too had their own checks and balances on the use and abuse of power. None of these peoples, such as the Tiv of central Nigeria or the Tallensi of northern Ghana, appeared to the first Europeans who saw them to have any regular means of self-rule above the level of family headmanship. But appearances were misleading. Tiv and Tallensi governments, and others like them, were revealed on closer acquaintance to possess an intricate and effective structure of interlocking relationships between descent-lines, villages and groups of villages.

It was indeed in these 'small societies' that the specific African genius for self-rule was generally bodied forth. More or less completely ignored by non-African commentators, then or since, this genius flowed in modes of effective local self-government and what is often now called, usually quite misleadingly, 'rural development'. The right term, now coming into increasing use by African thinkers who have won free from external guiding-strings, would be 'participation'.

FIVE

New Encounters

North African Invasions

Towards 1100 the Berber kings of the Almoravid line brought all Morocco and western Algeria within their rule, as well as the fifteen or so little states of Andalusian Spain and southern Portugal into which the Western Ummayad Caliphate had previously sundered. This Arabized Berber dynasty now presided over a phase of civic and artistic brilliance. This was brief enough, lasting only until the beginning of Christian Spanish conquests in the 1230s, yet it glowed with serenity and calm, with intellectual energy and artistic daring, and with prosperity in town and countryside alike.

What the Almoravids had begun, the Almohads continued. Their story was much the same. Like the Almoravid kings, those of the Almohad dynasty drew their strength from the revolt of Berber peasants against kings, governors and traders of the towns and cities. Just as Ibn Yasin of Sijilmasa had called for a return to the pure teachings of the Quran, for an end to new forms of taxation imposed by rulers grown 'corrupt' through good living, liberal speculation and all the 'laxity' of city life, so in 1125, proclaiming himself the Mahdi, did Ibn Tumart do the same, recruiting to his *ribat* or hermitage all those who were prepared to fight for a 'purified' order of society.

Descending from their hills, the *muwahiddun* of Ibn Tumart, the Believers in One God, took the lead among the Masmuda and Zenata Berbers and quickly made themselves masters of Morocco. In 1147 the successor of Ibn Tumart, a Zenata called 'Abd al-Mumin, became caliph of Morocco, with his capital at Marrakesh in the High Atlas. By 1159, invading eastwards, his armies had unified the Maghreb—Morocco, Algeria, Tunisia—for the first time in history and, at least until the times do alter, also for the last; while Almohad rule soon displaced that of the Almoravids in Spain as well. At the crossroads of a powerful state controlling all the southern trade routes of the western Mediterranean, the Maghreb blossomed once again. Cities like Fez and Tlemsen rivalled the urban beauty and learning of Granada and Cordoba, unsurpassed by now throughout the western world.

At home in these comfortable cities, the Almohad rulers and their governors soon followed their Almoravid predecessors. They too became adherents of all those things, 'laxity and corruption and religious liberalism', against which Ibn Tumart had raised his banners of revolt. But they remained formidable rulers. Ambassadors of the English King John (1199–1216), visiting the Almohad sultan of his day, are said to have found him preparing for their visit by reading the letters of St Paul so that he could better argue the Muslim case; while the reputation of his military power was such that these ambassadors were even authorized, or so it was said, to declare John's readiness to accept Islam in return for Muslim aid.

This versatile and tolerant civilization could neither resist the onslaught of hungry Christian knights, thundering down the stony hills of Aragon and Castile, nor hold together within itself. In 1229 Tunisia broke away under its Hafsid governors. In 1235 a group called the 'Abd al-Wadids established a new kingdom of their own, weak and ravaged though it was by Beduin raiding and devastation, while Morocco after 1247 fell to the local rule of another Zenata family, the Marinids. Riven by these internal conflicts, incapable of finding any lasting solution to the rivalry of town and countryside, Berber civilization never recovered its strength and unity. Most of Spain was lost in the 1230s; Valencia in 1243, Seville in 1248, Cadiz in 1262. Only the little southern kingdom of Granada held out till 1492.

Having recovered Spain and Portugal, the Christians passed to the assault of North Africa itself. In 1415 an expedition set out from the Tagus and captured the north Moroccan port of Ceuta, thus reversing for the first time in seven hundred years the northward tide of conquest across the Mediterranean. Launched now upon the wide world, the Portuguese would maintain their progress and drive their keels far to the west and south. But the early fifteenth century saw them fixed on less remote ambitions. After Ceuta there were other nearby ports inviting plunder. Slowly gathering strength and maritime efficiency, the Portuguese attacked and took Tangier in 1471 as well as Arzila and Larache. In 1508 they seized Safi and Argouz far down the coast. In 1513–14 they captured more Atlantic ports, while the Spanish in the western Mediterranean possessed themselves of Melilla in 1497 and other coastal towns in 1508. Only with the decisive battle of al-Ksar al-Kabir in 1578 did the Sharif of Fez make an end to European hopes of conquest, and lay foundations for the revival of Morocco under his energetic son Mulay al-Manṣur, Mulay the Victorious.

By this time a new power had made its mark in the eastern and central Mediterranean. Having established themselves in the Crimea and the Balkans as well as Anatolia, the Ottoman Turks had turned southward in 1515. In 1516 their Sultan Selim I (1512–20) acquired the plains of northern Iraq, engulfed Syria and Palestine, and secured a foothold in Algeria three years later. In 1517 these Turkish armies occupied Egypt and evicted the Mamluk soldier caste which had ruled there since 1250. Suleiman the Magnificent (1520–66) thrust his famous cavalry and musketmen to the very outskirts of Vienna, enclosing most of Hungary and Slavonia within his domains. He also pushed westward through Africa, adding Cyrenaica in 1521, Tripoli in 1551 and a part of Tunisia, conquest of the latter being completed in 1575. With Morocco remaining under its Saʿadid rulers, the

Ottoman frontier at the time of the battle of al-Ksar al-Kabir, in 1578, was established along the western boundary of modern Algeria.

What had happened, essentially, was that the Almohad empire in the Maghreb had broken down once more into the three main parts of Barbary which had existed since time immemorial; and the Ottoman conquests had confirmed this disintegration. For the generality of folk, little changed. Ruling from afar and indirectly, careful of the susceptibilities of their Berber vassals, Muslims like themselves, the Turkish sultans were content to promote local kings or governors wherever convenient dynasties could be found. Their authority in Egypt was scarcely more foreign, after all, than that of the Mamluk generals who had preceded them. In Tripoli they set up Turkish governors who were expected to sustain good relations with local Berber rulers and keep the trade routes open. In Tunisia there emerged a line of beys who had strong Turkish connections but could also count on local support, and it was the same with the deys of Algiers.

These tributary states of the Ottoman empire, strongly controlling the trans-Saharan trade at its northern terminals, well supplied with cereals and fruit and mutton from their fertile coastlong plains and hills, were harassed only by the activities of Christian navies, pirates and trading rivals. Traditionally described by these, but especially by their great competitors of Venice, as being little more than nests of pirates and ruthless sea-hawks, the North African polities were in fact a good deal more tolerant in their laws and easy-going in their customs than most of the European states of the day. The Protestant English, who were outside the influence of Catholic policy in the Mediterranean, admired their prosperity and made friends with them. Thomas Dallam found Algiers in 1559 'a great place of trade and merchandise', while Mainwaring, reporting on Tunis in 1616, spoke of it as a place where peaceful men were safe from molestation. 'In five months together, when I was coming and going there, I never heard of murder, robbery or private quarrel. Nay, a Christian, which is more than he can warrant himself in any part of Christendom, may on my knowledge travel 150 miles into the country, though he carry good store of money, and himself alone, and none will molest him.' Other visitors described these cities as being girt about with well-tilled market-gardens and vineyards, and with white-walled farmhouses set amid groves of burdened fruit trees, while Algiers early in the seventeenth century was said to have as many as three thousand merchant families and two thousand shops.

These states were invaded by the French in the nineteenth century. How prosperous they had remained may in some degree be measured by the contents of the treasure of the dey of Algiers, looted by the French in 1832, of 15,500 pounds of gold and 220,000 pounds of silver.* How solidly their traditions of independence still held firm may be seen convincingly in the long and bitter struggle they opposed to foreign conquest.

In the sixteenth century, however, it was the security and regularity of trade that suffered most. The western trans-Saharan routes by way of Morocco and Mauretania were especially hard hit. Great market-towns decayed. Sijilmasa, which for long had been the most important of them all, failed utterly to recover from the ravages of war. Yet this far-going ruin of the western routes was not repeated elsewhere.

Trade was interrupted along the central routes by the Moroccan invasion of Songhay and its immediate consequences, but a measure of general recovery in the wake of Ottoman conquest soon exercised a remedial effect. This was especially true of the eastern routes between the Fezzan and Bornu-Hausaland. It was now a duty of the Turkish governors of Tripoli to remain on good terms with the rulers of the Saharan oases, and with those of the Western Sudan whom they could reach; while Mai Idris Alooma of Kanem-Bornu exchanged ambassadors with the Ottoman sultan, and even imported Turkish technicians to instruct a company of Bornu musketeers. The general effect, in short, was to shift trade from the western routes to the central routes, and, though in

*Quoted from N. Barbour (ed.), A Survey of North West Africa, Oxford, 1959.

lesser degree, from the central routes to the eastern routes. By the eighteenth century the central and eastern routes were probably carrying as much trade as ever, together with an increase of slaves now demanded by rich Ottomans for their harems, households and armies. But the old western routes, once the most important of all, were so far reduced by the 1790s as to be carrying, according to French traveller Venture de Paradis, only one big caravan every two or three years.

This temporary decline and permanent geographical shift in the Saharan trade was a factor of growing importance in West Africa as a whole. Hand-in-hand with it went a vast expansion of the maritime trade along the coast of Guinea. Taken together, these changes soon combined into a comparative eclipse of the old Saharan trade. More and more it was the sea-going trade that really counted.

East Coast Disasters

Early in December 1497 three Portuguese vessels rounded the Cape of Good Hope and sailed into the Indian Ocean. Nine years earlier Bartholomeu Diaz had come as far but had turned back. Quelling the fears of his men, da Gama held stubbornly on, determined to reach India. Yet the brilliant discoveries for which he hoped began earlier than that. Five months before sailing eastward from the African coast, da Gama stumbled on a civilization neither seen nor known before by any European. Along the whole seaboard from Quilimane onwards, he and his crews touched at city after city and were repeatedly astonished by their wealth and urban comfort, by their tall ships from unknown eastern countries, and by their commerce in gold and ivory with equally unknown African countries which lay behind the coast-long plains.

In truth these cities had flourished for some three hundred years before da Gama saw them. And their flourishing was no mere figure of speech. Even today one may stand among their

ruins and remain surprised at the lavish wealth that could raise
such palaces and dwellings, pave them with the carpets of Isfahan
and Gujerat, line their walls with the swan-necked ware of Sung
China or the floridly superb platters of Mesopotamia and Persia,
and generally endow these cities with that air of world-
experienced sophistication which the Portuguese, before rushing
in to plunder them, took time to stare at for a moment and
admire. 'Moorish' in the Portuguese records—for the Portuguese
casually called any Muslim a Moor, however distant from Andalusian Spain or Morocco his place of birth might be—these
cities and their peoples afterwards became 'Arab' in the books of
European historians. In fact they composed a markedly African
variant in the wide traditions of Islamic culture.

Their economic achievement was that of urban polities whose
prosperity lay not in production but exchange. Kilwa in the south,
Malindi and Mombasa in the north: these were 'city-empires' in
the same sense as medieval Venice or Genoa. Their genius lay
in buying and in selling. They protected their monopolist positions by maritime enterprise which laid hold of key points for
purchase or trans-shipment. Kilwa, for example, made sure of
its overriding command of nearby rivals—notably of the important island-port of Kisimani Mafia—as well as of its firm dominion over Sofala, the principal export harbour for the gold of
the inland country. They seem to have manufactured little or
nothing for sale, but they must have had skilled craftsmen in
metals, because some of them struck copper and silver currencies.
There is also evidence that they grew cereals for export, or at
least for provisioning the cargo ships upon which their prosperity
depended, as well as for their own needs.

Very distant from any other centres of urban civilization, they
do not appear to have developed a written literature, whether in
Arabic or in Swahili using an Arabic script, until the seventeenth
or eighteenth century, during their period of post-Portuguese
recovery. But the quality of this later literature, some of which
has survived, suggests that their unwritten work in epic and lyrical
composition was copious and distinguished. For the Arabs from

the north, coasting down this seaboard in the years of its prosperity, these were always cities of strange and surprising adventure, markets where a man might see marvels or make his fortune by some turn of luck or magic. To all of this the legends of *The Thousand and One Nights*, of Sinbad the Sailor and his kind, pay an eloquent tribute.

But their attention to the opportunities of commerce was anything but magical. Like the Venetian Council of Ten, the rulers of Kilwa and its sister-cities took a severely unromantic view of the needs and duties of monopoly. Knowing their harbours to be vital for the ships of India and Arabia, and their markets not much less important for the producers of the inland country, these kings and their merchant-councillors erected a mercantile system whose rigidly oppressive tariffs must seem impossibly restrictive today, but whose efficacy can be gauged by the relatively high standard of living these cities gradually achieved. Strong on the northern part of the coast during the latter part of the fifteenth century, the king of Mombasa imposed on all seafaring merchants who used his harbours an import rate of great ferocity. For each thousand lengths of Indian cotton imported into Mombasa, he exacted a *mitqal* of gold and then, says an early Portuguese account which refers to pre-conquest times, 'they divide the thousand lengths of cotton into halves; of these the king takes one half while the other remains with the merchant . . .' Since the cottons had come from India, this seems extraordinarily harsh. Yet the point here—as with early European trade on the Guinea coast—was that gold could be bought at prices which were extremely cheap, notwithstanding such duties, when compared with the values which this gold could realize when sold again in India and elsewhere.

Kilwa tariffs, imposed in respect of the southern stretch of the coast, were of the same high order. 'Any merchant who wants to trade in the city', runs the same Portuguese report, 'has to pay an import duty of one *mitqal* of gold for every five hundred lengths of imported cotton, no matter what the quality. The king of Kilwa then takes two-thirds of the imported merchandise, while the

third which remains with the merchant . . . is again valued, and
pays another duty of thirty *mitqals* for every thousand *mitqals* in
value.'* Even then the patient Indian merchant had not finished
with import tariffs. Moving on down to Sofala to buy his gold
and ivory, he had to pay one length of cotton to the king of Kilwa
(that is, to the king's agents) for every seven lengths he sold.
Returning up the coast again, he was supposed to revisit Kilwa
and pay another fifty *mitqals* in gold for every thousand *mitqals'*
worth of precious metals that he had bought. If he tried to get
out of paying this final 5 percent impost by the device of sailing
past Kilwa, but then stopped at Mombasa before setting out for
India on the trade winds, he might have to pay the duty at
Mombasa instead. Similarly heavy duties were applied to the
export of ivory.

No doubt these exactions were often evaded by subterfuge or
bribe. Until we have a fuller story from the Indian end, the
details of the trade must remain something of a mystery. But
what is clear and certain is that it greatly prospered. Through
many centuries East Africa was a principal source of gold for Asia
and Arabia, while East African ivory, valued for ritual or ceremonial purposes both in India and China, was irreplaceable.
Bursting through grey ocean doors upon this brilliant scene, the
Portuguese almost at once began to loot and burn. They broke
into city after city, sacking and stealing. Da Gama ravaged Mombasa. D'Almeida fired Kilwa. Da Cunha ruined Brava and Zeila.

On his first voyage da Gama had missed Kilwa. But Alvares
Cabral sheltered there in 1500. Five years later the largest of all
the Portuguese fleets that would ever sail for India, commanded
by the future Viceroy d'Almeida, replied to this hospitality with
war. A German or Hollander who was with d'Almeida has left
an eye-witness account of it. They took this golden city of 'many

---

*The *mitqal* was the accepted weight of one gold dinar, monetary standard of this
whole inter-continental system of long-distance trade. Though its weight varied over time
and local circumstance, it stood originally at 4.233 grams. The best summary of this
matter is in S. D. Goitein, A *Mediterranean Society*, University of California, 1967, vol.
1, p. 359. A modern echo of this ancient and prestigious standard of value is the *mitical*
coinage adopted by the independent republic of Mozambique after 1975.

strong houses several storeys high' without opposition from the surprised inhabitants, and as soon as this was done 'the Vicar-General and some of the Franciscan fathers came ashore carrying two crosses in procession and singing the Te Deum. They went to the palace, and there the cross was put down and the admiral prayed. Then everyone started to plunder the town of all its merchandise and provisions.' Two days later they set it on fire.

At Mombasa, says the same witness, d'Almeida 'ordered that the town should be sacked and that each man should carry off to his ship whatever he found: so that at the end there would be a division of the spoil, each man to receive a twentieth of what he had found. The same rule was made for gold, silver and pearls. Then everyone started to plunder the town and to search the houses, forcing open the doors with axes and iron bars. There was a large quantity of cotton cloth for Sofala in the towns, for the whole coast gets its cotton cloth from here. So the admiral got a good share of the trade of Sofala for himself. A large quantity of rich silk and gold-embroidered clothes were seized, and carpets also; one of these, without equal for its beauty, was sent to the king of Portugal together with many other valuables.'

Writing in 1518, Duarte Barbosa remembers how da Cunha had treated Brava on the Somali coast. This 'great town of very fine stone and mortar houses' was 'destroyed by the Portuguese, who slew many of its people and carried many into captivity, and took great spoil of gold and silver and goods. Thenceforth many of them fled away towards the inland country, forsaking the town . . .'

This looting and burning need not have been fatal to these cities. Some of them, like Brava, did in fact recover quickly while others, such as Kilwa, knew another period of lesser but relatively fair prosperity after the power of Portugal had vanished from the scene. But what proved much more serious to them, and what finally undermined Kilwa and nearly all the other cities of the southern stretch of the coast, was the wrecking of their Indian Ocean trade.

Having stolen all the portable wealth they could find or carry—

and this they did in parts of India as well—the Portuguese set about trying to seize the ancient trade between western India and eastern Africa. In this they singularly failed. Having blundered through all that network of commercial intercourse, they found it beyond their strength or understanding to restore the customs and contacts of a score of enterprising countries. At one end of the network, they interfered grossly with the trade of inland Africa, or with such of it as they could reach by way of the Zambezi; at the other end, across the Indian Ocean, they seized or simply ruined the import-export trade of India and Ceylon. They did their best to stop all maritime enterprise not conducted under their own flag or sovereignty, and although many Indian Ocean sailors and traders continued to evade them, Portuguese intervention gradually proved fatal.

Even so, the Portuguese might still have managed to remould this Indian Ocean trade to their own advantage if they had been able to supply it with enough ships. They manfully tried; but the effort was beyond their means. Portuguese records show a total of 1,231 sailings to and from India between Vasco da Gama's first voyage of 1497–99 and the year 1612, or an average of about ten a year. Although considerable when viewed against the background of Portugal's comparative economic weakness, the number was far too small for any effective replacement of the manifold maritime operations in Asian bottoms which the Portuguese had interrupted or stopped. By as early as 1550 they were finding it very hard to supply the trade. Old ships grew unserviceable but were seldom repaired; the rate of new building slipped dangerously low. No fewer than sixty-six total wrecks were noted for the years 1500–1600, and other ships were lost through enemy action. After the first flush of loot, crews were almost as difficult to find as ships.

Ousted by the commercially thriving Dutch and afterwards by the English and the French, the Portuguese by 1650 could do little but cling to a few strongpoints such as Mozambique Island and Mombasa, or Tete far up the Zambezi and several inland markets of smaller value. In less than a hundred years of destructive effort they had gone far to ruin the work of centuries. If the ravages of the Portuguese were not everywhere of prolonged effect, and even gave way in the eighteenth century to a measure of civic recovery among the northern Swahili cities, this was due to the insistent strength of the long-distance trade from which these cities had taken their initial rise.

Most marked in the north, among the cluster of city-states on the offshore islands of Lamu and Pate, whence the earliest known written Swahili poetry was to come in the eighteenth century, this recovery was aided by an uneasy alliance with the Arab rulers of Muscat in Oman. After ridding themselves of their own Portuguese garrisons, the Omani helped the Swahili to oust the Portuguese from every foothold north of Cape Delgado, and finally, in 1728, from the great Mombasa castle of Fort Jesus. Having performed this service, however, the Omani conceived imperial ambitions of their own. They tried to dominate the Swahili seaboard and to monopolize its ocean-borne trade. Such was the pressure of their ambitions that some of the Swahili cities, notably Kilwa, tried to call back the Portuguese, just as later on they would attempt to call in the British and the French. Much of the eighteenth and early nineteenth centuries was filled with battles against the Omani, and with inter-city conflicts along the coast. These ended only in 1840, when a ruler of Muscat, the remarkable Sayyid Said, transferred his capital to Zanzibar and presided over a flourishing commercial system in which many of the Swahili cities, though not without protest, were able to find a not unprofitable place.

The cultural recovery of the eighteenth century was in any case a limited one. It was notable in literature, but architecture never again achieved its earlier distinction. New towns and palaces, such as those that were built on Kilwa Island and in the Mafia Islands, showed little of the curious beauty of carved coral* that had once been the delight of earlier times, although the fine

*This refers to the *porites* coral found along the coastal shelf of East Africa. Cut from the shallow seabed and dried out in the sun, this naturally soft material becomes extremely hard and useable as sawn masonry.

carving of wooden doors and other objects in wood remained a
cherished art. Behind this decline lay the steady impoverishment
of cities whose ocean trade and taxation were now a mere fraction
of what they had been before the coming of the Portuguese.

Further to the south, meanwhile, another arrival had set in
train a series of events that would lead to modern South Africa.
Outplaying the Portuguese, outsailing the French and English,
the Dutch had entered the Indian Ocean in 1595, had consol-
idated their maritime enterprises in 1602 with the foundation of
the Dutch East India Company and now carried all before them.
Far superior to the Portuguese in ownership of capital, commercial understanding and knowledge of the world of trade, the
Dutch lost little time in gaining a supremacy that was afterwards
to be seriously challenged only by Britain. One of their early
steps was to establish a base in southern Africa for their east-west
shipping. At first they tried to seize the Portuguese base of Mozambique Island. Failing in this after repeated attempts, they
picked on the Cape of Good Hope, and made it into a refreshment
station for the Far Eastern route. In 1652 Jan van Riebeeck was
landed there with orders to grow fresh vegetables and meat for
Dutch crews on their way to the East and back. Few in number
and little noticed, these settlers were merely servants of the Dutch
East India Company; and to begin with they all but starved. In
an effort to remedy their helplessness, the Company decided in
1657 that the settlers should try their hand at farming on a bigger
scale. Nine of their employees became landholders, 'free bur-
ghers' in the language of the day, each with thirteen acres and
an exemption from all taxes on condition they could and would
supply food for a minimum period of twenty years. Once again
the experiment all but failed. Gradually, however, these new
farmers adapted themselves. They found that the answer to their
problems of production lay in using local labour at next to no
cost. Soon they had turned the local Africans, who were Khoisan
(Hottentots), into their slaves. The era of *apartheid*, of racial
segregation and discrimination based on slavery or on very cheap
African labour, had begun.

Even in these early years the accents of Boer prejudice were clear enough. 'Their native barbarism and idle life,' wrote Willem ten Rhyne of the Khoisan Africans of the Cape in 1686, 'together with a wretched ignorance of all the virtues, impose upon their minds every sort of vicious pleasure. In faithlessness, inconstancy, lying, cheating, treachery, and infamous concern with every kind of lust they exercise their villainy . . .' But in those early days, contrasting with later times, doubts cropped up from time to time. 'From us,' commented Johannes de Grevenbroek in 1695, 'they have learned blasphemy, perjury, strife, quarrelling, drunkenness, trickery, brigandage, theft, ingratitude, unbridled desire for what is not one's own, misdeeds unknown to them before, and, among other crimes of the worst sort, the accursed lust for gold.' This was an aspect of 'race relations' which southern Africa's new settlers were quickly to forget but not to forgo.

West African Adventures

Late on an August afternoon of 1578 a few score Portuguese soldiers got narrowly away from the bloody Moroccan battlefield of al-Ksar al-Kabir, leaving behind them some 25,000 dead and all hope of further invasion of North Africa: not for another three centuries would Europe repeat the effort here. Dying in the hour of victory, the Sharif of Fez was succeeded by his son Mulay. Faced with the need to rebuild his fortunes, the new king looked for new resources. Not surprisingly, he thought of Songhay and the wealth of the Western Sudan.

Past years had already seen a Moroccan attempt to oust the Songhay rulers from their influence over the western trans-Saharan routes through Mauretania and over places like Taghaza, the great source of Saharan salt. Relieved of European pressure, Mulay now meditated conquest. Energetic and imperious, short of revenue and determined to obtain it, he decided that where merchants could go soldiers could surely follow. 'You talk of the perilous desert we have to cross', he is said to have told his advisers, scoffing at fainthearts who urged him to desist. 'You talk of the fatal solitudes, barren of water and pasture. But you forget those defenceless and threadbare merchants, mounted or on foot, who regularly cross the wasteland which caravans have never ceased to traverse. Far better supplied than they, I can do the same with an army that will inspire terror wherever it appears.'

Yet he moved carefully, planning ahead. Three thousand yards of English cloth were brought to Marrakesh to line the tents of his best regiments. Fresh units were armed and trained with the most modern weapon of the day, a firearm called the arquebus that was capable of killing at fifty or even eighty yards, not much of a performance by later standards and yet one that would be scarcely bettered for another hundred years. In November 1590 the army of invasion marched out of Marrakesh under command of a Christian Spaniard, Judar, who had turned Muslim and had earned for his services the rank and title of pasha. With Judar went 1,500 Moroccan light cavalry and 2,500 arquebusiers and spear-carrying troops, most of whom were Christian or Muslim mercenaries from Spain, together with a transport train of 1,000 pack horses, 8,000 camels, 1,000 stablemen and 600 labourers. Crossing the desert in about twenty weeks, a remarkably good performance for so large a host of men and beasts, this army met the Songhay forces under Askia Ishaq II (1588–91) at Tondibi, near Gao, and won an immediate victory. This success Judar owed mainly to his firearms and the better discipline of his troops; but he also seems to have been aided by divided counsels on the Songhay side.

Pressing into Gao and afterwards Timbuktu, the Moroccans were disappointed in their hopes of easy and profitable conquest. Gao proved to have little worth the looting. In Timbuktu they soon ran into trouble with its Muslim leaders. These had tended to welcome the Moroccan incursion as a means of reasserting their independence of Songhay overlordship. One of their Gao colleagues, Alfa Bukar Lanbar, is even said to have counselled Askia Ishaq II to abandon the field at Tondibi. But they were by no means content to accept Moroccan overlordship instead. Taking advantage of a moment when the Moroccan forces, now under Mahmud Pasha, Judar's replacement, had quit Timbuktu for another attack on Ishaq's still resisting army, the leaders of Timbuktu stirred up a revolt which was eventually settled only by Moroccan compromise.

There followed two years of profitless fighting up and down the Songhay empire as Mahmud Pasha sought to pin down his opponents and destroy them. In this he had some temporary success, and was able to regain Timbuktu in October 1593, when he at once set about breaking the political power of its religious leaders. Four months later Mahmud had most of these arrested, and sent the more rebellious in chains across the Sahara to Marrakesh. Among them was the famous Ahmad Baba (1556–1627), one of those sixteenth-century scholars of Timbuktu whose works still enjoy respect among the learned of the Western Sudan. After two years in a Marrakesh prison, Ahmad Baba spent another twelve under open arrest before returning to his native city in 1608. By then the Moroccans had relinquished any serious effort at close control there.

The task of exploiting Songhay proved beyond them. They tried hard, but succeeded only in completing the ruin of the empire. Their rule over Timbuktu and Gao proved stifling and disastrous: never again would these ancient cities see the restoration of their old prosperity. Much of the cultivated area around them fell waste as Songhay peasants fled from Moroccan control. Populations dwindled. The schools of learning were emptied of teachers and their students. The busy traffic of the Western Sudan was for long disrupted as revolt after revolt swept through these Middle Niger lands. There followed a decisive shift in power from the peoples of the towns to those of the countryside.

Effective Moroccan control, even of Timbuktu, came to an end early in the seventeenth century when Sultan Mulay Zidan, Mulay's successor, complained bitterly that the whole enterprise had cost 23,000 Moroccan lives. He decided to cut his losses. The government of Timbuktu devolved to a local pasha who was at first appointed by Marrakesh and owed the sultan a close loyalty;

but gradually the ties slipped and were lost as the Timbuktu Moroccans, little reinforced from home, married local women and lost their identity. Their records, available in the *Tedzkiret en-Nisian*, a Timbuktu history published in 1750, show no fewer than 156 pashas in 160 years. By the end of the eighteenth century they and their *arma* community, as this Moroccan-Songhay mixture had come to be called, possessed only a shadow of their former authority.

But the Songhay empire was beyond recovery. Although the southern provinces remained under the command of Songhay chiefs, the region of the Middle Niger—crucial for the trading connection—was left to the push and pull of local pressures. Prominent among these were the efforts of the Saharan Tuareg to win grazing land along the north banks of the Niger and to milk its cities of tax and tribute, while south of the river there were other peoples, Dogon and Mossi and Bambara, with similar ambitions. The year 1600 may be taken as a major turning point throughout these lands. The old history of the medieval Sudan had ended. A new period had begun.

There were other adventures along the coastland as European sailors came over the horizon. By contrast with the vast upheavals of the inland country, these coastal operations were still of small importance. Yet they marked the gradual onset of other changes which were to prove, in the end, of more formidable influence for West Africa than the overthrow of Songhay.

Early European voyages down this coast were little more than an extension into ocean waters of the piratical manners of the Mediterranean. They are usually said to have begun in 1441, when Antam Gonçalves seized 'two Moors' who were no doubt Sanhaja Berbers on the coast of Rio d'Oro, north of Senegal, and took them with seven other captives back to Lisbon. Two years later Nuno Tristão carried out another little raid near Arguin, a little further to the south. Other pirates quickly followed. Their forays against defenceless fisher families or cattle nomads were, as the annals published in Lisbon by Zurara in 1453 amply and dramatically reveal, anything but glorious.

Somewhere south of Arguin, where the long biscuit-brown edge of Saharan Africa crumbles into Atlantic surf and spray, a certain Fernandes went ashore with two swordsmen and met five women walking near the beach. These, say the Portuguese annals, Fernandes and his bullies 'took with right good will, as something that increased their capital without toil; and led them with other captives to their ships'. Southward again, lying off and on the rising land near Cape Verde,* another captain not long afterwards put seven men into a ship's boat and 'ordered them to row along the coast. As they went, these men caught sight of four Guineas seated by the water's edge. Seeing themselves unnoticed, six of the men in the boat jumped ashore, hiding themselves as well as they could until they were near to the Guineas, when they began to run to capture them.' But the 'Guineas', at least on this occasion, ran faster and escaped.

Violence and deception were never to be entirely absent from the Guinea trade in sailing ships throughout its four centuries of vivid experience. Yet the hit-and-run raiding of early voyages soon gave way to a more or less regular partnership in trade. The Europeans were in any case far too weak, and the Africans too strong, for violent methods to offer a satisfactory profit on these hazardous expeditions. Here along the Guinea Coast there were no rich cities to be pillaged and put in fee, but only a string of fisher hamlets and little states whose warriors were capable of beating off any attack that could be mounted through the surf.

Soon after 1445, accordingly, the Portuguese built a little trading fort on Arguin Island just south of Cape Blanco, near the site of the modern Port Etienne; and 'henceforth the affairs of these parts were treated more by trafficking and bargaining of merchants than by bravery and toil in arms'. A Venetian who sailed on this coast in 1456 could note that the Portuguese at Arguin were already buying and sending back to Lisbon about

*On the Senegal coast near the port of Dakar, not to be confused with the archipelago and, since 1975, modern republic of Cape Verde, some 350 miles into the Middle Atlantic, though still an African archipelago. For its history, see B. Davidson, *The Fortunate Isles*, Trenton and London, 1989.

one thousand slaves a year, and this within a dozen years after
Gonçalves had taken the first captives. What had really happened
was that the Portuguese, having sailed round the Muslim monopoly established along the North African coast, had now entered the trans-Saharan slave trade by the back door.

Their next effort was to get themselves into other forms of
trade, especially in ivory and gold. By 1472 their ships had sailed
as far as the Bight of Benin, and brought back news of large and
wealthy kingdoms near the seaboard. In 1482, as part of the
Portuguese plan to secure a safe way station to the east while
taking full advantage of local opportunities for buying gold and
other goods, a local chief at what was to become Elmina (at the
western end of the coast of modern Ghana) was asked for land
on which to build 'a house' for the storing of merchandise. Having
reluctantly agreed, he was surprised to find the Portuguese erect-
ing what was obviously much more than 'a house', and that they
were building it, moreover, on a piece of land traditionally held
as sacred. The Portuguese account of this affair says that Azambuja, who was in command, managed to buy himself out of the
fighting which then ensued and that 'the work was pressed on so
fast that within twenty days the walls of the fortress were built up
to their full height, and so was the tower . . .' After this Azambuja
remained 'in the castle for two years and seven months, during
which he set up a gallows and a pillory and made other ordinances
and agreements with the Negroes to the great honour and service
of the king of Portugal'; and not neglecting, as a fine early example
of Portuguese policy in Africa through years to come, to burn
down the local chief's village.

Though it would long remain without much significance for
the inland country, this early trade upon the coast expanded with
surprising speed. From the first it fell into a geographical pattern
that was to hold firm in later times. Three main areas of useful
contact were recognized. Westward, there was the long coastline
between the mouth of the Senegal and Sierra Leone; and here,
'when the trade is well organized', Pereira was writing in 1506,
'we can look every year for more than 3,500 slaves, many tusks

of ivory, some gold, fine cotton stuffs and numerous other goods.'
In this 'windward' region, so-called because the prevailing winds
blow from the west and south-west, trading contact was with
Dyula merchants operating from their markets in Mali, with the
Wolof states in Senegal, and with a host of lesser chiefdoms along
the coast.

Next there was the central region based on Elmina Castle and
other such coastal stations established by African agreement and
against the payment of a yearly rent. Into these a little of the gold
trade of the Akan forestlands now began to flow. The Portuguese
were able to expand their trade here by augmenting the supply
of porters, bringing in for this purpose a continual flow of slaves
purchased at Benin and selling these for gold to their African
partners in business, who also used them as mining labour. Here
this new connection promised so well that the English and the
French began pushing their way into a trade which the Portuguese, arguing papal consent to their monopoly, regarded as
entirely their own. There was much skirmishing at sea, but the
interlopers could not be stopped. An early English voyage of
1553, consisting of two ships and a pinnace, brought back 400
pounds of gold to the port of London, 36 barrels of peppercorn
and some 250 tusks, the English being surprised to find that a
basin of brass or copper could be exchanged for gold to the value
of as much as thirty pounds sterling in the currency of the day.

Eastward lay a third region of trade, the empire of Benin. This
commercial contact dated from 1485 when d'Aveiro was received
at court and opened diplomatic relations between the king of
Portugal and Oba Ewuare. Here the export trade was largely in
peppercorns, later supplanted by a better product found in the
Far East, as well as in ivory and in slaves for sale at Elmina on
the Gold Coast. The Benin trade in peppers and ivory was entered
by the English in 1553, but English and French vessels were few
in these waters until the seventeenth century, and even then it
was the Dutch who took the lead.

Eight hundred miles further down the west coast, Diogo Cão
paralleled the diplomatic efforts of d'Aveiro at Benin by visiting

the court of Mani Kongo, ruler of the Bakongo empire near the estuary of the Congo River. Here too envoys were exchanged and Portuguese missionaries allowed to settle at the capital. For a while, as at Benin, all promised well for this new partnership and alliance. 'Royal brothers', African and European, dictated polite letters to each other and exchanged their thoughts about the future. But the courtesies were not to last.

The Atlantic Trade and Slavery

Passing through Cairo in the 1320s on his way to Mecca, the great Mansa Musa of Mali had told a dramatic tale of maritime adventure. He said that his predecessor had sent two big expeditions, one of four hundred ships and the other of two thousand, across the ocean in order to discover what lay on the other side, but only one of these ships and its crew had ever returned. Even if these expeditions really took place, it is clear they were altogether exceptional. The coastal peoples of West Africa were skilful in building large canoes for inshore fishing and at handling these across thundering surf; but this was the obvious limit of their need. Until the coming of the Europeans, they faced an empty ocean. In this respect, of course, they were very differently placed from the Swahili peoples of the East Coast, who had long since learned ship-building and sailing skills from the Arab and Indian sailors of the Indian Ocean.

During the sixteenth century, however, there evolved in the Atlantic a trading community that was parallel to the much older and in many ways vastly different system of the Indian Ocean. From 1500 onwards the western seas were increasingly traced by sailing ship routes linking western Africa to western Europe, and soon afterwards to the eastern seaboard of the Americas and the islands of the Caribbean. In this new trading community West Africans played almost from the first an indispensable part. This was not as ship-builders or ship-masters, for they had none of the necessary skills, experience or incentive to impel them in that

direction; and the carrying trade remained a European monopoly
of skill and ownership. With rising European technological supremacy, this was the period in which the foundations for Africa's
future dependence on Europe, whether economic or political,
began to be laid.

Aside from unruly outbreaks here and there, European piracy
along the Guinea Coast had given way to trading partnership
well before 1500. But the partnership took a very different shape
and meaning from that of East Africans with the Asian traders
of the Indian Ocean. There along the East Coast, so far as all
known records indicate, slaving remained a minor aspect of trade
or one that was sometimes altogether absent. None of the Arab
writers of the medieval period speaks of the slave trade from East
Africa as being of any importance, and some of them do not
mention it at all. If slaves were wanted, they could be needed
only for household work, for there was no plantation system in
the East which could absorb large quantities of manual labour;
and the number required for household work or military service
in Muslim armies could never be enormous. *

At first it was the same in the West. Though the Portuguese
might be taking home several thousand slaves a year, they were
still only supplementing the supply of domestic labour fed by an
already existing and profitable trade in European slaves. So profitable had the Venetian Republic found its sale of Christian slaves
to Egypt and other Muslim countries, indeed, that its merchants
had not been deterred even by Pope Clement V's edict of ex-
communication for this offence, nor by his authorization to all
other Christian peoples to reduce the Venetians to slavery in their
turn.

But this use of slaves and slave labour, familiar in medieval
Europe as in Africa, became an altogether different matter once

*A contested view. For what seem to me conclusive arguments against there having
been large slave exports from East Africa before the nineteenth century on anything like
the scale of the Atlantic slave trade, see B. Davidson, 'Slaves or Captives? Some Notes
on Fantasy and Fact', in N. I. Huggins, M. Kilson and D. M. Fox (eds.), *Key Issues in
the Afro-American Experience*, New York, 1971, and reprints.

the Americas were discovered. Only hard work could open mines and make plantations flourish; and work was the last thing envisaged by the conquerors, at least for themselves. Yet even if Portuguese and Spanish soldiers and settlers had cared to labour in mines or plantations, they were desperately short of the necessary skills. They knew nothing of tropical farming; and although they had miners of their own at home, these were few and could seldom be spared. Consequently it became necessary to find labour; and, if possible, skilled labour.

They started by impressing the 'Indians'—the native peoples whom they found—and the results were appalling. When Hispaniola was discovered, 'it contained 1,130,000 Indians', a Spaniard well placed to make his guess wrote in 1518. 'Today their number does not exceed 11,000. And judging by what has happened, there will be none of them left in three or four years' times unless some remedy is applied.' The remedy, in fact, had already been found. European slaves being in too short supply, and Amer-Indians incapable of filling the need for labour except with their corpses, recourse was had to Africa. Within a few years of Columbus's first voyage in 1492 the Spanish were taking West African captives for enslavement across the Atlantic: few enough to begin with, and yet sufficient to cause the governor of Hispaniola to complain in 1503 that too many Africans were escaping and 'teaching disobedience to the Indians'. They were also breaking away from enslavement in sudden and successful revolts, terrifying the local settlers; and it would be better, the governor thought, not to send any more. But no such counsels could prevail over the pressing need for labor, and above all for African labour skilled in tropical farming and in mining.

Two years later, in 1505, a caravel sailed from Seville with seventeen Africans and some mining equipment. Five years after that the sale of Africans in the Americas was legalized by the Spanish crown. In 1516 Spain received its first shipment of slave-grown sugar from the Caribbean; and in 1518 a ship in Spanish service carried the first cargo of Africans directly from the Guinea Coast to the Americas. With this there opened a regular slaving system which was to endure for three and a half centuries, and deliver across the ocean some 10 to 12 million Africans, as well as killing many other millions before departure or on voyage. This peculiar form of trade, immensely valuable to western Europe but increasingly disastrous for western Africa, was to overshadow the whole commercial system of the Atlantic Ocean. It formed the major factor of difference, in so far as Africa was concerned, between the Atlantic system and its older counterpart of the Indian Ocean.

One may turn aside for a moment here and look at the conditions under which this overwhelming tide of forced emigration became so large a part of the African scene. While ashore on Grand Canary in the 1550s, John Hawkins of Plymouth heard not only that 'Negroes were very good merchandise in Hispaniola', but also that a 'store of Negroes might easily be had upon the coast of Guinea'. Why easily?

The answer lay in the social systems of Africa. Like other systems based on economies of subsistence which were qualified but not essentially changed by a certain amount of production for trade, these had no wage-labour of any regular kind at their disposal. Having no labour market, they functioned either by organizing men and women of certain 'age-sets'—men and women born at about the same time as each other—for traditionally accepted forms of labour, such as porterage among forest peoples who had no draught animals; or else by imposing free-labour services on certain groups and individuals. The latter might arrive at their servile condition through conquest, capture in war or punishment for crime. More often, though, they would be peasants whose status differed little in essence from that of the serfs or villeins of medieval Europe, and who were regarded as inseparable from the land they tilled. As in Europe, it became customary to use them for household or military services, for the accumulation of food or handmade goods, and for gifts or a means of exchange. In 1493, for example, the new emperor of Songhay, Askia Muhammad, inherited from his predecessor a number of 'slave peoples' whose slavery consisted in the obligation to provide certain stipulated goods or services. Blacksmiths had to provide spears, fishermen had to deliver fish or canoes or canoe-crews, cattle-breeders had to bring in forage or cattle, others had to perform household services.

There is no doubt that this use of tied or wageless labour increased, though for the most part only in the Muslim areas of the Western Sudan, after the fifteenth century. It was one of those aspects of Iron Age growth which steadily transformed the old equalities into new forms of exploitation and privilege. Muslim kings imposed heavier labour-services, accumulated wealth in kind through wider use of slave labour, and raised slave armies to protect their authority from lineage rivals, usurpers or popular revolt. All this, going hand-in-hand with the growth of trade and the expansion of money-currencies but generally stopping short of early forms of capitalism, occurred in the Western Sudan from at least the time of Askia Muhammad. Later it spread southward into the forest regions under the Alafins of Oyo and the powerful kings of eighteenth-century Asante.

Yet these 'wageless workers', one should note, were seldom or never mere chattels, persons without rights or hope of emancipation. They might be bought and sold, given away and accepted as gifts. Yet their condition was different from that of the African chattel slaves who would labour in the Americas. They were not, as these were, outcasts in the body politic. On the contrary, they were integral members of their community. Household slaves lived with their masters, often as members of the family. They could work themselves free of their obligations. They could marry their masters' daughters. They could become traders, leading men in peace and war, governors and sometimes even kings. 'A slave who knows how to serve', ran the old Asante proverb, 'succeeds to his master's property.'

These systems, then, were not 'slave-based economies' such as had existed in parts of Europe or Asia. They lacked the wholesale alienation of land into private ownership that could deprive the mass of people of their independent livelihood. If they had many forms of currency, notably the cowrie shell, these remained

marginal to economic life as a whole. While skilful in trade and
trading techniques, their merchants were by no means numerous
or strong enough as yet to play a dominant role in the state.
Horizontal divisions in society were increasingly apparent and
important; but they could exercise political and economic influence only at certain points and in certain situations, none
of which was capable of transforming these economies from
predominantly subsistence systems to full-blown 'money-and-
market' systems.

In the context of slavery, however, these systems manifestly
provided many forms of obligatory servitude. Some men had
much power and status, while others had little; and those who
had little were increasingly, as the process of horizontal social
stratification continued, at the service of those who had much.
Comparatively large numbers of men and women became 'dis-
posable' for one reason or another, mainly by capture in war or
sentence of the criminal courts. And it was out of this situation
that the trans-Saharan slave trade, and afterwards the increasingly
larger trans-Atlantic slave trade, were born and made to flourish.
However deplorable it may appear in the light of what happened
later, this 'disposing' of 'persons of inferior status' can have seemed
no more shocking or immoral to 'persons of superior status' in
Africa than the arbitrary sacking and starving of workers seemed
to the English employers of the industrial revolution. The one
form of servitude appeared as 'natural' as the other.

Neither buyers nor sellers therefore found it strange that a
demand for slaves should be met whenever the balance of interest
led that way: meeting this demand, indeed, became part of the
traditional economies of those concerned, whether they hailed
from America, Europe or Asia. Who generally bought and who
generally sold was determined for the most part by the relative
strengths of the economic systems in play. During the early Middle Ages the flow of slaves had gone from Europe to the Muslim
states of the Near East and Egypt in exchange for the finished
goods of those then more advanced regions; later, with Europe
growing more developed, the flow was reversed and went from

Africa to Europe. Only with the coming of wage-labour was slaving brought to an end; and wage-labour during many of its early years, characteristically for the attitudes out of which it had grown, imposed conditions which were seldom better and were sometimes worse than the outright enslavement of old.

The point to be noticed here is that the early sale of Africans to European sea-merchants departed in no way from previous practices of exchanging servile persons within Africa, or, indeed, within Europe. The only difference was that servile persons were now sold for transport overseas instead of transport overland, a change that was of no importance (at least for many years) to the traditional economies and social systems either of sellers or buyers. And had the European demand remained at the minor level of interest where it stood before the American discoveries and enterprises, the slave trade with West Africa could never have exercised any major influence on the course of events. But the American discoveries changed everything.

Not only were Africans plentiful. They were also skilled in tropical farming and in mining, being in these respects far superior not only to the Amer-Indians but often to the Europeans as well. As the years went by, they became so valuable and their rapid replacement so necessary, because of the hardships to which they were ruthlessly submitted, that the Portuguese from Brazil were even bringing gold to the Gold Coast, during the eighteenth century, in order to purchase with it slaves who could not otherwise be had. 'There remains only to tell you', wrote an English buying agent on the Gold Coast in 1771 to his directors in London, 'that gold commands the trade. There is no buying a slave without one ounce of gold at least on it . . . Formerly, owners of ships used to send out double cargoes of goods, one for [buying] slaves and the other for [buying] gold. If slaves happened to be dearer than usual, the cargo for [buying] gold was thrown into the slave cargo in order to fill the ship. On the other hand, if slaves were reasonable the gold cargo was disposed of for gold and ivory at a profit of thirty, forty, or fifty per cent . . . How strangely things are reversed now . . . [when] we scarcely see a ship go off with her complement of slaves, notwithstanding her cargo [is arranged to allow for payment of] eighteen to twenty pounds sterling [per slave] on the average . . .'

By this time the trade had become thoroughly engrained in the commercial system of the coastland. Its customs and regulations were almost a matter of tradition. From selling a few slaves in the early years, the Africans in the business—a 'business of kings, rich men, and prime merchants', as Barbot rightly called it in the 1680s—found themselves gradually edged and pressured into providing more and more. Far outstripping the early demand for household servants and porters, the business now called for enormous numbers. These could be provided, as we shall see, only by warfare and capture, so that from the middle of the seventeenth century it is almost always more accurate to speak of this trade as dealing in captives and not in slaves. Increasingly, the victims were prisoners-of-war whose enslavement began only with their sale to Europeans: few, any longer, had been in any servile status before they were sold. What had happened, as Walter Rodney has observed, was that the African 'ruling class [had] joined hands with the Europeans in exploiting the African masses': at first light-heartedly and without any notion of the consequences, and then, after the American discoveries, with an eye to their own increasing personal profit and power. It was not long before thriving coastal polities were founded on the sale of captives to the Europeans.

Some of the 'kings, rich men, and prime merchants' who had thus embarked on selling 'common folk' to the Europeans soon found reason to hesitate. The Kongo king Nzinga Mbemba, baptized soon after 1500 as King Affonso I, had welcomed the Portuguese, who came with promises of trade and useful knowledge, and made them many gifts of household servants and other persons of servile condition. But he found the Portuguese appetite for slave labour, whether for growing sugar on the offshore African island of São Thomé or for transport to Brazil, entirely insatiable. Portuguese agents rode roughshod over his authority among the coastal chiefs, dealing separately with each rather than through

his own agents, and carrying off anyone they could get their
hands on, including members of the king's own family. They
spread such 'corruption and licentiousness', this Kongo king complained in a letter to Lisbon of 1526, 'that our country is being
completely depopulated'. Two centuries later a king of Dahomey
even offered to allow Europeans to establish plantations along
the coast if they would cease to carry men away.

There were other such attempts at reducing human exports,
but none of them availed. To obtain European goods, especially
the firearms whose use was now spreading through West Africa,
it was necessary to meet the European demand for captives; and
if one local chieftain or 'prime merchant' should refuse, his rival
or neighbour would undoubtedly comply. Only a major shift in
European demand could have brought the traffic to a close.

No such shift came until the early years of the nineteenth
century, and even then only with the British and the French.
On the contrary, the trade repeatedly expanded with the invention
of new techniques of exchange. Crucial among these was the so-
called 'trade ounce'. The early chartered companies of the seventeenth century had all failed financially for one reason or
another of bad management, but mainly because they were
obliged to buy goods in Europe for cash, and to sell them in
Africa by processes of barter. It proved extremely hard, and often
impossible, for a captain to assure himself of a profit, since the
costing of a barter deal, involving many items of unfixed monetary
value, often defeated even the most cautious calculations of self-
interest.

To meet this difficulty the trade ounce was invented. It had
nothing to do with an ounce in weight, except that its value in
goods was related to the price of an ounce of gold in England
(the French worked to a different system). What was done, as
nearly as possible, was to assemble a package of goods, which
might consist of a mixture of iron bars, copper basins, cheap
cottons, muskets, ammunition, gunpowder, that was known to
cost, *in toto*, about half the value of an ounce of gold. This
'ounce' was then exchanged for a captive or captives (their price

in trade ounces varied widely according to place and time) whose approximate selling value was also known. Together with the 100 per cent 'mark up' on the gold value of the goods exchanged—notionally costing an ounce of gold, but actually only half an ounce—this allowed a captain to 'see his profit' in a barter deal, as well as allowing for the death of slaves during the voyage across the Atlantic.

Other techniques were invented on the African side. Those of the Fon kingdom of Dahomey are particularly interesting. Rising to power in the 1720s, the Fon secured control of most of the ports in the 'Benin Gap', the stretch of open scrub country which divides the forests of southern Nigeria from those of southern Ghana. Their kingdom was peculiar in that it was based on an extreme centralization, so that there are certain ways in which Dahomey may be said to have been the first nation-state in tropical Africa. Like some other kingdoms in contact with Europeans, the Fon developed what Polányi has called a 'port of trade' at Ouidah. Through this they successfully concentrated all dealings with Europeans, thus enabling them to make a clear division between the 'state sector', dealing in export and import, and the 'private sector', which remained, throughout most of Dahomey, one of subsistence and merely local trade. With this device the kings of Dahomey were able to profit from the European trade, especially in the import of firearms, while isolating the greater part of their country from the impact of European influence. There was no scope here for sub-chiefs to break away from royal authority, as happened in Kongo, and go into business on their own.

None of this reduced the inhumanity of the system in itself. Brutality grew worse after about 1650 when the trade got thoroughly into its stride. Coarsened by dealing in men, women and children whose value was only what they could realize for cash in the Americas, and whose fate promised only a quick death or perpetual servitude, the sailing-ship captain soon came to treat his captives like cattle. He bought them for size or strength or handsomeness, applied crude tests for ensuring that the goods were 'as per invoice', crammed and chained them in stifling misery below decks, and sailed for the Americas with such slow speed as he could muster, hoping that losses on the way would not exceed 10 or 15 per cent.

'As the slaves come down to Ouidah from the inland country,' Barbot wrote of the familiar scene, 'they are put into a booth or prison, built for that purpose near the beach, all of them together; and when the Europeans are to receive them, they are brought out into a large plain, where the ships' surgeons examine every part of every one of them, to the smallest member, men and women being all stark naked. Such as are allowed good and sound are set on one side, and the others by themselves: these rejected slaves are called Makrons, being above thirty-five years of age, or defective in their lips, eyes or teeth, or grown grey; or that have the venereal disease or any other imperfection.

'These being set aside, each of the others passed as good is marked on the breast with a red-hot iron, imprinting the mark of the French, English or Dutch companies so that each nation may distinguish their own property, and so as to prevent their being changed by the sellers for others that are worse . . . In this particular, care is taken that the women, as the tenderest, are not burnt too hard.' A week or so later if ships were to hand, or many weeks later if they were not, these luckless captives would start the 'Middle Passage' across the ocean, and with this again there were traditions of outrageous brutality. Every ship's captain feared revolt on board, and with good reason, for revolts were many. He would normally cause all his slaves to be chained below decks, sometimes bringing them up into the air once a day and making them jump about to restore their circulation. This was thought so necessary for health, the House of Commons was told in 1789, that the prisoners were 'whipped if they refused to do it'. Anti-slavery campaigners rightly pointed to the horrors and demoralization of these terrible voyages. They canvassed seamen in the great slaving ports of England and came back with gruesome evidence. 'Men on their first voyages usually dislike the traffic', Clarkson found after researches in Liverpool and

Bristol. 'But if they went a second or third time, their disposition
became gradually to be accustomed to carry away men and
women by force, to keep them in chains . . . and to behold the
dead and dying.'

Slave Trade Consequences

The degradation went beyond the slaving ships and plantations.
Ramifying through European and American society, it formed a
deep soil of arrogant contempt for African humanity. In this soil
fresh ideas and attitudes of 'racial superiority', themselves the
fruit of Europe's technical and military strength, took easy root
and later came to full flower during the decades of nineteenth-
century invasion and of twentieth-century possession of the
continent. Even men and women of otherwise thoughtful and
generous disposition came to think it well and wise that Africans
should be carried into slavery, since they were carried at that
same time, it was said, out of an 'endless night of savage barbarism' into the embrace of a 'superior civilization'.

But other men and women disagreed. British and French abolitionists played an admirable part in bringing the trade to an
end. Often treated by their opponents as subversive revolution-
aries who should be hounded from society because, in wishing
to destroy a valuable national trade, these abolitionists had clearly
'sacrificed their national feelings', they undoubtedly hastened the
day when slaving was declared illegal. Men like Sharp, Clarkson
and the Abbé Grégoire deserve the more honour because their
task appeared so hopeless. In 1775 the British secretary of state
for the colonies, a certain Lord Dartmouth, could still tell Parliament that his government was unable to allow a check or
discouragement 'in any degree' to a 'trade so beneficial to the
nation'.* Thirty-two years later, all the same, another British

*Polemicists will not fail to note that the British (and indeed United States) governments
were still using this same argument in defending their refusal during the 1960s to impose
effective sanctions or other measures against *apartheid* rule in South Africa.

government forbade any British ship to carry slaves; and the abolitionists could rightly claim that the victory was theirs.

Yet it was not, of course, only theirs or essentially theirs. Great changes in society may be hastened by good will; they have their origin in deeper pressures. The truth was that predominant British interests were no longer the same. The times had passed, as Eric Williams has explained in his classic study of this subject, when

Negroes for Sale.

A Cargo of very fine stout Men and Women, in good order and fit for immediate service, just imported from the Windward Coast of Africa, in the Ship Two Brothers.—
Conditions are one half Cash or Produce, the other half payable the first of January next, giving Bond and Security if required.
The Sale to be opened at 10 o'Clock each Day, in Mr. Bourdeaux's Yard, at No, 48, on the Bay.
May 19, 1784. JOHN MITCHELL.

Thirty Seasoned Negroes
To be Sold for Credit, at Private Sale.

AMONGST which is a Carpenter, none of whom are known to be dishonest.

Also, to be sold for Cash, a regular bred young Negroe Man-Cook, born in this Country, who served several Years under an exceeding good French Cook abroad, and his Wife a middle aged Washer-Woman, (both very honest) and their two Children. *Likewise,* a young Man a Carpenter.

For Terms apply to the Printer.

American advertisement for the sale of slaves in 1784.

King Sugar could rule the day at Westminster. Having embarked on manufacturing industries at home, the British were more interested in their own labour market than in any that might exist elsewhere. By the final years of the slave trade in British bottoms, its main work was finished. The capital it had helped to accumulate and nourish by the triple profits of the 'triangular trade'—cheap goods to West Africa for the buying of captives, slaves to the Americas for the buying of sugar and tobacco, and these in turn to western Europe for cash—had gone far to float the industrial revolution off the shoals of doubt and speculation. Europe changed. And when the British and the French next looked for adventures overseas, they went in search of raw materials, prestige and military advantage, and not in the least for slave labour.

A massive aid to the founding of mechanical industry: such was the main result of the overseas slave trade for western Europe. What the African chattel slaves had begun, the European wage slaves of the late eighteenth and early nineteenth centuries continued.

Across the Atlantic the results were very different, but in any case so great as to be knitted deeply into the fabric of daily life in every American land or island except Newfoundland in Canada. By 1800 half the population of Brazil was of African origin. There was not a single Latin American or Caribbean community without its numerous black or partly black component. Many of the more prosperous North American states relied on black labour. And such was the rate of replenishment from Africa, following the rate of mortal wastage of the slaves, that these Negroes were for the most part much more than 'Africans by descent'. They were often Africans *tout court*. At any rate up to 1800 the rate of mortality was such that whole 'slave populations' had to be replaced every few years. More than half the soldiers of Toussaint Louverture and Dessalines, those rebels who carried through the anti-slavery revolution in Saint Domingue and defeated the armies of France and afterwards the armies of Britain, had made the Middle Passage and were 'first generation Americans'.

Just the same may be said of those Africans, mostly from

Angola, who had fled in earlier times from captivity in north-eastern Brazil, and had established their own free republic of Palmares in about 1605. Palmares was defended successfully against repeated Dutch and Portuguese attacks for nearly a hundred years, and was governed by methods and customs that were drawn from the native land of its inhabitants, and even provided, according to Freyre, a Brazilian, a 'forerunner of the diversification of crops in contrast to the predominant mono-culture of the white planters'.* And the same could be said of many lesser bids for trans-Atlantic freedom by men and women who, whether in the Caribbean or on the mainland of the Amer-icas, built or tried to build other republics of the same kind. To omit these peoples from the scope of African history would be like excluding the early New Englanders, Australians, Canadians and New Zealanders from the history of Britain.

On Africa itself, the home and source of all this slave labour, the long-range effects of the Atlantic trade remain harder to eval-uate. They were undoubtedly very great, and far transcended the effects of other slave trades. The trans-Saharan trade in human beings never achieved a volume that could have any large con-sequence for West African society, however painful might be the individual consequences; while the Indian Ocean or East Coast trade in slaves was of even smaller significance up to the 1840s, though its influence for evil in the relatively brief but disastrous period of about 1840–80 became frequently extreme. In contrast with these, the Atlantic trade had grown to such a size by 1650 that for at least two centuries it did unquestionably bring a major influence to bear on many coastal and near-coastal peoples from the mouth of the Senegal to the southern borders of Angola, a territory of varying and generally narrow width but more than three thousand miles in length.

Although depopulation might seem the most obvious effect of a trade which probably involved the deportation or death of sev-eral tens of millions of Africans over three or four centuries—

*G. Freyre, *The Mansions and the Shanties*, New York, 1966, p. 40.

even if captives 'safely landed' in the Americas may not have
exceeded some ten millions*—a good deal of evidence suggests
otherwise. It is perfectly true, as Hrbek has argued, that African
populations (so far as anyone can guess) seem to have grown by
1900 much less rapidly than European, American or Asian populations. But to infer conclusions about the slave trade from this
is to overlook two objections: first, that colonial population estimates (as counting in Nigeria and Ghana strikingly confirms)
have probably been far too small, and second, that a number of
African populations suffered disastrously from the upheavals and
invasions of the years 1800–1920.

Some peoples must certainly have lost much of their strength
to the slave trade. Wherever slaving struck at a people who were
comparatively few or economically weak, it left an empty land:
here the right comparison is with the forced migration of peasants
from the Scottish Highlands during the nineteenth century, an
operation from which the population and economy of that region
have never been able to recover. But the parallel with emigration
from Europe can also be extended to more populous countries
and stronger societies; and the conclusion will be different. It
seems unlikely, for example, that there was any more serious
effect on the birth-and-survival rates of Iboland, through the
forced emigration of the slave trade, than on those of southern
Italy, Ireland, or England itself through an emigration forced not
by outright violence but by hunger and unemployment.

Depopulation of Africa there undoubtedly was; yet the main
damage lay elsewhere. Essentially, the Atlantic trade was a large
and long-enduring exchange of cheap industrial goods, mainly
cottons and metalware and firearms, for the 'raw material' of
African labour. (The quotation marks are also necessary because
the labour was in fact often skilled in those very techniques most
required in the Americas: tropical farming and metal-working.)

*A total arrived at by P. D. Curtin, in his important *The Atlantic Slave Trade, A
Census*, 1969, but probably an underestimate by a few millions. For discussion, see J.
E. Inikori (ed.) *Forced Migration*, Hutchinson, London, 1982.

Every question of humanity apart, this trade struck at Africa in two ways, both of which spelt impoverishment.

By providing Africa with cheap substitutes, the Atlantic slave trade undermined the local production of cotton goods and metalware; against this partial benefit of cheaper imports, it discouraged expansion from the handicraft stage. In the sixteenth century the Portuguese had imported the cotton stuffs of West Africa for sale in Europe; now the flow was reversed. Secondly, the Atlantic trade deprived a large number of African societies of many of their best producers, the youngest and strongest of their men and women; and it did this not spasmodically but continuously over several centuries.

One may therefore regard the overseas slave trade as an early type of colonial economy: of the exchange of European goods for African raw material and, by extension, as one of the reasons why a prelude to capitalism failed to develop in Africa until the latter part of the nineteenth century. No one can say how far African societies could or would have moved into cash economies and industrial methods of production if their early partnership with Europe, the partnership of the sixteenth century, had continued into later times. Yet there are some interesting pointers to an answer. When living in Kano a century ago, Heinrich Barth observed that handicraft production of textiles had reached such a high degree of 'cottage industry' as to be able to supply the whole of the Western Sudan from Senegal to Lake Chad. Far outside the slaving network of the Atlantic trade, Kano had clearly developed to the point where a new economic development could begin to unfold.

Later on, even within that network, a number of African societies adjusted to forms of capitalism with remarkable speed. They changed over from selling slaves to selling palm oil, cleared plantations of their own, traded enormously by credit, accumulated large reserves in cash or goods, even embarked on the business of chartering ships and crews. With Europe needing more and more soap as her factories grew in number and her cities in filth, palm oil exports from the Guinea Coast expanded from a few tons in 1800 to several thousand tons a year by the 1830s. This was not yet industrial production. But it was certainly an approach towards capital accumulation and productive investment, the necessary parents of industrialism, such as had never been possible in slaving days. To this structural development, the colonial period then put a full stop.

If the economic effects were generally bad, some of the political effects surpassed them. Because the demand for slaves far exceeded the supply of those who actually lived under servile conditions—whether from capture in war, from sentence of the civil courts for crimes of one kind or another or from any other reason—it was necessary to supply captives. And since African kings and merchants were generally hindered by their own social norms or political expedience from supplying their own people—though they certainly sold their political rebels, as being 'criminal', in much the same way as European governments transported European rebels across the seas—they could obtain sufficient captives only by warfare or violence. Knowing that without captives they could not hope for European trade, the chiefs of the Niger Delta armed their great canoes and sent them on expeditions into the populous inland country. The lords of near-coastal states plundered their tributary peoples for the same purpose. Wars and raids multiplied. At the same time, a close-knit system of commercial interest ensured the buying of any captive who was brought for sale. If many regretted the trade which had led to this, none could long withstand its pressures. Among those pressures, the need for firearms and ammunition now became the foremost.

By 1700, if not before, few coastal or near-coastal kings or chiefs could feel safe in their country without a supply of troops equipped with firearms. Only with these could slaving wars be carried on and European trade assured; only with these could the slaving raids of their neighbours be resisted. Having no mechanical equipment that was capable of the manufacture of firearms, African kings were obliged to buy them from the Europeans. But the Europeans would sell firearms only in part-exchange for captives. So the need for captives led to the need for firearms; and the need for firearms led to the need for still more captives, and still more firearms, in a vicious circle there seemed no means of breaking. Many of these coastal peoples became totally enmeshed in this spiral of mounting violence.

The Dutch agent at Elmina explained the roots of the system in a letter of 1701 to a friend in Amsterdam. Having described the skill with which Africans managed their 'muskets and carabins', Bosman wrote that 'Perhaps you will wonder how the Negroes come to be furnished with firearms? But you will have no reason to do so when you know that we sell them incredible quantities, thereby obliging them with a knife to cut our own throats. Yet we are forced to do it. For if we did not sell firearms, the Negroes would be easily provided with them by the English, Danes, or Brandenburghers. And even if we [the official trading companies of these nations] could all agree not to sell firearms, still the English and the Dutch interlopers [private traders] would abundantly do so. In any case, since gunpowder and firearms have been our chief selling goods for some time now, we should have done a poor enough trade without them . . .'

But what was true of firearms on the European side was likewise true of captives for enslavement on the African side. If one king refused to supply them he knew that his neighbour might not be so delicate. Even if all the kings could have agreed against supplying them, still there would have been plenty of individual operators to fill the need. And since slaves were what the Europeans chiefly and urgently wanted, no king or merchant along the coast would have hoped for anything but a 'poor trade', as Bosman explained, without making his contribution in captives. European and African rulers and merchants were thus involved in a trade that was morally degrading for both but was also, for Africa, often economically destructive and sometimes politically disastrous. Above all, the overseas slave trade both introduced and confirmed an underlying dependency that the colonial period was going to complete.

Towards the Crisis of Today

The Seventeenth and Eighteenth Centuries

Just as the sixteenth century may be regarded as marking a certain point of climax in the history of old Africa, at any rate to the south of the Sahara, the long period which followed may best be understood as one of transition—of several stages of transition—to the situations and problems, whether political or economic, of Africa today. This is not to say, of course, that Iron Age structures had fully realized their inner potentialities of growth by 1600, nor that the years which followed saw nothing but the gradual decline of 'classical structures' until, with the 1950s, a new world could break its way through colonial doors: on the contrary, some of the 'classical structures' continued to evolve and expand. Nor was there at 1600 any more obvious break in continuity than at most other convenient dividing-lines in history. Life for a majority of folk went on much as before. The old traditions held firm. Families of ancestors, vanished from this world but well remembered, continued to give self-assurance and identity to their descendant peoples. The ancient customs were observed.

Looking back, though, one can see that new elements were at work. However obscurely or indirectly, more and more populations were now drawn within the orbit of a continental crisis, slowly gathering, slowly widening, of unexampled magnitude: a crisis whose full and terrible effects would become manifest only

late in the twentieth century. This slow but menacing development—or process of under-development, of de-development—
is especially evident for the peoples who lived south of the Sahara.
Up to the sixteenth century their civilizations had evolved out of
their own unfolding dynamic in large though never complete
isolation from the outside world. They had reacted in a variety
of ways to the influence of the outside world, as the trading records
most obviously show, but the reactions had been very much their
own. They had built up new polities and systems of self-rule,
but these had followed an emphatically African pattern. The
many new answers they had found to many new problems of
everyday life had developed within an indigenous framework little
shaped by foreign pressure or example. Even where the universal
religions of Islam and Christianity had made some headway these
had rapidly acquired an African accent and appearance. 'Out of
Africa there is always something new', ran the old Roman tag;
and it was echoed down the years by men who observed that
whatever came out of Africa did indeed seem different from
anything known before.

This 'African Middle Ages'—this Mature Iron Age, as I have
suggested we may call it—came to an end around 1600, and
there now began an equally lengthy period that was to culminate
in European colonial invasion and its aftermath. The actual
'point of change', if any such moment of break can be sensibly
extracted from a process so very complex, occurred at different
times in different places. For the Western Sudan it may be placed
in the 1590s with the destruction of Songhay. For the Guinea
Coast it came a little later with the wide expansion of the Atlantic
trade. For the East Coast it struck as early as 1498 with the arrival
of Vasco da Gama and the years of ruin that immediately followed. In North Africa, less identifiable than elsewhere, the 'point
of change' may be thought to occur at the Ottoman conquests
of the early and middle sixteenth century, while for southernmost
Africa it can be fixed as late as 1652, when the Dutch made their
first small settlement on the Cape of Good Hope.

Whether early or late in the sixteenth or seventeenth century, large regions of Africa were now pulled ever more closely and continuously into the affairs and ambitions of a rapidly changing world around them. Reservations must always be necessary in any statement as bold as this; yet the period which now opens, even when allowing for such reservations, does indeed appear to support this dominant and deepening trend. Africa is carried by successive stages into an ever greater economic and technological inferiority over against the industrial nations, and finally into a political subjection which goes on until the 1950s. Then at last Africans can begin to face the direct challenge of all those post-medieval skills which have fashioned the modern world, and have formed a common ground for human equality.

This Age of Transition is therefore one of slow revolution, of gradual movement and enlargement in the forms and limits of Iron Age society—pre-industrial, non-scientific, based on economies of low production—to the threshold of participation in the knowledge and techniques of the world of today. It is an Age of Transition which obviously still continues in these present years. Just as clearly, it is one that has displayed the resolution, or attempted resolution, of many inner conflicts and contradictions. Some regions suffered disaster. Others built new and effective systems of self-rule. Yet all of them, early or late, directly or indirectly, were caught within the same great underlying process of many-sided change. All were subjected to a growing dependency on industrialized powers outside Africa.

New States in Guinea

Allied to the arms trade, the Atlantic slave trade had disrupting consequences which gradually spread after 1650 from the seaboard to the lands immediately behind the coast. Yet one must be careful not to exaggerate these consequences. The disruptions they caused at certain points along the coast and near the coast were undoubtedly very great. Further inland, however, these disruptions were either almost absent until the nineteenth cen-

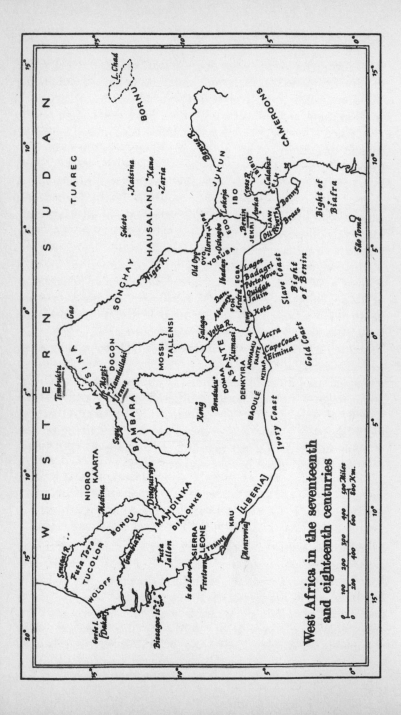

West Africa in the seventeenth
and eighteenth centuries

tury, or merely ancillary to other and much greater conflicts of political and economic power and interest. There was increasing warfare and insecurity in near-coastal West Africa. But to see this merely as the imposed result of slave raiding and 'tribal fighting' is to fall into the old Euro-centric myth of pre-colonial chaos or stagnation. In truth, this warfare should rather be seen as the outcome of power conflicts, state conflicts, which were and are as politically intelligible as those of contemporary Europe.

And where some peoples lost, others undoubtedly gained. 'There is', remarked Pereira in 1506, writing of the long low line of mangrove creeks that leads away south-eastward from the river of Benin, 'no trade in this country, nor anything from which one can make a profit.' So it would remain for another century. The scattered peoples of this water-logged delta of the Niger, mainly Ijaw, had nothing to offer but fish and salt; and no ships crossed the ocean for salt and fish. But when they crossed the ocean to buy captives, the position of the delta singularly changed. For behind the delta villages on their tufts and clumps in the swampland lay the fertile country of the Igbo, one of the most densely populated areas in all Africa.

During the sixteenth century the population of the delta began to grow for a number of reasons. Refugees arrived from the wars of Benin with its tribute-states or rivals. The chance of trade with sea-merchants attracted others. Little states began to take shape at the mouths of the estuary. Gradually these became partners in trade with Europeans. Often their organization took highly original forms, reflecting in this their great diversity of peoples, Ijaw and Jekri and Oron, Igbo and Ibibio, Edo and many more. What became vital to the stability of a Niger delta state was not to find means of expressing and safeguarding ethnic separateness, for any such course would soon have ruined its unity and welfare, but to find ways of knitting different peoples into a new community.

This was skilfully achieved, especially after about 1750. Delta society became something entirely new in West Africa. In these small republics and monarchies the most powerful traditions and

customs of previously separate identity were set aside in favour
of new techniques of union. Foremost among these techniques
was the 'canoe house', a kind of cooperative trading corporation
governed by men of strong political authority, sometimes numbering a few hundred people of varying ethnic origin and social
status, sometimes numbering many thousands. At Brass, Bonny
and elsewhere, at the four main towns of Old Calabar on the
Cross River, there emerged political and commercial systems of
great resilience and originality where, in earlier times, none but
little groups of fishermen had lived.

In this there was both development of potentialities inherent
in Iron Age society, and, by the influence of European trade, a
certain adaptation to new forms that may possibly be called early
capitalist. Traditionally government and trade in the delta had
rested with the authority of lineage groups that were little interested in economic expansion. As elsewhere in Iron Age Africa,
the production of a food surplus had supported the emergence
of many specialist workers who produced not food, or little food,
but useful articles instead. This specialization in the delta had
seen the development of groups concerned with wood-carving,
smithing, salt-making, potting, trading, divining-and-doctoring
and many other useful activities. But these specialists had remained for the most part within the limits of a subsistence economy: they produced for immediate needs and not for
accumulation.

With the eighteenth-century development of the 'canoe
house', however, accumulation became to some extent a deliberate aim in itself. What an enterprising man in the delta would
be likely to attempt now would be to buy or otherwise attract
enough dependants to man a war canoe, a vessel requiring up
to eighty or a hundred rowers and fighters, so as to embark upon
the slave trade in a regular way. 'A potential founder of a canoe
house', G. I. Jones points out, 'could use his wealth to buy more
dependants; and the work of these dependants in turn produced
more wealth to buy still more people. It was a cumulative process . . .' Having thus 'filled his canoe', in the saying of the time,

he would apply for acceptance as the chief of his own canoe house or trading corporation. If the established canoe houses found it in their interest to help him, they would recognize him as a trading chief.

In these and other new ways the city-states of the delta built their commercial strength on strict monopoly of the coastal trade. No doubt there are parallels here with the history of the East Coast city-states, although these dealt mainly in ivory and gold, and not in slaves, and little is known of how they actually did it. In the delta, however, the long Afro-European partnership has left copious records. They show clearly how these ingenious systems worked. Well armed, the delta states saw to it that the inland peoples respected their monopoly. Perfectly capable of uniting among themselves when the need arose, they repeatedly forced the ships' captains and supercargoes of several European nations to pay scheduled taxes, to honour local customs, to moderate prices and generally to treat as equals men like King Pepple and King Eyo and others of their energetic sort. Only the military oppressions of the colonial period changed that.

For their own law and order, and the needs of their commerce, they relied on an adaptation of traditional sanctions. Among the Efik of the Old Calabar towns, for example, the effective government of society became that of Ekpe, the 'Leopard Society'. Men of substance were organized at several levels of authority, commanding the obedience of men of lesser substance, to the point where Ekpe could administer laws and apply punishments, settle disputes, organize business agreements and act as an effective civil power. Reflecting its great concern with trade, Ekpe was not an aristocratic or ancestral organization but one whose several grades of membership could be entered by meeting a fixed scale of payment. Its hierarchy of authority, like those of other such politico-religious associations in Africa, was thus achieved by means closer to those of the City of London than the House of Lords. It was a flexible system designed to meet the needs of a new type of society.

The trouble with these prosperous little states was that their trade was built largely on the sale of captives. 'All that vast number of slaves which the Calabar Blacks sell to all European nations', observed Barbot in the 1680s, and much the same observation would be true for another century and more, 'are not their prisoners-of-war, the greatest part of them being bought by those people from their inland neighbours.' Or when the inland trade faltered, as it sometimes did, the strong 'houses' of Bonny, Brass and other city-states would simply arm their war canoes and send them upstream to kidnap on their own account. Hence it came about that the ending of the slave trade, gradually from 1807 onwards, plunged some of these city-states into a crisis from which they found it extremely hard to emerge. Others among them, seeking new outlets, embarked on plantation economies of their own and began exporting palm oil. But even these, very successful though they often were, failed to escape the general crisis of the region, since by this time the pre-colonial movement of British territorial encroachment had begun.

Elsewhere along the Guinea Coast the Atlantic partnership had varying but more or less comparable effects. Other little states prospered along what Europeans called the Slave Coast—the seaboard of modern Dahomey and Togo—and were active in the seventeenth-century slave trade. 'So diligent are they', Barbot remarked of Ardra and Jakin and their neighbours along this coast during the 1680s, 'that they can deliver a thousand slaves a month.' Though generally tributary to Oyo, they contrived a fair measure of independence until the 1720s when, as we shall see, they became involved in the great rivalries of the inland country.

It was much the same on the Gold Coast, the seaboard of modern Ghana. Here the growing maritime trade was conducted by Europeans, mainly English and Dutch and Danes, through some forty castles established on the coast with local consent and against the payment of a fixed rent; and from all this a dozen coastal states, led by the Ga, Fante and Nzima, drew steady profit. But here too, as we shall see, the balance of power turned not on European influence or presence, but on the varying fortunes of large states and empires in the inland country.

Further westward, beyond the inhospitable coastline of modern Liberia, the good harbours of Sierra Leone were likewise the scene of political development based increasingly on the opportunities of maritime trade, though little disturbed by the affairs of the lands behind them. Beyond these again the northward-trending coast of the modern Republic of Guinea, Gambia, Senegal—the coastland that Europeans came to know as Senegambia*—continued to be dominated by the Mandinka, Serer and Wolof but acquired some special characteristics of its own. These were later to be of great importance, in that Europeans established themselves here on a number of 'sovereign' islands, such as Gorée near modern Dakar.

While these small states along the coast were reinforcing their trade and evolving new means of exploiting their contact with the European sea-merchants, large changes were under way in the lands behind them. There, repeatedly, Iron Age society wrestled with new factors. These were visible in more advanced techniques of government and warfare; in larger commercial ambitions (though still linked mainly to the northern and not the maritime trade); in the drive for greater political power coupled with a need for more abundant revenue from tribute and taxation; and, as seems likely, in the pressures imposed by steadily growing populations. These new factors brought new and widening struggles for supremacy. And these are the struggles that dominate the whole complex story of the forest and near-forest lands of western Africa during the two centuries between about 1650 and 1850.

More and more enclosed within its stifling 'divine kingship', the once prestigious empire of Benin plays surprisingly little part in all this. East of the Niger the Igbo were always too strong for it. And west of Benin there was the Yoruba empire of Oyo, far exceeding it in size and strength. Based on Old Oyo, in open country where their heavy cavalry could operate, the *alafin* and his nobles now had dominion over many of the Yoruba states as

*And which Britain actually ruled as the Province of Senegambia between 1765 and 1783, with a governor at Saint Louis on the mouth of the Senegal River and a deputy on James Island in the estuary of the Gambia.

far southward as the dense forest near the coast, a region where
their power never securely ran. They greatly expanded this power
in the eighteenth century, conquering much of modern Dahomey, where open country comes right down to the sea, and
dealing with Europeans through Porto Novo, which they called
Ajase.

This large and orderly empire, administered by a non-literate
but highly integrated system of chiefs and sub-chiefs, fed by
revenues of tax and tribute from many prosperous farming peoples
and defended by its cavalry as well as by its prestige, formed a
political achievement of impressive size and scope. Little interested either in the slave or firearms trade, at least until the late
eighteenth century, Oyo was able to prevent this commerce from
inflicting much damage in Yorubaland. After enduring for nearly
a century and a half, it fell apart for detailed reasons which are
still in dispute, but which immediately derived from oligarchic
strife and local breakaways. The first clear blow came with Dahomey's successful refusal to pay tribute in 1818. There quickly
followed a damaging war of succession, and then, most fatal of
all, an invasion of Muslim-led cavalry from the new Fulani
empire in Hausaland.

These armies destroyed Oyo influence north of the Niger-
Benue line, detached Ilorin from Oyo loyalty, raided and ravaged
the northern Oyo towns and thrust many thousand Oyo subjects
southward into the refuge of the forest. After 1840, when the
northern invasions were finally halted at Oshogbo, the power of
Old Oyo was gone. Efforts were made to re-establish it from a
new capital further south, also called Oyo, under Alafin Atiba,
'a tall, charming, soft-spoken man, an imaginative conservative',
in Ajayi's words, who was 'a little pathetic in his undying belief
in the force of tradition in a world of revolutionary changes'.
These efforts failed. From 1840 onwards until the British invasion, the lands of the Yoruba were the scene of a continuing
struggle for power between the successor-states of Oyo. In this
Ibadan gradually took a hard-fought lead. And then the British,

profiting from these rivalries, came in with military expeditions
and fastened a new kind of unity on these divided lands.

The inland and coastal country of Dahomey,* west of Yorubaland, was the scene of a comparable struggle for power with
the Fon state based on Abomey, not far from the coast. The Fon
were eventually able to achieve a supremacy which lasted until
the French invasion at the end of the nineteenth century. This
Fon state, as we have noted, had interesting characteristics of its
own. It was organized on strongly military lines, its hierarchy
depending not, as in Oyo, on membership of an aristocracy but
on service to the state. Taking its rise at about the same time as
Oyo, and much stimulated after 1700 by an effort to throw off
Oyo suzerainty, the Fon for a long time remained both tributaries
of Oyo and victims of slave raids by the city-states of the Slave
Coast. Early in the eighteenth century, however, they grew strong
enough to make a bid for independence from Oyo, and to forge
their own partnership with the sea-merchants. Under Agaja
(1708–32) they captured the coastal markets of Ardra (Allada),
Ouidah (Whydah or Fida) and Jakin, and thus brought themselves
into direct contact with the source of firearms.

Agaja seems also to have wanted to cut down the export of
captives from which his own people had suffered: from this time
onwards, at all events, the Slave Coast began ceasing to deserve
its name. Captives continued to be sold abroad, but no longer
in such large quantities as in former times. A regular supply of
firearms, coupled with growing power in the inland country,
brought the Fon to the height of their power under Agonglo
(1790–97) and Gezo VIII (1818–58). They could now at last
turn the tables on their Yoruba overlords. Refusing the tribute
demanded of them by Oyo, they invaded eastward into Yorubaland, making two great raids or Egba country.

West of Dahomey, meanwhile, a third great area of conflict

*Dahomey became a colony of France, but after its independence changed its name
to the Republic of Benin (not to be confused with the Nigerian place of that name).

had opened in the central and coastal lands of modern Ghana. Here again the same internal factors of political and economic rivalry came to a climax in the long and remarkable supremacy of the Asante empire.

Rise of Asante

By about 1650 the gold trade of the Akan forestlands, still facing largely to the northward, was divided among a number of producing and trading groups of Twi-speaking folk. Bono survived in Takyiman. East of it was Domaa. South of Domaa lay a number of fragmentary Akan peoples under tribute to Denkyira, then the strongest among them.

Two lines of development now emerged. After 1700, Denkyira was increasingly submerged by the rising power of Akan groups who called themselves Asante. Secondly, though beginning a little earlier, the south-eastern part of modern Ghana saw the rise of the strong state of Akwamu. Under a famous king called Ansa Sasraku, the Akwamu successively enclosed the Ga cities of the coast, Great and Small Accra, and other states to west and east. By 1702 the king of Akwamu had more than nominal overlordship through some two hundred miles of country and coastland between the Fante state of Agona, his main vassal on the west, and the Slave Coast city-state of Ouidah, his distant though briefly held boundary on the east.

Akwamu maintained its primacy among the states of the Gold Coast and Togo seaboard through nearly half a century. Challenged by the Danes at Christiansborg, soldiers of Akwamu seized the castle and held it for a year, trading under their own flag, until handing back the castle to the Danes in exchange for a smart ransom. Yet their political organization rested on no sufficient principle of unification. So long as the king's armies were loyal and successful, his vassals fulfilled their obligations and paid their tribute. Otherwise they remained little more than a collection of defeated neighbours awaiting their chance of relief. No such empire could long withstand the fissuring pressures of new rivalries. These soon appeared from the inland country. Jostled by the Asante, now nourishing imperial ambitions of their own, another Akan group or rather three groups, the Akim branches of Abuakwa, Bosume and Kotoku, began pushing into Akwamu territory from the north-west. After many battles the Akim made good their penetration. Akwamu by 1731 had practically vanished from the scene.

With Asante, though, the story is notably different. Emerging in the latter part of the seventeenth century, the Asante Union deserved its name. It was far more than a collection of defeated neighbours, though in course of later expansion it became this as well. After 1700 the Asante turned themselves into a group of peoples so closely self-identified that they were at once called a nation by European observers, and became sufficiently powerful and tightly organized to rule the greater part of modern Ghana for nearly two centuries.

Like the divine kingship of the old Mesopotamian legends, the mystical bond of the Asante groups of the Akan or Twi-speaking people of central Ghana 'came down from heaven'. This happened when the priest Anokye caused the Golden Stool of Asante to alight gently upon the knees of King Osei Tutu. The Stool became the sacred object which symbolized not only the union of separate traditional groups and loyalties but also the guarantee of their united wealth and welfare. So long as the Golden Stool was safe, its adherents would prosper: but the condition of this safety was unity, and it was precisely the close-knit union of these groups which most distinguished them from their neighbours. Beyond this legend there is the evidence, misty and yet persuasive, of a conscious effort to weld together those who would otherwise, if left apart, have fallen to the continued exploitation of their more distant neighbours, Denkyira or Domaa. Thus it is known that Osei Tutu enacted laws by which all previous and separate traditions must be forgotten, or at any rate consigned to silence.

With these laws of 'common citizenship' every man of the Asante Union, publicly at least, was to place loyalty to the Golden Stool above all else.

Behind this legend there lay in any case a network of new commercial interests. Those chiefly families who led the Asante Union appear to have come from country to the south. Perhaps they had looked for new land with which to grow new crops. Trans-Atlantic maize, sweet potatoes and pineapples were now spreading through West Africa with increasing fruitfulness. Or perhaps they had wished to fasten on the profits of the gold trade. Undoubtedly the gold trade became central to their polity. It is even reasonable to see in the Golden Stool a sort of livery or corporation badge of loyalty and function in this trade. So long as the Asante held the upper hand over the gold trade, they would prosper, and the condition of their holding it, quite certainly, was their unity of action.

Facts about the Asante Union begin to become available around 1700, thanks largely to the survival of records made by the English and Dutch trading companies along the Gold Coast. Putting these together with Asante tradition, it seems clear that Osei Tutu died at an advanced age in about 1712, having completed the forging of Asante groups into a nation and successfully thrown off the overlordship of Denkyira. Under Opoko Ware (1720–50) and his successors, Asante became the greatest power in the central forestlands, dominating an area as large or even larger than modern Ghana, and trading extensively with the Western Sudan as well as with the Dutch at Elmina and the English at Cape Coast. Only with the reign of Osei Tutu Kwame (c. 1801–24) did the European element enter in any large degree into Asante strategy and foreign policy. But with the second half of the nineteenth century, this European element came gradually to overshadow the future and led, eventually, to British conquest. *

---

*For all this, see the classic and indispensable study in Ivor Wilks, *Asante in the Nineteenth Century*, Cambridge, 1975.

The European cloud was at first a small one on the ocean skyline. In 1637 the great Portuguese castle at Elmina had passed into Dutch hands. Whether by receiving rent from the Dutch for Elmina's ground, or merely by close economic relations, the king of Denkyira had taken the Dutch as his commercial partners. Now this partnership passed to Asante with its defeat of Denkyira after 1700. From now onwards the Dutch were dependent on Asante, not Denkyira, and so came to regard Asante as their principal commercial ally. But their English neighbours at Cape Coast, by contrast, were dependent on the Fante, a coastal group of the Akan who were unwilling to admit their vassalship to Asante. In 1805 the Asante came down with their armies to subject the Fante. In this they easily succeeded. Pursuing their objective, Asante regiments attacked the little English fort at Abora under the walls of which a number of Fante fugitives had taken shelter. This tough skirmish had no further violent results, however, since the English were far too weak to contrive any (even if they had then wished to, which they did not), while the Asante merely insisted on recognition of their coastal sovereignty. Later on the clash was to repeat itself in different circumstances. An imperialist Britain would invade Asante and bring the greater part of that state within colonial control.

Asante upheld its widespread peace and power for nearly two centuries. Safe and busy trading trails went out westward through Bonduku and Kong to the cities of the Middle and Upper Niger, eastward through Salaga to Hausaland, southward to the Europeans on the coast; and all these made Kumasi, the capital established 'under the shade of the *kuma* tree', into a market of far-reaching influence and a place of majesty and sure protection. When European agents were allowed to come here—and nine of them came in 1817–20, of whom five have left accounts of what they saw and heard—they were impressed by the king's liberal trading policies, the city's comfortable urban spread and the agreeable condition of the people there.

'The rubble and offal of each house', noted Bowdich in 1817, 'was burnt every morning at the back of the streets, and the inhabitants were as nice and cleanly in their dwellings as in their persons', a comment that could then have been made with some difficulty of most of the big cities of Europe. Many caravans arrived and left for distant markets. Many visitors came from still more distant countries. A record of 1815, for example, shows a Muslim dignitary as having arrived from Arabia with two companions who left for Timbuktu and Tripoli in the following year, while the dignitary himself returned to Mecca.

These Muslims who came to Kumasi did not convert the Asantehene and his court, though some of them seem to have tried their hand at doing so. They had freedom to worship as they pleased, and were not without a certain local power, being in command of most of the distributive trades or in service as clerks to the royal administration. A European visitor in 1824 even found that some of their leading men 'enjoyed rank at court, or were invested with administrative powers, entitling them even to a voice in the senate'. The head of the king's civil service, the Gyaasehene, employed a Muslim secretary who was literate in Arabic, while other such men served on government staffs in distant provinces, helped to draw up treaties and maintain political records and generally formed the skeleton of a literate chancery system.

In these and other ways the Asante empire formed another and outstanding example of the gradual transition of Iron Age political systems, during the eighteenth and nineteenth centuries, to more centralized, modern and expansive forms of power and organization. There is much in this to recall the earlier experience of the centralized states of the Western Sudan. As early as the reign of Osei Kwadwo (1764–77) there were administrative innovations which opened the way to greater central authority through the growth of the king's civil service. Enterprising men now began to be appointed by the king to posts of commercial, financial and political authority, on the basis of good and efficient service and not by virtue of their birth into chiefly families. If this bureaucracy affected most of the peasants and villagers of the empire very little, it was nonetheless increasingly influential at certain decisive points. Household troops recruited from enslaved captives or mercenaries, and designed to bolster the king's power against his chiefs and governors, became part of this centralizing apparatus by as early as the reign of Osei Bonsu at the beginning of the nineteenth century. So did eunuch officials. A militia called the Ankobia was kept for special service in the capital—a city of some 40,000 inhabitants by the early nineteenth century—and its control reserved for appointed men who could be relied upon, if the need arose, to act against hereditary chiefs. Not only Muslim Sudanese, but also Christian Europeans, were taken into royal employment. Facing British invasion in the 1870s, the Asantehene engaged a German or Dane called Neilsen to raise and train Hausa troops for his army. Another early 'expatriate technician' was a Frenchman called Bonnat, co-governor of a province. A third was a Scots-American.

By the nineteenth century, Wilks tells us, 'the central government had assumed control of a wide range of activities'.* Among these was a state trading organization maintained by the king alongside the 'private sector' in trade and mining. Down to 1873, in Casely Hayford's words, 'a constant stream of Ashanti traders might be seen daily wending their way to the coast and back again . . . The trade chiefs would in due course render a faithful account to the king's stewards, being allowed to retain a fair portion of the profits.' Officials were kept at royal expense, paid for their services and sometimes given an old-age pension. Foreign affairs and other state business were administered by strong central control, while communications were upheld throughout the far-flung empire by a rapid system of messengers across long miles of road. The king in Kumasi, Bonnat could observe, 'knows each day what is happening in the most humble villages of his empire. From all sides he receives reports and minute details . . . [while] conversely, day and night, the orders of the king are despatched in all directions.'

*I. Wilks: Seminar paper (Legon) on 'Aspects of Bureaucratization in Ashanti', June, 1965.

Like Oyo before it, the Asante empire had trouble with its constituent populations. Around 1750 a breakaway group of Akan marched westward into the inland country of the Ivory Coast, there to found a state under their new name, the Baoulé. Distant peoples tended to revolt or disobey. More important, the early Asante towns established around Kumasi in the late seventeenth century retained a largely autonomous character, so that 'the king's administration', Wilks explains, 'possessed no jurisdiction within the territories of the chiefs of Bekwai, Juaben, Kokofu, Nsuta and Mampong'. Such weaknesses as these counted for much during British invasion. Even so, the empire remained great and powerful throughout most of the nineteenth century. Only the superior firepower and military organization of the British were able to subdue and finally destroy it.

Peasants and Prophets

While Oyo and Asante gathered strength and grew into states and empires, the Western Sudan entered a long period of rebellion and structural change.

Under Moroccan rulers the men of Timbuktu lost their old freedom of action and enterprise. Their city dwindled in wealth and prestige. Their trade declined. Their schools of learning shone no longer as in the days of Ahmad Baba and his contemporaries of the sixteenth and early seventeenth centuries. When Europeans came here two hundred years later they would be astonished that so poor a city could ever have enjoyed so glittering a reputation. The old Songhay capital of Gao suffered even more from Moroccan invasion and occupation. This once dynamic trading centre, where the emperor Askia Muhammad had his tomb, fell to little more than a provincial market-village, dusty and ill-considered, easily forgotten. Jenne, the third of the great Middle Niger cities, remained important, as the northern terminal for much of the trade of the forest lands, but slowly fell away in size and wealth.

This shrinking of the cities was fatal to any hope of remaking the power of the Songhay empire. For more than a century they had given Songhay its motive power and cohesiveness. Once they were lost, the empire sundered into pieces. The long-service soldiers of the Askia melted away, returning to their villages or taking service with other lords. The careful edifice of bureaucratic control vanished from the scene. In tune with this collapse the early seventeenth century saw the rebellion of tributary peoples of the empire. Groups thrust into servile status by the lords of Songhay threw off their bonds. There came a time of reassertion for all those peasant folk, generally hostile to the cities and to Islam, who had felt the pressure of Songhay exploitation in wide regions lying on both sides of the Niger.

One by one the gates of urban order and authority were forced or smashed. Out of the northern oases there came the lean Tuareg of the Sahara, battering at Gao and Timbuktu, taking their revenge on the power which had long subdued them or held them at bay. Out of the southern lands, the grasslands marked by their lofty baobab trees, there pressed other riders bent on the same looting purpose, Mossi and Dogon and Bambara and their like, men who had long awaited their moment and seized it now with fury and the glint of spears. Discouraged and defeated, the Moroccans in the cities lost all heart for further conquest, and far away in Marrakesh and Fez, were soon forgotten or abandoned to their fate. Nothing remained of Songhay power but a few centres of resistance in the south from whence, now and then, desperate raids were launched upon what yet remained of Moroccan military strength.

But gradually, from all this tumult and dismay, a new pattern began to emerge. Country folk transformed themselves from raiders into settlers. Having done so, some of them borrowed Songhay traditions and techniques of central government, and began, after their own fragmented fashion, to build new systems of non-Muslim law and order. Among these were Bambara peasants who lived along the Niger west of Timbuktu. Not long after 1600 these farmers founded new settlements beside the river west of

Jenne and the Niger lakes. Towards 1650 we hear of them being
led by an enterprising chief called Kaladian, probably a historical
figure though possibly the traditional name for several 'founding
heroes'; and Kaladian reigns until about 1680, founding a little
state that is based on the river port of Segu. From here Kaladian
sends expeditions against neighbouring folk, obliging them to pay
tribute in the manner of the old empire. But this early Bambara
'empire' has no systematic framework of authority to sustain it,
and disappears with Kaladian's death.

Yet the process continues. In about 1712 the little Bambara
state of Segu comes under the rule of another bold and ambitious
leader who is certainly an historical figure, the famous Mamari
Kulibaly, Mamari the Biton, the Commander, at first the captain
of a raiding band but soon a king of substance. Mamari outwits
or outfights his rivals and enemies, and lays far stronger political
foundations in Segu. It is not for nothing that he has his military
title. He borrows defensive techniques from Songhay tradition,
forms a long-service army several thousand strong, adds a long-
service 'navy' of canoes to patrol the Niger, using for these purposes men who have been captured in war and thus reduced to
servile status.

With these forces Mamari the Commander challenges and
defeats his close neighbours—Soninke, Fulani, Mossi and others. In 1730 he beats back an invasion by the Muslim king of
Kong, a southern trading state which no doubt disliked this Bambara interference with ancient Muslim channels of trade and
influence. Mamari also attacks far down river and briefly holds
Timbuktu. He makes the little state of Segu into a miniature
successor-empire of Songhay along the river. In 1753, smarting
under his tough rule and monopoly of power, a section of his
subjects quit Segu and march north-westward, forming another
Bambara state in Kaarta and Nioro, the old homelands of ancient
Ghana.

Both of these Bambara states remained important in their region until the middle of the nineteenth century. But their history
was a troubled one. After Mamari's death in 1755 there followed

eleven years of swashbuckling chaos under the rule of one usurping general after another. Then Ngolo Diara seized the throne in 1766, put an end to army ambitions, and ruled over a reconstituted state until 1795. Two years after Ngolo Diara's death a solitary Scottish traveller made his way to the city of Segu through many hostile boundaries and not unreasonable suspicions, and revealed by what he found that Ngolo Diara's reign had done much to regain the old prosperity of the Middle Niger towns. Mungo Park found Segu with a population of about 30,000, as he thought, inhabiting four residential quarters composed of clay-built houses of one or two storeys. 'The view of this extensive city,' he wrote, 'the numerous canoes upon the river, the crowded population, and the cultivated state of the surrounding countryside, formed altogether a prospect of civilization and magnificence which I little expected to find in the bosom of Africa.'

Elsewhere, the accent on reconstruction in the Western Sudan had once more become specifically Muslim. There now begins a long attempt, or series of attempts, to rebuild once more a grand Muslim polity which is aimed at bringing the whole of this vast region, from the Atlantic to the Nile, within the borders of Islamic law and order and thus recovering the power and splendour of the old Western Caliphate. For a hundred and fifty years this vision will glow with varying success and brilliance. It will inspire one bold enterprise after another, sometimes with high success and at other times with none. Often unleashing bitter warfare, always posing the conflict between Islam and the traditional religions of West Africa, now with one people in the ascendant and now with another, the Muslim effort is driven and led by a long succession of memorable leaders from the early imams of the far west of the Sudan, almost within scent and hearing of the broad Atlantic, to the Mahdi of the Nile and of the wastes of Kordofan.

The earliest exponents of Muslim revival came from an unexpected quarter. They were Fulani and other cattle-driving folk who had given up their old religion together with their nomadic habits, had settled in towns and accepted Islam and had acquired

chiefs and political ambitions. Profoundly influenced by the
Islam of the western Arabized Berbers which had reached them
by steady infiltration through Mauretania after the fifteenth century, they set out to build new Muslim states. The first of these
was situated in the hills of Futa Jallon, near the middle of the
modern republic of Guinea, and was established in about 1725
by a mixture of Muslim peoples under Fulani leadership. These
subdued the local Dialonke, who were Mande-speaking farmers,
and ruled on military and theocratic lines. They drew their chiefs,
or *almamys*, from two senior families, the Alfa and the Sori, and
provided for the imposition of armed service on men who served
as their *mujahiddin*, their warriors of Islam. Other groups also
met this call to power through religious revolution. A second
imamate was founded in 1776 in Futa Toro along the south bank
of the Senegal. This was by a Tucolor* group called the Torobé.
They defeated the ruling king of the old Denianke line (itself
founded in 1559 after an earlier Fulani-Mandinka invasion), and
set their leader, Suleiman Ba, in his place. At about the same
time a third Fulani imamate emerged in Bondu, the grassland
plains which lie along the modern frontiers of Senegal and Mali.

   Something of the depth of this Muslim revival can be glimpsed
from the memoirs of Mungo Park, who passed through the imamate of Bondu at the end of the eighteenth century. He speaks of
the country's growing trade and farming production, but also of
its attitudes of tolerance. 'Religious persecution', he says, 'is not
known among them, nor is it necessary; for the system of Muhammad is made to extend itself by means more abundantly
efficacious. By establishing small schools in different towns,
where many of the pagan as well as Muhammadan children are
taught to read the Quran, and instructed in the tenets of the
Prophet, the Muhammadan priests fix a bias on the minds, and
form the character of the young disciples, which no accidents of
life can every afterwards remove or alter. Many of these little
schools I visited in my progress through the country, and observed

---

*Takrur in Arabic; these people were and are in fact Fulani.

with pleasure the great docility and submissive deportment of the children . . .'

With this Muslim schooling of the countryside there now developed, as it would seem, a gradual blurring of the sharp edge of conflict between Muslim towns and non-Muslim countryside, so that later on, during the nineteenth century, it was to become possible for Muslim leaders to raise the religious loyalty of peasants who must often have refused it in the past. The sociology of all this will be better explained as scholars now visit the libraries of the devout, and study the many thousands of documents, some old and some new, which are there collected and preserved. Even at this stage of knowledge, however, a few points stand out clearly.

Penetrating the countryside, Muslim missionaries and teachers gave Islam a broader base. In doing this they prepared the way for a change in their teachings. There occurred a certain process of democratization. The older attitudes had contained an element of exclusiveness well suited to Dyula traders and other Muslim groups who travelled the length and breadth of West Africa; or to city-merchants and rulers for whom Islam offered an ideological basis, both for central government in multi-ethnic states and for the techniques of trade and credit. Relatively new Muslim states like Kong, for example, were built on a hierarchy of privilege that was buttressed by Islam, and from which the rank-and-file were distanced if not actually excluded. Particular forms of West African Islam tended to strengthen these tendencies towards social rigidity. Taking over the characteristically African concept of spiritual power vested in a particular person—priest or wizard or soothsayer—Muslim leaders sometimes acquired a mystic authority denied to them by the orthodox tenets of Islam. After the manner of Sunni Ali of Songhay, for example, they tended to be revered as magicians even more than as Muslims. Hence the very special—and often highly privileged—position of Muslim marabouts, as they are called, in certain regions of West Africa, notably Senegal.

Perhaps the most interesting of these changes within West

African Islam was the steady political eclipse of the Quadiriyya
brotherhood—traditionally conservative, hierarchical and con-
temptuous of the heathen—by the Tijaniyya, a new brotherhood
which became an 'Islam for the poor'. Here too West Africa
worked its own pattern into ideas whose original content had
been very different. The Tijaniyya was founded as a proselytizing
movement by a North African teacher, Ahmad al-Tijani (1737–
1815), who was himself no revolutionary. Transplanted to the
Western Sudan, however, the Tijaniyya was to supply the religious means *par excellence* whereby the later Muslim revolutions
of the nineteenth century were carried through. It was to be the
instrument for conversion of many peoples of the countryside
hitherto inimical to the 'Islam of the towns'.

Yet the reforming movement, perhaps needless to say, was
never a simple single-stranded thing. Men's motives were as
mixed as in other movements of reform in other lands. Towards
1800, when the influence of religious change was present in one
form or another right across the Western Sudan from the Futa
Toro to the Hausa states, Uthman dan Fodio led a largely Fulani
movement of revolt against the rulers of Hausaland.* Like his
companions, Uthman was a member of the Qadiriyya brotherhood, not the Tijaniyya, the latter wielding influence in the
Western Sudan only after the rise of its caliph, Haj Umar Tall,
in the 1840s. Here there were many elements, whether of Muslim
revival, social reform or political ambition. Yet it is worth noting
that Uthman's writings and those of his companions placed great
importance on the reform of government and the end of administrative abuse as practised, at least according to Fulani accusa-
tions, by the Hausa kings. And the success of Uthman's revolt
rested to some extent on his achievement in winning support
from many Hausa people. He and his companions preached
against autocracy, political brutality, everyday injustice. They
denounced the 'collecting of concubines and fine clothes and

Fodyo or *fudi* means a senior grade of Muslim teacher in the language of the Fulani.

horses that run in the towns, not on the battlefields, and the devouring of the gifts of influence, booty and bribery'. They set themselves against bad rulers 'whose purpose is the ruling of countries and peoples in order to obtain delights and acquire rank . . .' They wished, on the contrary, to rule by the principles and teachings of the great Islamic tradition of the Rightly Guided Caliphate; and there was always in their attitudes, at least in the beginning, a powerful note of personal abnegation and moral regeneration. This note is repeatedly struck in their early writings.

But having acquired power, these Fulani reformers in Hausaland were faced with the practical problems of wielding it. They stepped into the place of the Hausa kings and, in so doing, were led to compromise between their ideals and the fruits of office. Religiously inspired revolution could demolish an unpopular and stagnant polity; lacking any new *material* policies, it found the task of building a better social structure altogether another problem. Dissension over the land distribution among Fulani leaders quickly followed; and Uthman's son Muhammad Bello, who became the Amir al-Mu'minin of Sokoto, had to impose his imperial authority by force of arms over dissident leaders like 'Abd al-Salam. Before long the new Fulani hierarchy had taken over the administrative system of their Habe-Hausa predecessors. But they had also been driven, like other usurpers and conquerors elsewhere, to corrupting the representative elements of the system they had seized into something very near autocracy.

There was perhaps nothing else they could do within the limits of their situation. Sultan Bello and his peers had to deal with acute and pressing rivalries among the 'family groups' which had led and largely formed the *jihad*. These 'standard bearers' demanded land and power. Necessarily they were given both. In receiving them they deepened the social divisions of Hausaland. Hausa rule had evolved in some four centuries of state and city government into a form of constitutional monarchy that was hedged about with many checks and balances. The Hausa *sarki*, or king, could act only when assured of a sufficient consensus of his nobles and officials. This was not democracy; but it was certainly not absolutism. In a city-state like Zaria the king's political control was limited by the power of hereditary officials, the latter being in turn limited by the parallel power of appointed officials. In the end the king was sovereign; meanwhile, he had to move in everyday affairs with studious care for the equilibrium of a system of which he was also, in the end, only the elected head. Perhaps the position of Elizabeth I of England, at any rate in relation to her nobles and officials, had been not so very different.

Yet the Fulani conquerors, having to impose their minority rule upon this system, could have no such delicate regard for precedent and balance. The exercise of new possession carried its own imperatives. 'After Fulani conquest,' M. G. Smith has explained, 'the government of Zaria changed from a constitutional monarchy to a qualified absolutism'; and this absolutism, at Zaria as elsewhere among the conquered Hausa states, 'grew and persisted as a system, although its personnel changed with each reign as an effect of dynastic rivalry'.

Once again one may note the failure of Islam's utopian illusion. The *mujahiddin* of Uthman and his standard bearers might in their better moments wish for a new social and religious equality such as could restore the Rightly Guided Caliphate of legendary times, Abbasid times, or even the 'golden age' of the Western Caliphate in the Sudan. Reality was different. Great though its civic achievements had often been, that 'golden age' of Mali, Kanem and Songhay had not rested on a growing equality between rich and poor, weak and strong. On the contrary, it had rested on a growing inequality; and this was the intensified stratification of society between rulers and ruled, bond and free, poor and privileged, out of which the political and military triumphs of the past had come. If the Hausa rulers had made themselves oppressive to ordinary folk, forming armies, building palaces, exacting labour services, they had done so only in the wake of

الحمد لله والصلاة والسلام على رسول الله

مـن عبد الله تعالى عمر بن محمد الامير فكائمي
المعظمة الاجل الأ عظم . الأعز الأكرم الا كمحه امير
قومه . ، وما لك زمام ارضه . عمنا السلطان معلا لا
ابر التقى محمد يقرأ المرحوم السلام الشام ورحمت
الله تعالى وبركاته اما بعد وأما واصل اليـك
كتابنا هذا فاننا نعلمك به ابراننا ابا بكر
قد اعلمنا بانقطاع التنازي بينه وبيى وزبرك
صاحب كتا فم فى شار ايدو والتى بهمنا
وبينكم وجار ثبنت علم ما توافقنا عليه ورضيت
به . فقد استقام الامر ورجع السير الراصلـه
ولا يكمر من جهتنا ار شا . الله تعالى الا تخـيم
وتأكيد العهد والا مانة على الوجه السابق
هذا ما اعلمتك به و بقنا الله وابا كم على
رعاية العهد والميثاق يوم يوم السفر . والتداو .
يباه اجر الثنى على الاطلاو . سيد نا محمـد
عليه صلاة الفلف التداو . اميرن والسلام

A letter from the chancery correspondence of Sultan Amin of Bornu, writing on a boundary dispute to his neighbour, Sultan Mu'azz of Sokoto, about 1877–80.

their great exemplars of the Western Caliphate, the *askias* of Songhay and *mais* of Kanem-Bornu. Herein lay the essential and enduring contradiction of this Muslim revival: in their best ideals, and in their genuine reformism wherever this existed, the revivers of Islam necessarily set themselves against the very patterns of society which provided Islam with its strength.

Even so, the new power in Hausaland offered impressive evidence of what may happen when philosopher-kings ascend the throne, and it was here that the *mujaddidin*, the revivers of Islam,* reached their zenith of intellectual distinction. When the British explorer Clapperton had audience of Sultan Bello it was no accident that he found the latter reading Euclid in Arabic, and was then engaged in a difficult discussion on the merits of Christianity. These new rulers in Hausaland were scholars of stature, eager to reform abuse and render justice. To Uthman, his brother Abdullah and his son Muhammad Bello are attributed some 258 books and essays on a variety of theoretical and practical

*As distinct from the *mujahiddin*, the warriors of Islam.

subjects, while the chancery correspondence between Sultan Bello and his rival of Bornu, Shehu Muhammad al-Amin, bears witness to the high level of literate education in which these men were trained.

Their system of training was far from merely local or provincial. It rested on practices of Islamic learning that were centuries old. F. H. El Masri has described it: 'After having attained a basic knowledge of religion, reading and writing in boyhood, the aspirant scholar (talib) would then travel about to learned men and stay with them till he had perfected with each the particular science in which that scholar had gained his fame; having completed his studies to the satisfaction of a master, he would then be given a license (ijaza) to teach the subject he had been taught, on the authority of the master. In this way the talib would go round to collect ijazas and thus establish fame as a recognized scholar. This process would not normally cease at a certain stage or age, for whenever a scholar was to be found, who had excelled himself in a branch of knowledge no matter whether a local man or a foreigner, others would go to study under him.'

Cities like Sokoto now offered, in this widening community of religious reform and scholarship, this bodying forth of a new Dar al-Islam,* a magnet of attraction for every man who shared their ideals and wished to emulate their distinction. One such arrived in 1826, coming from Mecca, a Tucolor scholar named Umar bin-Said. Newly appointed caliph of the Tijaniyya brotherhood in the Western Sudan, al-Hajj Umar was to build himself a career on the grand scale. Yet he took his time. He settled in Sokoto and lived there for eleven years, playing some part in public affairs and marrying, among other wives, a daughter of Sultan Bello's. In 1837, pursuing his slow-maturing plans, he

*Muslim jurists had from early times divided the world into two contrasting regions. The first of these is the Dar al-Islam, where Muslims are full citizens and non-Muslims tolerated only as tributaries or visitors. The second is the Dar al-Harb, the Home of War, where Muslims are not in the ascendant and against which they are supposed to be in a state of permanent war. Medieval Christianity had of course much the same view of the world as divided between Christendom and Heathendom.

went to live in Futa Jallon a thousand miles to the west. And still he waited. Only in 1848 did he launch his *jihad* from Dinguiraye in Upper Guinea, where he had formed a small imamate. But then his success was rapid and far-reaching. Leaving his son Habibu (by Sultan Bello's daughter) in command of his little imamate at Dinguiraye, Umar marched northward with his *mujahiddin*, his warriors of Islam, and overthrew the Bambara rulers of Kaarta and Nioro. In 1861 he took Segu from the Bambara successor of King Ngolo, and established there his son Ahmadu at the head of another imamate.

In mastering Segu, however, Umar was launched upon a career of political unification which could take no account of the precept that Muslim must not war on Muslim. Down river from Segu lay the potent little Islamic state of Hamdullahi ('God Be Praised'). Founded by one of Uthman dan Fodio's followers after 1805, and based principally on Fulani people of the torrid grasslands to the south of the great Niger Bend, this Massina state had evolved through half a century of strong Muslim rule into a theocratic imamate of considerable social achievement. In 1862, ruthlessly moving for power in the whole country of the Middle Niger, Umar struck at this state and destroyed it, only to be killed himself, two years later, during an expedition against the people of the Bandiagara hills. For a while, the empire he had built survived him. His son Ahmadu, though with many difficulties and facing many revolts, remained in substantial control of Segu, Kaarta, Nioro and Dinguiraye.

Yet the great vision of social and religious reform and unification had sadly faded by now. Though originating in that vision, the Tucolor system had become a family business incapable of maintaining the wide popular appeal from which its military strength had sprung. More and more, the wars for Islam degenerated into mere slaving raids and forays after plunder. Perhaps it might have been otherwise in less critical times. As it was, the Muslim revival now clashed fatally with a new power that was to sweep everything before it. As early as 1856 al-Hajj Umar's

Some West African peoples have long written their languages in an Arabic script. This is from a late fragment of local history written in Kotoko, a language of Chad, in about 1900.

troops had skirmished with a French garrison, thrust far forward from its base on the Atlantic coast, at Medina on the Upper Senegal River. Gradually the French now edged their way eastward into the Sudan. In 1890 they forced their way into Segu itself. Soon they had completed the subjection of the Tucolor system and of all rival systems, while the British, marching northward from the Nigerian coast, did the same a few years later in the lands of the Sokoto empire.

Given the balance of wealth, arms and experience of war, this would no doubt have come about in any case. Yet internecine quarrels greatly helped to open the gates of the Sudan. And this characteristic failure, this poverty of political achievement when compared with moral and religious aspiration, reappeared in the Eastern Sudan with the comparable reforming movement of the Mahdi Muhammad Ahmad ibn 'Abdullah. There, true enough, the circumstances were somewhat different. The Mahdia or Muslim Reformation in the Eastern Sudan began in 1881 after a long period of Turco-Egyptian rule aggravated by British and other foreign interventions. In a sense which was not true in the Western Sudan, where no such outside rule had yet existed but for the brief Moroccan interlude after 1591, the Mahdi was also 'Abu'l-Istiqlal, the Father of Independence.

Yet the Mahdi and his companions were no less concerned

with religious and moral renewal than their forerunners in the Western Sudan. And Muhammad Ahmad went further than other reformers—than Uthman dan Fodio or Umar bin-Said or Muhammad al-Wahab in Arabia—precisely in that he declared himself the Mahdi, the Appointed of God; and his vision was correspondingly wider than theirs. He saw himself as the central figure in a reformed and united Dar al-Islam that should embrace the whole of West as well as North Africa. His trouble came in translating this highly political vision—and what, after all, could have seemed more worthy of achievement than the unification of the African Muslim world?—into political practice, especially at a time when European imperialism had already started on its road to conquest.

Looking back on these grand enterprises, one may well think that the Mahdi and his near-contemporaries in the rest of the Sudan were above all unfortunate in their time. Much misunderstood or calumniated in Christian European records, they were undoubtedly men of outstanding vision and memorable purpose. Their tragedy was that they came too late to re-establish the wide Islamic systems of the medieval world, and yet too early to reconstruct any large region of Africa upon a scheme of rational multi-ethnic union. Their vision and their purpose foundered in the oncoming disaster of European invasion.

East Africa: After the Portuguese

Having wrecked the Afro-Asian trading system of the Indian Ocean during the sixteenth century, the Portuguese had made some effort to restore it to their own advantage. In this they failed and were quickly superseded by the Dutch. But the Dutch bothered not at all with East Africa or its trade, finding the Golden East more profitably attractive. From these events there followed two developments along the coast in the eighteenth century.

The first was a dwindling or vanishing of Portuguese garrisons

and settlements. The effort of those that remained was reduced
to occasional expeditions by little groups of armed settlers far up
the Zambezi or along the Mozambique seaboard, while most of
the gold-bearing country of the central plateau remained, as before, beyond their reach. Stiffly encased within a monopolist
system directed from Lisbon by way of viceroys in Goa, the
governors and captains in Africa had a care for little more than
the fortunes they could hope to make during the brief periods of
appointment they had bought, usually for three years. Those who
served in lesser positions understandably followed suit. Indifference and boredom reigned over all. English naval visitors at
Mozambique Island in 1812 found themselves greeted at the
governor's residence 'by the clashing of billiard balls and the
confused clamour of contending voices, so that we at first took
it to be a tavern or gambling house'. But the governor, they were
told, had gathered a fortune worth £80,000, a vast sum in those
days.

The second development, partly a product of the first, brought
a measure of African recovery in the wake of Portuguese indi-
gence. This was especially the case among the cities of the Somali
and Kenya (northern Swahili) coastline. These successfully
evicted their Portuguese garrisons and destroyed any further obligation to pay tribute to the Portuguese, having for these purposes
allied themselves at the end of the seventeenth century with Arab
fellow-Muslims from Oman and Muscat in southern Arabia.
There would now be at least a partial reforging of old commercial
ties with countries beyond the Indian Ocean. This was the period
of partial recovery when the northern Swahili cities, and notably
Lamu, developed the writing of their eloquent and epic literature
in ki-Swahili written with a modified Arabic script.

Along the coast south of Mombasa the recovery was slower.
At Mombasa itself the Portuguese continued to garrison their fine
castle of Fort Jesus until 1728. Then they were at last ousted in
the wake of many troubles, and, after an abortive effort in 1729,
were never again able to return. Since their early days of piracy

they had done little here but maintain themselves and exact such tribute as they could. An English visitor in 1667 had found it 'a place of no great traffic . . . while the inhabitants are so squeezed perpetually by the governor that they seldom or never come to be worth anything of an estate. Nor are they suffered to trade . . . without the governor's licence, which to be sure is never given whenever he can get anything by using it himself.' Yet the people of Mombasa seem otherwise to have been left to their own devices, and the city remained a lively centre of Swahili culture.

The old and once prosperous entrepôt of Kisimani on Mafia Island, off the Tanganyika coast, still existed in the sixteenth century and was then, as often before, a dependency of Kilwa. Natural disaster in the shape of ocean encroachment brought its life to an end not long after that. Nowadays there is nothing to be seen there but the fragments of a few mosques and other buildings and a scattering of broken Persian and Chinese pottery along the beach. Nearby on Juani Island, lying a little to seaward along the coral-paved ocean shelf on which these islands rise, a new town called Kua appeared in the seventeenth or early eighteenth century. Very probably based on older but more humble foundations, Kua became a small but well-built city of some importance until it was ruined, around 1822, by Sakalava raiders from Madagascar.

As at Kua, the ruins of Kilwa Kisiwani—Kilwa of the Island—show that there was still enough wealth and power in the old coastal trade after 1700 to allow the construction of mosques, merchants' houses and quite extensive royal quarters. Compared with the earlier buildings, however, these are relatively crude: the mosques have lost much of their fine decoration in carved coral, while there is little in the palace or residential structures to indicate the sophisticated comfort of medieval Kilwa. Life had evidently lost its old self-confidence of earlier days. The trading routes were sorely fouled or altogether cut, and Kilwa had suffered at least one highly damaging raid by people from the interior.

Little or no gold came any more from the distant mines. Such Chinese wares as continued to arrive were only of the cheapest kind.

To complete this decline, slave trading and raiding now became an important part of East Coast commerce. In earlier times, so far as all the evidence can show, slaving had never been more than a minor aspect of East African trade. Now it vastly expanded. The Portuguese turned for slaves to the East as well as the West Coast. Others followed them. As early as 1754 a French captain was buying captives in the Kilwa region both for use in the Mascarene Islands, Mauritius and Bourbon (later renamed Réunion), and for transport to Saint Domingue (afterwards Haiti) in the Caribbean. In 1776 another Frenchman even concluded a treaty with the sultan of Kilwa, a much reduced monarch when compared with his forebears. This treaty allowed the French an exclusive right to purchase slaves from Kilwa as well as to build a fort there if they wished. But the fort was never built, and the whole seaboard fell to dominant British naval influence after the Napoleonic wars. Early in the nineteenth century, Portuguese slave exports from the Mozambique coast were running at the rate of about 10,000 a year, very much higher than in any previous period.

A much heavier curse of slaving also developed along the central and northern sectors of the Swahili coast. This followed the growing commercial enterprise of the Arabs from Oman and Muscat. Their Imam Seyyid Said, operating with a small but well-found naval force from his Arabian capital of Muscat, now brought the more important harbours of the coast under his tributary control, claiming a right derived from the Omani share in expelling the Portuguese a century earlier. A man of energy and vision, Said set out to rebuild the old Indian Ocean connection between Africa, Arabia, India and the Far East. With this he had good success, and in 1840 took the bold and intelligent step of transferring his court from sun-scorched Muscat to the pleasant climate of Zanzibar.

By this time Zanzibar was already the greatest slaving port on the whole East Coast, far eclipsing any in Mozambique. A British estimate of 1839 put the total number of slaves who were sold there every year at between 40,000 and 45,000. Sayyid Said pushed it higher. Ceaselessly energetic, he made Zanzibar into the world's biggest producer of cloves, a spice that was sure of a good sale in several continents. Local labour proving insufficient for the new clove plantations, the Zanzibari Arabs went into partnership with Swahili traders to obtain slave labour from the interior. By the 1850s these Arab-Swahili slaving pioneers had pushed their way far inland from the coast of Tanzania, and had even come into contact with other slaving agents who had walked eastward from Angola on the other side of the continent. It was along their trails that European explorers would soon begin to penetrate inland Africa. Meanwhile havoc often accompanied the traders. Slaving fired local wars through Tanzania and Kenya into Uganda, and beyond Uganda into the forests of the eastern Congo. The tolerance of the past vanished in these raids and ruthless forays. There occurred here the same kind of political degeneration as in other parts of Africa affected by the war-like search for captives who could be sold as slaves. Peoples ceased to trust their neighbours. Every foreign traveller, whether Arab or European, became a likely enemy to be met with spears or flight.

The zone of crisis broadened rapidly in the 1850s. Between the Arab-Swahili slaving network in the north and similar Portuguese arrangements in the south, no people who lay anywhere near the main caravan trails—eastward from Zanzibar to Lake Tanganyika and beyond, or up the Zambezi and the Shiré into the old lands of Malawi or the vanished empire of the Monomotapa—could now feel itself safe. Here the old Portuguese trading settlements, concerned in the past with the gold and ivory trade and with local plantation farming, fell easy victims to the get-rich-quick temptation of slaving, and came soon to a sorry end. 'When the slave trade began,' commented the Scots explorer-missionary Livingstone on the situation along the Middle Zambezi in the late 1840s, 'it seemed to many of the merchants a more speedy mode of becoming rich, to sell off the [plantation] slaves, than to pursue the slow mode of gold-washing and agriculture; and they continued to export them until they had neither hands to labour nor to fight for them. It was just the story of the goose and the golden egg. The coffee and sugar plantations and gold-washings were abandoned, because the labour had been exported to the Brazils. Many of the Portuguese then followed their slaves, and the government was obliged to pass a law to prevent any further emigration . . .'

In such ways as these, and in others closely related to them, many remaining points of inland stability were sucked within a torrent of violence and death. Further to the southward, in the lands of the Karanga state beyond reach of these rapacious appetites, life continued for a time to be much the same as in the past. But even here the slave trade and colonialist incursions had their fatal consequences. After the beginning of the nineteenth century, the crisis of southern Africa engulfed the peaceful lands of the Karanga as well.

Madagascar lay outside these upheavals. Colonized by Indonesians at the beginning of the central-southern African Iron Age, Malagasy harbours welcomed their shipping for long after that. It was from Java and neighbouring islands, Idrisi tells us in about 1150, that people went to south-eastern Africa for supplies of iron they could sell to Indian armourers.* By the fourteenth century the greater part of the island was divided among a number of peoples of partly Indonesian stock, some of whom, like the

*Really from Java? The relevant passage in Idrisi's *Nuzhat al-Mushtaq fi' Khtiraq al' Afaq* (Palermo, *c.* 1150) has been variously read, according to the several manuscripts available. Among these manuscripts, however, Arabists seem to agree that the best is the one in Paris (Bib. Nat. No. 2221); and this one has Zabaj for the islands in question (S. Maqbul Ahmad, *India and the Neighbouring Territories in the Kitah Nuzhat, etc.*, Leiden, 1960 p. 23). Al-Biruni defined the Zabaj Islands as Java and Divah. This is not to say that the mariners of Java sailed directly to East Africa, though they may have done so. Throughout the Middle Ages, the whole Indian Ocean seaboard was interlinked by ports in all its maritime countries. As late as 1512–15 the Portuguese trader Tomé Pires found in Malacca, where he lived for those years, East Africans as well as Indians and West Asians, and mentions, among others, 'peoples from . . . Kilwa, Malindi, Mogadishu and Mombas . . .' Maritime links between East Africa and South-East Asia were many and of great antiquity.

Hova, were strongly established in the interior of the island. New immigrant groups, some of them from Africa, were still arriving, but their numbers were evidently small. 'Their historical importance derives above all', Deschamps observes, 'from the new political conceptions they brought with them, leading as these did to the foundation of kingdoms' in the Madagascar of the sixteenth century.

Southern Africa: The Wars of Dispossession

The term 'southern Africa' came into wide use during the 1950s to indicate all those lands and their peoples to the south of the west-to-east flowing Zambezi River, or, in some usages, south of the great rain-forest and grassland belt of the Congo Basin. These were lands and peoples that became directly or indirectly subject to the influence or control of Britain, and then of white-ruled South Africa and its successive whites-only forms of dictatorship. Historians of this vast region have thus had to come to terms with a theme always dominant since the eighteenth century, if not always recognized. This is the theme of white dispossession of black liberty and land: in other words, the gradual extension of European or locally immigrant-white control or ownership over all exploitable sources of wealth, and even, in many cases, over all exploitable sources of mere subsistence. This work of dispossession began in the seventeenth century and continued, sometimes at a headlong pace, into and through the twentieth. No important aspect of history in southern Africa for the last three centuries can be understood without confronting this enormous fact of dispossession.

Unfortunately, students of southern African history have not always been well served by a succession of writers, commentators, diarists and conventional historians who have taught and published on this subject. They were at times the willing or unconscious victims of an extreme form of what may be called the 'imperialist delusion': the self-deception so powerfully at work

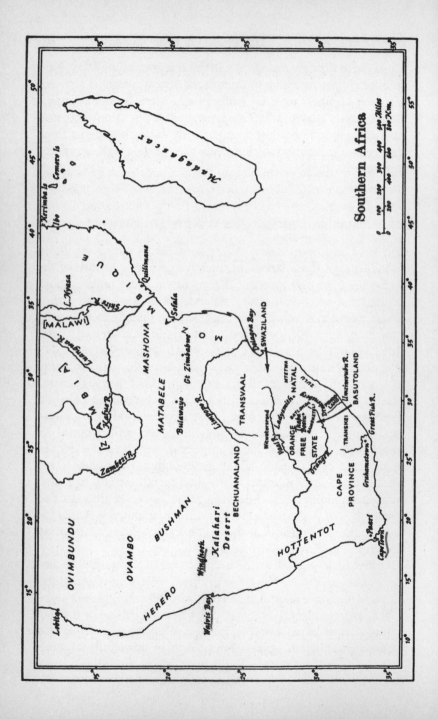

Southern Africa

0   100 200 300 400 500 Miles
0   200   400   600   800 Km.

among European peoples in justifying the colonialist invasions and enclosures. This self-deception taught that Africa must be 'saved from itself' by the European imposition of control. And in the case of southern Africa, as to some extent in other regions of the continent, the self-deception was repeatedly confirmed, and made to seem an obvious truth, by the confusions, violence and misery which spread among African peoples in the wake of the slave trade and its destructive consequences. White explorers and missionaries, and in due course colonial officials and various private travellers 'penetrating the bush veld', returned to 'civilization' and spoke of the death and devastation they had witnessed there or heard about, seeming to prove to the white man's world that these African communities lacked the skills and intelligence to rule themselves in peace, let alone achieve a moral or material progress.

None of this is to say that pre-colonial Africa was a kind of Utopia, or that African peoples were not in need of new ideas and new structures of social and economic life. What it does mean is that much of the accepted historiography of the southern regions, and above all of South Africa itself, has to be read with a prudent scepticism as the product of special pleading by those who have wished to defend, or at any rate to justify, this process of dispossession to which most of southern Africa's peoples have been subject. It is only in recent years that historians in South Africa, as to some extent elsewhere, have begun to question the accepted views of 'white history'. This, again, is not to say that 'black history' has done much better, if only because of its frequent tendency, by reaction, to read into the past the kind of 'triumphs and glories' that European nationalism has so often indulged in. But the 1970s, and still more the 1980s, brought a vigorous spirit of inquiry into play; and southern African historiography began now to tackle the story of the past, even the recent past, with a degree of insight not usually available before.

This task of revision has been difficult, and is still far from complete in the 1990s, because the records of the process of dispossession have relatively little to tell us, or little that can be accepted as usefully reliable, about the history of indigenous African peoples before the European or Afrikaner (local Dutch-descendant) impact struck them. What exactly were their social structures before, say, AD 1700? How did they govern themselves, settle or fail to settle their disputes? What then were their problems of development, their means of self-adjustment to change and renewal, their ideologies of self-assertion and self-acceptance?

About crucially interesting questions like these we can learn a little from such oral history as has been collected, from the guesses and conclusions of a handful of social anthropologists, and from applying the lessons of a more detailed historiography available to us from other African lands and peoples. But the conventional histories will help us rather little. Greatly embarrassed as they have been by what I have called the enormous fact of dispos-session, these histories have tended to take refuge in a convenient mythology where pre-colonial African history has been con-cerned.

Of these myths the crudest—in South Africa but also to some extent elsewhere—has been that most African peoples passed south of the Limpopo River into the territories which have be-come South Africa only 'at the same time' as the Europeans began to arrive by sea in 1652. Archaeology has disposed of this nonsense for all but fanatics of the racist sort. But other myths have filtered in to take its place. Perhaps the most persuasive of these, if only because of its meed of truth, is that most African communities—those, that is, belonging to one or another branch of the Bantu language-family—are simply the product in South Africa of successive 'waves of migration' from central Africa. The picture has been conjured up of 'marching hordes' pushing ever southward to the 'bottle-neck' of the southern coast (of what is now Cape Province), only to find that they could go no further unless they dived into the waves. Whereupon they duly collided with each other in the manner of Lord Macaulay's brave Etrus-cans on their march to Rome—'those behind cried forward, and those in front cried back'—with the tumultuous result one might expect. And at this point of confusion, lo and behold the Europeans arrived to restore order, greatly to the advantage of the natives, even if these, benighted as they were, could not see how they had gained.

So what meed of truth lies behind this improbable picture of the past?

South Africa Is Born

The Early Iron Age, as we have seen, did indeed promote a long and complex migration of cultures and to some extent of actual peoples, as the techniques of stock-raising, cultivation with iron tools and long-term village settlement spread, broadly, from north to south after their initiation in Middle Africa some two and a half thousand years ago. By about AD 300, as we have also seen, they were installed in important areas of what is now South Africa to the east of the Kalahari Desert and of adjacent deserts or semi-deserts.

Very little is as yet known, and very possibly can ever become known, about these cultural migrations. But we may reasonably infer from what is somewhat better understood elsewhere that they produced, in South Africa as in other African regions, a network of clan-and-lineage communities. These communities grew slowly in numerical size of settlement. They evolved their own ideologies of self-acceptance and worked out their own patterns and customs of mutual tolerance. In this southern land of beaming climate, good and often virgin soil for crops or cattle, and abundant extra protein in the form of game both big and small, they evidently prospered; and this prosperity is what their remembered history, in so far as very distant years are ever remembered, certainly combines to suggest.

The Iron Age Bantu-language peoples were not the only inhabitants. Stone Age peoples had preceded them by a vast number of centuries. Speaking Khoi or other languages, these Stone Age peoples were hunters, stock-breeders and food-gatherers (but seldom food-growers) who had yet to come into contact with the technologies of the Iron Age. Organized in family networks and dependent on stone tools and weapons, they had remained thinly spread across these lands south of the Limpopo. In 1652 the incoming Dutch settlers at the Cape of Good Hope found them there in ancient possession, but easily drove them out or else used them as subject labour.

Gradually pushing northward from their Cape settlement and its immediate surroundings, these Dutch farmers—Boers in Dutch—had a hard time surviving. Little by little they thrust inland for more land and labour. They formed what then became their ingrained habit of subjecting or expropriating any Africans they found in their way. Their movement inland was slow but steady. By 1760, however, their pioneering hunters, with farming settlers to follow them, had already crossed northward over the Orange River into the heartland of what was to become South Africa. Along the Great Fish River, meanwhile, they ceased to clash with Khoi groups (Bushman or Hottentot in the colonial literature), and clashed instead with Bantu-language groups. That proved a different matter. These Bantu-language peoples were numerous, strongly self-organized, and equipped with iron-tipped spears. Soon, like their dispossessors, they would also have fire-arms. Unlike the Khoi, they had a powerful capacity to defend themselves.

The earliest big clash, or war, between 'Boer and Bantu', came as early as 1779 while Boer incomers strove to expand their settlements beyond the Great Fish. The result was inconclusive. Many such wars followed during the next hundred years. Gradually, however, the frontier of white settlement was edged north-eastward through the good farming lands of what is now Cape Province, and, as this usually violent eviction of the inhabitants continued, other changes came. Stronger forms of self-organization emerged among local African clan-and-lineage communities, whose ancestors had opened these lands to cattle and cultivation many hundreds of years earlier. Kingships and military captaincies took shape. Early forms of state grew more capable of self-defence. We know little of all that, but the general picture is clear enough. Clan-and-lineage loyalties held firm. But the pressure of white aggression now gave them a coherence they had probably not had before.

At the same time, the Dutch settlers also began to conceive of themselves as a people distinct within itself. Soon they were no longer calling themselves Dutch or Boer but Afrikaner; and with this they evolved a dialect of Dutch, their *taal*, into a fully fledged language, Afrikaans. Partly these developments were in response to the needs of their community, increasingly conscious as this now was of having become something more durable and solid than a scattering of farmers, each settled 'out of sight of his neighbour's smoke', as their saying went. And partly these developments met an increasingly felt need for new disciplines that could buttress their seizure of African land and labour. By 1800 their characteristic ideology of nationhood was well established. Born of an extreme Calvinism and a crude self-interest, this ideology encouraged them to build their farming economy and their social morals on the curious notion that all Africans, the biblical 'children of Ham', were designed by God to labour as the white man's slaves. Immense sufferings would flow from this unyielding racism; and it would be no aberration that so many of the spokesmen of this ideology should in due course, in 1940, speak of hope for a Nazi victory.

Their movement inland was erratic, but it continued. In 1795, with the ending of Dutch East India Company rule (wherever, that is, this distant rule had been able to make itself felt), two little Afrikaner republics were proclaimed near the Cape of Good Hope, those of Graaff Reinet and Swellendam, setting the pattern for much that was to follow. These local Dutch claims were now succeeded by British imperial claims riding on the tide of history. After defeating the French in tremendous land and sea wars for world hegemony during the period 1793–1815, the British assumed the colonial government of the Cape and opened their long-sustained bid for imperial control of the whole of southern Africa. The Afrikaners, like the Africans, faced a new enemy.

The Britain that took over governance of the Cape settlements was intent on continuing its campaign to abolish the slave trade which an earlier Britain had done so much to introduce and sustain. The reasons for this campaign are outside the scope of this book; but the point here is that it was now accepted, in Britain, that abolition of the maritime trade in slaves demanded, sooner or later, abolition of the whole system and institution of slavery. Almost from the first, this being so, the slave-based system of the Afrikaners clashed in the Cape with the anti-slavery policies of British colonial rule.

Resisting the legal limits that were placed on their 'God-given right' to enslave Africans, Afrikaner farmers began shifting still further into the interior lands of the Cape, intending in this way to escape the anti-slaving reach of British colonial power. It availed them little. Drawn reluctantly into the raids and wars that continued along this northward-shifting 'frontier of settlement', British colonial power went after the Afrikaner wagons and horse-mounted commandos. But the land was vast, and passions were high. In 1820 the British even planted some 5,000 British settlers along the inland 'frontier' in a vain hope of keeping the peace between raiding Afrikaners and retaliating Africans. But the wars of dispossession continued as the British, like the Boers, pushed further northward.

White history has called them the 'Kaffir wars', the word *kaffir* being a borrowing, with the sense of 'heathen', from East Coast Muslims. The year 1799 saw the third of these wars of aggression and retaliation, 1812 the fourth, 1818 the fifth and 1834 the sixth, with other and even larger 'Kaffir wars' to follow. But 1834 also brought, at last, a British governmental decision to outlaw slavery in Cape Colony. Outraged by this new denial of their 'rights' to subjugate the 'children of Ham', Afrikaner farmers under a man called Louis Trichardt (his first name marks the presence of French Huguenot settlers) led the biggest of all the Afrikaner invasions of the inland country, the so-called 'Great Trek' of several thousand wagon-riding families, northward, over a period of several years, across the Vaal and other rivers into the 'promised lands' of what was then the far interior.

With this the wars of dispossession were again shifted towards the north, and the servitudes of modern South Africa were already taking shape. 'I have myself been an eyewitness of Boers coming to a village', David Livingstone wrote of inland South Africa during the 1840s, 'and, according to their usual custom, demanding twenty or thirty women to weed their gardens, and have seen these women proceed to the scene of unrequited toil, carrying their food on their heads, their children on their backs, and instruments of labour on their shoulders. Nor have the Boers', continued Livingstone, 'any wish to conceal the meanness of thus employing unpaid labour; on the contrary, every one of them, from Mr. Potgeiter and Mr. Gert Krieger, the commandants, downwards, lauded his own humanity and justice in making such an equitable regulation: "We make the people work for us in consideration of allowing them to live in our country" '. It was a 'generosity' that would continue for many a weary decade, spanning the end of the nineteenth century, and practically outlasting the twentieth.

These long-sustained and violent aggressions struck at the whole panoply of African peoples in these lands; and the consequences were lethal. Whether of one language community or another, 'Sotho' or 'Nguni' to use the accepted European terminology, they had been generally at peace with one another, or else their internecine wars had been typically small affairs of champions and cheers, and soon ended. Short-range stabbing-spears might be used, but the favourite weapon had been the long-range throwing-spear, casualties being thereby prudently limited to a few. Neither side seems to have had any interest in systematic or massive elimination of its rivals. European historians in South Africa have again told little about all this, but a few European missionaries, having collected oral history through long years of residence in the last decades of the nineteenth century, have given us something to go by. One of them, and the most prolific, was the Reverend A. T. Bryant, whose remarkable book of 1929, *Olden Times in Zululand and Natal*, is a not unprejudiced but certainly indispensable source.

'A day having been mutually arranged beforehand', Bryant records of the traditional customs of warfare between these southern peoples, 'each clan turned out en masse to enjoy the excitement. A core or two of warrior youths—for single clans were mostly small before the [Zulu-led] union—bearing assegais and shields, marched proudly and gleefully forth, with as many women and girls to stand behind and cheer . . . Each party, drawn up at a distance from the other . . . would send forth its chosen braves to single combat in the arena. Such a champion falling wounded would become the prize of the victors and be taken home by them to be ransomed, perhaps before sundown, with a head of cattle . . . Over the slain, mutual condolences would be exchanged . . .'

No doubt the picture is somewhat romanticized; but there is little or no reason to believe the later white-racist stereotype of 'tribal massacre' among pre-colonial African clans. What we know of their ideas of justice, usually preferring punishment by compensation to any other sanction, and of the emphasis they placed on the conservation of manpower, always in short supply, suggests customs of warfare among these peoples that could have had no tolerance of mass killing.

Yet the wars of dispossession and their consequences changed all that. Bloodstained years followed as the constant pressure of advancing white settlement thrust one community against another in a sort of 'shunting process' which, by copious evidence, became ever more destructive through Cape Colony and neighbouring Natal. Advancing white settlement was not the only disruptive factor. As historians in South Africa began to make clear in the 1980s, even while the implications of their findings remained controversial, a second great source of violent upheaval was also present after the 1820s.

While the trans-Atlantic trade in captives for enslavement in the Americas had began to fall away, eventually to vanish in the 1880s, a second major export of captives for enslavement meanwhile developed along the East African coast and its interior lands. This spread southwards into Mozambique and became extensive in the 1820s and later. As we have seen elsewhere, slave-trading spread violence and insecurity, misery and even devastation wherever it touched; and now, from Mozambique, it struck at neighbouring Natal.*

This set in motion what may best be seen as a second 'shunting process'. Facing acute problems never met before, and for which their history had in no way prepared them, threatened communities strove desperately to take themselves beyond the slavers' reach. That became increasingly difficult. Some of the Nguni-speaking peoples, divided into clan communities of which the Zulu were to become the strongest, had now found it worth their while to participate in the hunt for captives and in the delivery of these captives to Portuguese and other slaving vessels on the Natal coast. This was bad; but worse followed. Spears now gave way increasingly to firearms; and firearms were being rapidly improved in their effectiveness. Relentless killing could become the rule.

Other disasters accompanied this breakdown of traditional securities: among these were drought and its mortal consequences for people as well as cattle. There seems to have been no *massive* depopulation, but countless thousands died. Flourishing communities vanished in the chaos. Old constellations of political power and coherence gave way to new ones, often born in pain. The Zulu kingdom associated with its leader Shaka emerged; so, a few years later, did the Basuto kingdom associated with another strong leader, Mosheshwe. Militarized new peoples, fruit of the union of hitherto disparate populations, black and white, were also on the scene, adding to the rivalry for place and power; among these were the Griqua and the Koranna.

Gradually, after about 1830, the situation grew somewhat calmer even though new wars of dispossession were still in pros-

---

*See especially Patrick Harries, 'Slavery, Social Incorporation and Surplus Extraction: The Nature of Free and Unfree Labour in South-East Africa', *Journal of African History*, 22, 1981.

pect. But the ravages had been ferocious in their devastation. Those who lived through them, or saw their consequences, seem to have felt that nothing like this had ever occurred before; and surely they were right. Crossing the grassland plateau of the 'high veld' in 1833, the French missionary Casalis and his companions afterwards remembered the 'solitary and desolate aspect of the countryside . . . On every hand we saw human bones whitening in the sun and rain, and more than once we had to turn our wagon out of its course so as to avoid passing over these sad remains . . .'

The South Africa that would take formal and constitutional shape in 1910, the racist-ruled South Africa of the twentieth century, was thus born in the bloodshed that its system of government, its ideology, and its intentions were to guarantee. The reasons and responsibilities for all this were various, since nothing in such great calamities is ever reducible to simple explanations. Greed and fear, the great sowers of violence, were at work on each side of the 'racist divide'. Yet the persistent culprit remained the process of dispossession. This, above all, was what set these peoples violently against each other. Inescapable collisions wrought greater destruction. Further warfare and subjugation followed.

Orthodox history in South Africa, until the 1990s the history written by the victors, has understandably preferred another explanation. Just as the prolonged horror of the Atlantic slave trade was justified by its operators and profiteers with the argument that Africans when left to themselves were incapable of civil and therefore peaceful self-government, so now, in South Africa, it came to be explained that the killings and the chaos, especially after about 1800, were the product of African anarchy and thirst for violence. It was said that these 'savage tribes' suddenly militarized themselves and took to slaying each other because of a new and severe competition between them for grazing and sowing land. This in turn was held to be the result of 'over-population'. The outcome was said by white historians and commentators to have 'carried death and destruction far and wide' even before, as well as after, the northward-moving impact of white settlement on African land.*

Little real evidence for any general 'over-population' has in fact been found. What is evident in hindsight is that an appearance of 'over-population'—in the sense of a strong pressure on grazing land—was created by the 'shunting and crowding' process set in motion among South African peoples after about 1810 by dual pressures from outside their communities. One pressure was a dispossession of land, the other a dispossession of labour. A South African historian working with a post-*apartheid* approach, an approach which remained controversial but gained fresh ground in the 1980s as the racist system lost ground, has summed up this dual pressure of dispossession. 'After about 1810 the black peoples of southern Africa were caught between intensifying and converging imperialistic thrusts: one to supply the Cape Colony with labour; another, at Delagoa Bay [on the eastern coast where Portuguese and other slavers became active] to supply slaves particularly to the Brazilian sugar plantations, then rapidly expanding in size and in the need for labour'. The true initiators of the 'tribal chaos' of those formative years of South Africa were external pressures of imperialist dispossession.†

A pause in the process of dispossession came after 1830, but was brief. By this time the British imperial plan was to secure overall control not only of lands already seized but of the whole of what was to become South Africa. In order to realize this plan, they would first have to crush remaining African resistance, and this they set about doing with military reinforcements. In 1879,

*The quote here is from C. W. de Kiewiet in his *History of South Africa*, Oxford, 1951, p. 50. He was not a racist-minded historian, but like others in this instance, including myself in earlier editions of this book, he was misled by conventional South African historiography.

†Julian Cobbing, 'The *Mfecane* as Alibi', *Journal of African History*, 29, 1988, pp. 486–519. The word *mfecane*, translated as 'the wars of crushing', for which devastation the Zulu and their warrior-king Shaka were said to have been the prime initiators, was invented, Cobbing tells us, by the white South African historian Eric Walker in his *History of South Africa* of 1928. This attribution of wholesale guilt to Africans for the devastations rapidly became, as Cobbing argues, a 'hold-all' alibi to exculpate the principal culprit, namely, violent white dispossession of African land and labour.

after many provocations, Britain duly invaded the kingdom of
the Zulu, then under the leadership of one of Shaka's successors,
King Cetshwayo. Initially defeated by Zulu regiments at Isan-
dhlwana, the invading British army was successful at a second
battle, that of Ulundi, and Zulu resistance ceased. A year later
the same tactics of invasion failed against the Basuto kingdom of
Mosheshwe. But the general enclosure in South Africa continued.

Meanwhile the British were challenged from another quarter.
Having managed to form their little republics of the Transvaal
and the Orange Free State, the Afrikaners were determined to
keep their independence. For a while they succeeded. In 1881
the Transvaal Afrikaners shattered a British force at Majuba and
were able to impose a compromise whereby, in the so-called
Pretoria Convention of 1881, they saved the substance of their
sovereignty. But this only postponed still greater conflict. In 1899
the Afrikaner republics were provoked into war by the British
imperial government. This time they were defeated, in 1901,
after a long and very costly struggle.

Defeat for the Afrikaners in this Anglo-Boer War was in ret-
rospect a victory for them. They were rewarded by being granted,
in effect, their greatest aspiration: the limitless subjugation of the
black peoples and therefore the free availability, to whites, of
black-owned land and black labour. To this the British imperial
system readily consented now that it had the upper hand. There
was much talk about 'defending civilization' against black con-
spiracies; meanwhile the harsh truth of the new laws, introduced
as soon as the country was handed over to the white minority,
made sure that all operative power—legislative, executive or customary—should be guaranteed to the English-speaking and Af-
rikaans-speaking communities of European origin.

With the Act of Union of 1910—uniting the two British colonies of the Cape and Natal and the two Afrikaner republics of
the Transvaal and the Orange Free State—the British Crown
shed all its rights and responsibilities in a land now subjugated

to a rigorous racist rule by 'whites only' and governed by laws in the making and applying of which the black majority, whether of African or immigrant Indian or mixed origin, was to be allowed no voice. The next eighty years were to demonstrate the ruthless violence of this system. It was to be called *apartheid*, 'separateness', after an eventual victory for the Afrikaners at parliamentary elections in 1948. But in all essentials this racist system was present in the Anglo-Afrikaner 'settlement' of 1902, ending the war between 'Boer and Briton', and enshrined in the Act of Union a few years later.

Its rationale was simple. Extremely valuable deposits of gold had been discovered in the Transvaal during the 1880s. Research soon showed that foreign but mostly British capital would become available for commercial exploitation of these deposits only if large supplies of cheap black labour could be provided for work in deep mines. Extensive white agriculture would likewise depend on continued supplies of cheap black labour, even of semi-slave labour, if this 'new country' was to be able to produce the resources to support itself. So it was argued; and the argument was accepted without hesitation by the British, just as in earlier times it had been accepted by the Boer farmers, who had made 'the people work for us in consideration of allowing them to live in our country'.

Buttressed by brute force, the system proved durable. Not until the 1980s could its overthrow seem possible.

The Colonial Invasions

This enclosure of South Africa within a racist system, essentially a colonialist system, came after most of the great colonial invasions of the later years of the nineteenth century, and was justified by the same mythology. This taught that 'ravaging and desolation' were natural and endemic in 'savage Africa' before the advent of European rule. 'Tribal chaos', said this mythology, would continue to reign supreme unless and until it was stopped by European intervention. And what was said to have happened in South Africa during the early years of the nineteenth century seemed to bear this out.

Largely, as the study of African history has since revealed, this picture was false. Much of Africa was not in turmoil before the colonial invasions. There were vast regions of this massive continent where the old ways held firm, and where little occurred to disturb the quiet unfolding of traditional precedent and custom, as one generation after another issued from the loins of its ancestors, accepted its responsibilities, and forged its vital link between the dead, the living and the yet unborn. 'There is perfect security for life and property', David Livingstone found in lands of the Upper Zambezi during the 1840s and early 1850s, 'all over the interior country'. Other travellers reached the same conclusion.

Yet this was not the only truth. Another truth was that the crisis of continental transition which was to grip Africa in the twentieth century was already in its opening phases. In other large areas the slave trade had wrought its mischief, most latterly in eastern regions from the coast to the great lakes and beyond: and this slave trade, far from disappearing early in the nineteenth century, continued its baleful spread even into the 1880s. Elsewhere, especially along the western seaboard and the shores of North Africa, the challenge of new and different systems of commerce and production was actively at work, overthrowing old customs, brashly introducing new ones, almost always with the effect of more or less violent dislocation.

New problems arose for which old solutions were no longer adequate. Resultant strains, whether social or economic, began to prove too much for the frameworks of traditional Africa. The old ways, the ways of the long and in many ways profoundly successful Iron Age, could no longer meet this challenge of the times, and would now be swept away on a tide of unavailing protest and misfortune.

Part of this gathering crisis of system and structure arose from the dynamics of Iron Age success, which at least in several large regions, can be seen to have reached a maturity beyond which further expansion or economic development was going to need radical revisions of ideology and system. To these inherent strains of purely indigenous growth and transformation, however, others were added with dramatic speed and violence. Musket warfare was one of these. Other European imports, demanding payment in new and larger African exports of food or raw materials with all their economic and therefore social consequences, produced another.

The great fact now was that Africa and its neighbour Europe, with North America increasingly in the picture, were sorely out of step with each other in terms of what we think of as development. The gap in effective technological capacity and military power had been narrow in the Middle Ages, and barely existent earlier. Now it was an abyss. For at least three centuries, Europe had known a many-sided and fruitful speculative and scientific experience. But this was an experience that Africa had not shared.

Onwards from the 1830s European intervention unrelentingly deepened and widened. European governments might not welcome this, and sometimes they tried to oppose it, but intervention nonetheless continued. The year 1840 saw the French applying a system of regular administration to the scattered points they had long held along the far western coast of what was to become Senegal. In 1849 the first British consuls were appointed at Lagos (Nigeria) and elsewhere. These new authorities were increasingly drawn into action against African authorities. After the consuls came the gunboats and the troops.

In 1860, to cite one significant example among many, we find the British naval commander on the West African coast suggesting that British officers be sent to 'train' one neighbouring African army against another so that an ally might be reinforced. In that same year the French occupied the port of Dakar on the Senegal coast, and began pushing their troops inland. One year later the British seized and occupied Lagos Island on the coast of what was to be Nigeria. The invasion of Africa became national policy in western Europe; and this national policy, however unwelcome it might seem to budget-minded ministers in charge of European governments, soon swept away all obstructions to it.

Small annexations inexorably continued. But with annexations came the need for revenue, and revenue could best be had by taxing trade. Yet taxation supposed frontiers, and soon it grew clear that the wider the frontiers the higher the revenue could be. So we have Consul Beecroft of Lagos declaring in 1862 that Badagry on the mainland should be brought within the Lagos tariff. A year earlier Consul Foote had got the British navy to bombard Porto Novo, likewise on the mainland, for reasons basically the same. Little by little, coastal encroachment led to coastal seizures, deepening the involvement of Europe; and coastal seizures led step by step to inland invasion.

The demands of traders and governors for privilege, extended monopoly, more local revenue: these were one thing. Another was the pressure to end the slave trade by means of punitive expeditions into neighbouring and as yet unannexed territories, a military exercise which had the agreeably convenient by-product of extending the reach and power of traders and governors at the same time. Under these various pressures, wrote a senior British colonial official in 1863, 'we are insensibly sliding into a new policy (or rather a new practice, for it never seems to have received deliberation enough to deserve the name of a policy) of trying to stop the slave trade by means of soldiers instead of sailors'.* Stopping the slave trade, in short, became a means to quite a different end; from merely naval action against European, Brazilian and United States slavers on the high seas, Britain passed to military action on land. Later on, when slaving was no longer the issue, the process of enclosure still continued. Now it became a question of 'keeping the peace', and African traders who protested against the loss of their trading rights, to the benefit

---

*Quoted in J. D. Hargreaves, *Prelude to the Partition of West Africa* (London, 1963, p. 41), a book in which this whole coil of cause and effect is most effectively described.

of European traders, soon found themselves in the dock.* Little by little, annexation on one pretext or another crept ahead.

Ministers and officials in London and Paris, fearing the cost, might dislike and oppose this process. Their hesitations made little difference. Though largely concealed as yet, the machinery of imperial expansion was already in gear and could not be stopped. In 1865, a Select Committee of the House of Commons recommended British withdrawal from all parts of West Africa 'except, probably, Sierra Leone'. But nine years later the Gold Coast stations, far from being abandoned, were embodied in a new British colony. Even after the discovery of the anti-malarial properties of quinine, during the 1850s, the Niger River was officially regarded as of little value. But no fewer than twenty-one British firms had stations in the Niger Delta by 1864. Within another seven years there were five British steamers on the river.

When considering the records of this astonishing period one is repeatedly struck by how little the politicians understood the movement of their times. They sat at the controls, thinking themselves in full command, believing they knew the immediate course on which their ship of state was moving; and time after time they were wrong. Only in the 1870s did they begin to understand. Even then the French government was still proposing to the British that most of the French stations on the western coast as far as the Congo should be exchanged for the Gambia enclave. This might seem eminently sensible to officials in Paris and London, but it did not work and it could not work. For now the fury of imperial expansion had become a public fever. 'In the present tone and temper of the public mind,' a British minister regretfully observed in 1873, and it was soon to be true of France as well, 'no abandonment of territory would . . . be permitted by Parliament, or sanctioned by public opinion'. Even the Gam-

---

*See, for example, Sir John Kirk's commentary on the Brass (Niger Delta) disturbances of 1895, where he points out that the rules imposed by British imperial power had become 'practically prohibiting to native trade, and the Brass men are right in saying that this is so . . .', the main beneficiary being Goldie's Royal Niger Company. (HMSO Africa 3 of 1896, page 20 *et seq.*) The flag, in short, followed trade; and not the reverse.

bia enclave, though with barely a score of Englishmen living
there, must stay British; and even though it cost Britain the Ivory
Coast.

This fury carried all before it. The imperial scene was set in
western Europe by an atmosphere of frantic national competition
for overseas possession. European imperialism acquired a driving
power of its own. 'I do not know the cause of this sudden revolution,' Lord Salisbury, the British foreign minister, was com-
plaining as late as 1891, 'but there it is.' Others understood better.
Pursuing their interests and ambitions, they blew the trumpets
of patriotism and banged the drums of national rivalry. Ministers
gave way reluctantly; but they gave way. They made concessions,
hoping the cost might still be small. There was nothing else they
could do. 'Protectorates are unwelcome burdens,' a British official
explained to his government in 1883, 'but in this case it is, if
my view is correct, a question between British Protectorates,
which would be unwelcome, and French Protectorates, which
would be fatal.' A single gunboat in the Bights of Benin and
Biafra, he thought, would be sufficient to 'keep the protégés in
order'. Little did he know.

If British and French ministers failed to read the signposts of
the times, African leaders were even more at a loss. They watched
the erratic course of European policy and action, and could
seldom make head or tail of it. They accepted the alliance or
friendship of this or that European country, seldom seeing how
they had thus opened the gate to later conquest. Some kept their
heads in this most puzzling situation, and tried to draw what
benefit they could from European presence and pressure. Others
lost their heads and flung the gate open still wider. The ideologies
of Iron Age life had provided for many contingencies, but not
for an explanation of nineteenth-century Europe. The lesson was
to be long and harsh.

SEVEN

Conquest and Colonial Rule

Prelude: The Explorers

Systematic exploration of inner Africa may be said to have begun
with Mungo Park's journey of 1795–97 into the Western Sudan.
Park's travels, like those of other brave men who soon followed
him, had nothing to do with ambitions of conquest, and little
with those of commerce. Rather were they the fruit of philan-
thropy and the pursuit of science. The latter, indeed, came first.
When the British African Association was founded in 1788, what
Sir Joseph Banks and his companions chiefly wished for was an
understanding of the shape and layout of the African continent.
Armed with such knowledge, the philanthropists afterwards
worked to realize a policy of 'Christianity and commerce' that
should finish off the slave trade and 'civilize the Africans'. Imperialism was still in the future.

The exploring effort was for a long time understandably spasmodic. The difficulties were immense. More than thirty years
were to separate Park's confirmation that the Niger flowed to the
east, and not westward, from the Landers' fixing of the Oil Rivers
as the Niger's outflow to the sea. René Caillié made this great
journey from the Gambia through the Western Sudan and the
Sahara to Morocco in 1827–28, but not until 1889 would Binger
thoroughly investigate the countries which bordered Caillié's route
to the interior. Yet the effort went gradually forward. By the
1860s a handful of successful expeditions had mapped all the

main features of the West African interior, while the beginnings of a systematic study of its peoples had appeared with the writings of Heinrich Barth in 1857. Meanwhile in southern and central Africa the journeys of David Livingstone, embarked on in 1841 and heroically continued for a quarter of a century, had fired the imagination and ambition of many other explorers, whether missionaries or not. In 1857 Burton walked a thousand miles from Bagamoyo on the Tanzanian coast to Lake Tanganyika, while his companion Speke continued northward to Lake Victoria. With Grant a few years later, Speke reached the upper waters of the White Nile at the same time as Samuel Baker, coming down from Khartoum, was marching into the western uplands of Uganda. After the 1860s it became largely a matter of correcting errors and filling in the map.

Nineteenth-century missionary enterprise had the same slow spasmodic growth. Here too the difficulties were very great, not least those of physical resistance to malaria and other fevers. Yet the call for recruits was answered in spite of all attendant dangers. As many as fifty-two missionaries are said to have succumbed to one or another fever along the West Coast in 1825 alone, but the flow of volunteers never failed. In 1804 the British Church Missionary Society began operations in Sierra Leone. Twenty-three years later, marking an important step forward, the Fourah Bay Institution was founded for the education of promising pupils. One of the first of its pupils was Samuel Ajayi Crowther, later bishop of the Niger, an outstanding student of West African languages and translator of part of the Bible into Yoruba. In 1846 mission stations were established in Yorubaland, and in 1865 as far upriver as Lokoja.

The Catholic Church and many Protestant denominations took part in similar ventures in several coastal lands of Africa, gradually pushing their solitary way into the interior. By 1900 there were few large regions where Christian missionaries had failed to arrive and settle. Early Catholic endeavours of the sixteenth and seventeenth centuries were now reproduced on a continental scale. They did much to promote the emergence of a new Christian-educated élite. This was to play a part of some importance, even before 1900, in the formation of anti-colonial trends of thought. *

Invasion: 1880–1900

European imperialist rivalries and ambitions culminated in the 1880s in what *The Times*, with a justice that would stick, contemptuously called the 'scramble for Africa'. Looking back on that hasty and haphazard process of enclosure, some historians have detected its driving motive in Anglo-French agreements arising from British seizure of Egypt and the Suez Canal. Others have pointed to the provocative actions of Leopold II of Belgium in carving out for himself an enormous central African colony under the very noses of his far more powerful contemporaries.

Yet to see this astonishing adventure in merely diplomatic terms is to play Hamlet without the Dane: behind all the diplomatic and political moves lay more decisive pressures. These were released by the tremendous growth of western European capitalism, and were embodied on the African scene by what Mary Kingsley, a shrewd observer of the 1890s, called 'our great solid understuff, the merchant adventurers'. It was above all men like Goldie and Rhodes who ensured that governments in Europe should underwrite imperial enterprise beyond the seas. And it was out of their efforts, consciously or not, that the strenuous ideologies of European imperialism now took shape and action.

When these pressures finally exploded into many-sided invasion, the powers of western Europe found themselves with a number of critical advantages. They possessed useful footholds along the coast. They had long-standing ties with several coastal peoples. They disposed of over-whelming industrial and military strength against a continent still largely enclosed within the nar-

*For a further discussion, see my *Africa in Modern History*, Allen Lane, 1978 (U.S. title, *Let Freedom Come*, Little, Brown).

row productive limits of Iron Age economy, of pre-capitalist production by handicraft methods. Except for the years between 1914 and 1918, they were also able to control their rivalries in Africa within a general agreement among themselves. No matter how much they might quarrel elsewhere, they were usually careful not to quarrel in Africa. The broad limits of expansion for each of the interested powers—for Britain, France, Germany, Belgium (though as yet only through its king), Italy, Portugal and Spain— were defined with little trouble at the Berlin colonial conference of 1884–85.

An effective agreement on partition had in fact long preceded this conference. In North Africa the French had established their 'priority of interest' as early as 1830 with a sudden invasion of Algeria. This was continued at the eastern end of the Mediterranean by Britain, for whom Lower Egypt and the Red Sea also became of major importance as a channel of communication with the British empire in India. Here the British, following on the revolt of Arabi Pasha, finally asserted their primacy over the French by an invasion of 1882. This was ostensibly aimed at restoring the earlier Anglo-French financial control of Egypt. But having got into Egypt, the British stayed, declaring a protectorate in 1914 and finally evacuating the country only in the wake of the Second World War and the rise of a new Egyptian nationalism. Meanwhile the French had established a protectorate over Tunisia in 1883. Twenty years later, partly as the outcome of a deal with Britain which confirmed the latter's free hand in Egypt, France turned her attention to Morocco. In 1904 this ancient country was divided into 'zones of influence' by France and Spain, and colonial subjection soon followed.

The same process was repeated elsewhere, and often against the same tough resistance. No doubt it may be true that those regions of Africa worst plunged in crisis during the nineteenth century—the East African slaving zone is an obvious example— gained something from an imperial control which could at least stop internecine warfare. Yet a stiff price had to be paid even for this. With every internal war that could be stopped, another and

uglier war of invasion or pacification was likely to be started: and
the records of all this are dark with slaughter and destruction.
King Leopold and his agents of the strangely named Congo Free
State—intended to imply free trade there for European merchants—might reasonably claim to have put an end to the Arab-
Swahili export of slaves. They achieved this, unfortunately, at
the cost in death or misery of no mean fraction of the peoples
over whom they set their rule.

Like the British in the lands behind Lagos and the Gold Coast,
the French encountered strong peoples who were proud of their
independence, and were ready to fight for it. Their resistance
failed in the end because they possessed inferior equipment and
military organization, and because they could never achieve any
substantial unity among themselves. Yet it needed nearly twenty
years of warfare for the French to make good their claim to the
lands of ancient Ghana, Mali and Songhay.

One may note here that although the motivations of French
imperialism were basically the same as those of the British, they
were characterized in practice by the effects of a weaker supporting
capitalism. The French too had their 'great solid understuff' of
merchant-adventurers, but these were neither so great nor so solid
as men such as Goldie and Rhodes. Much more was left to local
entrepreneurs among settlers and careerists who, often enough,
made good or tried to make good with very small means. From
an economist's standpoint, accordingly, the French conquests in
Africa appear even more haphazardly guided than those of Britain. For while the bankers of the Third Republic were content
to invest in African enterprises if these could be shown as probably
profitable, they were unwilling to risk much of their capital,
preferring surer fields in Europe and Asia, and they had generally
little confidence in winning a secure return in Africa. * To compensate for this, however, there appeared as a powerful 'imperial
factor' the ambitions of an army and a bourgeoisie which related

* In her classic examination of French commercial enterprise in the French equatorial
colonies, C. Coquéry-Vidrovitch has brought much new light to this subject. See her
Le Congo au Temps des grandes Compagnies concessionnaires, 1972.

overseas conquest even more closely to national prestige than
their British counterparts. *Gloire* and *patrie* helped where bankers'
finance failed. The results were in substance much the same,
but the styles became altogether different; and this was a difference
that would mark itself deeply into subsequent developments when
it came to the period of political decolonization.

Lesser invaders found their task no easier even though their
ambitions might be smaller. Protected by Britain, the Portuguese
were allowed to assert spheres of influence over inland Angola
and Mozambique, countries where until now they had never
exercised more than a very occasional power by means of rare
military expeditions. Now they set about proving 'effective occupation' for the first time. * Stronger but also newer on the scene,
the Germans likewise acquired footholds in South-West Africa,
the Cameroons, Togo and Tanganyika. Though sometimes ac-
cused of a greater brutality than other invaders, they used methods
essentially the same. Like their competitors and partners—for
this great imperial share-out had the aspects both of competition
and partnership—the Germans moved inland from their coastal
footholds by a process of encroachment and aggressive provo-
cation, seizing on every African riposte as a means of extending
their military action and thus their 'effective occupation'. While
it was by no means only the Germans who practised such attitudes, there is some ground, as we shall see, for arguing that the
Germans outdid the others in their bland assumption of being
justified in what they did.

Though often prosecuted against long-enduring resistance by
many African peoples, colonial conquest was also carried forward
by more peaceful means. Of these the most effective was a process
of infiltration, steadily advanced until the stage of 'effective occupation' could be reached, behind a screen of 'treaties of protection'. These were 'signed' with one or another European power
by chiefs who could seldom or never have understood the intentions of their new 'protectors'. With these and other methods the

*Background in B. Davidson, *In the Eye of the Storm: Angola's People*, 1972.

European powers gradually partitioned Africa. They then drew up a large number of treaties among themselves, especially during the 1890s. These inter-imperialist treaties formalized the recognition of frontiers which for a long time would remain little more than mere lines on the continental map.

Having settled their own potential conflicts, the European powers next proceeded to the detailed penetration and subjection of the lands to which they had thus assured each other of 'effective occupation'. If the years 1880–1900 were broadly those of conquest and the 'establishment of presence', the decades 1900–1920 may reasonably be defined as the 'period of pacification' during which installation of colonial rule was made complete.

The System Installed: 1900–20

At the European end the consequences of this new form of imperialism were liable to be measured by an accountancy of monetary profit and loss. For Africans, however, they varied by the actual techniques that were adopted. Within the new frontiers a number of different methods of colonial rule were introduced according to the strength, wealth and particular political tradition of the new rulers. Though at first little more than hand-to-mouth expedients, these methods or 'doctrines' gradually evolved into different theories of government and were generally collected under the labels of 'direct' or 'indirect' rule.

Much influenced by their experience of governing India through local kings and princes, the British hoped to try the same economical method in Africa. They looked for kings or princes who might be ready to act as intermediaries. Here and there, as notably with the Fulani emirs of Northern Nigeria, they conveniently found them. Elsewhere they tried to create such chiefs by nomination. Both kinds of effort tended to pervert existing institutions. The Fulani emirs, for example, became little more than outright dictators ruling by foreign power, something they had scarcely been before, while 'nominated chiefs'—sometimes called 'warrant chiefs'—either failed dismally to win authority among their people or else reduced themselves to mere agents of the new imperial power. All this advanced the long if often partially concealed dismantlement of traditional forms of rule.

The French acted somewhat differently in the wide grassland countries of the Western Sudan. Here they had come into prolonged and hard-fought conflict with the kings and peoples of several states. Like the British with relation to the Mahdi and his troops in the Eastern Sudan, they faced stubborn and intelligent resistance. Neither the kingdom of Segu nor that of Sikasso, nor the strong power erected by Samori Turay in the 1880s, nor most of the lesser states whether Muslim or pagan, gave in without a fight. The wars were bloody and long sustained, and repression was conducted with a harsh and often indiscriminate brutality. Few rulers were ready to act as agents of the French. And the French therefore tended to destroy traditional authority wherever they met it, concentrating all power in the hands of their own commanders or administrators. Even where they felt it wise or found it possible to maintain local rulers, these were deprived of all effective authority. 'In the Mossi country', claimed an official report of 1905, 'indirect rule has produced its expected results. The people have accepted with confidence the substitution of our authority for that of the Moro Naba [king of the Mossi] . . . Stripped of his political powers, [the Moro Naba] Mouméni has nonetheless retained all his religious prestige in the eyes of the natives . . .' It was scarcely 'indirect rule'.

Yet the difference between direct and indirect rule, the supposedly different methods of colonial government generally ascribed to France and Britain, was far less obvious to the ruled than to theorists in far-away Europe. Both Britain and France were found to rely closely and in almost every case upon a combination of direct rule through a European officer and indirect rule through local collaborators or paid agents. And since the number of European officers could never be large—for their salaries and expenses had to be paid from local taxation, such being the basic rule of all this colonial enterprise—the quality of actual day-to-day government generally varied with the local collaborators or agents even more than with the political or personal attitudes of the Europeans.

Local policemen, nominated chiefs, interpreters, assistants of one sort or another: these were the men to whom 'pacified populations' were increasingly subjected. Where local societies had remained more or less intact, or had become integrated in the colonial system by treaties of protection rather than by outright conquest, this could work in their favour. Many a local chief and his counsellors were able to inform themselves punctually and securely of European intentions through the good will of *boma* clerks, capable of reading the local administrator's papers and quietly passing on their information. Often, though, and especially in areas taken after bitter fighting, the intermediaries added to the miseries of conquest. 'Established as masters in the villages,' a French report on the Western Sudan says of such African colonial agents during the 1920s, 'they are a burden on the inhabitants who must feed them: the favourite wife, the junior brother, the servant and the stableman, all folk with a taste for good living who demand good cooking and chicken at every meal.'

Little real difference, moreover, marked the methods of annexation and pacification. Just as European pioneers had relied largely on signing 'treaties' with chiefs who were then considered to have made over their land, mineral rights, or other attributes of sovereignty to this or that European power, so now the expeditionary forces, plunging ever more deeply into the territories thus 'assigned' to them, were prone to use closely similar techniques of subjection. Inevitably, they tried to split their prospective subjects along the grain of old rivalries or state boundaries, selecting this or that people to support against its neighbours in exchange for promises of later preference.

Characteristic of this was the British attack on Bida in the emirate of Nupe in 1897. This attack proved successful, thanks in part to the help of the Nupe against their Fulani overlords. The rest was done by superior fire power. 'The Fulani cavalry',

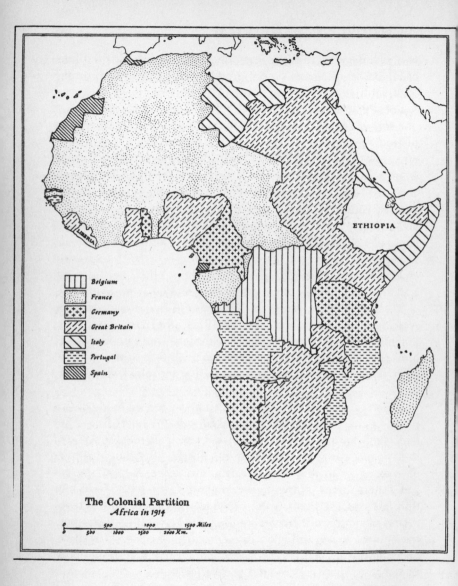

LIBERIA

ETHIOPIA

	Belgium
	France
	Germany
	Great Britain
	Italy
	Portugal
	Spain

The Colonial Partition
Africa in 1914

0   500   1000   1500 Miles
500   1000   1500   2000 Km.

runs a contemporary British account, 'made repeated charges on all sides, but were utterly nonplussed by the galling fire from the Maxims', machine guns of an early but most effective type in that time and place; and George Goldie, leader of the expedition, could then telegraph to London in the best style of earlier conquests in India that 'Bida is ours'. The Nupe, of course, were left to understand that their allies had arrived to liberate them from one imperial rule only to impose another. Having taken Bida, the same expedition repeated its success against Ilorin, whose emir also showed fight. 'The guns and Maxims having been brought into action, the [British-Hausa] square reached the riverbank without waiting, and the Fulah force broke up and retired within the city. Nothing now remained but to shell the place . . .'

Yet there were several important differences in the methods of exploitation. Here the equatorial territories suffered worst through the baleful example of the Leopoldian system in the Congo. This involved the handing over to European concession companies of sole rights not only to land and labour within a given region, often very large, but also to the fruits of the forest and the soil. Huge areas of the Congo Basin (enclosed after 1885 within the Congo Free State, so named because it was supposed to be free of discriminatory taxes for all the interested European powers) were opened to the most reckless despoliation of land and people. Here the concession companies included the Leopoldian administration of enormous 'Crown Lands'. King and businessmen reaped their rich harvest of profits, at least after 1895, from the export of rubber and ivory collected by forced labour and costing little more than the expense of transport and military administration. The results were undoubtedly appalling. An official Belgian commission reporting in 1919 reached the conclusion that the population of the Belgian Congo (transferred to Belgian sovereignty in 1908 after the dissolution of the Congo Free State) had been 'reduced by half' since the beginning of the European occupation in the 1880s. No such losses, we may note, had ever been caused by the East African slave trade, revolting though it was. The cure had proved far worse than the disease.

The same highly destructive system was applied in French and German equatorial Africa a little later. In 1900 the whole vast area of French Equatorial Africa (now the Republics of Chad, Gabon, Central Africa and Congo-Brazzaville) was divided among forty French concession companies which enjoyed a charter of thirty years. 'One idea dominates the system', declared a relevant French decree: 'All the products of the conceded territory, whatever they may be, are the property of the concession company . . .'

These products were gathered by Africans who could earn the means of paying their colonial poll-tax, collected otherwise by being transformed into direct forced labour, only by bringing in quantities of rubber, ivory and other commodities. In certain areas this system became one of what Coquéry-Vidrovitch has called 'an economy of pillage'; generally, in any case, the companies were purely parasitical on African life and labour, while the colonial state which ostensibly controlled the companies and guided the colony towards 'civilization' was in turn parasitical upon the companies, regularly taking 15 per cent of their (admitted) profits. Many companies were so ill-organized, purely speculative or under-financed that they made no profits at all; others persisted for a while, and then vanished without trace.

The state was consequently short of funds, for the notion of supplying from Paris what the local companies and taxed Africans could not provide seemed merely perverse to the masters of the French empire, as of other empires in Africa. The total effect, and not only in these equatorial colonies, was to stop or frustrate African economic effort at expanding pre-colonial African productive and trading activities, while, at the same time, impressing very large numbers of Africans into effectively wage-less labour on behalf of companies which had not the slightest interest in promoting African welfare, let along African development. Often the wastage—and again not only in these French colonies—was on a monstrous scale. There was the well-known but by no means unique case of the Congo-Océan railway in the southern part of these huge territories. Between 1921 and 1932 it was officially admitted that the state had recruited no fewer than 127,250 men for work on this line of rail. Of these, more than 14,000 perished, once again according to official figures, but the true total has been placed by Coquéry-Vidrovitch at around 20,000. 'The news of a recruitment, carried out with no gentle means by police operations in which the least robust men could not escape,' she tells us, 'created a "panic terror" for it signified, at least until 1928, a probable "condemnation to death" '.

It was a 'colonization', a *mise en valeur*, which had no more regard for the interests of African human beings than it had for those of African animals, and sometimes even less; besides which the animals, if hunted here and there, were generally left to themselves. Back in Europe, meanwhile, it was just as regularly said that colonization equalled civilization, and that the brave pioneers out in Africa were helping 'the natives' to a better life. And not only was this said in France: it was said in all the imperialist countries whenever the mood of benevolence seemed appropriate or useful, even though French colonial attitudes were no worse in substance from those of other colonizers. There were those who saw the truth and deplored it. 'In the course of a long life passed entirely in the colonies, during which I have had the honour to govern seven different colonies,' Governor-General Antonetti remarked sorrowfully of the French Congo territories in 1928, 'I have never seen such an abandonment of the rights of the State, whether in defence of the natives or in general questions of public interest. Such things explain much, and in a certain measure the failure of the French effort in the Congo.' But such voices were few, and their audience scarcely larger.

Other colonial interests did as well for themselves, although more briefly, in the German-occupied Cameroons. In 1898 the South Cameroons Company, its chairman the Hamburg financier Scharlach, but its capital mainly Belgian, received nearly 20 million acres where it could collect rubber free of all payment for all eternity. A year later the North-West Cameroons Company was given no less than one-fifth of the whole territory. Operations of this kind could not be conducted without brutality and gross abuse. Such were the scandals set loose by the German companies that their activities were largely wound up before the First World War, while the concessions of the French companies, although surviving to their full term in 1930, were mercifully not renewed.

Elsewhere methods varied. Often they were much less 'intense', especially where no obvious natural wealth could be collected by forced labour or where other methods could be successfully applied. Most West African peoples suffered a good deal less in this period than those in the central, eastern and southern regions. They were submitted to no powerful concession companies. Their territories were seldom regarded as fit for permanent European settlement. In southern Africa it was different again. Here the main British drive was for mineral deposits and for good farming land where Europeans could be settled. Here too the general method was through concession or chartered companies who were given far-reaching powers of government by their respective countries, but whose interests scarcely included the forced collection of rubber, ivory and other natural products, and whose impact was therefore less severe. The plateau lands between the Limpopo and the Zambezi were accordingly administered by the chartered British South Africa Company until 1923, when the colony of Southern Rhodesia was formed, ostensibly under Crown rule but in fact with a free hand for local European settlers.

Forced-labour practices might be less frequent here, but the end-result was to prove even worse than for the Africans of the French and other equatorial lands in the Congo Basin and its periphery. As the imperial structures took shape, Africans found themselves increasingly deprived of their best land, and often enough of all their land. So it came about that within three years of the Act of Union of 1910 which united the four South African colonies of the Cape of Good Hope, Natal, the Orange Free State and the Transvaal, and gave them independence as a British Dominion, another act was passed which deprived Africans of any rights of ownership, or even habitation, in some 88 per cent of the whole territory.

Sixty years later, in 1973, the amount of land recognized as being in African ownership was about the same: the only difference, now, was that these Native Reserves of African ownership and habitation were transformed into 'Bantustans' where, at least in theory, Africans would be free to run their own local affairs. In Southern Rhodesia the settlers acquired, or were allowed to acquire by imperial government, a much smaller proportion of the land, but what they did acquire always included the most fertile areas, while the status of Africans was steadily degraded to that of rightless servants and labourers.

Further north the lands between the Zambezi and Katanga, the latter now seized by Belgium, were similarly administered by the British South Africa Company until 1924, when this territory called Northern Rhodesia (Zambia today) passed under official British colonial control. Here and there, as in South Africa, Algeria and Kenya, especially favourable country was marked out for settlement by Europeans. The African farming lands thus engrossed were simply treated as 'vacant', and therefore as 'Crown property' to be disposed of as the colonial rulers thought fit. South Africa took its present shape in 1910, after the Anglo-Boer War of 1899–1902, when the British conceded all powers of government to the white populations of the Cape Province, Natal, the Orange Free State and the Transvaal, subtracting from this Union only the protectorates of Swaziland, Basutoland and Bechuanaland.

Some of the later consequences for southern Africa will be reviewed in the next chapter: they were almost invariably painful and with time they became worse. The process of enclosure, one may meanwhile emphasize, was by no means everywhere coercive. In some cases, as in Buganda, the British were able to assert their authority through alliance with the Ganda king against his rivals, notably the king of neighbouring Bunyoro, rather as the Portuguese had done in Kongo and Monomotapa in earlier times. Not a few peoples, such as the Bemba, were persuaded by Eu-

ropean missionaries to accept a European over-lordship whose
further consequences they could not be expected to foresee, and
which indeed most of the missionaries did not themselves foresee.
Other peoples accepted European over-lordship from a pure misunderstanding of the nature of the newcomers. Thus the rulers
of the Uganda kingdom of Ankole are said to have thought that
the first Europeans they saw were the descendants of their semi-
legendary Chwezi heroes, though it was not long before they
learned better.

Eastward in Kenya the Luo suffered for a while from the same
delusion, and so accepted British rule without armed resistance.
'This', Ogot tells us, 'was chiefly due to the injunctions that had
been issued by their diviners, who wielded considerable influence
in pre-European days, against such resistance. The coming of
marvellous "red strangers", who were supposed to emerge from
the sea, had been foretold by them, and the people were advised
against showing any hostility to the intruders lest they incur the
wrath of the ancestors. Hence the Luo people welcomed the
Europeans cordially, co-operated with the administration in all
possible ways and generally expected great things of the white
man. The prominent Luo leader, Odera Ulalo, for instance, gave
unflinching support to [the British] in the latter's effort to subjugate the warlike Nandi.'*

Yet it needs to be noted, in spite of these exceptions, that the
process of imperial enclosure was more often coercive than not,
and that in no few cases it was violently destructive. These things
may be disagreeable to remember. Yet no history can quite pass
them by without a word, for the violence and destruction were
also an influential part of the scene: their consequences, in fact,
are with us to this day. They should not be allowed to obscure
the humanitarian and civilizing efforts of many excellent men
and women, nor sully the reputation of those colonial officials
and soldiers whose principal sins were no worse than Victorian

*B. A. Ogot, 'British Administration in the Central Nyanza District of Kenya, 1900–
60', in *Journal of African History*, 2, 1963.

smugness, ignorance, and insensitivity to the claims of pre-industrial peoples. Nor should they, perhaps above all, form any sort of reason for modern Africans to 'blame their condition' only on the failings or excesses of colonialism. But the violence and destruction have to be remembered by any historian who wishes to arrive at a balanced view of the colonial period. One should recall, in this respect, the German imperial record in South-West Africa, the land of the Herero, Ovambo and Nama.

The Germans came relatively late into the 'scramble', but by much the same route as their rivals. Their beginnings in Africa, as with the British and the French, were by way of businessmen and financiers, such as Sharlach and Luederitz, who were primarily interested in trade and speculation. These found it difficult to win any governmental backing. Luederitz secured his first 'concession' in the gulf of Angra Pequena at a time when Bismarck, still in charge of German imperial affairs, was by no means convinced of its utility to the Reich. His notion of the matter, rather like Salisbury's in Britain, was that enterprising businessmen should carry their own cost and risk; and the most he wanted to agree to was the establishment by international agreement of a German 'sphere of interest', from which the competition of non-German businessmen would be effectively excluded.

The 'South-West' venturers behaved as others did elsewhere. They bought 'concession rights' for as little as they could, but generally in exchange for arms and ammunition, a deal that the German authorities would afterwards have reason to regret; and they played all the usual tricks of fraud and false promises. Thus the second Luederitz concession treaty of 1883, made with a Nama chieftain called Joseph Fredericks, provided for the purchase of a coastal stretch of about 250 miles, northwards from the mouth of the Orange River, in exchange for £500 sterling and sixty British rifles. According to the text of this agreement, the coastal stretch was to be twenty miles broad. Not unnaturally, the Nama took it for granted that these were to be English miles. But the agreement was in German, and the Germans declared that the miles were German miles. The difference was not a small one, the English mile being about 1.4 kilometres, and the German 7.4 kilometres. The Nama woke up suddenly to the fact that they had signed away, in the German view, the greater part of their whole territory. That Luederitz was deliberately tricking them is clear from his own surviving papers. *

Having got their concessions, the German businessmen were overtaken by bigger interests, notably the banks. Here again the uncoiling springs of European imperialism had their effect. Powerful pressure groups pushed for conquest in Africa. What had begun as commercial speculation grew into a thundering parade of nationalist prestige: the process acquired, as in Britain and France, explosive pressures of its own. Soldiers such as von François, and after him von Trotha and others, saw their duty in the assertion of German imperial rule no matter what the local cost might be; the process also acquired, here as elsewhere, a 'morality' of its own. The first serious clash came in 1893 when troops under von François's command put some 16,000 bullets into a sleeping Nama village, killing a handful of men but, according to the official records, no fewer than seventy-eight women and children. † From 1893 to 1903 there was scarcely a year without its 'punitive military operations' of one sort or another. In 1904 the Herero, driven to despair by the steady confiscation or suppression of their cattle, their lands and their rights to the benefit of German settlers, declared outright war on the Germans. A few months later, though without coordination, the Nama did the same.

What these peoples suffered in a repression which turned into a determined and long-sustained destruction of African people is patiently set forth in the imperial records. 'I know these African tribes', wrote von Trotha, the general entrusted with the task of putting down the Herero and the Nama: 'They are all the same.

*In *Die Erschliessung von Deutsch-Suedwestafrika durch Adolf Luederitz*: Akten, Briefen, Denkschriften: C. A. Luederitz, Oldenburg, 1945: especially p. 87.
†The whole dismal story has been told, from the inside of the German imperial archives (now assembled at Potsdam), by Horst Dreschler in *Suedwestafrika unter deutscher Kolonialherrschaft*, Berlin, 1966, published in English translation as *Let Us Die Fighting*, Zed, London, 1981.

They respect nothing but force. To exercise this force with brute terror and even with ferocity (*mit krassem Terrorismus und selbst mit Grausamkeit*) was and is my policy. I wipe out (*vernichte*) rebellious tribes with streams of blood and streams of money. Only by sowing in this way can anything new be grown, anything that is stable.'

He was as good as his word. Yet the sowing of destruction proved less easy than he had thought it would be. The Herero fought back with the courage of desperation. They forced von Trotha into the realization that he could not beat them, with the troops he had available, in pitched battle. He chose another way. To the horror even of his otherwise congenial civilian colleagues in the territory, he surrounded the main forces of the Herero in such a way that they could break out only towards the Kalahari. There in the waterless wastes of the Omaheke, he calculated, they could be left to perish. And they were left to perish, while German soldiers shot them away from the waterholes along the fringes of the Omaheke. 'The closing of the eastern frontier of the colony and the exercise of terror against every Herero who is sighted', insisted von Trotha against his principal civilian colleague's protests, 'will remain the policy so long as I am here. The [Herero] nation must disappear [*untergehen*]. If not through shooting then in this way': of death by thirst, that is, in the wastes of the Omaheke.

Those who had not entered the Omaheke, but had stayed behind within the limits of the German-proclaimed colony, were duly met with von Trotha's terror. They were relentlessly rounded up, and many of them, whether men, women or children, were shot. Others were put into 'concentration camps' (thus named in the records). Out of about 15,000 Hereros thus 'concentrated' and about 2,000 Namas, more than 45 per cent had died by 1907 when the risings ended. In 1904 there was estimated to be a total of about 80,000 Herero and 20,000 Nama; in 1911 the estimates showed 15,130 Herero and 9,871 Nama remaining alive. Nearly 75,000 had paid the price of imperial prestige.

However various the methods of colonial enclosure, the results were in one great aspect the same. They brought a new subjection by peoples who, unlike all previous and internal conquerors, regarded themselves as naturally superior to Africans, and who were also able to apply methods of oppression and exploitation of a range and intensity never known before. They evoked revolt after revolt. Some of these revolts, like those of the Matabele and Mashona in the early Southern Rhodesia of the 1890s, the Herero and Nama risings, the resistance of the Ovimbundu kingdoms in Angola during 1902-3, the Maji-Maji war against the Germans in Tanganyika a little later, or other revolts in other territories, were on a massive scale. Such revolts were of a kind with the earlier wars of resistance to actual invasion: with the struggles of Arabi in Egypt, with the stubborn fight put up against the French by the Algerians under Amir Abdelkader in the 1840s, with the defensive battles of the Asante, with the wars of Ahmadu and Samori in the Western Sudan and of the Mahdi in the Eastern Sudan and with the bitter resistance of the Abushiri and many others in East Africa. Other revolts were 'mere local troubles', little recorded outside the colonial annals. They were nonetheless numerous, and they continued for a long time. In them, indeed, lay some of the deeper roots of Africa's later consciousness of the need for a new independence. There is a large sense in which resistance to invasion, revolts against colonial rule and the rise of nationalist movements during the 1950s should be seen as part of a continuing theme of self-defence and self-realization among a wide range of African peoples confronted now, and for the first time, with the full weight and fact of the modern world.

The colonial wars and risings took their steady toll. Attempts were sometimes made in Europe—and would continue to be made for many years ahead—to justify repression on the grounds that it offered the only effective way of establishing a new peace over wide regions hitherto enmeshed in 'tribal warfare'. Yet another form of warfare had meanwhile caused more victims in four years than all those who may have died in pre-colonial 'tribal fighting' during twice as many decades. Some 46,000 Kenya Africans are estimated to have lost their lives in British military service between 1914 and 1918, a greater destruction, as a British critic noted at the time, 'than a generation of intertribal wars'. From West Africa the French mobilized no fewer than 211,000 Africans, of whom 169,000 were deployed in the fearful battles of the Western Front in France with an officially admitted total of 24,762 killed, this taking no account of a large number of others whose fate was never ascertained. Not even the most minimal effort was ever made to compensate the families of the dead.

The year 1935 brought a last though peculiarly vicious postscript to the chapter of invasion. On 3 October of that year, to the accompaniment of air attack on defenceless villages and a welter of bombastic propaganda, the armies of Fascist Italy invaded Ethiopia. The conquest was no easy one. Not until 1 April 1936 were the invaders able to reach Gondar; only on 5 May could they enter the capital of Addis Ababa. Even then their troubles were not over. Resistance continued. As late as 1 January 1939, the Italian Foreign Minister Ciano was noting that 'Asmara is still in a state of complete revolt.' Two years later the game was up. Beaten by British armies coming up from East Africa, Italy's Fascist legions vanished from the scene. The Emperor Haile Selassie re-entered Addis Ababa on 5 May 1941, almost five years to the day since he had gone into exile.

The System at Work: 1920–45

It was a curious system. The colonial powers—now without Germany, whose colonies were divided between Britain and France in the form of Mandated Territories of the newly formed League of Nations—possessed far more territory than they knew what to do with. Having seized much of this in order to prevent it from falling to rivals, they were often content with mere territorial possession, a fact which may help to explain their relative willingness to abandon mere territorial possession forty years later. Most colonies were expected to pay for their own colonial government, so that the degree of intensity with which territorial possession could be asserted was often dependent on local taxable capacity and the attraction of mining or other profitable forms of private investment. To this there were exceptions in land selected for European settlement. Here the intensity of territorial occupation was far greater. Local populations were driven into farming labour under semi-slave conditions, notably in South Africa.

All this being so, the general character of the central years of the colonial period was of hand-to-mouth administration, political decay and economic stagnation. Very little could be done to realize the humanitarian promises of 'civilizing Africa' that had sounded and resounded in the parliaments of Europe during the years of conquest. Yet the underlying pressures of European occupation—of occupation by powers which were the emanation of societies geared to industrial production and the search for private profit—were gradually having their profound if planless effect. Little by little, Africans were gripped by the economic system of their new rulers.

Methods of rule which imposed the need for money began to undermine traditional economies of subsistence where money had little or no place. Contrived in South Africa and rapidly applied elsewhere, such methods sought to raise revenue by money taxes. Even more, they sought to augment the supply of cheap labour. For British territories the precedent was legalized with the Glen Grey Act of 1894 in the Cape Province. This piece of legislation, introduced if not actually devised by an arch-apologist of empire, Cecil Rhodes, provided that African men must pay a 'labour tax' of ten shillings a year unless they could prove that during three months of each year they had been 'in service or employment beyond the borders of the district'. The idea, in short, was to force village Africans into wage employment for Europeans, while making sure that the wages remained on a far lower scale than European workers would demand. As Rhodes explained, 'if they could make these people work, they would reduce the rate [that is, the wage-rate] of labour in the country'. This 'labour tax' was widely applied after 1900 in many territories,

and became, as time went by, a major factor in the dismantlement
of traditional systems of life. Except in the territories ruled by an
industrially primitive Portugal, it had by this time come to be
accepted that directly forced labour, whether as forms of outright
or modified slavery, could not be profitably used in any systematic
way. As forced labour practises dwindled after 1920, it became
ever more needful to lever the African peasant out of his village
and oblige him to work in mines and plantations. South African
precedents were applied ever more widely. The village farmer
was generally mulcted of an annual tax which had to be paid in
cash. This could be earned only by going to work for Europeans,
while failure to pay could be met, and regularly was met, by
visits from the colonial police and spells of 'prison labour'.

Apart from this central method of collecting labour, the sheer
impact of European production also had its effect. A wide variety
of simple industrial goods, whether clothing or shoes or factory-
made trinkets or bicycles or the like, became available for the
first time; and men were increasingly willing to work for Europeans in order to earn the cash to buy them with. These diverse
pressures, directly coercive or not, led to a continual disintegration of traditional systems of community life, law and self-respect.
Wide regions were annually denuded of a significant proportion
of their 'fit adult males', to borrow one of the curiously zoological
phrases of the colonial era; and the effects were often disastrous.
'The whole fabric of the old order of society is undermined',
noted an official report of 1935 on the consequences of migrant
labour in Nyasaland (Malawi), 'when thirty to sixty per cent of
the able-bodied men are absent at one time . . . Emigration [i.e.
labour migration], which destroys the old, offers nothing to take
its place, and the family-community is threatened with complete
dissolution.'

In many other territories, especially in the central and southern
regions, the situation was not much better; in South Africa it was
generally worse. Nor was it even true that these migrant workers,
by moving into the European cash economy, also moved into
the European industrial system and learned corresponding skills

and an understanding of this new world they had to face. On the contrary, they were almost invariably used for unskilled or semi-skilled labour under colour bars which prevented them from learning anything but how to use a pick and shovel. Wages were paid at the minimal subsistence level for a single man, even when, as rarely, their families could accompany them; and it will never be known how many hundreds of thousands of African families were therefore crippled or destroyed. Not for many years would there be any serious colonial effort to mitigate or mend the damage of this migrant labour system.

Another solvent of traditional stability was the steady destruction of African handicraft industries. Reviewing the past, an official report on Nigeria observed, in 1948, that 'since the growth of European economic enterprise in Nigeria, native mining has been on the decline because of the *de facto* monopolization of deposits by Europeans . . . or through the competition of European products with the final products of native mineral industries'. The once flourishing handicraft industry of the Hausa had tinned its brassware with locally produced metal. Yet 'by 1923 this indigenous tin-producing industry had completely disappeared'. Much the same was true of Nigerian iron-smelting, practised here for some two thousand years; by the 1930s it had 'largely died out'. Traditional guilds of smiths, Forde was noting at about the same time, 'have decayed, leaving their members impoverished, and threatened with social degradation'. And it was no different in many other territories. Ibn Khaldun had reckoned the Algerian weaving centre of Tlemsen to have used some 4,000 hand-looms in the fourteenth century. By the middle of the nineteenth century, after French occupation, there were only about 500. In 1954 Tlemsen was found to have exactly 105 looms.

Under pressures such as these the heart of traditional Africa, its village life and economy, suffered lesion after lesion. Yet the new mining and urban centres had no real alternative to offer. In these it became the habit of employers to 'house' countless thousands of migrant village workers in barracks or compounds from which all women, married or not, were deliberately excluded. Any hope of earning more than the minimal wages of bachelor subsistence was blocked by colour bars, by bans on trade union organization, and by a more or less complete denial of training facilities.

The situation was most obviously bad in South Africa, though the reasons for this may be only that much more is known of South Africa than of other territories in the colonial period. There the expropriation of African land had reached a point by the 1930s where nearly nine-tenths of all cultivable soil was 'reserved' for European occupation. Outside their crowded tenth, Africans lived on sufferance, subjected to a host of petty persecutions, and debarred from selling their labour in anything approaching a free market.

It goes without saying that local conditions greatly varied. In the cities of Kenya, for instance, it was possible for African migrant workers to bring their families to town, and many did. Yet a man's wages continued to be calculated on the basis of bachelor subsistence, it being regularly supposed in the face of all the evidence that his family was happily supported on a farm in the countryside. As late as 1954 an official inquiry into wages paid to Kenya African workers found that these were 'generally insufficient not only to feed, house and clothe their families, but even for their own needs', and concluded that 'approximately one half of the urban workers in private industry, and approximately one quarter of those in the public services, are in receipt of wages insufficient to provide for their basic essential needs of health, decency, and working efficiency', a grimly bleak memorial to the benefits of sixty years of colonial rule.

Conditions tended to be better, even much better, in some of the western territories. There was little alienation of productive land in the French West African Federation (Senegal, Mauretania, Soudan [now Mali], Niger, Upper Volta, Guinea, Ivory Coast, Dahomey); or in Togo, formally a Mandated Territory of the League of Nations and later, until independence in 1960, a Trusteeship Territory of the United Nations; and none at all in the British territories (Nigeria, Gold Goast [now Ghana], Sierra Leone, Gambia and the British part of ex-German Togo, another Mandated and later Trusteeship Territory).

In contrast with countries of growing European settlement in eastern and central-southern Africa, the colonial economies in West Africa were effectively dominated by a small number of powerful trading and mining companies. These played a key part in fixing the terms of trade: the prices, that is, which African growers could realize for their products and the prices they were obliged to pay for European goods they might wish to buy. As elsewhere—except in a handful of countries such as South Africa and Algeria which were designed for European settlement on the grand scale—the general level of non-commercial investment remained very low, although movement of raw materials and crops from the interior (and of troops into the interior) was aided by the completion of a few railways.

These railways almost all ran inland from the coast, so that West Africa today lacks any effective inner-territorial network. In Nigeria a line linking points in the north had been completed as early as 1911 and was joined with a line to Lagos on the coast two years later. After 1920 the French carried their rail link through Senegal as far as the Upper Niger at Kayes and then to Bamako, now the capital of Mali. Another line joined Conakry with the plains of Upper Guinea. There were a few others of the same kind, such as the line from Lobito through inland Angola to the Katangan copperbelt, and the East African railroad from Mombasa. Some attention was given to ports, notably Dakar in Senegal, Freetown in Sierra Leone, and Sekondi on the Gold Coast; but systematic construction of wharf and dockside rail facilities came only during the raw material boom after the Second World War.

Western Africa was often less unfortunate in political affairs as well. While the governing ideology of 'white man's countries' like Kenya supposed that it must be 'hundreds of years' before 'the natives could be fit to take a hand in government', the outlook in West Africa was very different. The Gold Coast had enjoyed

at least the shadow of a form of self-rule through legislative council from the early years of the colony; and the absence of European
settlers could also sometimes mean less pressure by an ideology
of racist superiority on the part of the administrators. In Nigeria
the Lagos colony had likewise had its advisory council from the
1860s. A new colonial constitution of 1922 provided for advisory
executive and legislative councils. If the unofficial members of
these councils were almost invariably 'safe men' from the colonial
standpoint, they were still Nigerians. Even in early days there
existed a Nigerian and Gold Coast political public opinion which
repeatedly exercised its influence, however indirectly and partially, on methods of government, not least through energetic
newspapers like the *Gold Coast Independent*. One of the undoubted achievements of this public opinion was to prevent the
freehold sale of land to Europeans. Generally, the political and
social suffocation of the colonial period was felt less severely along
the coast of West Africa than in other regions.

French policies of 'assimilation' introduced another variant,
but these became important on the political scene only after 1945.
Before the Second World War the only 'French West Africans'
who had managed to acquire citizenship rights in the French
Republic were the inhabitants of the old colonial municipalities
of Dakar, Gorée, Rufisque and Saint Louis along the coast of
Senegal. These were admitted to the community of French civilization and allowed to elect an African deputy to the National
Assembly of the Third Republic.

Gain or Loss

How one measures the African balance of loss and gain through
this gruelling episode of European colonial rule will depend, no
doubt, upon who one is. Most Africans, or at any rate those not
privileged in belonging to an élite of *beati possidentes*, have probably seen in it little but loss for their continent. Most Europeans,

even when thinking not solely of their own interests, have claimed
for it little but gain. A just balance will in any case vary from
one territory to another and even from one colonial power to
another. Besides, it was nothing if not a contradictory process,
mostly dialectical by nature, and individual judgements will accordingly vary about the weight or value to be placed on one side
or the other of the scales.

The matter becomes even more elusive in the sphere of moral
judgements. Could there ever be a moral justification for invading
and expropriating the territory and possessions of other peoples?
The Victorians generally thought there could, provided always
that the invading and expropriating were done outside Europe.
Adhering to a vulgarized Darwinism, they held themselves so far
superior in the human scale to these 'tribes without the law',
these 'fluttered folk and wild', as to be in duty bound to save
such benighted populations from the darkness in which they were
supposedly plunged. It appeared to Richard Burton, perhaps the
most successful propagator of such views, that it must be 'egre-
gious nonsense' to question the natural and inherent superiority
of Europeans over Africans: 'everyone who has studied the natural
history of man', he opined in his usual tone of declamation, the
hectoring tone of a man who has travelled much but understood
little, 'must have the same opinion'. Yet there were others, less
insensitive and self-regarding, who also believed in the moral
imperatives of colonial rule; and not a few of these others were
men deserving of respect.

Today we can look at these things a little more objectively.
Nobody now will care to argue in Burton's tone, or nobody at
any rate who is likely to be worth hearing. Even gentler views of
the same kind will be hard to sustain in the light of the colonial
record. Among Africans there was disillusionment almost from
the first. While the diviners of the Luo may have instructed their
people to accept and aid these 'red strangers' from the sea as
beings of a marvellous benevolence, closer acquaintance brought
a different view, and the twilight of those particular gods was as

swift as the African dusk itself. Even before 'full occupation' had been assured, there were movements of protest against European rule: among the Luo, for example, as early as 1913. Then it was that Onyango Dunde relayed to his followers a message from their god Mumbo, pronouncing that 'all Europeans are your enemies, but the time is shortly coming when they will all disappear from our country'.

Yet the Victorians had a point. However confusedly, they saw that Africans really were in a different, an earlier, phase of sociopolitical growth; and the best of them wished to make it possible for this phase to be followed, as painlessly as might be, by an advance into the technology and attitudes of the industrial world. There was, very clearly, a great need for the 'modern' reconstruction of African life and thought: not, as we may easily agree today, because the industrial world was inherently capable of offering more happiness than the old world of rural subsistence, but because the old world of rural subsistence could not possibly withstand the strains of exposure to the consequences of technological change in the rest of the world. That old world must either transform itself, or collapse in helpless ruin. Africans, in short, could no longer defend themselves on the basis of their old traditions and modes of organization. The 'power gap' between Africa and the industrially advanced nations, those that had begun to reduce Africa to an underlying dependence during the slave trade, had by now become disastrously wide.

This gap had appeared long before. When Affonso of Kongo, back at the beginning of the sixteenth century, had vainly pressed the king of Portugal to send him shipwrights, or at least to sell him a ship for ocean-going travel, he was only expressing the inability of African society to adapt itself to the needs of building ships and sailing them. When Kalonga Mzura, a hundred years later, had invited 'his' Portuguese to send in carpenters who could build sailing boats for Lake Malawi, he was really saying that his own people neither possessed the requisite skills nor were even interested in winning them. The further self-defence and self-

realization of Africa required, in brief, a closing of the technological power gap in ways that could only result from new social
attitudes and structures.

On one side of the balance, then, there was this need for a
creative revolutionary break with the long unfolding of African
Iron Age society. The need was not a new one. It had been there
from as far back as the time when modern engineering took its
rise in western Europe. It had steadily widened. And now, with
the direct confrontation of European colonial presence, it became
an urgent need. This is another way of saying that there had been
nothing in the prolonged Afro-European contact of pre-colonial
times that was able, much less aimed, at producing any such
crucial transformation. These chapters have suggested several
reasons why this was so.

One of them lay in the dynamic strength of African systems
of self-rule which had enabled mankind to populate and master
the continent by methods and ideologies native to itself. Those
systems had only begun to exhaust their social value when the
general crisis of the nineteenth century moved over their horizon.
They had revealed themselves capable of an almost infinitely
subtle adaptability to shifting circumstances and challenges; although, as it happens, only in the last twenty to thirty years,
when so few of them remained intact, have the reports of social
anthropologists begun to reveal their full qualities of flexibility,
tolerance and psychological insight into the problems of man-
in-community. Little had come from outside that could have
seemed in any way socially preferable.

Not surprisingly: for what had come from outside was often
the worst that outside civilization could offer. Islam made an
exception. The value that large numbers of Africans found in
Islam, whether for the overleaping of ethnic conflicts, for the
development of new techniques of trade and credit, or the organization of new forms of self-rule, suggests that Islam, on the
whole, was often a factor of constructive transformation. 'On the
whole', however, there were many exceptions. Islam also led to

forms of oligarchical despotism which had not existed before, to
the introduction of slave labour and to the extension of the overland slave trade. And it did all this without 'breaking the mould'
of Iron Age continuity: without breaking it, that is, either because
the Muslim powers of North Africa and the Middle East lacked
the necessary know-how, or because Islam in Africa, in order to
succeed, had to naturalize itself to African attitudes and beliefs.
Early Christianity in Africa, aside from the special cases of Christian Nubia and Ethiopia, made no such concessions, and failed
almost everywhere to achieve more than a fleeting and eventually
insignificant impact, as anyone may see who cares to read the
Papal records. *

For the rest, what came from outside arrived in the guise of
settlers of a persistent rapacity and arrogance, whether in the
manner of the Portuguese along the Zambezi or of the Boers in
the far south, or of traders, plying the Atlantic trade, whose
capacity to transfer cultural progress was always, to put it mildly,
minimal. None of these could help towards any constructive
transformation, towards any far-reaching change, such as could
move African society from its pre-industrial subsistence base to
one which could absorb the early possibilities of modern technological progress.

Even the European settlers along the Zambezi brought nothing
new except firearms and an often gross ambition for personal
wealth and power. Far from helping to transform the structures
of African life, they merely degraded these structures, or else
themselves became adapted to African modes. The most successful among them, indeed, were precisely those who turned
themselves into local potentates by adapting African political processes, built up private armies, and set about the task of conquering or terrorizing their neighbours. Perhaps their one true
claim to distinction was their ruthlessness. Standing outside the

*In, for example, Cuvelier and Jadin, *L'Ancien Congo d'après les Archives romaines
(1518–1640)*, Brussels, 1954.

moralities of Africa and Europe alike, such settler groups became little more than armed bandits. Commenting on the reasons why the king of Urozwi had expelled all Portuguese from his lands in the 1690s, the king of Portugal's viceroy in Goa wrote of the many troubles that had overtaken the Portuguese. 'These wars', he observed in a dispatch to Lisbon, 'are caused by the arrogance of our own people, who have many Africans [as slaves] and commit excesses which drive the [African] kings and princes to revolt . . . Everybody [among the Portuguese] wants to be a ruler . . .'

The Boers were different, for they were often skilled and laborious farmers, producing wealth by their own work as well as purloining it from the Africans whom they enslaved. Yet the Boers were just as incapable of transmitting any of the technological progress of western Europe, for they knew nothing of it. Fastened within their own pre-industrial ideology, they behaved according to the teachings of a religion which was set in its principles and practices against anything that was not of an extreme conservatism, and they had accordingly nothing useful to give Africa. Only much later, when faced themselves with a violent challenge from Europe in the shape of the Anglo-Boer War of 1899, did a few of them begin to understand that they, too, might have to move with the times. When they did so move, however, their old conservatism simply acquired a new form, and the outcome for Africans was even worse than before.

If the Atlantic trade produced some changes among coastal peoples who engaged in it, these were changes which remained within the pre-industrial mould. The peoples of the Niger Delta, of the Guinea Coast and Senegambia, proved well able to adapt their social structures to the handling of a vast and various trade with Europeans. These adaptations were often ingenious. Yet they, too, could produce no decisive shift towards technological advance. Not a single one of these peoples, for example, ever embarked upon ocean trading on their own account until the latter part of the nineteenth century; and then, of course, it was too late: the mounting pressures of European monopoly saw to that. King Ja Ja of Opobo, the shrewdest of those who tried it, ended his career in British imperial captivity.

If one asks, all the same, just why it was that these coastal peoples, faced as they were for so many years with the clear evidence of technological superiority on the European side, still failed to learn its lessons and launch some kind of technological revolution of their own, one is brought back again to the nature of the systems within which they lived. To the strength of these systems; but also to their weakness. They were strong because they were the product of centuries of successful trial and error by which men had worked out ways of living in the tropics and the forests, in the grasslands and the mountains of this often harsh continent. These systems were, if you like, the outcome of a long period of natural selection of a social kind: they enclosed men within frameworks of spiritual and moral behaviour, collective duty and individual responsibility, that rested on traditions of inherently sufficient power and persuasion.

It is easy to forget the self-confidence that was undoubtedly engendered by these tried and tempered modes of life, although the resilience and durability of African cultural attitudes repeatedly remind one of it even in the changed world of today. Earlier observers did not fail to notice this self-confidence, though seldom with admiration: somehow or other, and disconcertingly, the 'savages' stubbornly refused to see how miserable they were. 'These nations', complained Father Cavazzi da Montecuccolo after some experience of northern Angola during the seventeenth century, 'think themselves the foremost men in the world, and nothing will persuade them to the contrary. They imagine, for never having been out of Africa, that theirs is the biggest, happiest, most agreeable and indeed most beautiful part of the world . . .' The systems were strong, in other words, because within the limits of the world they knew they worked manifestly better than anything that was offered them in exchange. They worked better not only at a material level but also in terms of spiritual, moral and socially constructive behaviour.

These traditional systems were weak for at least two large reasons. First, and above all, because they were the victims of their own success. They might be flexible in day-to-day adjustment. Towards all questions of structural change they showed a fundamental hostility. They were conservative by the strictest definition. They were the result, after all, of long years of careful experiment which had had to balance one danger of disintegration or failure against another, and often in circumstances of great ecological difficulty. Having reached stability, structures such as these were bound to induce an extreme distrust of far-reaching change. Although the outcome of a great deal of daring experiment in the past, they had reached a self-perpetuating level where further large experiment seemed not only unwise, but also, given the spiritual sanctions that helped to stay them up, positively wrong.

Secondly, these systems were very numerous. Pre-colonial Africa lived within a multitude of petty frontiers; exceptions such as the wide empires of the Sudan, Guinea, Central Africa, only prove the rule. Underlying unities of culture there might certainly be; seldom or never did they lead to unities of action. This was the political weakness of Africa in face of the slave trade, and afterwards of the slave trade's natural successor, colonial invasion. Individual kings and merchants might perceive the damage of the slave trade. They could never prevent it, or turn it to more than local or immediate profit, because they could never achieve unity with rivals and competitors; and the same was to be true of the European imperialist challenge. Africans, in sum, did not build their own ships and sail the ocean seas (except for the Swahili of the East Coast, who sometimes did), or otherwise embark on revolutionary technical experiment, because they saw no sufficient reason and interest in doing so, or, when European pressure taught them differently, because they lacked the social power to command or invent the necessary means. They needed a structural revolution in the content as well as in the form of their societies; and the circumstances in which this could take place were not yet present.*

Yet was it not, precisely, *these* circumstances that the colonial intervention actually provided? Apologists for European colonial rule have liked to say so. They have pointed to the innovating aspects of the experience and found in them the great apology for invasion and occupation of the continent. 'For the integration of East Africa with the general progress of mankind in the world outside,' to quote the words of an English historian, 'a drastic simplification of the old political diversity was an inescapable necessity. It was a problem which, judging by historical precedent, only a period of colonial tutelage could solve.' Clearly there is something in this. The reduction of East African states from several hundreds to a dozen or so was undoubtedly a by-product of colonial enclosure; and this may reasonably be regarded as lying on the positive side of the dialectical equation which has given us the Africa we know today. But the argument, as apologia, depends on use of the word 'tutelage', supposing a process of deliberately beneficent action on behalf of 'wards in guardianship'. This was indeed what used to be said about colonial policy in moments of ideological afflatus. Yet the record, as it happens, can be made to bear this gloss only with the greatest possible difficulty. What this argument is really saying is that *any* major intervention, no matter how blindly carried out, can have positive results. Goethe said it long ago:

*None of this, of course, is to say that there were no technological innovations, but only that the innovations were exceptional, and, in the situation which obtained, could not be generalized. Of the exceptions, few are more instructive than the firearms industry set up by the 1890s by the defender of the Western Sudan against the French, Samori Turay. This is said to have employed 300–400 blacksmiths capable of producing twelve guns a week and some 200–300 cartridges, and these guns, though smooth-bored with rifling only near the muzzle, possessed, in one French professional military opinion, a 'breech mechanism which worked easily'. (See M. Legassick, 'Fire-arms, Horses and Samorian Army Organization 1870–98', *Journal of African History*, 1, 1966.)

Sollte diese Qual uns quälen,
Da sie unsre Lust vermehrt,
Hat nicht Myriaden Seelen
Timur's Herrschaft aufgezehrt?*

The gains of colonial rule can be argued: to say that they were part of a deliberate process and could not have been achieved by other means, is to mistake the nature of the experience, as well as to ignore the losses.

There would seem, in fact, to be two mythologies at work. One of these reflects a wish to believe that only a period of foreign rule could bring Africa fully into the modern world. The other, opposing the first, is that all the ills and troubles of the continent today are due to its colonial heritage. Muting the emotional overtones, and standing as far as one may outside apologetics, we should be able to recognize that truth lies somewhere between these extremes. The colonial experience was undoubtedly heavy in its consequences. Most of these consequences were bad for Africans. But the total experience was dialectical by nature. The ills of Africa today derive partly from the colonial heritage, but also partly from Africa's still existing need for profound structural transformation. This need must have been present in any case, colonial period or not.

Seen from this standpoint, and eschewing moral aspects of the matter, it is the negative sides of the experience that seem likely to command the judgement of history. Even when considered from the relatively narrow aspect of a reduction in the number of self-governing units, in the quantity of frontiers, it cannot be said that the central result of colonial rule was to reconstruct Africa on modern lines, on the lines that were necessary to Africa's

*Must this torture be tormenting
When it brings us greater law?
Were not souls beyond the counting
Eaten up by Timur's maw?

(*West-Oestliche Divan*, Insel, 1953, p. 58.)

reconstruction from the Iron Age limits of the past. If there was virtue in a simple reduction—supposing, of course, what cannot be supposed in the light of the evidence: that the reduction was made with a view to African benefit and not to imperialist convenience—there was little or none in the way it was achieved. Vast areas such as the Congo Basin were casually clamped within a single system of colonial rule, while others were fragmented, as in western Africa, into a scatter of little colonies for which a viable independence was never even considered to be possible, much less desirable.

Viewed from other aspects, the answer appears to be the same. What the central consequence of colonial rule proved to be was not the modern reconstruction of Africa, but the far-reaching dismantlement and ruin of the societies and structures which the invaders had found.

Nobody need doubt that by 1900 the greater part of Africa most urgently required a renovation in terms of industrial science, mechanical production and new social relationships. But it was not the colonial system that provided or ever could provide this renovation. Potent to destroy, the bearers of the white man's burden proved helpless to rebuild, and the troubles of post-colonial Africa after the 1960s were to confirm this point with a weary insistence. All that was achieved, in general, was a deepening of that very large crisis of change and transformation which much of Africa had already entered before the invaders came on the scene. The invaders could and did widen this crisis. They proved unable to resolve it. Nor, for the most part, did they try to resolve it.

A Crisis Unresolved

Of course there is more to be said than this. There is scarcely a single chapter in the colonial experience that does not have its inner contradictions. To see only the destructive essence, the undermining of Iron Age society, would be to ignore a number of lesser consequences, of side-effects, that were not negative, or at any rate not purely so. While the impact and value of these varied with the nature of the metropolitan society from which the rulers came, they were present even in colonies, such as those of Portugal, that were governed by an attitude almost pre-industrial or even pre-capitalist. Though wastefully and planlessly, with reluctance or contempt, the colonial rulers nonetheless opened a few new doors to the outside world. They helped to overcome the comparative isolation of the past. Their paternalist yet persevering Christian missionary endeavour and self-sacrifice—all this being very much akin to the comparable Christian effort among the British working classes of the nineteenth century—became a powerful influence in awakening a minority of Africans to their true situation and in preparing for a different future.

Even in this educational field, however, the balance of gain was not a simple one. There was public education, true enough; but throughout the colonial period this was never more than sparsely available, even at an elementary level, and was couched most clearly in the concepts and prejudices of the educators. Even if it may have been rare that French history books taught Africans that their ancestors were Gauls, the spirit of the teaching was exactly in that vein: it taught African inferiority and European superiority. For the greater part, moreover, it was designed to do no more than provide a little primitive literacy and counting for hewers of woods and drawers of water. It ranged from a relatively high percentage of children at primary schools, after 1945, in the British and French territories and in the Belgian Congo, to the pathetic levels of the Portuguese 'civilizing effort' in Angola and Mozambique, where less than 1 per cent of African populations ever saw the inside of a school, no matter how rudimentary, before the wars of resistance began in 1961.

So far as secondary education is concerned, there is no exaggeration in saying that the whole of tropical Africa possessed only a handful of secondary schools up to the time of political independence in the late 1950s. Some of the characteristic examples must make painful reading for Europeans who have wished to believe in the reality of 'trusteeship'. After forty years of British administration in Tanganyika, a population not far short of 10 million people was able to enroll exactly 318 pupils in the class of standard 12 (the last in the four-year secondary course), while the number of school-certificates, permitting pupils to carry on with their studies, was 245. Taking the three British East African territories together—Kenya, Tanganyika and Uganda—the official figures show that populations totalling some 24 million people were able to achieve, after several decades of 'trusteeship', fewer than 2,000 school-certificates every year: fewer than one, that is, for every 12,000 people. In West Africa the position was generally rather better; elsewhere, it was often much worse. After thirty-three years of Crown Colony rule in Southern Rhodesia, official figures for 1958 showed that 12,158 African children entered school at the bottom of the scale, in sub-standard A, while the number who got through to the top, standard 12, totalled exactly 13; and this, one may note, for an African population of approximately 3 million. *

For the majority, then, colonial education either had no meaning, because it did not touch them, or none that was useful as an instrument of cultural enlightenment. Mass participation in anti-colonial struggles of one kind or another was a continuous feature of colonial life, but little of it owed anything to the influence of what was learned at school. The great revolts rested on their own traditions of political independence. The anti-colonial prophets, whether of African religion or separatist Christianity, founded their Messianic teachings upon ideas that lay outside the paternalist lessons of the schools.

It remains true that colonial education, or the means of achieving education overseas, was sometimes useful in providing small élites with a better understanding of the world they were in, and

*A factual appraisal of the whole situation, from which I draw these figures, is in *The Educated African*, ed. R. Sloan and H. Kitchen, London and New York, 1962. See also my *Modern Africa*, Longman, 1991.

that some of these élites, notably in West Africa, played an influential and distinguished part in campaigning for the rights of Africans. Even so, such voices were few and far between.

Most of the élites were content to accept the values of their masters. They tended to live double lives, in their 'European' guise and in their 'native' guise—and to prefer the first to the second, since the first carried with it not only comfort but also a certain prestige. This often meant a clear break between the colonial and native milieu, and a corresponding incapacity of the élites to use the education they possessed for the task of transforming African dependence into independence. An African leader has summarized all this. Colonial education, he points out, 'was not designed to prepare young people for the service of their own country; instead, it was motivated by a desire to inculcate the values of the colonial society and to train individuals for the service of the colonial state . . . This meant that colonial education induced attitudes of human inequality, and in practice underpinned the domination of the weak by the strong, especially in the economic field.'* It was education for the *status quo*, but a strictly colonial *status quo*. For even where a better understanding of the world helped to undermine the authority of the colonial régime, it also undermined the authority of all those Africans who stood for traditional methods and therefore, in the circumstances, for continued subjection, technological inferiority and poverty of social power. And it carried on this undermining process so effectively, at least in the minority field of educated African opinion, that what often came to matter during much of the colonial period, as Oliver has noted, was no longer what went on in the palaces of traditional potentates but what went on in the mission schools.

These are among the reasons why the colonial conquest was unique, and why it must be judged as such. Many African empires had arisen in the past, many innovating régimes, many strong reformers. Yet these had remained within their Iron Age

*Julius K. Nyerere, *Education for Self-Reliance*, Dar-es-Salaam, 1967, p. 3.

framework even though, as the nineteenth century wore on, some of them were beginning to escape from it. Many outside influences and even a few outside invasions had arrived in previous centuries. But these had never been sufficiently large or long-enduring, or launched from a sufficiently different social system, to resist more or less rapid absorption into the adaptive patterns of indigenous African life. With colonialism it was altogether different. After that, Africa could never again be the same. The patterns of indigenous life simply could not contain, much less absorb, these eruptive methods and technologies; they wrecked the old framework beyond hope of repair. In this destructive and preparatory sense the colonial experience may be said to have performed a considerable transformation, however blind and painful. By 1945 the whole complex structure of Iron Age society, so greatly out of step as it was with the world from which the conquerors came, had suffered a collapse so fatal that it could never be put together again.

Even remotely in the continental heartlands, far within the rain forests of the Congo, a skilled Belgian sociologist could find by 1946 a decay in traditional norms so far-reaching that 'nowhere any more, it may be said, does the chief really administer his tribe; nowhere is the traditional grouping still intact'. Just as the industrial revolution had swept away the confining bonds of pre-industrial society in Britain a century and more earlier, and had done this in a comparably planless, violent and blindly painful way, so too did the colonial hurricane level to the ground every great polity it found, shaking them to their very roots, and leaving in its wake the need not only for new structures, but for structures of an altogether different and expansive type.

Yet there remained, one may repeat, a profound difference between the consequences of the industrial revolution in Europe and those of the colonial system in Africa. The first destroyed but also, after its fashion, mightily rebuilt afresh; the second, having gone far to ruin what it found, could only leave for Africans the task of making a new society. No such new society came into being during the colonial period. Little was left behind but an utter impoverishment of the old society, a chaos of ideas and social relationships. Nothing could be less true than the oft-repeated statement, heard so often during the last years of the colonial period, that 'we have at least prepared these peoples for their own emancipation'. When the principal colonial powers eventually withdrew, everything of basic social meaning remained to be renewed or built afresh.

This theme of a necessary post-colonial reconstruction was never more clearly sounded, perhaps, than by a British Royal Commission which reported on the affairs of East Africa in 1955. That was at a moment when the pressures of disintegration had gone far towards wrecking the structures of traditional life. The commissioners looked at the situation and came up with conclusions which will be remembered. These dislocated 'tribal units', they opined, 'cannot revert to a past which offered to their members no prospect of material advancement'; there could be no going back to the 'simple life' for peoples who had tasted the appetites and glimpsed the possibilities of a different world. But, continued the commissioners, there could be no going forward, either, from the situation that these peoples were now in: from the basis, that is, laid down by half a century of colonial rule. 'Nor . . . can they go forward, or even stand still, under their present customary, legal and economic organization of land, labour and capital.' There could only be going back, so long as there was no 'common level of education and wealth, irrespective of divisions of tribe or race': so long, in other words, as the situation resulting from colonial rule was allowed to persist.

It would be possible, and even easy, to show that the situation described by the East African commissioners in 1955 was that of the greater part of colonized Africa. In almost every direction, but for some parts of West Africa, dismantlement of traditional society had been continuous over many years, though especially after 1939. The old world was being relentlessly swept away, with all its weaknesses but also with all its strengths. There might be few outside the ranks of the traditional rulers who regretted it. Yet the new world which was 'struggling to be born', as the commissioners put it, had still to see the light of day. Such was the sad condition of its parents, by the 1950s, that many observers could reasonably fear a miscarriage. This was the condition that made it all too certain that Africans, taking stock in the first years of their new political independence, would tend to lay all their troubles at the feet of colonialism, whereas, in truth, these troubles were inherent in the need to undertake and carry through the far-reaching reconstruction of Iron Age society which colonialism had provoked but never realized. What political emancipation did in the 1960s was to provide the opportunity for reconstruction: not from colonial confusion alone, but above all from modes and structures which could no longer satisfy or defend the interests of a majority of men, and above all of a majority of women.

EIGHT

Towards Liberation

The Forerunners

The tides of nationalism have flowed through many fogs and shadows up and down the world. But it may help to explain some of the special features of nationalism, as they developed afterwards in Africa, if one remembers that these furious currents of opinion took their initial rise during a dawn that was in many ways generous and lucid. Up to the time of the Napoleonic empire, at least, European nationalism was the child of the Enlightenment and the Rights of Man: even later, during the middle years of the nineteenth century, it was still the poets and philosophers of the 'submerged nationalities', whether Italian, Slav or Magyar, who sang most potently of human equality and therefore of human freedom. And it was in much the same spirit of emancipation, and even by way of many of the same modes of expression, that the tides of nationalism took their rise in Africa; for in Africa, as in Europe, the driving inspiration was not that all men should be divided by becoming nationals, but that all men should be united by becoming free. The actual results of nationalism were going to be different, and lead to disaster, but that was not at all what the anti-colonial liberation foresaw or could have foreseen.

What the 'morning stars' of the African awakening, men like Africanus Horton and Edward Blyden, the latter from the Caribbean but long settled in Africa, were concerned to achieve was not the nationalist mosaic of Europe—not the European 'tribal nationalism' of the late Hannah Arendt's lapidary phrase—but the abolition of all those artificial barriers against equality, and therefore against freedom, that racism and imperialism had imposed. 'Why should not the same race who governed Egypt', wrote Horton in his *Vindication of the African Race*, published in 1868, 'once more stand on their legs and endeavour to raise their characters in the scale of the civilized world?'

This was the egalitarian tradition of thought, often markedly Christian in its African expression, that held firm until the very threshold of nationalist achievement and even after the threshold was crossed. 'What is the difference between a white man and a black man?' asked an African missionary in the Nyasaland of 1911 where the difference in power and wealth had become enormous: 'Are we not of the same blood and all from Adam?' And this was the tradition that would inspire new leaders in another generous and lucid dawn, little more than three decades later, during the sharp awakening and release which accompanied defeat of the Nazi-Fascist aggressions and their racist ideologies.

This line of thought may be traced through every phase of the colonial period. Involvement in the First World War gave it a new strength. If the African volunteers who suffered on the battlefields of European conflict 'were good enough to fight and die in the Empire's cause', wrote the *Gold Coast Independent* in 1921 (and the Gold Coast had given 3,000 men to the Empire's cause, as well as the price of eleven aeroplanes), 'they were good enough . . . to have a share in the government of their countries'. Others felt the same. Although the period of full colonial installation had scarcely begun, and the last wars of pacification were still in progress, the year 1920 saw a meeting in Accra of African spokesmen from each of the four British West African territories, and the formation of a National Congress of British West Africa. 'We desire,' announced the Gold Coast leader Casely Hayford in his inaugural address, 'as the intelligentsia of our people, to promote unity among our people'; and the aims of unity, however tentatively stated, were equality and freedom.

During the weary years after 1920 more Africans escaped from stagnation at home into a wider world. Some went to western Europe, where they could compare their own situation and struggles with those of other 'depressed classes'. Others travelled to the United States, where they could learn from the teachings of Afro-American thinkers such as William Burghardt Du Bois and visionaries such as Marcus Garvey. Still others reached the newly founded Soviet Union, where they could imbibe the stronger medicine of social revolution. By the early 1930s the political awakening had begun to ripen into new and wider forms of thought and action. What now mattered most was no longer what happened in the mission schools, but what happened in a host of little centres of political discussion and incipient trade union organization.

Ideas of change had great diversity of form. In Egypt, as in Tunisia and Algeria, national movements became largely the work of middle-class intellectuals acting within the Islamic tradition, even while, as with Egyptians like Ali 'Abd al-Razaq and Taha Husain, they questioned much Islamic doctrine taken formerly for granted or above discussion. Like the nationalist party of the Wafd in the field of politics, al-Razaq opened the way for an ideological rebirth of purely Egyptian nationalism by challenging the right of the Caliphate to consider Egypt merely as a unit of the 'Islamic empire'. Elsewhere the same ferment was at work. Founded in 1920, the Tunisian Destour, or 'Party of the Constitution', aimed at national emancipation from French rule, and was supplanted in 1934 by a new party, the Néo-Destour, under more determined leaders such as Habib Bourghiba, who later became Tunisia's first president. Algeria saw the crystallization of its first modern nationalist movement in 1925, when Messali Hadj formed the Etoile Nord-Africaine, the Star of North Africa. This was displaced in 1934 by the more militant Parti Populaire Algérien, duly banned by the French in 1939 but kept alive underground.

Westward again, the early 1920s saw the great Moroccan revolt of Abd al-Krim. But Moroccan nationalism, grounded in a move-

ment of Islamic reform promoted by the Salafis, the 'Good or
Pious Ancestors', is usually dated from 1930. Like other Muslims
elsewhere, the Salafis had seen the invading French army in the
light of a Christian power seeking to suppress Islam. But they
advanced to more directly political ground in 1930, when the
French caused the promulgation of a *dahir*, or sultan's decree,
whereby the Berber peoples of Morocco were removed from the
jurisdiction of Islamic courts. Salafism blossomed into nationalism. Then it was that Allal al-Fassi formed a secret society
called al-Zawaiyya which soon became the core of a nationalist
movement, the Istiqlal, or Party of Independence.

At the other end of Africa the 1930s likewise saw the spread
of new ideas of emancipation among many Africans of South
Africa who had previously stood within traditional frames of
thought: among peasants now enclosed in squalid rural slums,
among migrant workers labouring in the gold mines of the Wit-
watersrand, and, gradually, among fast-growing peri-urban mul-
titudes as well. In less harried lands the spread was slower, but
it stubbornly continued. If ideas of emancipation still lay in the
future for most of the peoples of central Africa, this was no longer
true in the eastern or western regions. Thus the Kikuyu of Kenya,
whose land included fertile and healthy uplands increasingly enclosed by European farmers, had embarked on the politics of
protest as early as 1921. This was when the Young Kikuyu Association was formed under the lead of a Nairobi telephone op-
erator called Harry Thuku. Its message, as framed by Thuku,
was clear enough. 'Hearken, every day you pay hut tax to the
Europeans of Government', was one of the points in his 1922
programme: 'Where is it sent? It is their task to steal the property
of the Kikuyu people.'

Now too there came a widening breakaway from Christian
church communities seen as dominated by Europeans for their
own ends. By 1929 there were many independent African
churches whose message proclaimed 'Africa for the Africans', and
was as much political as religious. Meanwhile the politics of
protest in West Africa had continued to assume ever more de-

termined forms of directly political organization. When the Second World War once more shook the prestige and power of the colonial rulers, and thrust many thousands of Africans into new patterns of thought or action, the ground of popular understanding was well and widely laid.

After 1945: The Struggle Against Colonial Crisis

In its consequences for Africa the Second World War greatly accelerated that general dismantlement of traditional society which had begun with colonial invasion in the 1880s. The evidence, as before, is complex and even contradictory; yet its negative aspects were now increasingly apparent, as the following fairly characteristic piece of evidence may be enough to show. 'For five years,' Father van Wing could write of the Belgian Congo in 1945, 'our populations were subjected to a war-effort that was extremely intense and varied. The whole black population was mobilized to produce as much as possible, and as rapidly as possible, in order to export what the Allies needed and to provide what they lacked. That is the dominating fact.'

This 'dominating fact' in mines and plantations was coupled with an often disastrous decline of the indigenous rural economy. Deepening poverty in the countryside drove men and women in ever rising numbers into towns and cities. The flood gained fresh strength as soon as the colonial powers had recovered from their own losses and disorganization. Wartime demand for raw materials was surpassed by a post-war boom in western European and American production. By the mid-1950s there was scarcely a single city in Africa which had failed to treble or quadruple its population since 1939. Vast numbers of peasants broke away from the misery of rural poverty and braved the different misery of life in hastily erected urban slums, 'locations' or, in the graphic French term for them, 'tin-can towns'.

Nothing like this had been seen since the British industrial revolution. Thrust suddenly into a cash economy far beyond their

control or understanding, these new townspeople made shift as
they could. However much they suffered, whether from colour-
bar discrimination in South Africa and in the colonies of white
settlement, or from sheer material and moral inanition elsewhere,
the flood continued. Something of the same picture could be
painted of these towns as of the English industrial cities of the
mid-nineteenth century. 'The evils associated with the absence
of family life, drunkenness, prostitution and venereal disease',
observed the British Royal Commission on East Africa in 1955,
'are rife in the towns with large African populations . . .' One
of the most illuminating series of statistics available for these years
concerns the rising rate of alcohol import. By 1951 official figures
show the French West African colonial federation as importing
fifteen times more strong drink than in 1938; and the French
territories were not unique in this respect.

As these trends uncontrollably continued, it soon became
clear, at least to the few who cared to look, that much of Africa
was now plunged in profound and widening social and economic
disintegration, and that none of the old colonial solutions could
any longer hope to work. The wiser heads in colonial administrations perceived the way the wind was blowing, and vainly
sought for means of subduing its force. For these colonies 'to go
back to the subsistence economy of the past', the East Africa
Royal Commission decided in 1955, 'or even to stand still in the
dawn between the old institutions which are dying and the new
which are struggling to be born, would be to court disaster.' Yet
how could any solution along colonial lines prevent this? In a
large sense it could be said that the partly latent crisis of the
nineteenth century and the colonial period itself had now reached
the explosion point.

A New Nationalism

This explosion took the form of struggles for national independence within frontiers drawn by the colonial powers. Earlier

demands for equality and emancipation now became nationalism in the narrower sense of the word. Gathering in Manchester in 1945, the members of the sixth Pan-African Congress, including Kwame Nkrumah, afterwards president of Ghana, Jomo Kenyatta, afterwards president of Kenya, and a representative of Nnamdi Azikiwe, afterwards president of Nigeria, still spoke (as some of them would afterwards continue to speak, but with a new authority) of the Pan-African cause, but they struck a markedly new note. Unlike their predecessors, they demanded not only respect for Africans, but also autonomy and even independence.

New and more radical nationalist parties were soon formed in colonies such as the Gold Coast, Nigeria and French West Africa where the ruling power was prepared, if still with great reluctance, to allow them to exist. The other side of the process of dismantlement—the growth of the politics of protest—became increasingly apparent. In colonies such as Northern Rhodesia the influence of the British Labour Party had paved a cautious but still possible path towards effective trade unions, invariably prohibited in earlier years; and trade unionism now played a part of growing importance in the effectiveness of national movements.

Little by little, and then with gathering speed, the nationalist cause spread far outside the limits of the educated minority which had first proclaimed it, and assumed mass dimensions as it drew within its orbit ever larger numbers of townspeople and peasants. These movements soon thrust ahead of the few concessions which British or French colonial governors were ready to accept as necessary; and the dozen years after 1945 were accordingly full of violent clashes and upheavals, repressions, shootings and imprisonments. Yet the onward drive of African opinion, coupled with a growing British and French awareness that nothing but major political change could meet this crisis, gradually achieved important constitutional changes.

North of the Sahara, the decisive point of change came with the Free Officers' *coup d'état* of 1952 in Egypt and the assumption of power by Gamal Abdel Nasser two years later; although, in

mere point of time, the former Italian colony of Libya had
achieved sovereignty under its Sanusi king, Idris al-Mahdi al-
Sanusi, in 1951. Morocco and Tunisia followed in 1955–56. In
1956, too, the Anglo-Egyptian Condominium over the Eastern
Sudan was brought to an end, and the Republic of Sudan was
proclaimed in Khartoum. The collapse of Fascist Italy had meanwhile restored independence to the ancient empire of Ethiopia,
adding an Eritrean province, and the new Italian Republic was
also ready to pull out of Somalia. South of the Sahara the pace
of constitutional change was set by the Convention Peoples' Party
of the Gold Coast under Kwame Nkrumah's energetic leadership.
Achieving internal self-rule in 1951, the country that was now
to be called Ghana acquired full political independence in 1957.
Nigeria quickly followed, with internal self-rule beginning in
1952 and independence in 1960.

Everywhere else the pressures for change grew immeasurably
stronger during the 1950s. The year 1960 saw the emergence of
an independent Somali Republic which combined the former
British territory of Somaliland with that of Italian Somalia. Tanganyika followed in 1961, and Uganda in 1962. Kenya, though
in the wake of bitter struggles between African and white settler
claims to hegemony, became independent in 1963, and Zanzibar
in 1964. This East African island followed its independence with
an almost immediate revolution against its sultan and its land-
owning minority, and joined with nearby Tanganyika in a union
which took the name of Tanzania.

After ten years of strife and frustration the European-dominated
Federation of the two Rhodesias and Nyasaland was abolished
in 1963; Nyasaland and Northern Rhodesia became the independent countries of Malawi and Zambia a year later. With Sierra
Leone achieving independence in 1961, Gambia in 1965, the
two High Commission territories of Basutoland and Bechuanaland, as Lesotho and Botswana, in 1966, and Swaziland in 1968,
there remained to the British Empire in Africa only a nominal
title to the rebellious settlers' Crown Colony of Rhodesia.

All this, historically, marked a turning-point that was neatly labelled by Harold Macmillan, then British prime minister, as the work of a 'wind of change'. Africans could at last speak for themselves and look forward to a future of their own shaping. But it was not always or even often noticed at the time that the 'wind of change' swept away far less than many supposed. It carried new men into office and power. But the desks they sat at were the same as before, and so were the files from which they worked. The rulers had changed, but not the institutions of colonial government.

It could not be long before these new rulers found that the peaceful transitions of reform had their strict limits, and that these limits made it hard, if not impossible, to carry on the work of unification and general progress, whether within countries or between countries, to which they were committed. Some of the new rulers accepted this situation and worked merely at turning it to the advantage of a new élite, a new bureaucracy, a new bourgeoisie whether civilian or military. Others, staying true to their vision of a different future, tested the limits of the framework handed on to them by the departing colonial rulers and prepared to try to break out of them. But for all of them the price of peaceful change, of a reformism which accepted independence within the existing institutions of colonial rule, was to prove a high one. Yet the starting atmosphere was one of solid hope: at least these lands were political colonies no longer.

The French colonies moved to the same end by a different route. After Germany's invasion of France in 1940 the pro-Nazi régime established at Vichy tried to maintain both the racist ethos of colonialism and the fact of direct imperial rule. Democratic France could offer little opposition to this until 1943. By then, however, the war had assumed an explicitly anti-colonialist form under the dual if very differently motivated pressures of the United States and the Soviet Union, and these had an increasing influence on the Free French movement led by General Charles de Gaulle. Suspected by the Americans as a British instrument, de Gaulle found himself played off against ex-Vichyist leaders in North Africa. Reacting to this, he spoke more and more sharply for republican ideas in the grand tradition of liberty and equality, and opened the way for some promise of change in those colonies where African élites had thrown in their lot with his cause.

Out of these manoeuvres there came the famous 'Brazzaville Declaration' of 1944, generally regarded as the beginning of the end of the French empire in Africa. Viewed in the light of later years, the Brazzaville decisions were extremely timid. 'The nature of the French colonial task', they announced, *'excludes all idea of autonomy, all possibility of development outside the bloc of the French Empire: even the distant establishment of self-government in the colonies is excluded.'* (Emphasis in the original.)

Yet the Brazzaville decisions offered 'participation'. Coupled with the spirit of the times, this helped to pave the way for provisions in the 1946 constitution of the new Fourth Republic whereby the French colonies were to elect, albeit by restricted franchise, a number of Africans who would sit as deputies in the National Assembly in Paris. Grasping this opportunity, a number of the nascent nationalist parties came together at a unity conference in 1946, at Bamako in the Soudan (later Mali), and formed themselves into a multi-territorial alliance called the Rassemblement Démocratique Africain. It was the leaders of this RDA who now made the running throughout French Africa.

In 1956 one of the last governments of the Fourth Republic proclaimed that each of the territories might have internal self-rule. This *loi cadre* or 'framework law', as it was called, did much to split the budding unity of the French West African movements while giving each of them more freedom of action within its own boundaries. Two years later, newly returned to power in France, de Gaulle offered all these territories a choice between immediate independence or membership in a new French Community run from Paris. Only the Guinea 'Section of the RDA', the Parti Démocrate de Guinée under the leadership of Sékou Touré, was strong enough to take advantage of this. Surviving a subsequent French boycott, Guinea pointed the way for the others, all of whom, including Madagascar, followed in 1960 after another shift in French policy that was greatly influenced by Félix Houphouet-Boigny of the Ivory Coast. With this the French Community was dead, although the hand of Paris was reaffirmed and strengthened by military and financial agreements under which France retained a predominant influence in nearly all these former colonies. Up to 1965 France retained some 20,000 troops in 'Black Africa'. Even after 1965 France continued to influence or control many of its economic and budgetary decisions and retained troops in a number of territories. Association with the West European Common Market further strengthened these ties with France.

These, for the most part, were withdrawals of political authority which affected little more than French prestige, or what was imagined to be such, and were conducted in a peaceful way. With the settler colonies, however, it was different; and here as with British colonies of the same type, the theme of underlying conflict between metropolitan and settler interests, struck so often in European history, was sounded in the notes of hatred, violence and disaster. Algeria was the worst case. As at much the same time in Kenya, the central equivocation in European colonial policy was made to erupt, or allowed to erupt, in great explosions of warfare.

It may be said that the French had never been as equivocal as the British in their expressions of solicitude for the 'natives'. They had frankly conquered Algeria for France. They had taken its fertile regions into the constitutional framework of the French Republic. They had poured in their settlers without the least respect for Algerian needs or culture. If they had occasionally claimed to be doing this for the benefit of Algerians, no such pallidly humanitarian improbability was allowed to influence policy. This policy was to give the power to their settlers. As businessmen or landowners, these settlers were interested in the maximum obtainable degree of exploitation of Algeria. As employees or skilled workers they were concerned to barricade their monopoly behind colour bars which would restrict Algerians to unskilled labour or low-paid handicrafts. Though in a French guise, the resultant system was perfectly South African or Por-

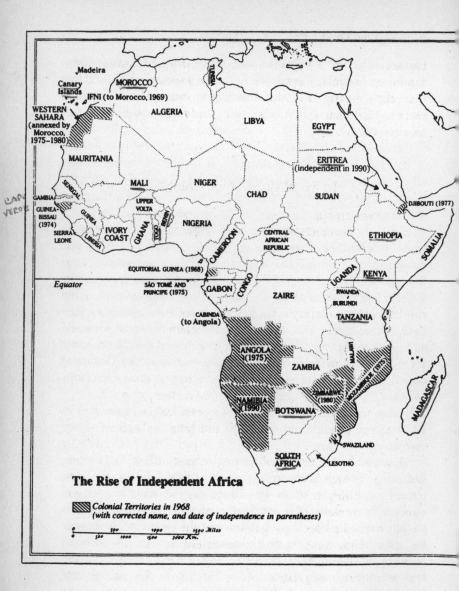

CAPE
VERDE

Madeira

Canary
Islands

IFNI (to Morocco, 1969)

WESTERN
SAHARA
(annexed by
Morocco,
1975–1980)

MOROCCO

TUNISIA

ALGERIA

LIBYA

EGYPT

MAURITANIA

MALI

NIGER

CHAD

SUDAN

ERITREA
(independent in 1990)

GAMBIA

SENEGAL

GUINEA-
BISSAU
(1974)

GUINEA

SIERRA
LEONE

LIBERIA

IVORY
COAST

UPPER
VOLTA

GHANA

TOGO

BENIN

NIGERIA

CENTRAL
AFRICAN
REPUBLIC

CAMEROON

ETHIOPIA

DJIBOUTI (1977)

SOMALIA

EQUITORIAL GUINEA (1968)

Equator

SÃO TOMÉ AND
PRINCIPE (1975)

GABON

CONGO

ZAIRE

UGANDA

KENYA

RWANDA

BURUNDI

TANZANIA

CABINDA
(to Angola)

ANGOLA
(1975)

ZAMBIA

MALAWI

MOZAMBIQUE (1975)

MADAGASCAR

NAMIBIA
(1990)

ZIMBABWE
(1980)

BOTSWANA

SWAZILAND

SOUTH
AFRICA

LESOTHO

The Rise of Independent Africa

Colonial Territories in 1968
(with corrected name, and date of independence in parentheses)

0   500   1000   1500 Miles
0 500 1000 1500 2000 Km.

336

tuguese. Out of it—just as in South Africa, Rhodesia, Mozambique, Angola, Kenya—there came a society of 'race' rather than class, nearly all whites tending to unite, no matter what sectional conflicts might otherwise divide them, against nearly all non-whites.

In the White-Settler Colonies

The stronger among these racist societies was to prove impossible to modify, in southern Africa as elsewhere, by any means other than the use of counter-violence. However deplorable this may have been, the fact was that the majority of settlers simply lacked the qualities required for the acceptance of peaceful change. Entrenched in their minority despotism, clinging to their extremely high standards of living, they closed their eyes to all else. Only where settler communities were relatively small or weak, as in Tanzania, Malawi, Zambia, was it possible for national movements to make headway without systematic or prolonged violence. But wherever the settlers were strong, they sufficiently believed in their own power of exclusive rule, or successfully looked to the support of metropolitan pressure groups; and progress became possible only through the bitter policies of armed revolt.

Algerians had often revolted in the past. There is a sense, indeed, in which some of them were always in more or less declared hostility to their French rulers, whether by outright violence or protests of a peaceful nature. They had never prevailed. Even the liberal governments of the early Fourth Republic, after 1945, brought no improvement in their situation. A growing population had less and less to eat. If the average Algerian had five quintals of grain a year in the 1870s, the amount had fallen to four quintals in 1900 and to little more than two in the 1940s. Rising population figures had much to do with this. But so also did French expropriation of the coastal grainlands for the growing of wine. From a mere 4,000 acres of vineyard in 1830,

the land under vines had grown to about 750,000 acres by the
middle 1950s. Economic degradation went hand-in-hand with
more or less complete denial of political rights. Such was the
nature of cultural oppression that Arabic, the language of most
Algerians, was neither permitted as a medium of instruction nor
even allowed to be taught in the schools.

Reacting against an *attentiste* leadership of their national
movement, a number of young Algerians banded together in the
early 1950s and decided upon another armed revolt. This was
launched in the Aurés massif of eastern Algeria in November
1954, and was finally successful after seven years of French military and civilian repression which cost about a million lives and
involved more than half a million French troops. It came to an
end, one may note, not when one side or the other had gained
an obvious victory—the military position at the end was much
nearer to one of stalemate—but when the metropolitan interests
of France were clearly shown by this resistance to be in conflict
with those of the settlers. Again, characteristically for these caste
societies, the last phases of the struggle were marked by increasing
hostility between the metropolitan country and the settlers. The
same was to be true of Britain and Rhodesia after the Rhodesian
settlers' revolt of November 1965.

This pattern was repeated on a smaller scale in Kenya. As in
Algeria, Kenya was conquered and enclosed as a 'colony of settlement', at least in the minds of the men who made the running,
and notably in that of Sir Charles Eliot, the first commissioner
of the East African Protectorate which took shape in the 1890s.
Excellent land most suitable for European farming was to be
occupied by a large number of settlers while the interests of the
'natives' could be ignored because, in the scale of civilization,
they were supposed to be people without claims, even without
identity. 'We have in East Africa', wrote Eliot in this connection,
'the rare experience of dealing with a *tabula rasa*, an almost
untouched and sparsely inhabited country where we can do as
we will . . .' It was Eliot's view that largely prevailed.

There emerged a caste system based on the paramountcy of European interests, and above all on those of a few thousand British farmers in the 'white highlands' of central Kenya. Most of these settlers thought that Kenya was to be another South Africa, and they behaved accordingly. In the end, as in Algeria, it was revolt alone that turned the scale in any decisive way. This was the revolt of the Kikuyu and some of their neighbours, beginning in 1953 and continuing until 1957, and leading, if through many and various paths, to independence under majority rule in 1963, but only after some 10,000 peasants had lost their lives. Elsewhere, caste societies proved less capable of resistance, and bloodshed could sometimes be avoided. In this spectrum of varieties the vast colony of the Belgian Congo made something of an exceptional case.

As late as 1959 the Belgians in Belgium, whose governments had given away no political power-positions to their settlers in Africa, were still asserting their intention of governing the Congo for another thirty years or more. Suddenly shifting their ground in January 1960, clearly hoping that in this way they could take advantage of African inexperience, they broke away from this traditional policy and conceded full political independence within six months. This duly came in the middle of 1960 with nothing prepared. Not only were there fewer than a score of Congolese university graduates at this time—and not a single one of these with any serious administrative experience—but, far more disturbing, no Congolese national party or movement had enjoyed more than a few months in which to organize and prepare itself for power. Without a single Congolese officer, its mercenary Force Publique (a colonial force raised by colonial methods in the days of the Congo Free State and used ever since for the woeful tasks of pacification) mutinied almost at once. The newly independent administration collapsed under these and other strains. Its most effective leader, Patrice Lumumba, fell victim to outside pressures and internal intrigues, and was murdered in 1961. Years of conflict and betrayal lay ahead.

Even so there remained, by 1967, few colonies outside the embattled 'white south'. The French still had the enclave of Jibuti (French Somaliland), but largely because its population of some 50,000 people were divided in their loyalties between Somalia and Ethiopia. The Spanish for a while still had their thinly populated colonies of the Spanish Sahara (Rio d'Oro), Sidi Ifni and Spanish Guinea (consisting of the West African island of Fernando Po and the nearby mainland enclave of Rio Muni); all these enclosed a population of fewer than half a million. The British retained a measure of control over a small southern African country, Swaziland, which was due for political independence in the near future.

Apart from Angola and Mozambique, where they faced a mounting nationalist resistance from guerrillas of the MPLA (Movimento Popular de Libertação de Angola, founded in clandestinity in 1956) and FRELIMO (Frente de Libertação de Moçambique, founded in 1962), the Portuguese still clung, though with growing desperation, to their small colony of Guiné in West Africa as well as to the historically related Cape Verde Islands. Nationalist resistance here had begun in 1956 with the clandestine formation of the PAIGC (Partido Africano de Independência de Guiné e Cabo Verde) under the inspired leadership of its remarkable founder, Amílcar Cabral (1924–73). These wars of counter-violence against a particularly retrograde Portuguese colonialism were long and painful, since they had to be conducted against a ruthless system supported by strong alliance with the industrial powers in the North Atlantic Treaty Organization (NATO).

Yet the wars of counter-violence proved consistently successful. Guiné became fully independent as Guinea-Bissau in 1974. Mozambique and Cape Verde won their independence in 1975, as did the two south Atlantic islands of São Tomé and Principe, which likewise formed a new republic. Angola declared its independence in 1975 but then had to win a 'second war of liberation' against South African and Zairean invaders. South

African military aggression continued in later years, but without overturning the new Angolan republic.

These achievements changed the balance of power in southern Africa, and enabled an anti-colonial counter-violence to succeed in Southern Rhodesia as well. Largely conducted by the Zimbabwe African National Union (ZANU), this guerrilla campaign led to negotiation and independence in 1980, wh- outhern Rhodesia became the republic of Zimbabwe. A corresponding campaign was in course, by then, in the virtual South African colony of Namibia, a campaign that was eventually successful in 1990, when Nambia became independent.

The Racist Bastion in South Africa

For many years now, with every technological advance in the workings of their caste society, the South African whites had taken, politically and socially, a corresponding step backward to an ever more oppressive dictatorship. By the 1960s they possessed an industrial machine of comparatively great power and wealth, fuelled and constantly expanded by steady inflows of private capital from the United States, Britain and other West European countries.

In many ways these whites could claim to have achieved an advanced civilization. Yet in many other ways, and in all those touching on its attitudes to non-whites, and on the condition of the non-whites, this civilization still rested on the presumptions of slavery. None of the ease and comfort that these whites increasingly enjoyed appeared able to give them the self-confidence of men who could seriously question their actions or ideas. On the contrary, their political retreat into a 'white fortress' continued year by year, and especially after the National Party of Afrikaner (Boer) extreme racism came to power in 1948. One after another the petty discriminations against non-whites were multiplied in terms of pass laws and everyday segregation. One after another

the major discriminations were strengthened in terms of education, political life and territorial segregation. One after another
the slender rights of non-whites were wiped from the legislative
map. When non-whites replied to this with political protest, they
were sent to prison. When they answered with passive resistance,
they were furiously assaulted by the police. When they grew tired
of passive action and passed to violence, they were tracked and
seized and executed without the least attention to the motives for
their violence.

By 1965 some kind of pattern was beginning to emerge about
the way in which the leaders of these whites now saw their future.
Within the bulk of South Africa (including Nambia, a land supposedly in 'trusteeship' from the League of Nations and then the
United Nations, but long since, in fact, a South African colony),
the whites were to rule as permanent masters of an African population some five times their number. Here, the non-whites were
to be tolerated as useful workers and nothing more.

Alongside this 'white South Africa' there were to be a number
of 'Bantustans', inhabited only by Africans, which were to have
a measure of domestic self-rule as satellites of white South Africa:
in fact, as labour reserves under another name. To these Bantustans, at least in the ideology of the white leaders, were to be
added the former British High Commission territories of Lesotho
(Basutoland) and Botswana (Bechuanaland), and Swaziland, as
well as new Bantustans in the large colony of Nambia. Over and
beyond these again, and in a situation not yet clearly defined,
there were to be the neighbouring and much larger satellites of
Rhodesia, Angola and Mozambique. These three would be ex-
pendable if outside pressures proved intolerably strong; meanwhile, South Africa would help them, if necessary, to gain a
local independence under settler rule, as well as advancing its
influence, if possible, still further into the 'black north'.

This pattern, it was believed, would be stable for three reasons:
first, because of the absolutely dominant position of the whites
in South Africa itself; secondly, because the outside world would
not in fact prove willing or able to intervene; thirdly, because

the 'black north' would remain, at least for the foreseeable future, too weak to intervene or even to defend itself.*

Seen from this perspective, 1967 showed both gains and losses. South African whites could take comfort from the success of their fellow-whites across the Limpopo, although it remained to be seen whether these settlers could make their rebellion succeed even with the steady help they were receiving from their South African patrons. Declared in November 1965, a rebellion against the Crown Colony status of Rhodesia had met with feeble British responses, irresolute British action and a merely half-hearted attempt to apply economic sanctions. Even so, the rebellion had had the effect, far from welcome from a white South African standpoint, of uniting the greater part of the world in at least formal opposition to a régime of the same type as that of South Africa; and it was still not sure who would win.

By 1980 the situation had greatly changed. The two great flank-guards of the South African system, Angola and Mozambique, had indeed acceded to their independence, but under powerfully radical African governments; and nothing that Pretoria was able to effect against them had so far done more than worry and disturb these new republics. The new republic of Zimbabwe might be economically vulnerable and politically divided; but it was very far from being the convenient pawn or subsidiary that Pretoria had planned. Even the directly colonial power that South Africa still wielded in Namibia seemed now to be under serious threat. And as black resistance widened within South Africa itself, a series of worldwide demonstrative boycotts of the *apartheid* state—for example, in sporting events—began to produce a new feeling of anxious isolation in segments of the white minority.

*No such pattern, perhaps needless to say, was officially acknowledged by any Afrikaner spokesman. Nor would it be true to say that Afrikaner leaders were themselves united on what their policies should be. Yet this was the pattern which came insistently from the record of those years. For perceptive hints from a skilled observer generally sympathetic to the white South African position, see E. S. Munger, *Notes on the Formation of South African Policy*, Pasadena, California, 1965; and, in wider perspective and greater detail, B. Bunting, *The Rise of the South African Reich*, repr. 1969; and R. First, J. Steele and C. Gurney, *The South African Connection*, repr. 1973; with their bibliographies.

The question now frequently posed, even by interests in the outside world that had previously taken *apartheid* for granted, began to be: how long can *this* South Africa survive?

The answer would clearly turn on three basic considerations: the strength of the régime; the degree of support that it could continue to command from external allies; and the counter-strength of black resistance.

Repression in the 1960s had appeared to silence all effective black protest. An initial effort at counter-violence by guerrilla sabotage had failed, and ended in the long-term imprisonment of black leaders, including Nelson Mandela. Yet the silence was broken early in the 1970s by successful strikes of black workers in manufacturing industries. In parallel with these successes, black students in 'tribally segregated' colleges—dividing Sotho from Zulu, Xhosa from Venda, and so on—began to evolve a unity of protest, across these largely artificial 'tribal barriers', under the banner of 'Black Consciousness'. This was an essentially morale-raising campaign which made its mark, even though its best-known spokesman, Steve Biko, was soon killed in prison.

Collapse of the Portuguese colonial system in 1974–75 was undoubtedly a factor in promoting the further recovery of black self-confidence in the *apartheid* state. In 1976 the scene of protest shifted, partly in response to that collapse, to vast African 'townships' such as Soweto near Johannesburg. School-students went on strike, and were duly shot down by the police in large numbers, reliably estimated at several hundred young men and women. This repression provoked something that came near, for the first time in recent South African history, to a mass uprising, again put down by police violence but, this time, denoting a new determination among wide strata of the black population (whether African, Indian or Coloured). Guerrillas of Umkonto wa Sizwe, the military wing of the African National Congress, now began to find an ever more effective support from that population, and guerrilla successes increased as a result. By 1982 it appeared that the process of armed resistance had possibly gone beyond the régime's ability to suffocate it, while the number of guerrillas now within South Africa, awaiting further stages in that process, was thought to be several thousand.

By this time, too, the racist régime had gone far towards a more or less complete militarization. Inherently, its condition had become one of endemic emergency, and there was little to suggest that this condition could be terminated by new forms of repression. Its military and economic strength were overwhelmingly powerful; yet they rested on an embattled minority of some 4 million whites in a total population now approaching 24 million. How far could this highly privileged minority support the strains and demands of militarization? There were those now who began to say that racist South Africa would not survive the century.

However that might be, the régime's external alliances continued to hold firm, offering no more than verbal protest against the intransigent violence of the *apartheid* state. Powerful interests, notably in the America of President Ronald Reagan, argued that survival of the *apartheid* state was essential to the stability of the Western economic system, relying as this did on South African gold, and having great investments in South African mining and manufacturing industry. The West would try to persuade the régime to moderate its discriminatory laws and customs, but it would not act to undermine a system which appeared vital to Western interests.

Here again a question was posed: within the *apartheid* state, was there or was there not any potential for self-correction, modification, constructive change? Earlier optimists had believed that the sheer expansion of the South African economy, calling for more and more black skilled and professional labour, must gradually lessen discrimination against blacks and remove colour bars on high-wage employment. Yet the great boom of the 1950s and 1960s had achieved no such change: on the contrary, every expansion of the economy had gone hand-in-hand with new measures of discrimination and segregation. No evidence of any 'self-correcting potential' within the regime had come to light. The condition by the middle of the 1980s was to be one of deepening apprehension, conflict and violence.

Towards a Liberated South

What was further clear by now was that the fate of much of the rest of the continent—its chances of exit from acute structural crisis, its hopes of diminishing impoverishment, its plans for a better future—was going to be decided in significant part by the fate of South Africa itself. So long as the régime of *apartheid* racism could continue its war of economic and military attrition against its neighbours, large avenues of possible development would remain blocked off. Abolish that régime, however, and the scope for intra-regional and even intra-continental co-operation, mutual aid and constructive solidarity of effort could be decisively widened.

If South Africa were thus de-militarized, perhaps other countries could be as well. If so, then there would be a chance to cut down on Africa's reckless spending on arms and armies. So long as that destructive waste continued, so also would the decline into ever harsher poverty for the mass of people. In 1960, when many colonies became independent countries, Africa as a whole spent $1 billion on importing arms; bad enough, but in 1987, incredibly, this overall African spending on arms imports had risen to $35 billion. The climb has continued. This has been another recipe for disaster.

Meanwhile the question of South African de-militarization remained an open one. The final years of the *apartheid* régime in South Africa threatened to be its worst, weighing bitterly on future efforts at reconciliation and reconstruction. Through the 1980s the régime continued to writhe and struggle against what now seemed its eventual defeat.

Internally, repression was made still more ruthless and indiscriminate. But this again proved incapable of silencing the protest of the black majority. On the contrary, defiant protest grew wider and still more confident of being able to secure democratic change. This protest came from trade unions previously illegal, from political alliances previously unheard of, from the great black townships around Johannesburg, Cape Town and other white-cored cities, from countless individuals and organizations previously silenced; and little of this defiant protest could be silenced any longer.

True to its nature, the régime found the lesson hard to learn. In its racism it continued to insist on using the big stick of repression, encouraged at home by most (though no longer all) of its white electorate, and abroad by powerful investing interests and groups who opposed the ending of *apartheid* racism because *apartheid* in South Africa seemed a sure guarantee of corporate and personal profit. In 1986, accordingly, the whole country was placed under emergency regulations. These gave the green light to repression by army and police. State terrorism against the black majority took new and sinister forms. It became clear that the last official restraints had been withdrawn. In 1986 alone, between March and June, some 40,000 arrests or detentions were made. Tight censorship muzzled critics. Openly democratic organizations of the black majority, notably an alliance of many black organizations known as the United Democratic Front, were harried, persecuted or banned, as the widely representative African National Congress had long been.

After 1986 the story continued as before: mounting repression was met by mounting defiance. Protest was of course hampered by the repression: for while a few of its leaders, including the veteran Govan Mbeki of the African National Congress, were released from long-term imprisonment under pressure both national and international, thousands of others were now thrust into jails. Ever more trigger-happy, the régime's police used more violence, and used it widely. This violence was now lethal and systematic in its assault on the black majority. For decades South Africa had been virtually a police state for most of its inhabitants. Now it became a shoot-to-kill state. Yet protest nonetheless con-

tinued, outfacing all threats and murders. Something would have
to give.

Externally, ramming home the same conclusion, the régime
met with other defeats. Its military forces of subversion had sponsored and promoted a vicious campaign of banditry against the
newly independent government and people of Mozambique, but
this campaign, though wreaking widespread havoc and starvation,
had still failed to overturn that country's independence. Across
on the western side of the southern continent, in Angola, a similar
campaign of violent 'destabilization' through another Pretoria-
sponsored and -financed organization known as UNITA had similarly failed, even though here it was reinforced by full-scale
South African military invasion. This invasion culminated in
1988, after months of highly destructive warfare, in a major defeat
of the South African army by the army of Angola supported by
units of Cuba's air force; and this time, given the severity of
South African military losses, it seemed unlikely that the South
African invasion could be renewed.

South of Angola, the régime had intended to maintain its hold
on its old colony of South-West Africa, now Namibia. But here
too there was defeat. In a complex series of diplomatic pressures,
coupled with internal pressures brought to bear by Namibia's
independence movement, the South African political position
was progressively undermined. Finally, in March 1990, the
South African flag was lowered in Windhoek, the Namibian
capital, and the country became free to envisage its own future.
With this, the last of racist South Africa's satellite neighbours
moved out of Pretoria's direct control. The vision of a liberated
south came a little closer.

At much the same time, inside South Africa, the result of all
these defeats began to take effect. There was a change in white
leadership, promising democratic concessions. The acknowledged spokesman of the black majority, the now world-famous
African National Congress leader Nelson Mandela, was at last
set free after nearly three decades of close imprisonment. The

world began to understand that the racist cause, however it might still struggle to survive, was decisively lost.

In all this, international pressures played a vacillating and contradictory role, of which the detailed history is still to be written. But, generally, it had already been shown that international protest and pressure, and above all an application of financial and other sanctions against the régime, could be highly effective measures in support of internal protest and the demand for democratic change. Here in South Africa, at least, these anti-*apartheid* sanctions opened light at the end of the tunnel.

The outcome, clearly, could now be a great chance for democratic liberties and equalities, but would not easily be reached. Majority black opinion—whether African (by far the biggest section), Indian or Coloured (of mixed origins)—was solidly and passionately behind its representative organizations, notably the now unbanned African National Congress and its political ally, the United Democratic Front. But there were threatening fractures in the black communities. Violent urban crime in crowded 'townships', such as Soweto (South-West Township) outside the Transvaal mining and business city of Johannesburg, was one of these fractures. It was hard to deal with, and meanwhile played into the hands of official repression. More serious, in the province of Natal, an organization called Nkata, based on a sort of 'tribal' and partly Zulu separatism, registered acute hostility to the ANC with outbursts of reckless aggression which could provoke (and clearly were intended to provoke) replies in kind. Product of the *apartheid* system's so-called 'Bantu' homelands policy, which elevated the old 'native reserves' to a purely theoretical 'independence' (in practice recognized nowhere), Nkata and some other 'Homelands' splinters might have no future in a democratic society; but meanwhile they offered a distraction from which the *apartheid* system could profit. Even civil war seemed possible.

The ANC itself, with the release of Mandela and other veteran leaders, replied with new efforts to defend its unity. Immediately, though, it faced some unavoidable dilemmas. With the govern-

ment at last prepared to come forward with what seemed to be
a serious plan of democratic concessions, negotiations would raise
basic issues of enormous importance for the future. At what point,
for example, could it be said that the *apartheid* system was abolished? Was this conceivable for the black majority before the
system's abandonment of its main principles of racist discrimination: the Group Areas Act, the Registration of Voters Act, and
the Land Act (of 1913, giving whites exclusive rights of ownership
in some 85 per cent of the whole country)? These were the three
great 'pillars' of the system. Even when these laws were repealed,
could the black majority be satisfied with an economic situation
in which most sources of wealth were securely concentrated in
white hands and ownership? If not, what measures of restitution
must be insisted on?

All these aspects of systemic discrimination represented the
legal framework of white supremacy. They were built into every
field of the country's life. They embodied the conscious and
determined violence of the system, just as did a reckless police
force and hugely inflated armed services. They must go if any
peaceful settlement were to be reached. Against them, over decades, the ANC and other black organizations had unfolded campaigns of peaceful protest and agitation, invariably put down by
intimidation and force. Since the 1960s, after long hesitation,
the ANC had also used an arm of counter-violence to the violence
of the system, Umkonto wa Sizwe (Spear of the Nation), in
repeated actions of guerrilla sabotage and the like. What transition
to a democratic society would now be possible, and how could
this be achieved?

Meanwhile the ruling National Party, the government party
and chief builder of *apartheid*, had severe problems within its
own Afrikaner community. Menacing among these problems was
an extremist breakaway faction which now pressed for a policy
of violent response to any meaningful concessions to democracy.
The new state president, F. W. de Klerk, now gave sign of wishing
to move towards a gradual dismantlement of the system. In this
he was supported by leading financial and business interests.

These were already hurt by world-wide isolation of South Africa in some selected fields where external sanctions had been applied, and were sorely fearful of external action—that is, action by the principal industrial powers—against South Africa's foreign debts, now very large. But how far would de Klerk and his supporters move towards dismantlement of the system, and with how much vigour and speed, given Afrikaner willingness to believe that time was still on the side of *apartheid*? The world waited to see. The omens for peace were better than ever before, but potent dangers still loomed ahead.

The Wider Picture

More generally, the continent in the 1980s had plunged more deeply into acute impoverishment and political confusion. The outcome had to be far ahead, but a brief overview may be useful.

While most of Africa north of the Zambezi had achieved political independence by the early 1960s, the further progress of these new states was beset with troubles. Many were small or very small in territory or population, and could never hope to prosper until they united with their neighbours. Most were tied so closely to the financial or commercial leading strings of their former rulers as to enjoy little but the appearance of sovereignty. Not a few were utterly without reserves of cash, capital and trained personnel; and some of them, having failed to settle acute internal rivalries, were deep in the toils of civil war. Only a handful of these nation-states had as yet begun, or seemed able to begin, the long and difficult task of reshaping and rebuilding their everyday life in such a way as to overcome, step by step, the deep crises of economic system and political structure they had been obliged to take over from the past.

The period after 1970 was accordingly one of puzzled dispute about the future, of setback and disillusionment, of search for new types of society which could offer genuine economic and social development as well as political freedom. In more than a

few of these new states there were dominant groups who were
entirely content to relapse into positions of personal privilege and
to repress, by reckless arrogation of all power to themselves, every
effective criticism or popular movement aimed at regeneration.
But even in these countries, abused though they were by political
frivolity or personal corruption, the hopes and pressures of liberation continued to exercise an influence towards expansive
change.

These hopes and pressures raised a ferment of new ideas, pro-
grammes, doctrines and ideological debate; and all this, however
immediately fruitless it might seem, could only promise well for
a continent of peoples long deprived of contact with the problems
and solutions of the rest of the world, or of any democratic
methods of discussing these. It soon became clear that political
and economic solutions accepted on the day of independence
could be regarded as no more than provisional.

Africans now began to move across barriers which had previously divided them. These were of many kinds, both old and
new. Although the societies of Iron Age Africa had possessed
profound inner unities of culture and formation, they had known
no more than partial and temporary unions imposed by internal
conquest or symbiosis. Since very distant times, in this continent
of most ancient human settlement, ethnic and language divisions
had fissured into a multitude of separate identities, each of which,
rooted in the centuries, had grown and flowered within its own
ambience. The depth of these roots of different identities has
been strikingly shown by the study of language: the three or four
'parent tongues' of most West African languages, for example,
may have begun their ramification more than 10,000 years ago.

Iron Age history nourished this process of separate growth. And
then for seventy years or more the European colonial system,
brief but huge in its consequences, placed nearly all Africans
within a multitude of new compartments above whose walls it
was difficult or impossible to hear or see anything of value about
neighbours near or far. Many Africans managed to travel abroad
during the colonial period. But inter-regional or even inter-ter-

ritorial knowledge remained minimal: East and West Africa could often seem further from each other than either was from Britain or France. Even the spread of education had its accompanying disadvantages, for one 'colonial language' or 'metropolitan culture' tended to be set in opposition to another, often acutely, so that there were moments when Africans seemed bound to become divided between English-speaking and French-speaking rivals.

Yet the boundaries and divisions began to be crossed. All these new states were linked to one another, whether they liked it or not, by the same colonial experience. They faced much the same problems, carried many of the same handicaps, often ran the same dangers. This community of experience helped them to come together. Inter-African conferences and encounters turned into meetings of genuine self-discovery. Conceived in the very different circumstances of Afro-American experience beyond the Atlantic, the unifying ideas of Pan-Africanism began to play a fertile role in Africa itself.

The essential thought behind Pan-Africanism, in its new and African guise, was that African countries must unite their energies and policies, or else forfeit even the slender freedoms of action they had gained from political independence. Singly or in small groupings, they would never be able to withstand the intrusive pressures of the outside world: of what Kwame Nkrumah, very much the standard-bearer of new ideas about unity, called 'neo-colonialism'. Various efforts were made in this direction.* They were variously frustrated, not least by the close ties which persisted between most of the French-speaking states and France. In 1963, both as a step forward and as a compromise, thirty-two governments agreed to form an Organization of African Unity, with joint organs for economic planning, political consultation and military defence. This disappointed Nkrumah and the few leaders who thought with him. They saw it as a feeble substitute for the

*Reviewed in R. H. Green and A. Seidman, *Unity or Poverty?: The Economics of Pan-Africanism,* 1968.

closely organized Pan-African government they believed was necessary; but they accepted it as a possible step on the road. Others
regarded the new organization as little more than useful cover
for continued separatism. If few cared or dared, at least in public,
to oppose the trend towards a functional unity of all the independent states, this was because Pan-Africanism had now won
wide popular support.

Along with this, the most influential thought which now gained
ground was the broadening conviction that nothing but radical
and far-reaching social and economic change along indigenous
lines, African lines, could advance these new nations from their
fragile and provisional status of the early 1960s. There arose a
belief that Africans must complete their transition to the modern
world by methods which could not and would not be the same
as the methods recommended by their late rulers. This conviction
deepened as the true weakness of their political independence
grew patently clear. There were many new departures. More
and more thoughtful people, tying up with the ideas of Pan-
Africanism, argued that foreign policies of 'non-alignment'—
meaning, in the language of the day, a refusal to concede loyalty
to any other international grouping—must be matched by domestic policies of non-capitalist and even socialist development.
Efforts at continental unity must likewise go hand-in-hand with
new policies aimed at internal unity. By 1965 three basic lines
of new thought and action had emerged: those of neutralism,
tentative forms aiming at socialism, and Pan-Africanism.

They were, of course, argued sharply and often confusedly;
and it could scarcely have been otherwise in a continent so suddenly, but also so partially, embarked upon the steering of its
own affairs. Neutralism swung between the interpretations of
those who wanted freedom to move in the direction of socialist
economies and those who wished merely to stay outside the military systems of the rest of the world. Single-party political systems, more and more the rule after 1960, everywhere faced the
major problem of transforming loosely organized anti-colonial
movements into political parties with a positive programme for

reconstruction and a democratic structure. Here too there was confusion and diversity of aim. A few countries really moved towards a larger measure of internal unity and democratic growth. Many saw the degeneration of their governments into 'group dictatorship' by small conservative élites who had taken over power from withdrawing colonial administrations, and who now used their relatively high degree of education and wealth to grow fat and idle at the expense of the majority of their fellow-citizens. Predictably enough, the scene was laid for *coups d'état* and popular upheavals; and these soon followed.

Ideas about socialism were no less various or sincere. Some leaders and parties thought of socialism as no more than a mild form of humanitarian restraint, inspired by ancient traditions of communal ownership and co-operation, upon economies that should otherwise become vigorously capitalist. Others used the slogans of socialism as a demagogic fig leaf for their personal exploitation of the state. Still others took the ideas of socialism seriously. These they saw as meaning a systemic effort to rebuild society on a new basis, and now, with one or another country in the lead, reached out for means of doing so. Here it was that the notion of a total reconstruction began to make some headway. Political freedom could be of little value, it was argued, unless it were completed by an institutional freedom from the confining limits of a pre-industrial past and neo-colonial present.

By 1980, no matter with what setbacks, the historical posture of Africa had very greatly changed from colonial times. All these ideas, together with the men and women who defended and enlarged upon them, had gone far to project a new atmosphere and sense of African identity and purpose. Whether they spoke of an 'African personality' which should express the underlying cultural unities of Africa, and endow all Africans with membership in a grouping clearly distinctive to itself; whether they campaigned for an African neutralism which might enable them to chart their course through the conflicts of the world, and promote a continental plan of common action; whether they argued for a socialism which should be specifically African in its forms, and yet open the gate to radical enlargement of every activity of daily life: in this way or in that, with profound conviction or with little, clearly or confusedly, large numbers of men and women throughout Africa were now thinking of their countries and their continent in ways which were entirely new.

After 1964, with political independence no longer a joyful novelty, the long period of transition had begun to descend once more into a crisis. But now in the 1980s the crisis was felt and analyzed more deeply than before. Many pressures drove this awakening to reality: above all, perhaps, the impossibility of things remaining as they were. Preventive medicine had unleashed a population growth which overflowed the capacity of any existing socio-political structure to meet the most elementary demands of modern life. Even the comparatively rich and fertile countries of coastal West Africa were still importing food to the tune of large sums of money they could not afford. Tens of thousands of boys and girls were vainly trying to enter secondary schools. Other thousands were leaving secondary schools with little or no hope of finding skilled employment. Countless urban workers were living on the brink of an extreme poverty. Rural reconstruction after the ravages of the 1940s and '50s was slow or altogether absent.

This crisis of the colonial legacy could now be seen and understood as the central challenge of the new independence. Deprived of their old securities, increasingly aware that far-reaching reorganization could alone save them from deepening poverty, from social confusion, and from dependence on the charity of others, ordinary people were now launched upon a conscious effort to grasp the nature of their plight and to work their way towards its resolution. In this massive and confused campaign, spread across a continent where one level of post-colonial development often contrasted strongly and even violently with another, they were assailed by contrary advice from every quarter. They were faced by many discouragements, whether in the grim confusions of Zaire, in the relentless packing of the prisons of South Africa, in the spectacle of self-appointed bureaucracies posing as the heroes of a new order, or in the growing knowledge of their immediate situation.

Examples and Exceptions

Meanwhile the deepening crisis of continental transition from pre-colonial and colonial structures and institutions to new and independent ones, a transition whose origins lay far back in time and whose potential looked far into the future, brought fresh evidence of the difficulties that now lay unavoidably at hand. The régimes formed by educated élites—by emergent 'middle classes' in the British usage—began to go aground in the shallows of their own relatively isolated positions within the states whose guidance they had assumed. Obliged by these positions to behave as 'middle classes' *in posse* (by no means always a thankless role, much less an uncomfortable one), they were consequently obliged to accumulate, as had their forerunners in Europe and North America, by whatever means might come to hand. Their popularity had to be correspondingly fragile. So far was this the case that many of the new nation-states appeared to have lost all legitimacy in the eyes of their citizens: corruption on one hand was answered by 'parallel' or illegal trade on the other, until military rule seemed the only means of keeping the peace and of giving these new states the semblance of an effective reality. Persisting with the nation-state mosaic inherited from the colonial partition began to look like a mistaken route, however difficult it might be to find a different and more useful way ahead.

Aside from this, these élites were also living within the structures of pre-colonial loyalty and kinship; and these historical structures now recovered much of their old vitality. The prestige of old chiefships and ethnic hierarchies glowed with a new insistence on their power and presence: it was rather as though the departure of the colonial rulers had blown upon their embers till they came alight again. Africa was fast recovering its own history, and they were part of it. This gave the ruling groups a dual nature:

modernizing on one hand, 'traditionalist' on the other. It was not an easy duality to manage or contain. And its inner contradictions, between loyalties to the past and different loyalties to the present, had been continuously reinforced by the consequences of colonial policy during the last period of colonial rule.

The case was very clear in the most populous of all the new states, the Federation of Nigeria, which acceded to full political independence in 1960. Governed at the outset of colonial rule as two countries, really as two different colonies, one in the northern grasslands and the other in the coastal regions, Nigeria took shape in the late 1940s as a colonial cosmos of three administrative regions: a very large one in the North and two others in the South, containing a great variety of distinctive cultures and local histories. By the early 1950s, when British reforms accepted the notion of internal self-rule within these regions as a prelude to a federal independence, Nigeria's regions were dominated by indigenous ruling groups whose major loyalty, no doubt naturally in the circumstances, was to their respective regions rather than to the Nigerian 'nation-in-prospect'. When independence duly came, the federal assembly in Lagos was consequently composed of rival parties whose members were above all spokesmen for their regions and not for trans-regional national parties. It was a guarantee of internal strife, and this soon followed.

It was a strife that many outside Africa were content to think of as a 'tribalism' to which Africans, it was held (ignoring all European experience, even in the most recent past), were somehow especially vulnerable. This was a misunderstanding that came partly from the differentiation of terms familiar to colonial paternalism: if Europe had 'nations', Africa had 'tribes', and whereas it might be natural for nations to quarrel, tribes should do nothing of the kind. In the case of Nigeria, as it happened, the major constituent peoples (if not others as well) had as much right to call themselves nations as any in Europe. The historical distinctiveness of Nigeria's constituent cultures was not in doubt.

But the strife of the 1960s came far less from that distinctiveness, with its consequences for the mass of people, than from rivalry between ruling groups.

The first five years of political independence saw the regions drawing ever more apart until their governments were practically behaving as separate states. Yet other interests and pressures still pulled towards the maintenance of Nigeria as a large federation of these states. There thus arose a struggle for power at the centre as well as in the regions. This came to a head when the central government, dominated by the spokesmen of the North, combined with a minority group among the ruling Action Party in the Western Region so as to oust the majority group in favour of the minority.

The details of what followed would be out of place here. But resultant upheavals in the Western Region were coupled with a general discontent at the get-rich-quick attitudes and methods of the new 'middle classes' now in power. The year 1966 saw a succession of military take-overs. These were followed by large disasters of inter-ethnic strife. By 1967 Nigeria was plunged into a long and painful civil war arising from these underlying factors, but, immediately, from the secession of the Eastern Region as the independent state of Biafra. Fighting continued until the end of 1969 when the Biafran state and its formative élite could hold out no longer, and peace was restored by a central government under the command of General Gowan. *

This peace was widely welcomed throughout the country, and was opened in an atmosphere of clemency and reconciliation.

---

*Much has been written, and still will be written, about this civil war. A good introduction, meanwhile, is J. de St Jorre, *The Nigerian Civil War*, 1972. Basic documentation on the subject is in A. H. M. Kirk-Greene, *Conflict in Nigeria*, 2 vols., 1971. Just how far and far-reaching was the federal government's policy of reconciliation may be seen in the fact that the senior Biafran commander, General A. A. Madiebo, was able to publish his memoirs in Nigeria: *The Nigerian Revolution and the Biafran War*, Fourth Dimension Publishers, Enugu, 1980: a book that may usefully be compared with memoirs of the commander of the federal side, General Olusegun Obasanjo, *My Command*, Heinemann, London, 1980.

There was the feeling that a new start could now be made. This feeling was reinforced by an important economic gain. Large deposits of high-grade oil in conveniently offshore deposits along the Nigerian seaboard were now finally proved. This was to become a factor of growing importance.

Politically, a new system of regional division into twelve autonomous states (in place of the existing four) had been proposed by General Gowan on the eve of the civil war; now it was brought into effect with a marked success. This did much to remove the old atmosphere of tension between north and south. It also gave scope for the use of far more talent than before.

Reaching for stability with capable hands, the post-war governments of Generals Murtala Mohammed and Olusegun Obasanjo went further along the same lines. The number of autonomous states within the federation was increased to nineteen, and afterwards to twenty-one, while revenues from oil were distributed among them with less friction than expected. In 1979 the military rulers made good their promise of 1976 to 'return to barracks', and, with this on their programme, set up commissions to prepare a new civilian constitution. This came duly into effect in 1980 with Alhaji Shehu Shagari presiding over a strong federal executive. But this renewed attempt to launch parliamentary government in the absence of a dominant 'middle class' fell victim, not surprisingly, to the same traps and failures as the last, and within a few years Nigeria was once again under military rule, latterly under the patriotic direction of General Ibrahim Babangida, who strove, once again, to find the way to a representative democracy. To this end he and others sought to build on the undoubted successes of Nigerian federalism, and, in broadening these successes, to give them the spur and life of a genuinely democratic participation.

The Nigerian case deserves reflection, historically, not only because of Nigeria's pre-eminent importance and weight upon the continental scene, but also because it has encapsulated many of the most severe of the continent's problems. These have centred on the need to forge new institutions capable—as the inherited institutions manifestly have not been capable—of meeting the challenge of further transition into viable units of self-development.

On a long view, the fundamental issue was evidently concerned with the transformation of 'mini-state Africa' into a number of large regional federations or co-operative unities. No other prospect now appeared to hold out any substantial hope of rescuing the continent from its worsening poverty and deepening institutional crisis. It seemed equally clear that any such advance must be far ahead, given the rivalry of nation-state rulers and bureaucracies and the drag of inertia. Yet it stood on the record by 1982 that two large enterprises were in hand that could at least point the way.

One of these was ECOWAS, a sixteen-country organization composing the Economic Community of West African States, formed in 1975, to promote a broad regional co-operation and gradual 'blurring' of frontiers and capable, already, of something more (if, as yet, of not much more) than good intentions. Another, launched in 1979, was a less ambitious and perhaps more realistic agreement among South Africa's neighbours to band themselves together for joint economic planning and investment. this was SADCC, or the Southern African Development Co-ordination Conference.

Both of these, of course—like the all-continental OAU itself—were mere organizations of government and not, as yet, of public opinion or of political parties. Yet public opinion, if in a very different and perfectly illegal dimension, was already recording its vote against the frontiers of the colonial partition by the regular and large-scale smuggling of goods across all of West Africa's national boundaries; and no government, as yet, had found any way of stopping this. However improperly, huge numbers of West African producers and traders were reverting to the old regional unities of pre-colonial times.

Partial and illegal though it was, this rejection of the legacy of colonial partition had become another factor in reinforcing the belief that basic institutional changes of structure must be inseparable from the achievement of long-term stability and over-all development. Within the purely national dimension, Ghana has provided another if sadly instructive example. The government led in 1957 by Kwame Nkrumah took over all the structures and administrative legacy of the colonial period, but, at least to begin with, succeeded in solving some bitter problems of 'trib-alism' and 'regionalism'. Yet when Nkrumah tried to proceed further in step-by-step transition from the colonial legacy, he was soon overthrown by a combination of sectional interests, political incompetence and external pressure. Thereafter, with every change of régime, Ghana declined still further.

The military who overthrew Nkrumah's regime in 1966, by which time the 'one-party' state had degenerated into a 'no-party' state, backtracked to the structures and institutions of 1957, be-came increasingly corrupt and ineffective and in 1969 made way for a new parliamentary régime under Dr Kofi Busia. This was widely welcomed, but not for long. 'Tribalism' and corruption reappeared. Busia's régime culminated in a 40 per cent deval-uation of the currency and was at once ousted by a new military ruler, Colonel Ignatius Acheampong. By this time the foreign indebtedness incurred under Nkrumah had been vastly swollen by new borrowings made under Busia, and the country was stum-bling from one crisis to another. This once prosperous land had become a ruined debtor. And who was to blame? Plenty of scape-goats were found as one *coup* succeeded another; but the answer at the end of the day, essentially, was that all the political legacies of the colonial period had failed to work in any sense valuable to a majority of the people.

The years since Nkrumah had convincingly demonstrated this harsh and difficult truth: various permutations of the 'Western model' had been tried, but they had not worked; and nothing stable had emerged since Nkrumah's overthrow in 1966 by 'West-ern-oriented' army officers. Meanwhile the 'Eastern model', par-tially tried during Nkrumah's last years, had produced no viable alternative. Co-operatives had failed. State enterprises had done no better, or had done worse. Besides which, bitter experience in several countries had shown (and would continue to show) that any attempt to construct an independent alternative to the 'Western model', influenced or not by the 'Eastern model', would at once be countered by externally directed subversions and interventions, as for example in official U.S. and other promotion of the South Africa–backed UNITA subversion in Angola, and the similar 'Renamo' subversion in Mozambique.

It was in these circumstances that there began to crystallize, early in the 1980s, a conviction that Africa's peoples must somehow find viable structures of self-government from the lessons of Africa's own historical experience. Tentatively at first, and with reverses, new structures began to appear as one or another attempt was initiated to 'deconstruct' the neo-colonial state and its bureaucratic carcass in favour of devolving administrative powers to locally formed and, prospectively, locally elected assemblies and executives. That was how, in now outmoded ways, precolonial Africa had governed itself. More modern forms of those old ways had already appeared during the 1960s in the anticolonial armed struggles of the peoples of the Portuguese colonies, and had proved their worth. There they had acquired the name of *participação popular*, 'people's participation'. Since then they had reappeared in various forms elsewhere. A corresponding body of theory and practice had begun to take shape.*

These ideas of devolution from the rigidly centralist state structures of neo-colonialism came to be widely discussed in a number of forward-looking countries, but their full potentials for success still remained to be explored. Any transition from 'foreign solutions', and above all from prestigious 'Western solutions', was clearly going to be fraught with problems of a politico-cultural kind, but also, no less, of an economic kind. In short, the profound structural crisis evolving in the 1980s called for radical

---

*See esp. the writings of Amílcar Cabral, published posthumously in a collection entitled *Unity and Struggle*, London and New York, 1979–80. For a succinct but authoritative statement on 'people's participation' applied in practice after independence, as it was in the Republic of Cape Verde (independent in 1975), see B. Davidson, *The Fortunate Isles*, Trenton and London, 1989, app. 2, and *passim*.

changes of culture and structure while at the same time rendering any such radicalism extremely hard to carry through. That was to be shown, tragically, in the case of the little inland republic of Burkina Faso (formerly the French colony of Haute Volta) when, in 1987, the reformist leader Thomas Sankara was shot down by political rivals.

Yet the group of reforming ideas loosely gathered under the heading of 'people's participation' nonetheless continued to express the conviction that Africa's problems must either find Africa's solutions or remain unsolved. In this ideological 'void' that opened between the incapacity of "Western" solutions and the crashing failure of "Eastern" solutions, as Thomas Sankara said shortly before he was assassinated, Africa 'must invent the future'.

Otherwise matters would grow still worse than they were already; and for this widening thought there was plenty of supporting evidence. This was seen to be especially the case wherever the rigidly centralizing structures inherited from colonialism were further reinforced or frozen, sometimes under the cover of a borrowed doctrine, at other times under no cover save that of brute force.

Of those systems or states that relied on brute force, there is little that needs to be said. They were intellectually hollow structures without the least moral substance, or none that could be taken seriously. They belonged to the detritus and debris of Africa's modern history. Régimes of bloodstained dictatorship in the 1970s, such as those of Idi Amin in Uganda and of Bedel Bokassa in his self-styled 'Central African Empire' (formerly the French colony of Oubangui-Chari), or that of military bullies persecuting Burundi or ferociously warring in Chad, were warlord tyrannies incapable of progress and, usually, incapable of thought. Here the sufferings of a majority of the affected populations were severe and often mortal.

It was noticed at the same time, reinforcing the ideas of necessarily African and indigenous reform, that most of such mindless tyrannies could scarcely have survived, or even come into existence, without crucial promotion or support from some power outside Africa whose interests they more or less directly served. Ethiopia now showed what miseries must follow on accepting or inviting Soviet support. Without the support of U.S. and European backers, the harsh régime headed by Mobutu Sese Seko in the vast land of Zaire (formerly the Belgian Congo) could not have fastened itself on Zaire's unfortunate peoples, nor have continued to suck their wealth into Mobutist coffers.

The case of Zaire might seem extreme; it was not alone of its kind. By the late 1980s, after more than twenty years of Mobutist dictatorship, Zaire remained a state without a nation, a geographical concept without a people; which of course was not to say that the people inhabiting Zaire had vanished into a political myth. On the contrary, their social and economic life outside the confines of the Mobutist state's kleptocracy—inside, that is, the widening scope of illegal trade and clandestine purposes— was apparently alive and even vivid. Yet little could be known of it. *

Of those tyrannies which used a borrowed doctrine to justify themselves and which, unlike the Zairean cases, claimed to assert a moral and intellectual purpose or at least a measure of dignity, there is more to be said. The most obvious of this type was that of Ethiopia after the 1974 overthrow of its long-outdated imperial system. Such cases were now in short supply anywhere in Africa, but the Ethiopian case would attract much consideration. It was typical in this context. But it was also *sui generis*, peculiar to itself and its course has been tragic.

Formed by conquest of neighbours during the big imperialist 'share-out' in the last years of the nineteenth century, the empire of Ethiopia grew from a quasi-feudal Abyssinia. To this ancient Abyssinia the warrior-monarch Menelik of the Amhara people, living mostly in the province of Shoa, added large regions to the north-east and south. Menelik did this in the 1890s by military

*See a large bibliography: e.g. relevant papers and references in papers by Crawford Young, Naomi Chazan, Janet MacGaffey, René Lemarchand and others in D. Rothchild and N. Chazan (eds), *The Precarious Balance*, Boulder and London, 1988. These deal largely with the case of Zaire, but parallel evidence for other cases is also copious.

conquest, with the agreement of two other 'share-out' powers, Britain and Italy, which between them 'shared out' the lands of the Somali and of peoples living in what then became the Italian colony of Eritrea. Menelik's shrewd and forceful successor, Emperor Haile Selassie, was narrowly able to survive the Italian Fascist invasion and takeover of 1935 to 1941. But he then set out to enlarge the empire.

In 1952 Haile Selassie managed to secure federal control of the former Italian colony of Eritrea, since 1941 under British military administration, and in 1962 he annexed that country outright. He failed to enclose the whole of Somalia (independent in 1960) as he intended, but hung on successfully to wide Somali lands seized by Menelik before him. All this redounded to the benefit of the ruling Amhara group with its capital at Addis Ababa. Although the Amhara constitute only a fraction of Ethiopia's whole population, their interests were generally treated as supreme, whether in terms of land enclosure or other benefits.

Haile Selassie meanwhile continued to ride the two horses of 'tradition' and 'modernization'. But they pulled increasingly apart. Misgovernment deepened. Natural setbacks such as cyclical drought became man-extended disasters. U.S. advisers, then with dominant influence, advised without real success. It could only be a question of time before the old system collapsed. Widespread peasant uprisings shattered imperial control, especially in southern provinces where large areas had been taken into absentee or 'settler' (*neftegna*) Amhara ownership, or its equivalent in peasant expropriation. In 1974 a military 'committee' (*dergue* in Amharic) declared a revolution, threw out the emperor, and initiated what was to be an immense confusion.

The revolution in itself consisted partly in the overthrow of the emperor and his dependents, and partly in peasant seizure of large estates. But the Dergue, then or later, was not otherwise revolutionary, and set itself to reconstitute an Amharic supremacy under new management. Other trends, notably drawn from student ranks in Addis Ababa, saw the need to give this management a genuinely radical and innovatory nature. But the military

Dergue suppressed them with ruthless bloodshed. In 1976 the Dergue, now under the leadership and soon the personal control of Colonel Mengistu Haile Mariam, an assimilated Amhara, turned for military and ideological aid to the USSR, evicted U.S. influence and introduced a dictatorial regime inspired by the stagnant and crisis-ridden Soviet system as it was under Leonid Brezhnev.

Reinforcing its Amharic hegemony, this 'new' Dergue of Mengistu's used its executive powers to carry through the strange project of subjecting Ethiopia and annexed Eritrea to a form of Stalinism, even at the very time when Stalinism—a personalist tyranny bedecked with Marxist-Leninist slogans—had manifestly come to grief in its home country. This deepened the social and ecological miseries of those peoples enclosed within Ethiopia.

Worst of all, perhaps, the régime refused to address itself to its greatest source of weakness, that is, to meet a whole series of 'national questions'—of non-Amhara demands for autonomy or independence—raised by various peoples in the empire. Bitter wars shook the empire, beginning with an Eritrean uprising in 1962 and continuing down the years with other uprisings by Tigreans and Somalis, Oromos and Afars, and others. These wars came to a head in and after 1985, when massive and repeated defeats of Mengistu's conscript armies were administered by the Eritreans and Tigreans. Even then the Dergue and its dictator persisted in their policies of military repression.

As these wars went on, the Eritrean independence movement (EPLF: Eritrean People's Liberation Front) developed a notable sophistication and good sense that the régime was lacking. In alliance with the Tigrean Liberation Front and other allies opposed to Amharic supremacy, the EPLF evolved structures of 'people's participation' that displayed an alternative to continued decline, and encouraged their development across large regions from which it had evicted the Dergue's troops.

Soviet military input had manifestly failed to save the Dergue, as even more clearly had Soviet political advice, which failed to reckon with the demands of Ethiopia's 'national questions'. More generally, Soviet or Soviet-allied advice, often through East Germans, failed to recognize and allow for all those social and economic aspects of rural change required to overcome the distortions of the colonial period. Dergue collapse followed. And in 1990 a new régime vowed itself to ethnic equalities and to grass roots participation.

The Challenge Renewed

The search for viability had meanwhile to continue as the 'solutions of the East' met with still greater disaster than the 'solutions of the West'. Meanwhile the crisis of structure continued to deepen. In this respect the Ethiopian case—and more widely, the case of the whole great region of the Horn of Africa—emphasized the fruitless profligacy of military governments, even those capable of political thought. In the matter of military spending, already touched upon, the Dergue régime knew no limits save the refusal of foreign lenders to throw good money after bad. In 1976, when Mengistu took power, the Ethiopian régime spent about $103 million on arms from abroad, or about $3.5 per Ethiopian. In 1979 military spending had risen to $525 million, or about $17 per head. Almost all of it can be safely said to have gone into mindless bloodshed.

By 1990 militarists and militarism—and the profits of supplying these—had become a source and guarantee of ruin in no few African cases.

Meanwhile the problems of impoverishment had begun to look well-nigh insoluble. Populations continued to grow at a rate which threatened to double their size by early in the twenty-first century. Yet this otherwise welcome increase in human wealth and potential was in no way matched by means of supporting it, even at a minimal level of nourishment and employment.

Food imports continued to grow in size and cost as cities spread, and as rural deliveries of food declined with widening peasant refusal to remain the price-victims of urban-based régimes. There were exceptions: newly independent Zimbabwe, for example, scored a major success in promoting greater food production by increasing prices paid to rural food producers. But generally, more people had less to eat in a continent still largely agrarian. Given a huge expansion of illegal trade through smuggling and other such operations, it was now difficult to know exactly what was being produced and sold. But increasing food shortage was in any case a fact beyond doubt.

Foreign aid in grants or interest-paying loans fell away in the 1970s, and seemed unlikely to recover, even where, as in the small but significant case of the Cape Verde Republic, it remained indispensable and was wisely used. The consequences of this general decline were worsened by a parallel decline in the terms of trade—the relationship between import prices and export prices—to Africa's overall and sometimes very painful disadvantage. It was usually the case by now that a ton of African exports could buy, from year to year, less and less of the foreign imports that were needed, whether of food or of manufactured goods.*

Foreign indebtedness accordingly rose steeply and, it had come to seem, unavoidably. But so, at the same time, did the soaring mountains of debt-service interest that African countries had now to meet. For a significant number of African countries, by the last years of the century, interest payments on foreign debt approached figures larger than the total value of those countries' exports. In 1984, for example, total African debt to foreign lenders stood at $81.7 billion; in 1989 that figure had grown to $256.9 billion, with an interest-service total of $25.3 billion. This burden of debt in 1989 represented 93.3 per cent of African GDP, and 328.4 per cent of total exports, while debt-service stood at 32.8 per cent of the region's export earnings, meaning that the less well endowed African countries, which were many, could no longer hope to pay their way.

Here, indeed, were crucial illustrations of the drama that was

*A complex issue. See, for example, the discussion in D. K. Fieldhouse, *Black Africa 1945–80*, London and Boston, 1986.

now being called the 'north-south' conflict of interest, the economic conflict between industrialized countries and formerly colonized countries. All those capital and other such goods needed to expand the productive technology and capacity of Africa became ever less obtainable at the very time when the requirements of infra-structural and primary-industrial development grew ever more acute and urgent. There were occasions now when it could even appear to pessimists that much of the continent must revert to a village economy, or starve on urban pavements. This was a 'doomsday scenario' that was unlikely to happen, for scenarios of that kind do not happen except in times of international war. But radical change and restoration now seemed not a choice but a necessity.

At this point the historian has to stand back. Searching for viability, Africans found other peoples doing just the same. The solutions handed down to them with such complacency—or with so much arrogance?—had after all proved to be no solutions. This was true of 'neo-colonial' regions outside Africa as well as of 'neo-colonial' regions inside Africa: for example, those regions of eastern and central Europe where a Soviet imperialism had followed the imperialisms of the nineteenth century, Austro-Hungarian or Tsarist Russian or Ottoman Turk. There too the solutions 'handed down' had not worked: neither the nation-statist solutions after World War I nor the Stalinist solutions after World War II. There too viable solutions had to be forged in what seemed an ideological void.

There was now a general sense that history in all these once colonized or subjected countries had reached some kind of 'turning point', and that the future, whatever it might hold, must bring new approaches. In Africa these new approaches had yet to mature, but seemed likely to acquire a dual thrust. One thrust already consisted in a widening critique of the post-colonial nation-state, now generally known as the neo-colonial nation-state. The second thrust, less mature and yet also present, suggested that a saving virtue could lie in the gradual but intelligent 'deconstruction' of the neo-colonial state in favour of two trends.

One of these trends should advance the cause of democratic structures of self-government 'at the base of society', generally along the lines of the 'people's participation' mentioned above. The other, still largely a matter of theory rather than practice, should look to the development of federal-type unities that might overcome the constrictions and reductions of post-colonial states cripplingly distorted by bureaucratic parasitism.

All these ideas and approaches came forward as a renewed challenge of sanity and courage to the crisis in which these once colonized peoples were inextricably caught. And because of this, no doubt, the general African mood of the closing century was not without its note of stubborn optimism.

Brief Guide
to Further Reading

The useful bibliography of Africa, and especially of African history, has continued to expand every week in several languages.

Those who wish to know more about the subject, but are not themselves specialists, may therefore like to have a short list of fairly new books, complementing sources mentioned in my footnotes. Nearly all of the following have specialized and lengthy bibliographies which can take the reader a long way in many African directions and deeply into many African subjects.

Those who mean to become specialists will read at least a selection of many professional journals, whether devoted to history, archaeology, linguistics or some other aspect of a ramifying science. Among these, on the more purely historical side, they will certainly read the quarterly *Journal of African History*, Cambridge University Press, also *African Archaeological Review*, London. Several African universities publish distinguished historical journals. Among regional journals mainly devoted to archaeology, mention may be made here of *Kush*, Khartoum, and *Azania*, Nairobi. The full list of all such journals, whether of one historical discipline or another, would be too long for inclusion here.

On the geo-physical and ecological background, three general works make a good starting point. They are:

G. H. T. Kimble, *Tropical Africa*, vol. 1, Land and Livelihood; vol. 2, Society and Polity, 1962.

L. D. Stamp, *Africa: A Study in Tropical Development*, 1958.

E. B. Worthington, *Science and the Development of Africa*, 1953.

A more specialized discussion of tropical farming problems and solutions will be found in:

P. H. Nye and D. J. Greenland, *The Soil under Shifting Cultivation*, 1960.

P. Richards, *Indigenous Agricultural Revolution*, 1985.

For a survey of literature on food-producing, see M. A. Havinden, 'The History of Crop Cultivation in West Africa: a Bibliographical Guide', *Economic History Review*, 23, 1970, pp. 532–55.

The last twenty-five years have seen great advances in the understanding of Stone Age African cultures. Here the reader will be well advised to begin with J. D. Clark's brilliant synthesis, 'The Prehistoric Origins of African Culture' in the *Journal of African History*, 2, 1964, p. 161. Dr. Louis Leakey's views are usefully summarized in number 3 of *Tarikh*, 1967, published by Longmans for the Historical Society of Nigeria. Several summarizing works may also be mentioned:

C. Ehret and M. Posnansky (eds), *The Archaeological and Linguistic Reconstruction of African History*, 1982.

J. D. Clark, *The Prehistory of Southern Africa*, 1959.

D. W. Phillipson, *African Archaeology*, 1985.

R. Lewin, *Bones of Contention*, 1987.

Still useful for the rise of farming and metal-using cultures is:

V. G. Childe, *New Light on the Most Ancient East*, latest edition, 1954.

Carrying on from there, good introductions to Pharaonic Egypt and its place in history are:

W. B. Emery, *Archaic Egypt*, 1961.

A. Gardiner, *Egypt of the Pharaohs*, 1961.

M. Bernal, *Black Athena*, 1987.

Especially to be recommended are the third and fourth volumes in the Fischer *Weltgeschichte* series, *Die Altorientalischen Reiche* II and III, 1966–67, edited by E. Cassin, J. Bottéro and J. Vercoutter: e.g. chap. 4 in II, 'Das Neue Reich in Aegypten' by J. Yoyotte and J. Cerny.

The history of Kush, of Christian Nubia and of other Sudanese achievements up to 1821 are well surveyed in:

P. L. Shinnie, *Meroe, A Civilization of the Sudan*, 1967.

B. G. Trigger, *Nubia*, 1976.

A. J. Arkell, *Short History of the Sudan*, revised edition, 1962.

W. Y. Adams, *Corridor to Africa*, 1982.

The latest findings in Kushite archaeology and history, at present a field of active and many-sided work, are regularly reported in the journal of the Sudan

Antiquities Service, *Kush*, published annually in Khartoum under the editorship of Thabit Hassan Thabit. See especially *Kush 1962*, F. Hintze, 'Preliminary Report on the Excavations of Musawwarat', and *Kush 1964*, W. Y. Adams, 'An Introductory Classification of Meroitic Pottery'. The best available chronology of Kushite rulers is that of F. Hintze, *Studien zur Meroitischen Chronologie*, 1959; see also F. Hintze, 'Nubien und Sudan—ihre Bedeutung für die alte Geschichte Afrikas' in *Spektrum*, vol. 7–8 of 1964. Anyone who wants to taste the excitement of modern archaeological discoveries in Kushite culture should also read J. Vercoutter, 'Un Palais des "Candaces" Contemporain d'Auguste' in *Syria*, 39, 1962.

On Ethiopian origins, especially Axumite, a sound introduction is still that of A. Kammerer, *Essai sur l'Histoire Antique d'Abyssinie*, 1926, but later discoveries require it to be supplemented by newer work. A useful general survey is J. Doresse, *L'Empire du Prêtre-Jean*, vol. I, Ethiopie antique, 1957; but those who wish to be up with the latest discoveries should consult *Annales d'Ethiopie*, 1955 onwards, and a brilliant essay by J. Leclant, 'Frühäthiopischer Kultur' in *Christentum am Nil*, 1963. See also a valuable new synthesis edited in its English edition by J. L. Michels: Y. M. Kobishchanov, *Axum*, Pennsylvania State University, 1979.

Basic works on the Berber bronze age and historical beginnings are:

    G. Camps, *Aux Origines de la Berbérie: Monuments et rites funéraires*, 1961; *Massinissa et les Débuts de l'Histoire*, 1961.

For Phoenician and Roman Africa see:

    G. and C. Charles-Picard, *La Vie Quotidienne à Carthage*, 1958.
    B. H. Warmington, *Carthage*, 1960; *The North African Provinces*, 1954.

For the general history of pre-colonial Africa, mainly of Africa south of the Sahara, there is now available a small number of introductory surveys, including:

    R. Cornevin, *Histoire des Peuples de l'Afrique Noire*, 1960; *Histoire de l'Afrique*, 1962. (Both are full of much valuable detail.)
    P. Curtin and others, *African History*, 1978.
    B. Davidson, *Old Africa Rediscovered*, 1959, paperback 1970. (An overall survey, based mainly on the archaeological record.) U.S. title, *The Lost Cities of Africa*, Little, Brown.
    H. Deschamps, *L'Afrique Noire Précoloniale*, 1962. (A very good pocket guide to the subject.)
    J. D. Fage, *A History of Africa*, 1978.
    R. Mauny, *Les Siècles Obscurs de L'Afrique Noire*, 1971.

R. Oliver and J. D. Fage, *A Short History of Africa*, 1962, and updatings. (This short synthesis contains a reading guide.)

R. F. Rotberg, *A Political History of Tropical Africa*, 1965.

Extensive multi-volume African histories are also available from the Cambridge University Press, and from UNESCO.

We also have two good atlases of African history:

J. D. Fage, *An Atlas of African History*, 1958; reprint, 1972.

R. Roolvink, *Historical Atlas of the Muslim Peoples*, 1957.

And a useful encyclopedia:

African Encyclopedia, Oxford University Press, 1973. Nelson's *Dictionary of World History*, 1973, has some 800 entries for African historical subjects and persons.

Some idea of the wealth of the written records of African history may be had from a number of modern anthologies, including:

C. Coquéry, *La Découverte de l'Afrique*, 1965. (A brief but attractive collection of extracts, beginning with Herodotus.)

J. Cuvelier and L. Jadin, *L'Ancien Congo d'après les Archives romaines (1518–1630)*, 1954.

B. Davidson, *The African Past*, 1964. (Chronicles from Antiquity to modern times: Africa south of the Sahara.) Revised and expanded as *Revisiting African Civilization*, Trenton, 1990.

G. S. P. Freeman-Grenville, *The East African Coast*, 1962. (Select documents from the first to the early nineteenth century.)

C. Fyfe, *Sierra Leone Inheritance*, 1964.

T. Hodgkin, *Nigerian Perspectives*, 1960; reprint 1975.

F. Wolfson, *Pageant of Ghana*, 1959.

As well as these, there are four anthologies of European exploration in Africa:

E. Axelson (ed.), *South African Explorers*, 1954.

C. Howard (ed.), *West African Explorers*, 1951.

M. Perham and J. Simmons (eds.), *African Discovery*, first published 1942.

C. Richards and J. Place (eds), *East African Explorers*, 1960.

And one anthology of especial value for early European voyaging:

J. W. Blake (ed.), *Europeans in West Africa, 1450–1560*, 2 vols, 1942.

Of great importance, the early Arabic sources for African history, otherwise available in out-of-date translations or not available at all, are now published in new translations with up-to-date introductions by V. V. Matveev and L. E. Kubbel of the University of Leningrad. Two volumes covering the seventh to twelfth centuries have so far appeared with extracts from thirty-nine authors:

> *Arabske Istochniki VII–X Vekov*, 1960; and *Arabske Istochniki X–XII Vekov*, 1965, the latter beginning with al-Makdisi, whose principal work dates from AD 966.

Essential in this field is: N. Levtzion and J. E. Hopkins (eds): *Corpus of Early Arabic Sources for West African History*, 1981.

This may be the place to mention a few introductory works on the side of language, religion or social and political ideas:

C. G. Baëta, *Christianity in Tropical Africa*, 1968.

D. Dalby (ed.), *Language and History in Africa*, 1970.

B. Davidson, *The Africans: An Entry to Social and Cultural History*, 1969; paperback, 1973; U.S. title, *The African Genius*, Little, Brown.

D. Forde (ed.), *African Worlds*, 1954. (Studies by a number of specialists in the cosmological ideas and social values of African peoples.)

M. Fortes and E. E. Evans-Pritchard (eds), *African Political Systems*; latest edition, 1958.

M. Fortes and G. Dieterlen (eds), *African Systems of Thought*, 1965. (Studies by a number of specialists.)

J. Greenberg, *The Languages of Africa*, 1963. (A concise survey of basic importance.)

I. M. Lewis (ed.), *Islam in Tropical Africa*, 1966.

The plastic and other arts of Africa south of the Sahara have been variously and sometimes curiously described. Scholarly and well-illustrated works on the subject include:

R. Brain, *Art and Society in Africa*, 1980.

A. Diop (ed.), *L'Art Nègre*, 1949.

E. Elisofon and W. Fagg, *The Sculpture of Africa*, 1958.

W. and B. Forman and P. Dark, *Benin Art*, 1960.

E. Leuzinger, *Africa, the Art of the Negro Peoples*, 1960.

E. de Rouvre, with D. Paulme and J. Brosse, *Parures Africaines*, 1956.

L. Underwood, *Bronzes of West Africa*, 1949; *Masks of West Africa*, 1952.

F. Willett, *Ife in the History of West African Sculpture*, 1967.

D. Williams, *Icon and Image*, 1974.

Study of the consequences for Africa of the slave trade is still in its infancy, though readers may care to consult my *Black Mother* (reprint, 1968; paperback,

1970) for a new review of the trade's leading phases and a discussion of its impact on social structures in Africa. For an extremely valuable documentation, see E. Donnan's four volumes of *Documents Illustrative of the History of America*, Washington, D.C., 1930–35. An indispensable inquiry into the trade's world consequences is E. Williams's *Capitalism and Slavery*, Chapel Hill, 1944 (reprint London, 1964). For further discussion of slavery themes, all of which still require much thought before any safe conclusions can be reached, see for example the report of a symposium on 'The Transatlantic Slave Trade from West Africa' at the Centre of African Studies of the University of Edinburgh in 1966; and W. Rodney, *A History of the Upper Guinea Coast 1545–1800*, 1970, with a relevant paper of Rodney's in the *Journal of African History*, 3, 1966. P. D. Curtin has lately revised previous estimates of numbers in his important *Atlantic Slave Trade: A Census*, 1969. For further discussion, see J. Inikori (ed.), *Forced Migration*, 1982.

Returning to the more narrowly historical field, the following is a brief list of basic or introductory works confined to one or another region or theme:

Muslim Spain (Al-Andalus):

E. Lévi-Provençal, *Histoire de l'Espagne Musulmane*, 3 vols, 1950.
R. Le Tourneau, *The Almohad Movement in North Africa in the Twelfth and Thirteenth Centuries*, 1969.

North and North-East Africa:

N. Barbour, *A Survey of North West Africa*, 1959.
H. I. Bell, *Egypt from Alexander the Great to the Arab Conquest*, 1948.
P. M. Holt, *A Modern History of the Sudan*, 1961.
S. D. Goitein, *A Mediterranean Society*, vol. I, 1967.
G. E. von Grunebaum, *Medical Islam*, 1946.
A. H. M. Jones and E. Monroe, *A History of Ethiopia*, 1955.
C-A. Julien, *Histoire de l'Afrique du Nord*, 1951.
B. Lewis, *The Arabs in History*, 1950.
J. Markakis, *National and Class Conflict in the Horn of Africa*, 1987.
E. Ullendorff, *The Ethiopians*, 1960.

Two volumes in the *Fischer Weltgeschichte* series provide a good overall survey of the history of Islam:

C. Cahen, *Der Islam I: Vom Ursprung bis zu den Anfängen des Os-manreiches*, 1968.
G. E. Von Grunebaum, *Der Islam II: Die Islamischen Reiche nach dem Fall von Konstantinopel*, 1971.

Much in these volumes is indispensable to an understanding of African Islam, and provides a reliable background introduction. In this respect, there are useful facts in J. S. Trimingham, *Islam in West Africa*, 1959.

West Africa:

J. F. Ade Ajayi, *Christian Missions in Nigeria 1841–1891*, 1965.

J. F. Ade Ajayi and R. Smith, *Yoruba Warfare in the Nineteenth Century*, 1964.

S. A. Akintoye, *Revolution and Power Politics in Yorubaland 1840–1883*, 1972.

E. A. Ayandele, *The Missionary Impact on Modern Nigeria, 1842–1914*, 1971.

D. Birmingham, *Trade and Conflict in Angola, 1483–1790*, 1966.

E. W. Bovill, *The Golden Trade of the Moors*, 1958.

R. Cornevin, *Histoire du Togo*, 1959.

M. Crowder, *The Story of Nigeria*, 1962; *West Africa Under Colonial Rule*, 1968.

P. D. Curtin, *The Image of Africa, British Ideas and Actions, 1780–1850*, 1965.

K. Onwuku Dike, *Trade and Politics in the Niger Delta 1830–85*, 1956.

C. Fyfe, *A History of Sierra Leone*, 1962.

J. M. Gray, *A History of the Gambia*, 1940, reprint 1966.

J. D. Hargreaves, *Prelude to the Partition of West Africa*, 1963.

P. Hill, *Rural Hausa*, 1972.

G. I. Jones, *The Trading States of the Oil Rivers*, 1963.

D. Kimble, *A Political History of Ghana, 1850–1928*, 1963.

J. A. Langley, *Pan-Africanism and Nationalism in West Africa*, 1972.

M. Last, *The Sokoto Caliphate*, 1967.

R. Mauny, *Tableau Géographique de l'Ouest Africain au Moyen Age*, 1961.

C. Newbury, *The Western Slave Coast and Its Rulers*, 1961.

K. Polányi, *Dahomey and the Slave Trade*, 1966.

J. Rouch, *Contribution à l'Histoire des Songhay*, 1953; *Les Songhay*, 1954.

A. F. C. Ryder, *Benin and the Europeans 1485–1897*, 1969.

M. G. Smith, *Government in Zazzau, 1800–1950*, 1960.

J. Suret-Canale, *L'Afrique Noire Occidentale et Centrale*, vol. I; Géographie, Civilisations, Histoire, 1961; vol. 2, L'Ere Coloniale, 1900–45, 1964. Vol. 2 is also in English trans.

T. N. Tamuno, *The Evolution of the Nigerian State*, 1972.

L. Tauxier, *Histoire des Bambara*, 1942.

Y. Urvoy, *Histoire des Populations du Soudan Central*, 1936; *Histoire de l'Empire du Bornou*, 1949.

W. E. F. Ward, *A History of Ghana*, 1958.

I. Wilke, *Asante in the Nineteenth Century*, 1975.

South and South-Central Africa:

H. Deschamps, *Histoire de Madagascar*, 1960.

L. H. Gann, *A History of Northern Rhodesia, Early Days to 1953*, 1963.

P. S. Garlake, *Great Zimbabwe*, 1973.

C. W. de Kieweit, *A History of South Africa*, 1950.

P. Mason, *The Birth of a Dilemma*, 1958. (Conquest and settlement of Rhodesia.)

J. D. Omer-Cooper, *The Zulu Aftermath*, 1966.

J. Vansina, *Kingdoms of the Savanna*, 1966.

A. J. Wills, *An Introduction to the History of Central Africa*, 1964.

M. Wilson and L. Thompson (eds), *Oxford History of South Africa*, 2 vols, 1969, 1971.

East Africa:

E. Axelson, *South-East Africa, 1488–1530*, 1940; *The Portuguese in South-East Africa, 1600–1700*, 1960.

B. Davidson, *A History of East and Central Africa to the late 19th Century*, 1968.

G. S. P. Freeman-Grenville, *The Medieval History of the Tanganyika Coast*, 1962.

J. Gray, *History of Zanzibar from the Middle Ages to 1856*, 1962.

V. L. Grottanelli, *Pescatori dell'Oceano Indiano*, 1955.

B. A. Ogot, *History of the Southern Luo*, 1967.

R. Oliver and G. Mathew (eds), *History of East Africa*, vol. I, 1962.

J. Strandes, *Die Portugiesenzeit von Deutsche- und Englisch-Ostafrika*, 1899. (English trans., 1961, *The Portuguese Period in East Africa*.)

The books cited above are concerned mainly or entirely with the pre-colonial period, and many others could now be added. On the colonial period itself there is a vast bibliography of very diverse value, whether of published official papers, individual memoirs, polemics, journalism or, latterly, analytical scholarship; and I can make no attempt to cover it here. But a few points may be useful. The administrative record from an orthodox imperialist standpoint is most effectively set forth and described in Lord Hailey's *An African Survey*, first published in 1938 but reprinted and revised in 1945 and again in 1957. A standard work on the French side is R. Delavignette, *Service Africain*, 1946

(English title, *Freedom and Authority in French West Africa*). A valuable short survey of French attitudes is contained in H. Brunschwig's *Mythes et Realités de l'Impérialisme Colonial Français 1871–1914*, 1960. Readers may also consult the *Encyclopédie de l'Empire Française; Encyclopédie du Congo Belge;* and the *Grande Enciclopédia Portuguesa e Brasiliera*, all of which present many articles on the philosophy, motivation and claims of European imperialism in Africa as seen by the imperialists themselves. Work on the actual 'mechanics' of imperialism has produced important books: among these are C. Coquéry-Vidrovitch, *Le Congo au Temps des grandes Compagnies concessionaires*, Paris, 1972; and J. Suret-Canale, *French Colonialism in Tropical Africa*, English edition, London, 1971.

In the reporting field there is a small number of highly critical works dating from the colonial period, notably H. W. Nevinson, *A Modern Slavery*, 1906 (Angola and São Thomé); E. D. Morel, *Red Rubber* (Congo Free State), revised edition, 1919; N. Leys, *Kenya*, 1926; and my own *African Awakening*, 1955. Between the extremes of acceptance and rejection there is a large number of works of varying merit from many standpoints.

The background to the South African situation of today may be found from a number of points of view, more or less critical, in B. Bunting, *Rise and Fall of the South African Reich*, 1964; G. M. Carter, *The Politics of Inequality*, 1958; B. Davidson, *Report on Southern Africa*, 1952; L. Marquard, *The Peoples and Policies of South Africa*, 1952; and H. Tingsten, *The Problem of South Africa*, 1955; while many statements in justification of *apartheid* may be had by application to the Government Publications Office of the Republic of South Africa, Pretoria. An excellent survey of Lesotho, Botswana and Swaziland is J. Halpern's *South Africa's Hostages*, 1965. Further north the most useful surveys of white-settler situations in south-central Africa are those of C. Leys, *European Politics in Southern Africa*, 1959; C. Leys and C. Pratt, *A New Deal in Central Africa*, 1960; and T. M. Franck, *Race and Nationalism* (in the Rhodesias and Nyasaland), 1960

For East Africa the second volume of the *History of East Africa*, 1964, edited by V. Harlow and E. M. Chilver, carries on the story into colonial times; while the *Report* of the East Africa Royal Commission, 1955, is of basic importance among British Government policy papers. R. Oliver's *The Missionary Factor in East Africa*, 1952, has many valuable insights; as does F. B. Welbourn's *East African Rebels*, 1961. The white-settler viewpoint is well expressed in J. F. Lipscomb's *White Africans*, 1965; while a contrary view may be found in P. Evans's *Law and Disorder in Kenya*, 1956; in J. M. Kariuki's *'Mau-Mau' Detainee*, 1963; in D. L. Barnett's and Karari Njama's *Mau Mau from Within*, 1966, an indispensable work on the Kenya Emergency of the 1950s; and in N. Leys above. The West African bibliography is capacious for this period; aside

from the books listed above under *West Africa*, all of which have good bibliographies, the reader may follow the story from the imperialist attitude of M.
Perham, *Lugard*, 2 vols, 1956 and 1960 (the first covering Lugard's ventures
in East Africa, the second in Nigeria); in J. E. Flint, *Sir George Goldie*, 1960;
and in R. Oliver, *Sir Harry Johnston and the Scramble for Africa*, 1957. On
the Congo Free State, R. Slade's *King Leopold's Congo*, 1962, may be compared
with E. D. Morel's *Red Rubber*, mentioned above, and with P. Joye and R.
Levine, *Les Trusts au Congo*, 1961 (dealing chiefly with the Belgian Congo).
A penetrating study of relations between the Belgian parliament and King
Leopold will be found in J. Stengers's *Belgique et Congo: L'Elaboration de la
Charte Coloniale*, 1963. Portuguese colonial enterprise in Africa covers a long
period of early contact, piratical or commercial, as well as later conquest, to
which Birmingham (op. cit.) and Duffy (op. cit.) provide good introductions.
Authoritative statements of Portuguese 'doctrine' for internal consumption, as
distinct from propagandist work for foreign eyes, will be found in M. Caetano,
Os Nativos na Economia Africana, Coimbra, 1954, and J. M. da Silva Cunha,
O Sistema Português de Politica Indigena, Coimbra, 1953, while a list of
essential works concerning Portuguese imperialism in Africa will be found in
B. Davidson, *In the Eye of the Storm: Angola's People*, 1972, an historical
overview.

For nationalist background in the nineteenth and early twentieth centuries
the chapters by D. L. Wheeler in *Angola*, 1971 (D. L. Wheeler and R. Pélissier)
are of great value. For later and contemporary developments see A. Cabral,
Revolution in Guinea, 1969, an indispensable collection of Cabral's writings;
B. Davidson, *The Liberation of Guiné*, 1969, and *In the Eye of the Storm*,
1972; J. Marcum, *The Angolan Revolution*, vol. 1, 1969; and E. Mondlane,
The Struggle for Mozambique, 1969. Also on the Cape Verde archipelago, an
independent republic since 1975, see B. Davidson, *The Fortunate Isles*, Trenton
and London, 1989.

German colonialism forms another chapter in this many-sided affair. The
best modern introduction is H. Brunschwig's *L'Expansion Allemande Outre-
Mer du XVe Siècle à Nos Jours*, 1957. Since the Second World War German
scholars have published a number of important works based on the German
imperial archives now collected at Potsdam: these include K. Büttner's *Die
Anfänge der Deutschen Kolonial-politik in Ostafrika*, 1959; F. F. Müller's
Deutschland-Zanzibar-Ostafrika, 1959; H. Stoecker's *Kamerun unter Deutscher
Kolonialherrschaft*, 1960; and H. Dreschler's *Südwestafrika unter Deutscher
Kolonialherrschaft*, 1966. For South-West Africa, see also H. Loth's *Die Christ-
lichen Missionen in Südwestafrika*, 1963; on the later situation and background,
R. First, *South West Africa*, 1963, and L. Lazar, *Namibia* (Africa Bureau,
London), 1972 (documentary record of international status of Namibia (South

West Africa) vis-à-vis the United Nations and South Africa, etc., and the rise of Namibian nationalism.

On the economic consequences of the colonial system, the bibliography has been remarkably deficient, but S. H. Frankel's *Capital Investment in Africa*, 1938, makes an important starting point for analysis. P. Hill has embarked on the little-known subject of African markets and marketing procedure in numerous papers: e.g. *Markets and Marketing in West Africa*, a report on a symposium at the Centre of African Studies of Edinburgh University in 1966. C. Coquéry-Vidrovitch has explained the French concessionary system in Equatorial Africa in a book of outstanding value: *Le Congo au Temps des grandes Compagnies concessionaires, 1898–1930*, 1972. Any profound study of precolonial economic systems has yet to be undertaken, but the interested reader will find useful insights in Polányi, *supra* (West Africa). Apart from books listed above which may touch on economic questions from the imperialist angle, the reader may also consult a critical study written from a Marxist approach, that of J. Woddis, *The Roots of Revolt*, 1960. An attempt at some conclusions may be found in my *Which Way Africa? The Search for a New Society*, 1968, chaps 6 and 7. A new general synthesis, emphasizing the indigenous economic background, is A. G. Hopkins, *An Economic History of West Africa*, 1973. For a critique of colonial economic structures, see Samir Amin, *L'Afrique de l'Ouest Bloquée*, 1971; and *Le Développement Inégal*, 1974. Important is C. Coquéry-Vidrovitch, *Africa: Endurance and Change South of the Sahara*, University of California, 1988.

For the rise of modern nationalism and the campaigns that led to political independence, the best short guides are T. Hodgkin's *Nationalism in Colonial Africa*, 1956, and his *African Political Parties*, 1961. See also my own synthesis: *Africa in Modern History*, 1978. More detailed studies of importance include D. E. Apter's *The Gold Coast in Transition*, 1955; J. S. Coleman's *Nigeria: A Background to Nationalism*, 1958; G. Shepperson and T. Price's *Independent African*, 1958 (origins, setting and significance of the Chilembwe rising in Nyasaland of 1915); and, for the Maghreb of North Africa, C. A. Julien's *L'Afrique du Nord en Marche*, 1952; while an essential documentation on the Algerian independence movement and war is that of A. Mandouze, *La Révolution Algérienne par les Textes*, 1961. A number of books by African leaders are of key importance: these include Sir Ahmadu Bello's *My Life*, 1962; Kenneth Kaunda's *Zambia Shall Be Free*, 1962; Julius Nyerere's *Freedom and Unity*, 1966; and Kwame Nkrumah's *Autobiography*, 1957, and his *Africa Must Unite*, 1963. For a view of the life and times of Nkrumah, a key figure in the early period of decolonization, see B. Davidson, *Black Star*, 1973; reprint, 1989.

Lastly, mention may be made of five useful handbooks to the current African scene. These are C. Legum's *Africa: A Handbook to the Continent*, 1961; H. Kitchen's *A Handbook of African Affairs*, 1964; R. Segal's *Political Africa: A Who's Who of Personalities and Parties*, 1961; Reuter's Guide to *The New Africans*, 1967; and, most detailed in its surveys, *Africa South of the Sahara*, Europa Publications, London, annually. C. Legum's excellent *African Contemporary Record* is published annually.

Chronologues

Up to about AD 1400 (or 803 of the Muslim epoch), the chronology of most African history can rely upon few dates that are surely fixed, though the position here is better to the north of the Sahara than to the south of it. The fixing of probable approximate dates by various scientific methods, above all by testing of the C-14 isotope of carbon, has fortunately done a great deal to fill gaps and can confidently be expected to achieve a great deal more: this also applies to the period after AD 1400 up to about 1750. Periodical lists of dates arising from C-14 tests are published in the *Journal of African History*.

After about AD 1400 the ascertained and probable chronology steadily improves, whether from documents in Arabic or several European languages, and this improvement becomes substantial after about AD 1600, at which point the relevant European documents begin to multiply. African unwritten history has similarly done much to help us.

The lists which follow here offer an approximately comparative outline of the continental chronology by which scholars now steer their course. They are, of course, subject to the reservations noted here, are necessarily few and thus selective and should in no way be taken as being comprehensive even for early periods. Their task is to serve, if possible, as a useful frame of reference.

Although there is no clear line of demarcation to be found in any general way, these charts omit the Stone Ages and begin with the outset of the African Iron Age (omitting a North African Bronze Age of well-known importance in the lower valley of the Nile, as well as among the Berber peoples of the Mediterranean littoral). With some possible but still controversial exceptions, there was no Bronze or Copper Age in Africa south of the Sahara. For users of this book who want an outline of the Stone Ages (as of Pharaonic Egypt), books listed in my brief guide to further reading will be adequate as introduction; while Thurstan Shaw has lately reviewed the existing evidence for Early Agriculture, a theme of great importance, in his article of that title in the *Journal of the Historical Society of Nigeria*, vol. VI, no. 2, June 1972.

Periodization

Writing history has generally been found to impose some acceptance of a periodization; and this seems to be the case of African historiography as well, at least where long-term syntheses are concerned. Older approaches that arose in the time of European paternalism tended to adopt a periodization based on European rather than African history: one was told of 'Africa in the Middle Ages', of 'Africa During the Slave Trade', of 'Colonial Africa', and so forth. A satisfactory periodization for Africa's history *per se* has yet to be agreed upon. Meanwhile I have framed the following lists within a periodization proposed in 1965*; it has, at least so far as I know, given rise as yet to no substantial objections.

With the large reservations that any periodization must impose, this one may be a helpful working tool for sub-Saharan Africa, though it fits less well in supra-Saharan Africa, where it sometimes will not fit at all; and once again, as with all such periodizations, there are few or no clear dividing lines. Users of these lists will be good enough to bear all such reservations in mind.

Early Iron Age	*c.* 350 BC–AD 1000
Intermediate Period	*c.* AD 1000–1300
Mature Iron Age	*c.* AD 1300–1600
Age of Transition	*c.* AD 1600–Present Times

The dates are those of the Christian calendar; users who want the corresponding Muslim dates after AD 621 should refer to G. S. P. Freeman-Grenville, *The Muslim and Christian Calendars* (Conversion Tables), Oxford, 1963.

Not believing in the value of a bare record of dates, I have constructed these lists somewhat discursively, and invented a name for such compilations: chronologues.

*Basil Davidson, 'Can We Write African History?', African Studies Center, University of California at Los Angeles, Occasional Paper no. 1, November 1965.

EARLY IRON AGE

	Western	Eastern/Central/Southern	Nile Valley/Northern
BC c. 350	Origins of earliest yet known Iron Age culture south of Sahara: Nok Culture of C. Nigeria. Presumed 'companion cultures' suspected, but not yet securely traced (1974).	Hunting and gathering cultures of Late Stone Age in many regions: populations very sparse, but widely spread.	Rise of the city and nearby satellites of Meroe as political and cultural centre of the Kushite kingdom (formerly centred on Napata to the north).
	Early trans-Saharan trade, between W. Sudan and N. Africa, by way of Berber middlemen, well established.	Probable period of initial 'Bantu' spread from supposed early areas of diffusion in southern grasslands of Congo Basin	Origins of Axumite culture in north-east Ethiopia by synthesis of local people and immigrants from southern Arabia.
	Rice cultivation well established in some western areas (Mandinka). Spread of early forms of forest agriculture.		Carthage a major power, though soon to be challenged by Roman Republic.
			332 Alexander enters Egypt: Ptolemaic dynasty follows.
AD c. 100	Further spread of early metal-using cultures, principally of iron.	Northerly points along East Coast become peripheral parts of Indian Ocean/Red Sea carrying trade, but as yet on very small scale.	Egypt, Tunisia and Algeria have become Roman colonies. Development of synthesis of Roman, Punic and Berber cultures in Tunisia and Algeria.
	Trans-Saharan trade expands with growing use of camels in place of horses and donkeys.	Early Iron Age cultures in C. Africa (e.g. Katanga, Zambia, Zimbabwe) begin to unfold.	Meroitic Kush remains a powerful state with widespread interests in the long-distance trade.
			Origins of Axumite kingdom of N.E. Ethiopia after c. 100 BC.

EARLY IRON AGE

	Western	Eastern/Central/Southern	Nile Valley/Northern
c. 400	Presumed emergence of early states of W. and C. Sudan, notably of Ghana in the former, as centrally ruled polities with a systemic interest in long-distance trade.	Continued spread of iron-using cultures associated with formation of Bantu-speaking peoples south of the Congo Basin. First settlements at site of Great Zimbabwe. These cultures have developed early forms of agriculture, but have not yet spread south of Limpopo.	Byzantine culture in Egypt Lower Nubia (formerly in Kush) under kings of 'X-Group' (beginning in third and fourth century). c. 325 (?) King Ezana of Axum invades Meroitic Kush. Axum has accepted Christianity as state religion (beginning with Ezana in early fourth century); origins of Ethiopian Christianity.
c. 800	Ghana a well-established trading state in W. Sudan, together with smaller trading states formed in parts of the Sahel by western Berber peoples. Some early trading towns, such as Kumbi, Audaghost and Gao, probably in existence, most of them probably on Neolithic foundations. Earliest southward penetration of Islam from Morocco and Central Maghreb.	Bantu-speaking chiefdoms in the Katanga are producing and trading in copper. Spread of Bantu-speaking peoples southward of the Limpopo: origins in South Africa of seSotho- and seZulu-speaking polities. Early formative migrations of peoples of Upper Nile into historical locations. Swahili coastal culture in formative period.	Rise of Islam: 622 Hijra of Muhammad. 641 Arabs take Babylon (in Egypt). 670 Uqba ibn Nafi occupies Ifriqiya (Tunisia). 683 Arabs reach Moroccan Atlantic. 711 Tariq crosses into Spain. 713 Abd al-Azziz reaches Tagus. 732 Charles Martel turns back Arabs at battle of Poitiers. 756 Caliphate of Cordoba.

EARLY IRON AGE

Western

Rise of early state of Kanem-Bornu.

Origins of Yoruba and Hausa states in western and northern Nigeria.

Eastern/Central/Southern

First Muslim settlements on East Coast, probably beginning with Lamu archipelago off north Kenya seaboard.

c. 900 Further development of early Iron Age cultures in central grassland regions, from Katanga southwards.

c. 917 Al-Masudi visits parts of East Coast and (943) describes having heard of a strong African kingdom somewhere there. Gold and ivory trade already well established with Indian Ocean partners of coastal and inland peoples.

Nile Valley/Northern

c. 800 Egypt under Abbasids.

Nubia divided into three Christian kingdoms, soon reduced to two (after conversion in sixth century).

Axum in decline, facing Muslim and Persian competition in Red Sea and western Indian Ocean.

c. 969 Fatimid rule established in Egypt. Major westward shift of maritime trade routes from Persian Gulf.

INTERMEDIATE PERIOD

	Western	Eastern/Central/Southern	Nile Valley/Northern
c. 1000	Ghana at height of its power in W. Sudan. Al-Bakri (1067) describes wealth and organization of kingship from good second-hand sources. Early polities of southern Mandinka-speaking people, southwards from Ghana. Gao under *dia* dynasty (Songhay). They accept Islam as a state religion (c. 1020).	Origins of Zimbabwe Culture in central grasslands (colonized in nineteenth century as Rhodesia). Beginnings of building in stone. Symbiotic Arab/Swahili culture continues to develop along Somali, Kenyan and Tanzanian seaboards. Early Bantu-speaking cultures well established south of Limpopo.	Egypt under Fatimids. 1171 Ayyubids oust Fatimids. 1250 Mamluks oust Ayyubids; rule Egypt until 1517. Formation of feudal kingdoms in central and northern Ethiopia. Flowering of culture, including written literature in Ge'ez after c. 1200. Christian Nubia: decline under Ayyubid attacks from north and infiltration of Arab pastoralists elsewhere. Fall not completed until fourteenth century or later in parts.
c. 1100	Similar developments in Kanem: its Saifuwa dynasty expand their power and also accept Islam as a state religion. 1054 Almoravid Berbers take Audaghost. They also take Ghana capital.	c. 1200 At Kilwa, King Ali al-Hasan mints earliest Kilwa coins.	c. 1200 Successor states in Maghreb. al-Andalus: 1031 End of Caliphate, followed by many successor kingships. 1061 Almoravid dynasty, unity largely restored. 1147 Almohad dynasty, unity largely maintained.
c. 1250	A 'time of confusion' sets in while successor states compete for power. Period of crystallization of many maturing Iron Age polities, including origins of Wolof states in Senegal, Yoruba states in western Nigeria, earliest kingship at Benin under semi-legendary Ogiso dynasty, etc. Sundiata becomes king of southern Mandinka state of Kangaba.	c. 1260 Husuni Kubwa palace built on Kilwa. Swahili ports now deeply engaged in long-distance trade between inland gold and ivory producers (mainly via Sofala for gold) and Indian Ocean mariners.	

MATURE IRON AGE

Western

c.c. 1400

Wolof empire well established in Senegal.

Crystallization of Mossi and other grassland kingdoms.

Emergence of Akan state of Bono-Manso, and of town of Begho on northern fringes of Asante (Ashanti) forest (modern Ghana), as important new centre of gold export trade. This develops the Middle Niger trading towns of Djenne and Timbuktu.

c. 1440

Benin becomes powerful under *Oba* Ewuare.

Eastern/Central/Southern

1415 Malindi sends a giraffe to the Emperor of China. This is followed by Chinese voyages to western Indian Ocean, including northern parts of East Coast of Africa.

1425 Dynastic disputes at Kilwa; they are overcome.

c. 1425 New Rozwi (Shona) dynasty in central grasslands (Zimbabwe Culture), known as Mwanamutapa, begins with Mutota (d. c.1450). Mutota shifts capital from Great Zimbabwe to area of Mount Darwin in north-east of modern Zimbabwe (Rhodesia), embarks on large programme of conquest.

c. 1450 Mutota's successor Matope completes conquests: establishes Shona suzerainty over most of present-day Zimbabwe and Mozambique.

Nile Valley/Northern

1498 Vasco da Gama reaches Swahili city-ports; sails to India with Arab pilot.

c. 1500 Fung Sultanate founded at Sennar on Blue Nile as successor state (Muslim) to southernmost Christian Nubian kingdom of Alwa.

1541 Portuguese land at Massawa and aid Ethiopia against invasion by Ahmed, sultan of Adel, who has Ottoman help.

1559 Ethiopian King Claudius killed while warring with Adel.

1563–97 Sarsa Dengel king of Ethiopia.

INTERMEDIATE PERIOD

Western	Eastern/Central/Southern	Nile Valley/Northern
		1269 End of Almohad dynasty: Christian conquest begins (but Granada holds out until 1492).
c. 1255 Mansa Uli (d. c. 1270) continues to expand Kangaba into state of Mali, which begins to 'take over' from successor states of Ghana as Mature Iron Age polity.		
	MATURE IRON AGE	Portuguese ocean voyages:
	c. 1300 Origins of new cultures in inland East Africa: e.g. Chwezi dynasty in southern Uganda, and others further south, arising on earlier 'small kingships' or chiefdoms.	1434 Gil Eannes sails south of C. Bojador.
c. 1312 Mansa Musa becomes king of Mali, which continues to expand in W. and C. Sudan, and develops new techniques of literacy, trade and credit adopted from Islam.		1441 First captives for Portugal taken directly from African peoples south of Morocco.
	Spread of *ntemi* forms of kingship through Tanzania (northern and inland plains).	1450 Portuguese on Senegal seaboard.
c. 1325 Musa takes Gao, dies 1337.	1331 Ibn Battuta visits Kilwa: finds it a strong and wealthy trading city.	1472 Ruy de Siqueira reaches Bight of Benin.
c. 1335 Songhay *sonni* dynasty begins at Gao.		1482 Portuguese build Elmina Castle (modern Ghana seaboard).
c. 1375 *Sonni* Suleiman-Mar makes Gao independent of Mali. c. 1400 Gao troops raid Niani, capital of Mali. Rise of Songhay power in C. Sudan at expense of Mali.	In central grasslands, Great Zimbabwe culture develops further. Origins of great stone buildings, which probably raised to near present (ruined) extent before AD 1400.	1483 Diogo Cão reaches estuary of Congo.
1375 Abraham Cresques, Jewish cartographer of Majorca, completes earliest detailed map of western Africa. European voyages foreshadowed.		1488 Bartolomeo Diaz rounds C. of Good Hope.

MATURE IRON AGE

Western	Eastern/Central/Southern	Nile Valley/Northern
1493 Songhay expansion. *Askia* dynasty founded by al-Hajji Muhammad (d. 1528; followed by nine other *askias* to Moroccan conquest in 1591). Songhay dominates C. Sudan.	c. **1493** Changamire breaks away from Mwanamutapa dynasty; sets up new state based on Bulawayo area (e.g. Khami and other sites).	Ottoman dates: 1512– Selim I. 20
c. **1504** Oba Esigie begins long and successful reign; adds Idah to Benin empire. Portuguese accepted as residents in Benin city.	c. **1500** Formation of Luba kingships in Katanga.	1517 Ottomans complete conquest of Egypt.
	Southern Bantu polities well established throughout fertile lands south of Limpopo and east of Drakensberg as far south as (modern) Cape Province of S. Africa. Origins of later Swazi, Ngoni and Xhosa states.	1520– Suleyman 'the Magnificent'. 66
c. **1507** Kanem-Bornu expansion: Mai Idris Katakarmabe reoccupies Njimi, old Kanem capital.		1529 Their power penetrates to Algeria.
c. **1525** Mai Muhammad continues wars with Bulala east of L. Chad.	**1505** Portuguese burn Kilwa, continue ravages up the coast; in following years attempt to monopolize Indian Ocean carrying trade, partly succeed. Beginnings of decline of Swahili city-ports.	1530 They occupy Yemen, dominate Red Sea trade, threaten Ethiopians, also Portuguese.
1570– Kanem empire at height of **1617** power under Mai Idris Alooma, 'the learned, just, courageous and pious Commander of the Faithful'.		1534 They secure Tunisia.

MATURE IRON AGE

Nile Valley/Northern

Eastern/Central/Southern

From base on Mozambique I., Portuguese begin slow penetration up Zambezi valley.

1520 Chronicle of Kilwa.

1585 Some Swahili cities revolt against Portuguese with hope of Ottoman aid; disappointed.

1593 Portuguese begin building Fort Jesus at Mombasa as main base in north.

Western

1553 English traders reach Benin.

1591 Moroccans invade Songhay.

Period of Portuguese raiding invasions of Angolan kingdoms. Large Portuguese slave trade to Brazil.

AGE OF TRANSITION

Western

c. 1600   Niger Delta peoples organize themselves into trading states as landward partners of European maritime traders, whether English, Dutch, Portuguese or French.

This trade develops into large and continuing sale of captives, for enslavement in the Americas. Here, as at many other points between the Congo estuary and Senegal, the Atlantic slave trade now gets into its stride, expands till c. 1750, remains at high level till c. 1800, gradually dwindles until it disappears in 1880s.

Firearms do not become an important political factor until c. 1700, but are of growing significance after c. 1650.

Eastern/Central/Southern

Seventeenth century opens against background of great changes, along coast, through Portuguese invasion, and in the inland country by further development of Iron Age structures.

1607   Dutch attack Portuguese on Mozambique I., fail here, but erode Portuguese control of Indian Ocean.

1628   Portuguese expeditions against Mwanamutapa: beginning of disintegration of that state.

1631   Mombasa rebels against Portuguese; fails.

Nile Valley/Northern

1549–   Saadi dynasty in Morocco.
1654   Portuguese evicted from seaboard footholds (Agadir, Safi, etc.). Songhay invaded (1591) and loosely held through *pashas* resident in Timbuktu.

1578   B. of al-Ksar al-Kabir: Iberian invasion of Morocco defeated.

Ahmad al Mansur sultan of Morocco (d. 1603).

1632   Basilides king of Ethiopia: Gondar period. Reorganization of kingship, eviction of Jesuits.

AGE OF TRANSITION

Western	Eastern/Central/Southern	Nile Valley/Northern
c. 1650 New constellations of power in inland country, largely unrelated to Atlantic slave trade but more and more interested in firearms. Expansion of northern Yoruba state of Oyo. Foundation in northern (modern) Ghana of Gonja, Buna, Wa; and, in south, of Denkyira and Akwamu; all as states more centralized than earlier states.	1650 Portuguese lose Muscat in S. Arabia: rise of Omani power there.	
Songhay disintegrates after invasion by Moroccan army under Judar Pasha (b. of Tondibi, 1591).	1652 Dutch settle at C. of Good Hope: *see below.*	
Rise of Fon state (Dahomey) under Wegbaja; Akaba continues expansion after 1685; Agaja after 1708.		
1727 Agaja embarks on conquest of small seaboard states which monopolize trade with Europeans (Gt. Ardrah, Ouidah, Jakin). Builds strongly centralized monarchy, maintains Ouidah as 'port of trade' with Europeans.		

AGE OF TRANSITION

Western	Eastern/Central/Southern	Nile Valley/Northern
1651 Courlanders build James Fort on island in Gambia estuary.	1661 Competing with the Portuguese at sea, the Omani raid them at Mombasa, and (1670) at Mozambique I.	
1661 James Fort seized by British Royal Africa Company.		
1677 Expansion of Akwamu (south-eastern Ghana) under Ansa Sasraku; expansion continues till 1702, when Akwamu briefly occupies Cuidah.	1695 Changamire Dombo evicts Portuguese traders from his (Zimbabwe Culture) kingdom of Urozwi. Northwards, in Zambezi Valley, Portuguese settlers expand plantation economy (prazos).	1671 First dey of Algiers: Ottoman suzerainty reduced.
c. 1680 Asante found strong state in forest of central (modern) Ghana, especially under first king of united Ashanti states, Osei Tutu (c. 1650–1712).		1689 Tenth dey of Algiers, Ali Chaouch, achieves title of *pasha*; autonomy again increased.
1701 Asante defeat Denkyira, secure direct trade with Dutch as Elmina.	1698 Omani evict Portuguese finally from Mombasa.	1710 Bey of Tunis recognized as enjoying hereditary succession, another reflection of waning Ottoman power.
		1729 Jesus II king of Ethiopia (d. 1753): period of feudal wars and of prelude to political reorganization in nineteenth century.

AGE OF TRANSITION

Western	Eastern/Central/Southern	Nile Valley/Northern
1702– Ashanti expands to control territory of most of Ghana under Opoku Ware (1720–50), Kwasi Obodun (1750–64), Osei Kwadwo (1764–77). Power reinforced under Osea Kwame (1777–1801) and Osei Bonsu (1801–24); latter greatly develops state organization.	c. 1700 New patterns of power and organization in many areas of C. Africa. Origins of Lunda kingships in south-western areas of Congo Basin; of Bemba and Lozi polities in (modern) Zambia; of gradual extension of use of certain trans-Atlantic food plants, notably cassava; apparent general increase of population at less slow rate than before.	1798 Egypt briefly invaded by French under Napoleon.
		1805 Egypt ruled by Muhammad Ali under loose Ottoman suzerainty.
1807 Future defensive wars with British foreshadowed, but no fighting yet.	Portuguese now in loose control of seaboard peoples of Angola from main base at S. Paolo de Loanda (Luanda).	1820 Semi-autonomous Turco-Egyptian régime in Egypt.
		1830 French seize Algiers: beginning of French occupation of Algeria.
1724 Oyo reasserts Yoruba suzerainty in S. Dahomey; again in 1730, 1739, 1748.	**South Africa:**	
1725 Imamate of Futa Djallon (Guinea) founded: complex reorganizations of Muslim states in W. and C. Sudan foreshadowed.	1652 Dutch make small settlement at Cape of Good Hope as way-station to East.	1855 Theodore II emperor of Ethiopia.
c. 1750 Baoulé kingship in S. Ivory Coast founded by Akan immigrants.	1688 First Huguenot immigrants. Gradual expansion of Cape settlement and slave labour.	1863– Egypt under Khedive Ismail. 85
1765– British Province of Senegambia (maritime Senegal and the Gambia). 83		

AGE OF TRANSITION

Western	Eastern/Central/Southern	Nile Valley/Northern
1770–89 Oyo under Alafin Obisdun, after whom state power begins to crack under external and internal strains.	1779 First of many wars of expansion, along the 'inland frontier', against Xhosa and other peoples established along and east of Great Fish River.	1867 British under Napier briefly invade Ethiopia; defeat armies of Theodore, who kills himself (1868); withdraw.
1775 Imamate of Futa Toro n. Senegal) founded: end of Denianke dynasty in Futa Toro (1776).	1789 Second such war.	1869 Suez Canal opened.
1787 Sierra Leone founded.	1799 Third such war.	1880 Period of rising Anglo-French imperialist rivalry; British generally prevail in Egypt.
1791 Freetown founded.	1806 British occupation of Cape settlement made good against French rivalry.	1881 French secure Tunisia.
1796 Mungo Park reaches Niger at Segu.	1836 Great Trek of Afrikaner settlers northward from British control.	Muhammad Ahmad proclaimed *Mahdi* in the Sudan, embarks on recovery of indigenous power.
1804–11 *Jihad* of Fulani reformer, Uthman dan Fodio, leads to Fulani hegemony over most of N. Nigeria under first Fulani *Amir al Mumenin*, Muhammad Bello, with cap. at Sokoto. Origins of Sokoto Caliphate.	1838 They found Republic of Natal.	
1807 British outlaw maritime slave trade.	1843 British annex Natal.	
1816 Foundation of Bathurst	1846 Seventh war against Africans.	
1822 Foundation of Liberia.	1859 First railway in Cape Colony.	
1851 British attack and occupy Lagos.	1860 Indentured Indian labour begins.	
	1867 Diamonds discovered.	

AGE OF TRANSITION

Western	Eastern/Central/Southern	Nile Valley/Northern
1852 Alhaj Umar begins *jihad* from Upper Guinea: founds Tuculor state on Middle Niger.	1877 Ninth war against Africans.	1882 British bombard Alexandria.
1854 Faidherbe French governor of Senegalese settlements.	1878 Zulu defeat British at Isandhlwana.	1885 British fail to relieve General Gordon at Khartoum.
1857 French occupy Dakar.	British penetration into lands north of Limpopo under (Rhodes's) British South Afica Company.	1889 Emperor Menelik and Italians sign Treaty of Ucciali.
1863 British at war with Asante.		
1864 British annex southern Ghana. Defeat Asante.		1890 British Protectorate declared over East Africa (north of Tanganyika); Germans rapidly follow in Tanganyika.
1884–85 Major congress of imperialist powers at Berlin: they partition Africa, and prepare to invade and take possession.	1880 First Anglo-Afrikaner (Boer) war.	
1878 French take Cotonou (Dahomey).	1884 First S. African gold fields opened.	
1884 Germans occupy Togo and Kamerum.	1886 Witwatersrand gold fields opened.	
1886 Goldie's United Africa Company (founded 1879) receives charter as Royal Niger Coy.		
1886 French occupy Ivory Coast.		

AGE OF TRANSITION

Western	Eastern/Central/Southern	Nile Valley/Northern
		1896 Italians invade Ethiopia; are defeated at Adua.
		1898 British destroy Mahdist power at battle of Omdurman.
	1895–96 French establish protectorate on Madagascar.	Kitchener compels Marchand to withdraw from Upper Nile (Fashoda). British rule Sudan in formal condominium with Egypt.
1893 French declare Guinea a colony.	1896–97 Ndebele (Matabele) and Shona rise against dispossession; are defeated with difficulty.	
1898 Final defeat of Samori Turay by French, after some twenty years of resistance by Samori and his armies.	German penetration of South-West Africa; followed by armed resistance and harsh repression.	1899 British and French agree on delimitation of 1,950 miles of frontier between Congo-Nile watershed and Tripoli. Most other colonial frontiers agree soon after.
	Penetration of British South Africa Company north of Zambezi (Zambia). Origins of Northern Rhodesia Protectorate.	
1900 British occupy Asante, Nigeria. Most colonial frontiers now settled, or in 1901–2.	1899 Anglo-Boer War begins.	1908 Italians declare Somalia their colony.
	1902 Ends at Peace of Vereeniging.	
	1901 Most internal frontiers agreed between colonial powers.	
	1908 Belgian State assumes authority in (Leopoldian) Congo Free State.	

AGE OF TRANSITION

	Western	Eastern/Central/Southern	Nile Valley/Northern
1910	Early period of Gold Coast (Ghana) cocoa export-boom.	1910 Union of South Africa constituted.	1911 French occupy Fez; 1912, declare protectorate over Morocco. Italians seize Libyan towns, declare colonies of Tripolitania and Cyrenaica.
		1913 Systematic legalized discrimination against Africans begins with Land Settlement Act (allocating African ownership to about 12 per cent of territory), and continues rapidly with acts in other fields.	
1920	National Congress of British West Africa formed.	1919 Tanganyika under British Mandate.	
		1923 Southern Rhodesia settlers achieve self-rule as nominal Crown Colony of UK.	1929 Italians reconquer Fezzan.
1930	Period of collapse of colonial export prices.	c. 1925 Portuguese complete colonial occupation of inland Angola and Mozambique.	1934 Tripolitania and Cyrenaica united in colony of Libya.
1946	Rassemblement Démocratique Africain formed.	c. 1946 General rise of African nationalism in wake of Second World War.	1935 Italy invades Ethiopia.
			1941 Italy evicted from Ethiopia: Emperor Haile Selassie restored.

AGE OF TRANSITION

Western	Eastern/Central/Southern	Nile Valley/Northern
1951 Internal self-rule for Ghana.	1948 Afrikaner National Party comes to power: origins of legalized *apartheid* system based on existing system of discrimination	1951 Libya becomes independent kingdom.
1952 Internal self-rule for southern Nigeria.	1952 In South Africa, African nationalists launch passive resistance to *apartheid*; are defeated by draconic laws.	1952 Free Officers overthrow Egyptian monarchy with strong nationalist programme. Gamal Abdel Nasser soon becomes supreme; British evacuate their last bases in Egypt.
	1953–63 Northern and Southern Rhodesia and Nyasaland in settler-controlled federation.	1954 Algerians begin war of independence.
1957 Ghana independent.	1954–57 Peasant nationalist rising in C. Kenya: defeated with estimated loss of 10,000 African lives, but preludes independence.	1955 Tunisia becomes independent.
1958 Guinea independent.		1956 Morocco becomes independent. Spain returns holdings except Ceuta, Melilla, Ifni enclave, lands south of Draa.
	Beginnings of modern nationalist organization in Angola and Mozambique.	Sudan becomes independent.
1960 Nigeria, all other French colonies (14 in number) except Djibouti, independent.	1960 Madagascar independent as Malagasy Republic; Belgian Congo, Somalia independent.	Egypt invaded, at Suez, by Israeli, British, French forces; they withdraw.

AGE OF TRANSITION

	Western	Eastern/Central/Southern	Nile Valley/Northern
1961	Sierra Leone independent.	Tanganyika, Rwanda independent. Angolan nationalist rising signals beginning of anti-colonial wars in 'Portuguese Africa'. Republic of South Africa constituted outside British Commonwealth.	
1962		Uganda, Burundi independent.	Algeria becomes independent.
1963	Guinea-Bissau nationalists open armed resistance to continued Portuguese rule.	Kenya independent.	Organization of African Unity (OAU) founded with headquarters in Addis Ababa.
1964		Malawi, Zambia independent. Zanzibar joins Tanganyika in United Republic of Tanzania. Beginning of armed resistance to Portuguese rule in Mozambique.	
1965	The Gambia independent.	Rhodesian settlers rebel against British Crown; declare unilateral independence under settlers' constitution.	
1966		Basutoland independent as Lesotho, Bechuanaland as Botswana.	

AGE OF TRANSITION

Western	Eastern/Central/Southern	Nile Valley/Northern
		1968 Mauritius becomes independent.
	1968 Swaziland independent.	
1970 New 12-state federation in Nigeria after end of civil war (1967–69).		1970 Egypt: Aswan Dam completed, Nasser dies.
	1972 In S. Rhodesia, strong armed resistance to settlers' regime installed in 1965 develops with aid of FRELIMO in Mozambique.	
1973 Nationalists in Guinea-Bissau declare independent state.		
1974 Guinea-Bissau fully independent.	1974 Overthrow of Portuguese dictatorship by young army officers opens way to acceptance of need to decolonize.	1974 Revolution in Ethiopia overthrows imperial government in favour of military rule, which, a little later, is reorganized under Col. Mengistu Haile Mariam.
1975 Cape Verde archipelago forms independent republic after complete withdrawal of Portuguese power.	1975 Mozambique and Angola become independent. South African troops and Zairean army invade new Angolan republic, but are defeated with aid of Cuban reinforcements.	
International Court at Hague finds that Western Sahara, decolonized by Spain, has right of self-determination; but Morocco and Mauritania decide to partition territory. Armed resistance by Western Saharans (Polisario Front) defeats Mauritania but war against Moroccan invasion continues, leading, in 1983, to serious split within OAU.		1976 Brief war between Ethiopia and Somalia over future of Somali-peopled Ogaden province of Ethiopian empire.

AGE OF TRANSITION

Western	Eastern/Central/Southern	Nile Valley/Northern
1975 15 W. African countries form Economic Community of W. African States (ECOWAS); Cape Verde Republic joins in 1977.	1978 S. African aggressions against Angola increased. Meanwhile armed resistance by SWAPO (South-West African People's Organization) to continued S. African rule in Namibia gains new strength. At same time, African National Congress of S. Africa launches new campaign of armed resistance, aimed chiefly at industrial targets, and scores successes.	1981 Eritrean nationalists enter their 20th year of armed resistance to Ethiopian occupation. Other armed struggles against Amharic supremacy within Ethiopia now in course by Oromo and in Tigre.
1979 Nigeria, now a 19-state federation, prepared to return to civilian rule, and does so successfully in 1980 with Alhaji Shehu Shagari as its first president.	1980 After various attempts at partial concession to African majority rule, settler government in S. Rhodesia capitulates in face of guerrilla pressure. General election gives sweeping majority to ZANU and Robert Mugabe becomes prime minister.	
1982 Civil war in Chad erupts again as local rivals are backed by various external interests.		

AGE OF TRANSITION

Western

1983 Nigeria expels 2 million illegal immigrants, mostly Ghanaian; holds elections; Shagari re-elected president but overthrown in December.

1984 Military régime in Nigeria under Buhari.

1985 Buhari régime ousted by military coup; General Babangida takes over.

Eastern/Central/Southern

1982 Nine states (Angola, Botswana, Lesotho, Malawi, Mozambique, Swaziland, Tanzania, Zambia, Zimbabwe) persevere with organization for economic co-operation formed by them in 1979; Southern African Development Co-ordination Conference (SADCC), with HQ in Gaberone, capital of Botswana.

1984 In S. Africa, new constitution makes electoral concessions to Coloureds and Indians, but none to Africans.

1985 While repression grows inside S. Africa, *apartheid* régime steps up military interventions in Angola and Mozambique.

Nile Valley/Northern

1982 Republic of Sudan makes progress with new major canal in the far south—Jonglei Canal—designed to conserve Upper Nile waters lost in Sudd marshlands since time began.

1985–88 Repeated military victories by Eritrean Peoples' Liberation Front, now joined by Tigray PLF. Régime under siege but continues to refuse to negotiate with dissident ethnic groups.

AGE OF TRANSITION

	Western		Eastern/Central/Southern		Nile Valley/Northern
1987	In Burkina Faso, President Thomas Sankara assassinated by rivals.	1988	S. African troops in Angola suffer major defeat, withdraw.	1989	Sudan continues to suffer great internal conflict, and civil war between north and south.
1989	In Chad, political conflicts unresolved but civil war abates.		International isolation of *apartheid* régime causes serious anxiety for régime.		
		1989	In S. Africa, President Botha replaced by F. W. de Klerk.		
		1990	Namibia becomes independent.		

Index